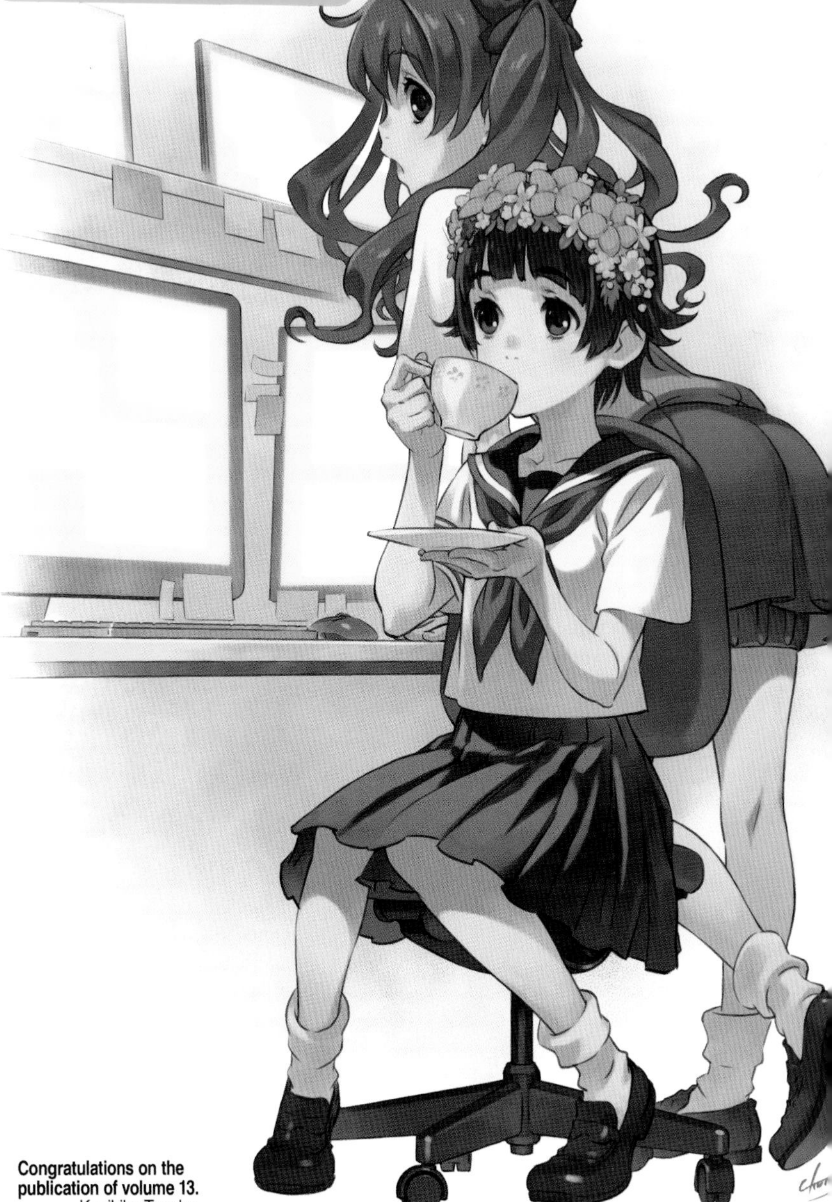

Congratulations on the
publication of volume 13.
–Kunihiko Tanaka

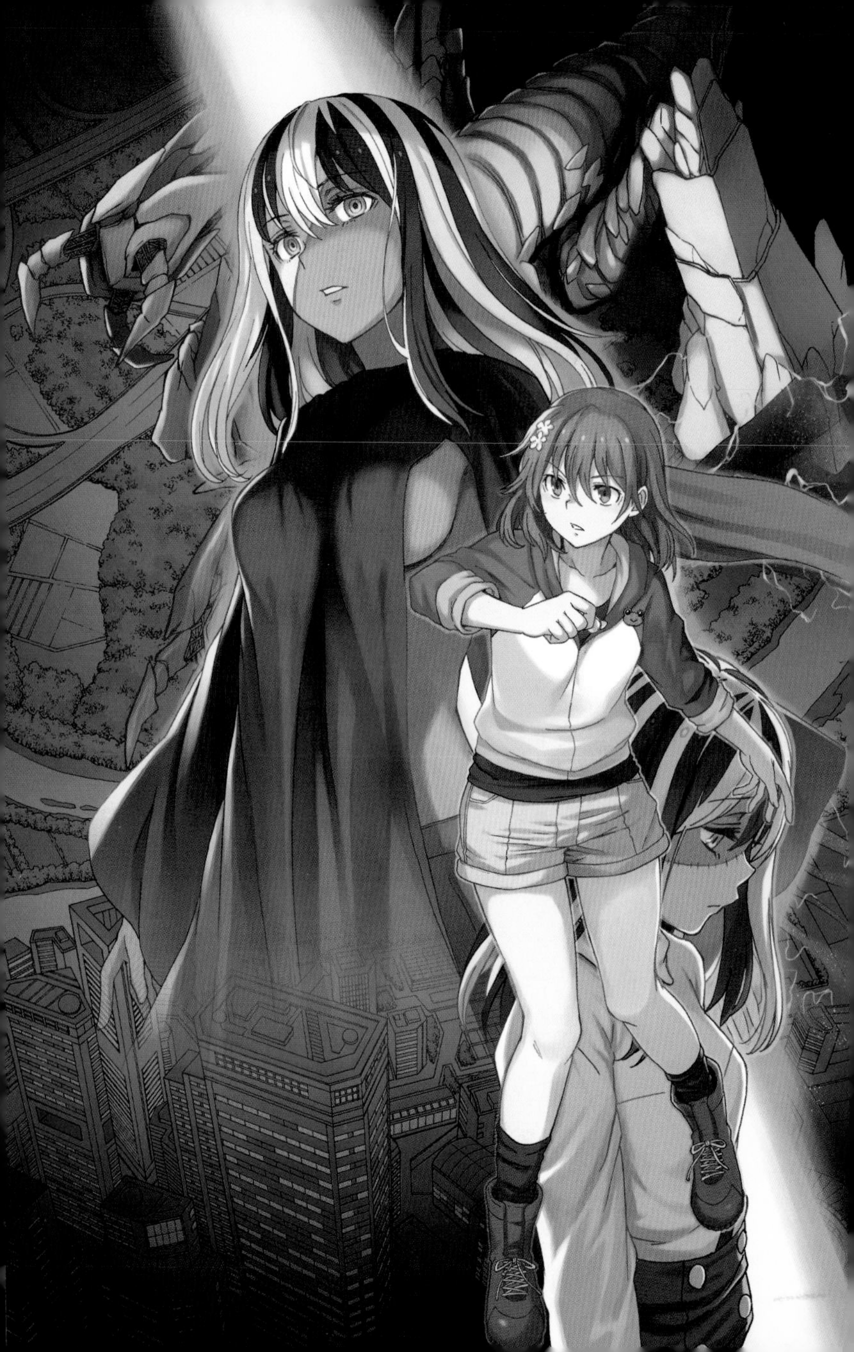

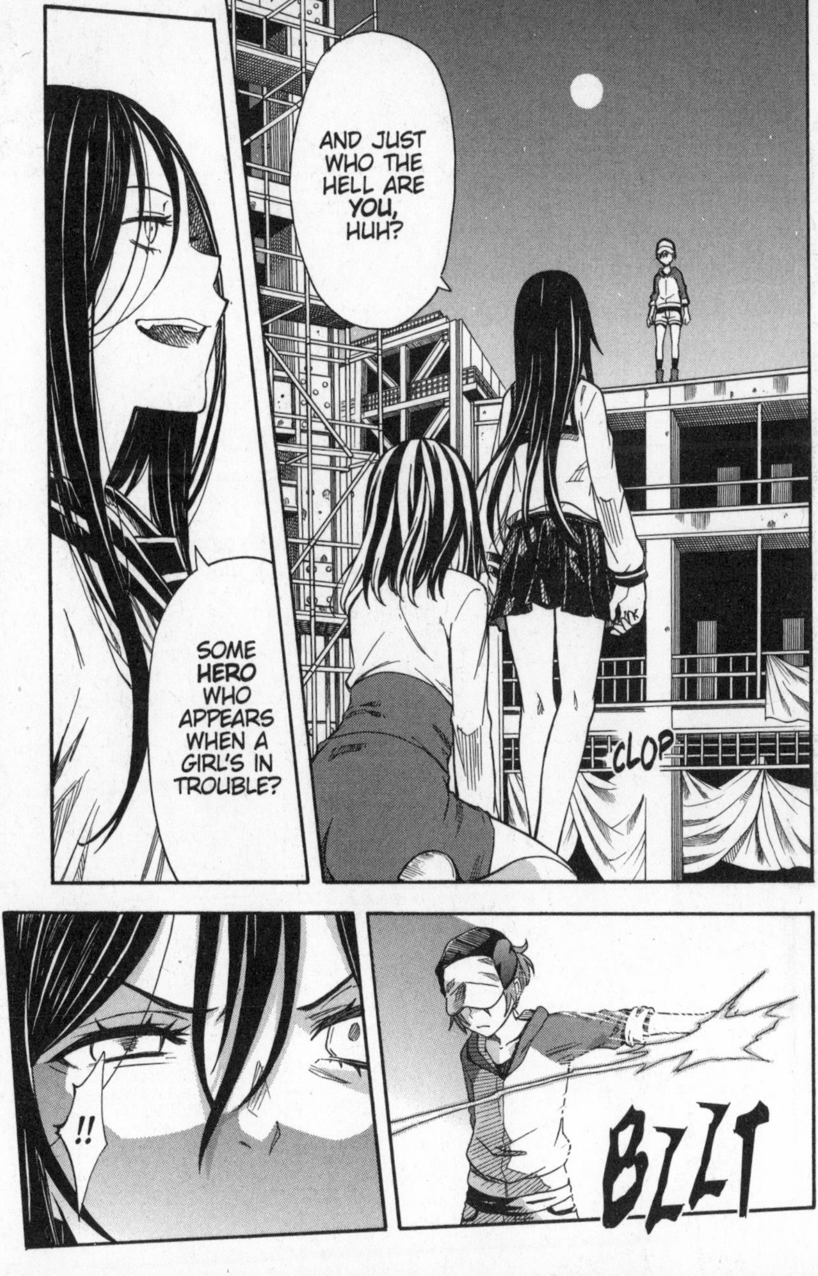
AND JUST WHO THE HELL ARE YOU, HUH?
SOME HERO WHO APPEARS WHEN A GIRL'S IN TROUBLE?
CLOP
!!
BZZT

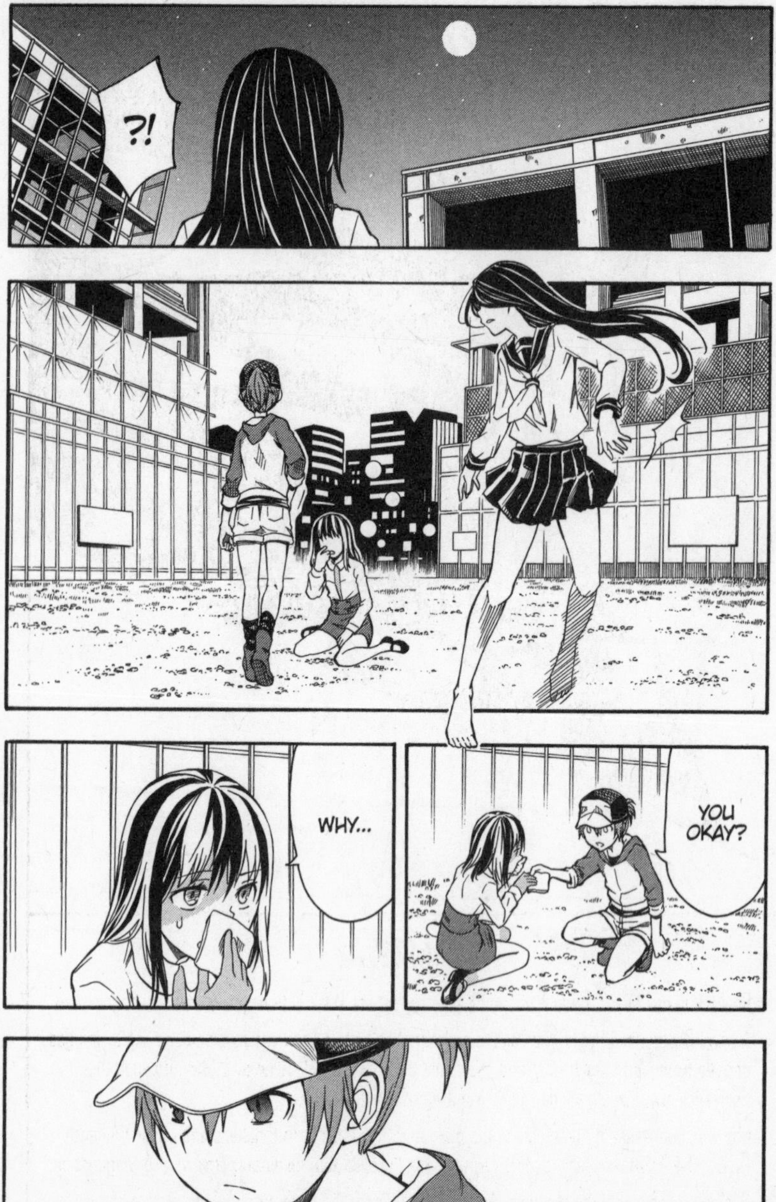
?!
YOU OKAY?
WHY...

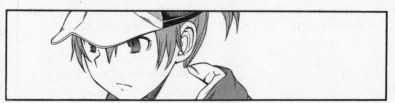

CHAPTER 89: UNLUCKY DAY

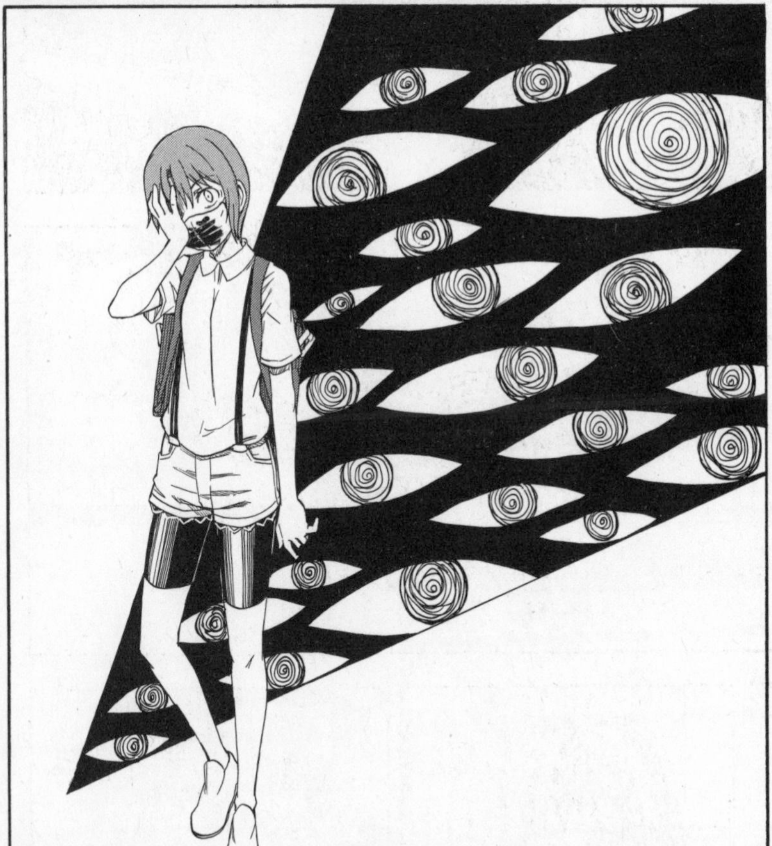

LEADER

- Real name unknown. The girl who acts as leader of the Dark Side organization Scavenger.
- A Level 3 who uses the ESPer ability Predator. When she closes one eye, she can deploy images of eyes to fill up the night sky, and she's able to survey a wide area by looking through them. Her efficiency drops considerably during the daytime, though.
- She was oppressed by teachers in the past, and thus sees both teachers and honor students (who fulfill those teachers' orders) as evil. She believes that eliminating them is serving justice.
- She has a habit of inviting people she likes--or people who have potential--to work with her.

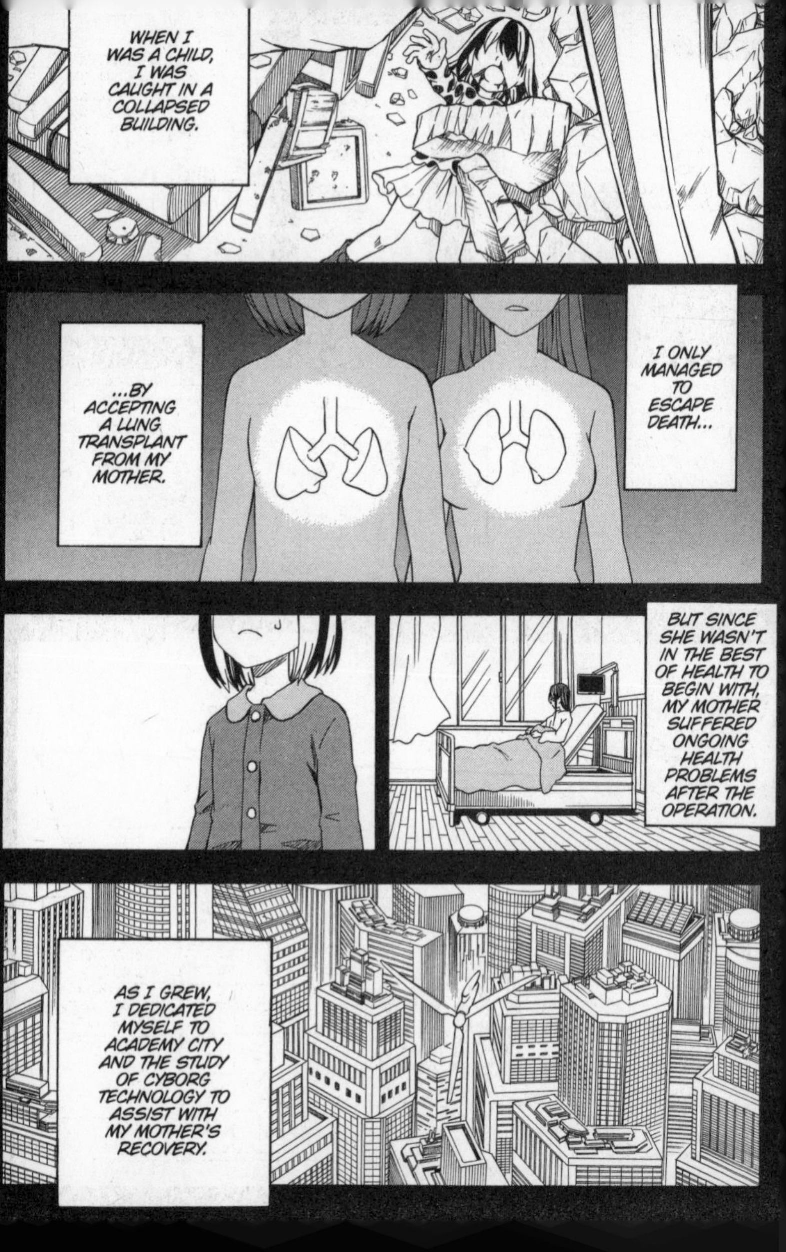
WHEN I WAS A CHILD, I WAS CAUGHT IN A COLLAPSED BUILDING.
I ONLY MANAGED TO ESCAPE DEATH...
...BY ACCEPTING A LUNG TRANSPLANT FROM MY MOTHER.
BUT SINCE SHE WASN'T IN THE BEST OF HEALTH TO BEGIN WITH, MY MOTHER SUFFERED ONGOING HEALTH PROBLEMS AFTER THE OPERATION.
AS I GREW, I DEDICATED MYSELF TO ACADEMY CITY AND THE STUDY OF CYBORG TECHNOLOGY TO ASSIST WITH MY MOTHER'S RECOVERY.

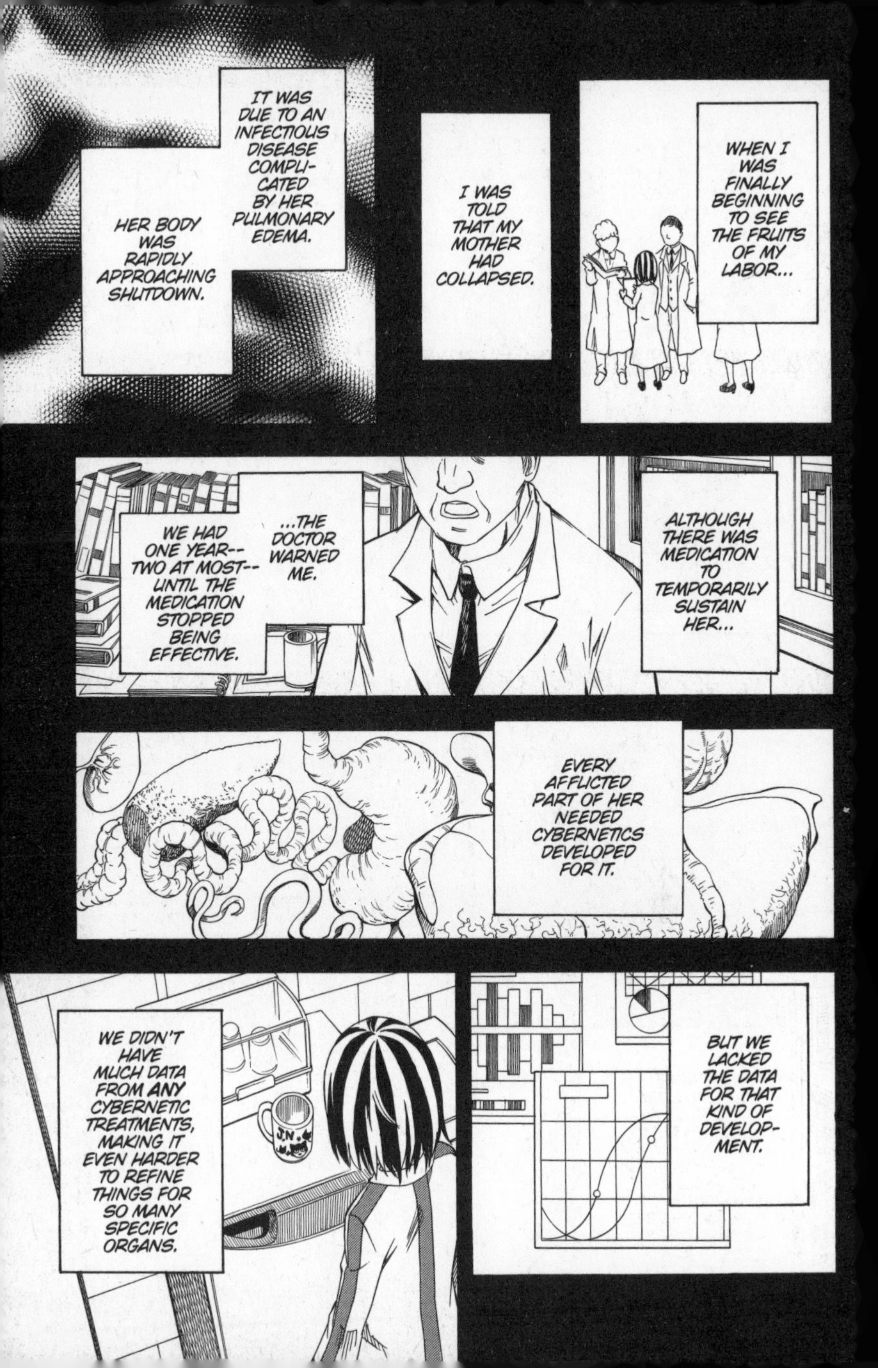
WHEN I WAS FINALLY BEGINNING TO SEE THE FRUITS OF MY LABOR...
I WAS TOLD THAT MY MOTHER HAD COLLAPSED.
IT WAS DUE TO AN INFECTIOUS DISEASE COMPLI-CATED BY HER PULMONARY EDEMA.
HER BODY WAS RAPIDLY APPROACHING SHUTDOWN.
ALTHOUGH THERE WAS MEDICATION TO TEMPORARILY SUSTAIN HER...
...THE DOCTOR WARNED ME.
WE HAD ONE YEAR-- TWO AT MOST-- UNTIL THE MEDICATION STOPPED BEING EFFECTIVE.
EVERY AFFLICTED PART OF HER NEEDED CYBERNETICS DEVELOPED FOR IT.
BUT WE LACKED THE DATA FOR THAT KIND OF DEVELOP-MENT.
J.N.
WE DIDN'T HAVE MUCH DATA FROM ANY CYBERNETIC TREATMENTS, MAKING IT EVEN HARDER TO REFINE THINGS FOR SO MANY SPECIFIC ORGANS.

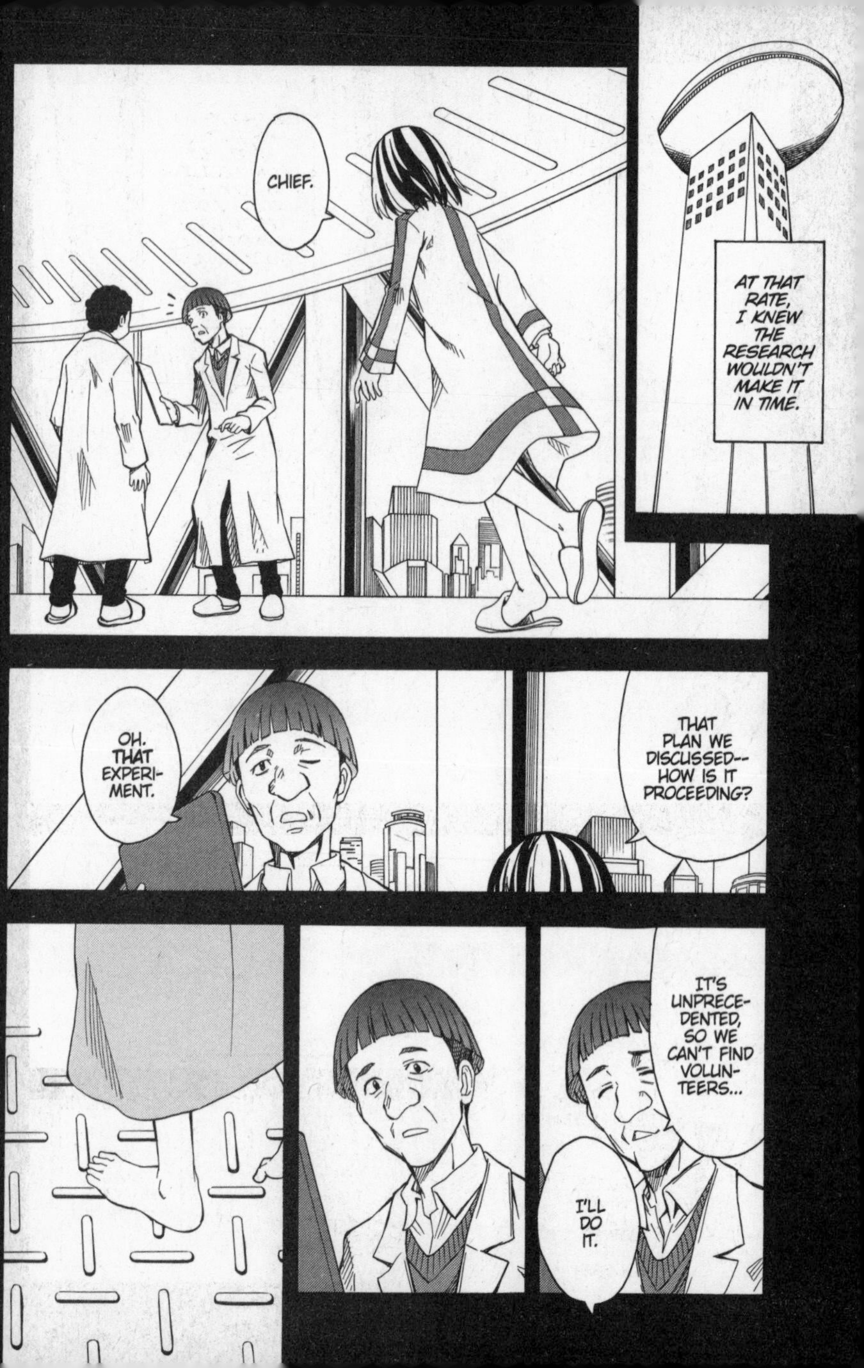
AT THAT RATE, I KNEW THE RESEARCH WOULDN'T MAKE IT IN TIME.
CHIEF.
THAT PLAN WE DISCUSSED-- HOW IS IT PROCEEDING?
OH. THAT EXPERIMENT.
IT'S UNPRECEDENTED, SO WE CAN'T FIND VOLUNTEERS...
I'LL DO IT.

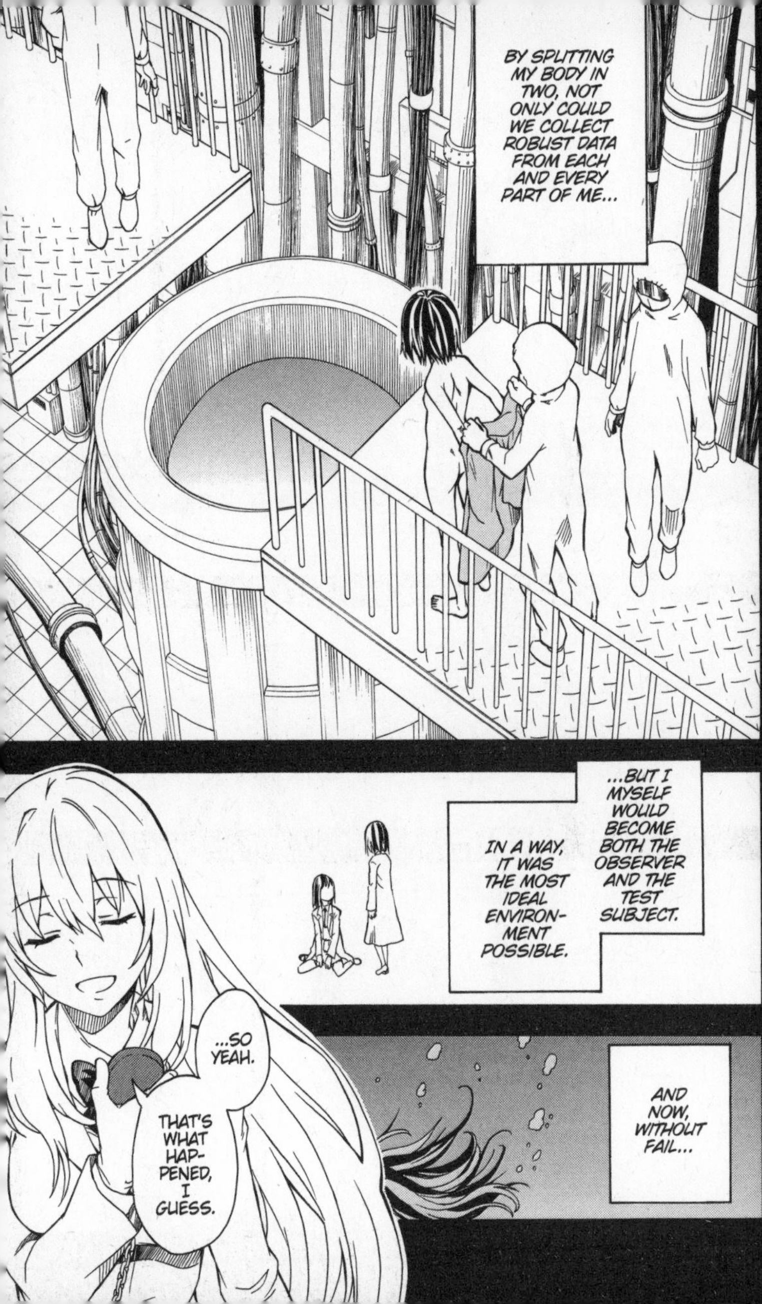
BY SPLITTING MY BODY IN TWO, NOT ONLY COULD WE COLLECT ROBUST DATA FROM EACH AND EVERY PART OF ME...
...BUT I MYSELF WOULD BECOME BOTH THE OBSERVER AND THE TEST SUBJECT.
IN A WAY, IT WAS THE MOST IDEAL ENVIRON-MENT POSSIBLE.
AND NOW, WITHOUT FAIL...
...SO YEAH.
THAT'S WHAT HAP-PENED, I GUESS.

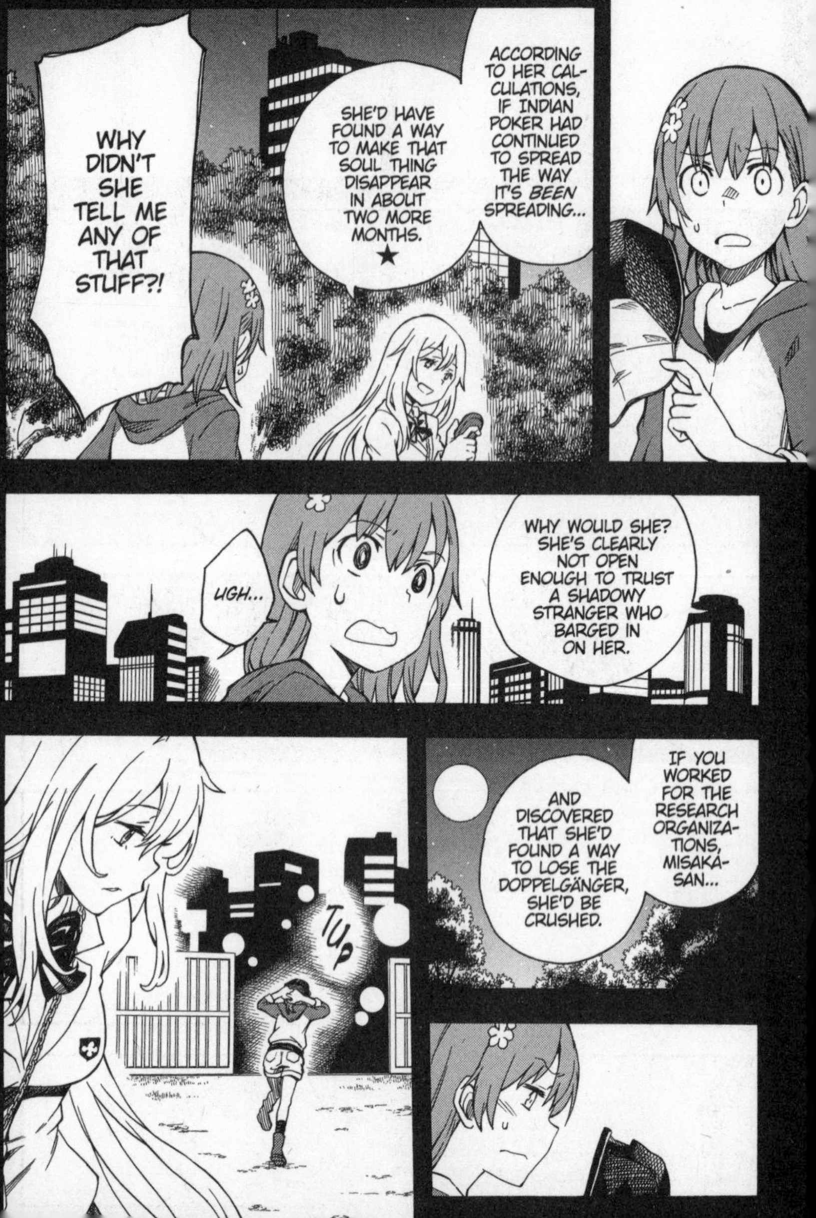
ACCORDING TO HER CALCULATIONS, IF INDIAN POKER HAD CONTINUED TO SPREAD THE WAY IT'S *BEEN* SPREADING...
SHE'D HAVE FOUND A WAY TO MAKE THAT SOUL THING DISAPPEAR IN ABOUT TWO MORE MONTHS. ★
WHY DIDN'T SHE TELL ME ANY OF THAT STUFF?!
WHY WOULD SHE? SHE'S CLEARLY NOT OPEN ENOUGH TO TRUST A SHADOWY STRANGER WHO BARGED IN ON HER.
UGH...
IF YOU WORKED FOR THE RESEARCH ORGANIZATIONS, MISAKA-SAN...
AND DISCOVERED THAT SHE'D FOUND A WAY TO LOSE THE DOPPELGÄNGER, SHE'D BE CRUSHED.
TUP

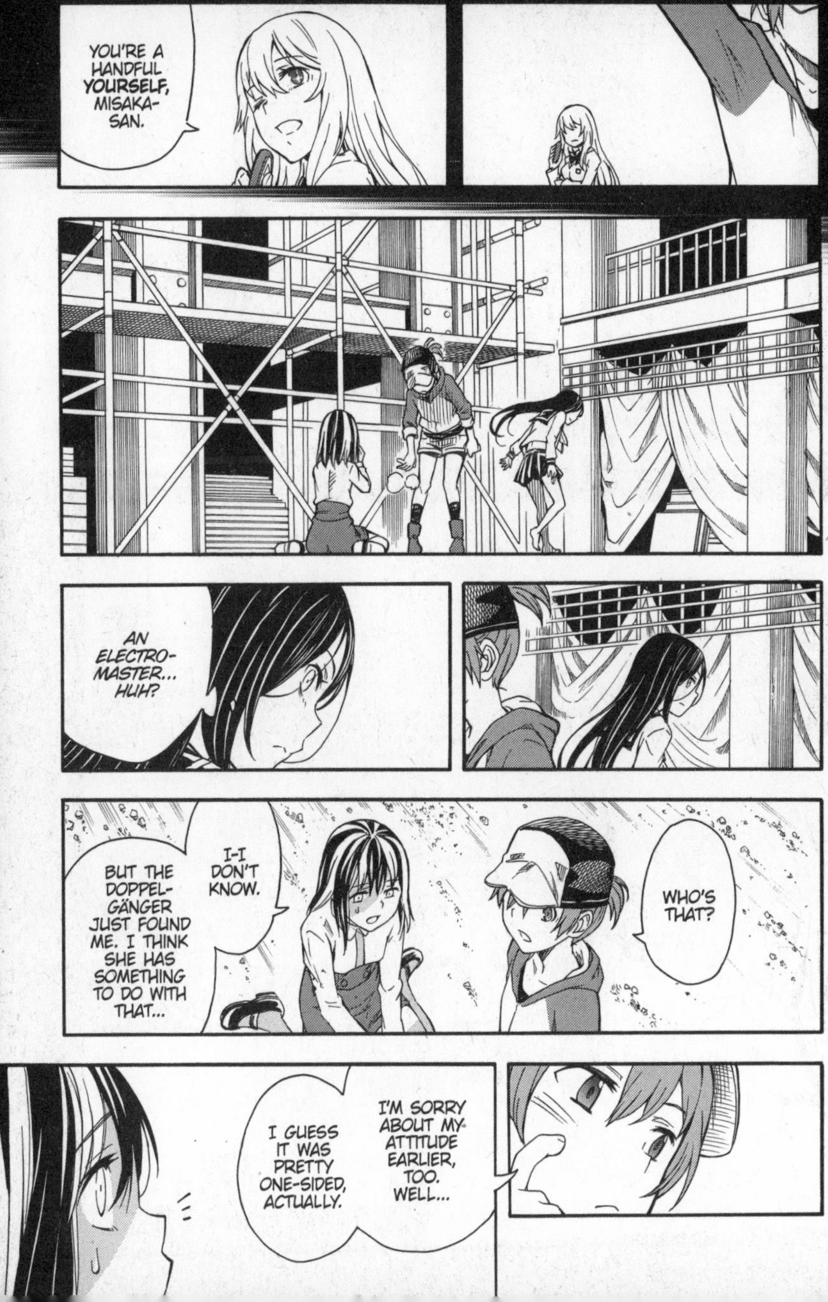
YOU'RE A HANDFUL YOURSELF, MISAKA-SAN.
AN ELECTRO-MASTER... HUH?
WHO'S THAT?
I-I DON'T KNOW.
BUT THE DOPPEL-GÄNGER JUST FOUND ME. I THINK SHE HAS SOMETHING TO DO WITH THAT...
I'M SORRY ABOUT MY ATTITUDE EARLIER, TOO. WELL...
I GUESS IT WAS PRETTY ONE-SIDED, ACTUALLY.

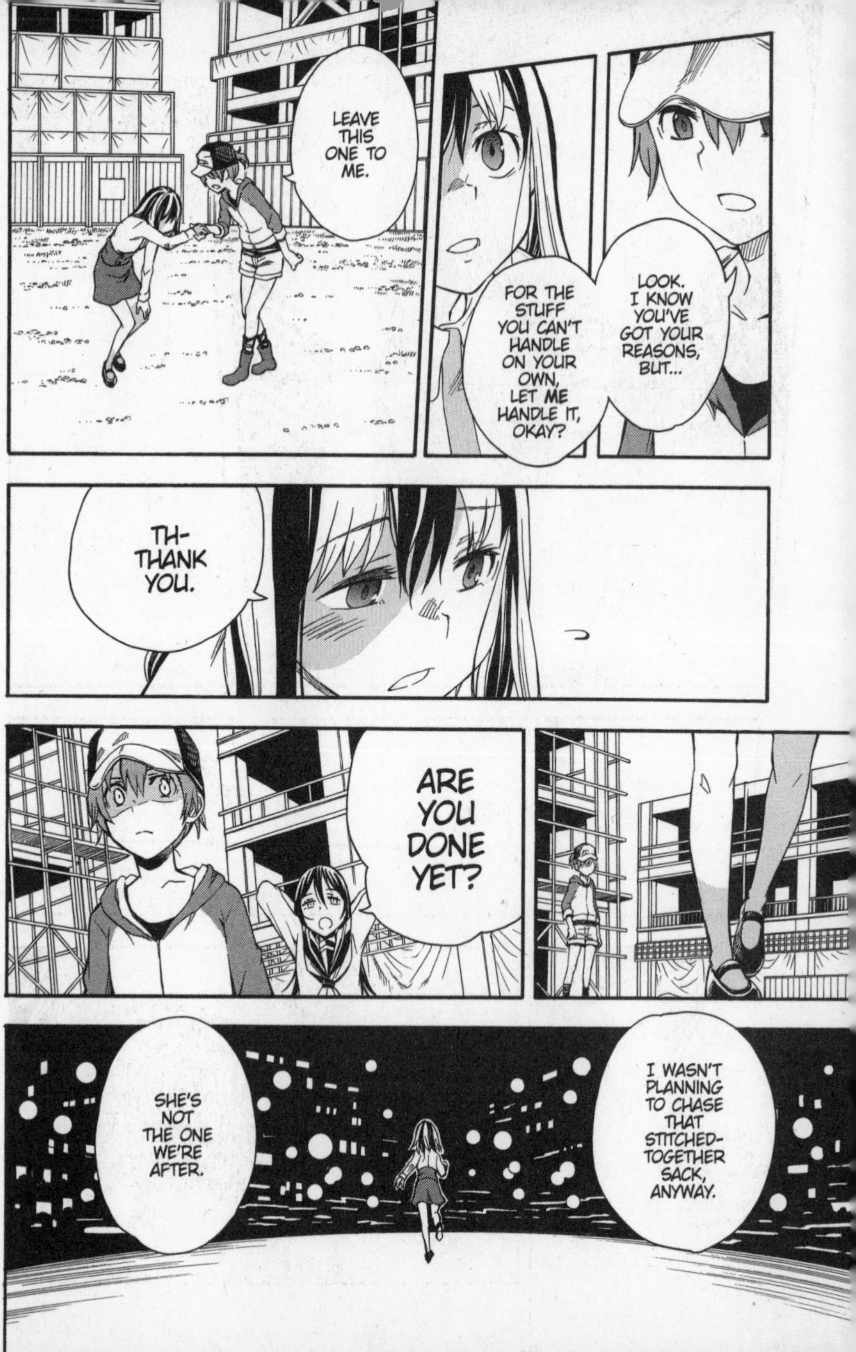
LOOK. I KNOW YOU'VE GOT YOUR REASONS, BUT...
FOR THE STUFF YOU CAN'T HANDLE ON YOUR OWN, LET ME HANDLE IT, OKAY?
LEAVE THIS ONE TO ME.
TH-THANK YOU.
ARE YOU DONE YET?
I WASN'T PLANNING TO CHASE THAT STITCHED-TOGETHER SACK, ANYWAY.
SHE'S NOT THE ONE WE'RE AFTER.

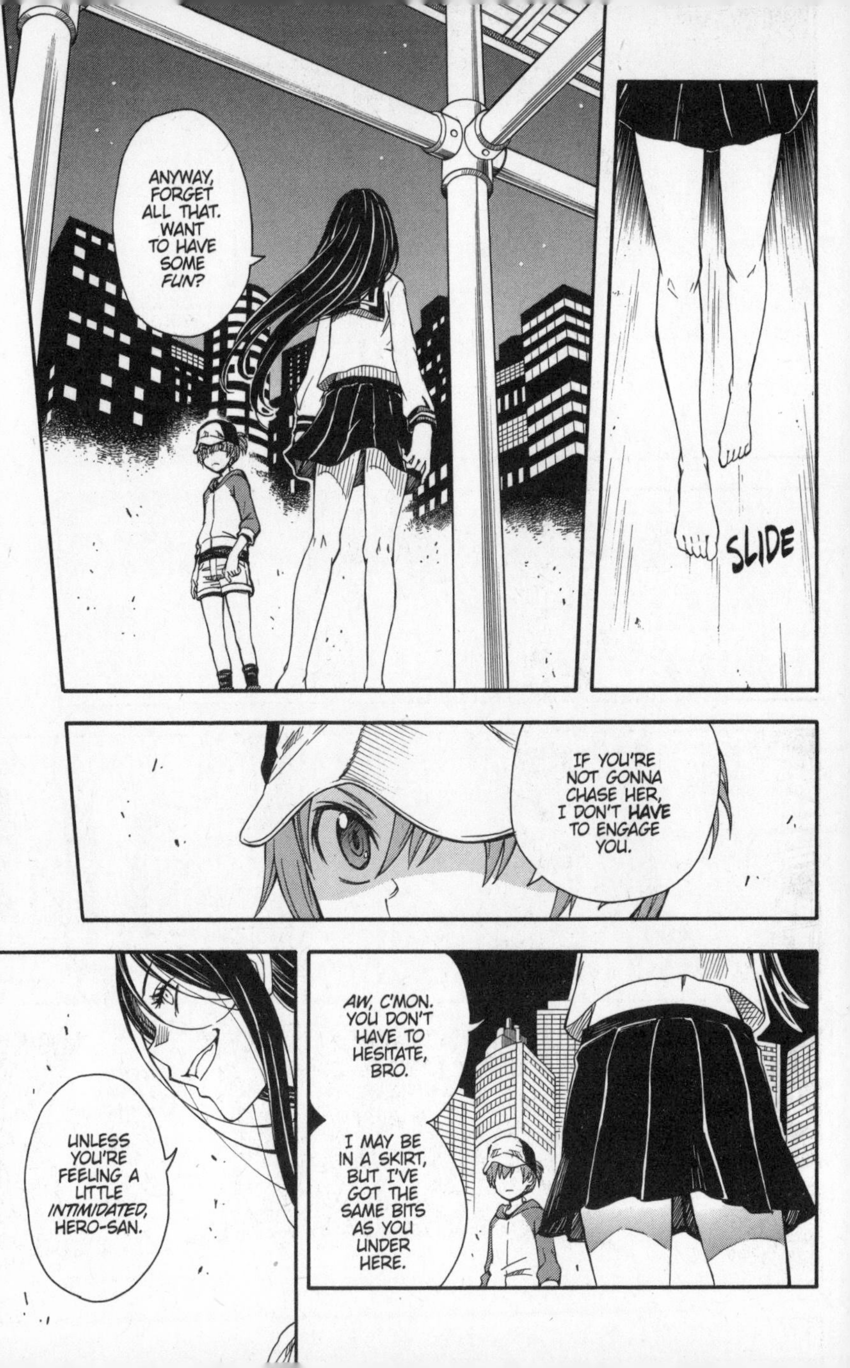
SLIDE
ANYWAY, FORGET ALL THAT. WANT TO HAVE SOME *FUN?*
IF YOU'RE NOT GONNA CHASE HER, I DON'T **HAVE** TO ENGAGE YOU.
AW, C'MON. YOU DON'T HAVE TO HESITATE, BRO.
I MAY BE IN A SKIRT, BUT I'VE GOT THE SAME BITS AS YOU UNDER HERE.
UNLESS YOU'RE FEELING A LITTLE *INTIMIDATED,* HERO-SAN.

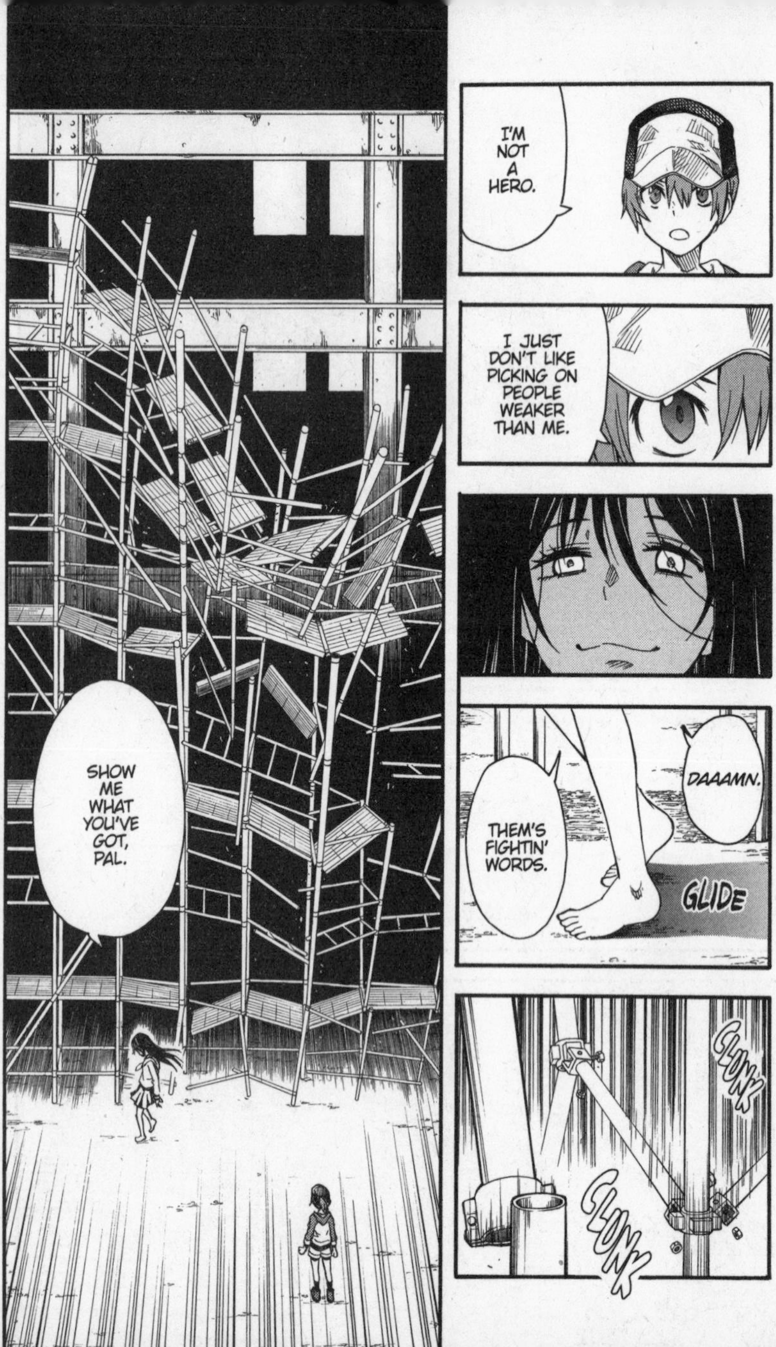
I'M NOT A HERO.
I JUST DON'T LIKE PICKING ON PEOPLE WEAKER THAN ME.
DAAAMN.
THEM'S FIGHTIN' WORDS.
GLIDE
CLONK
CLONK
CLONK
SHOW ME WHAT YOU'VE GOT, PAL.

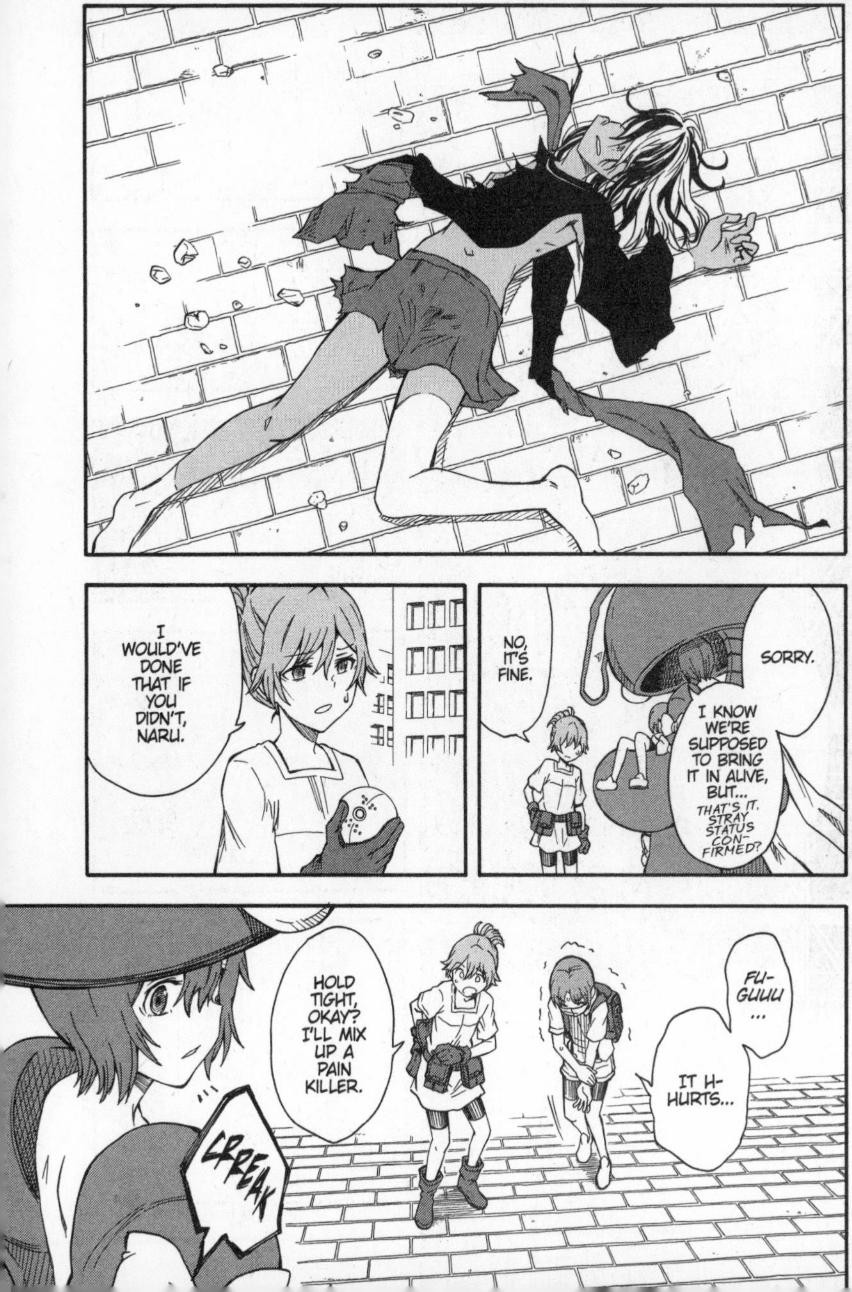
SORRY.
I KNOW WE'RE SUPPOSED TO BRING IT IN ALIVE, BUT...
THAT'S IT. STRAY STATUS CON-FIRMED?
NO, IT'S FINE.
I WOULD'VE DONE THAT IF YOU DIDN'T, NARU.
FU-GUUU...
IT H-HURTS...
HOLD TIGHT, OKAY? I'LL MIX UP A PAIN KILLER.
CREAK

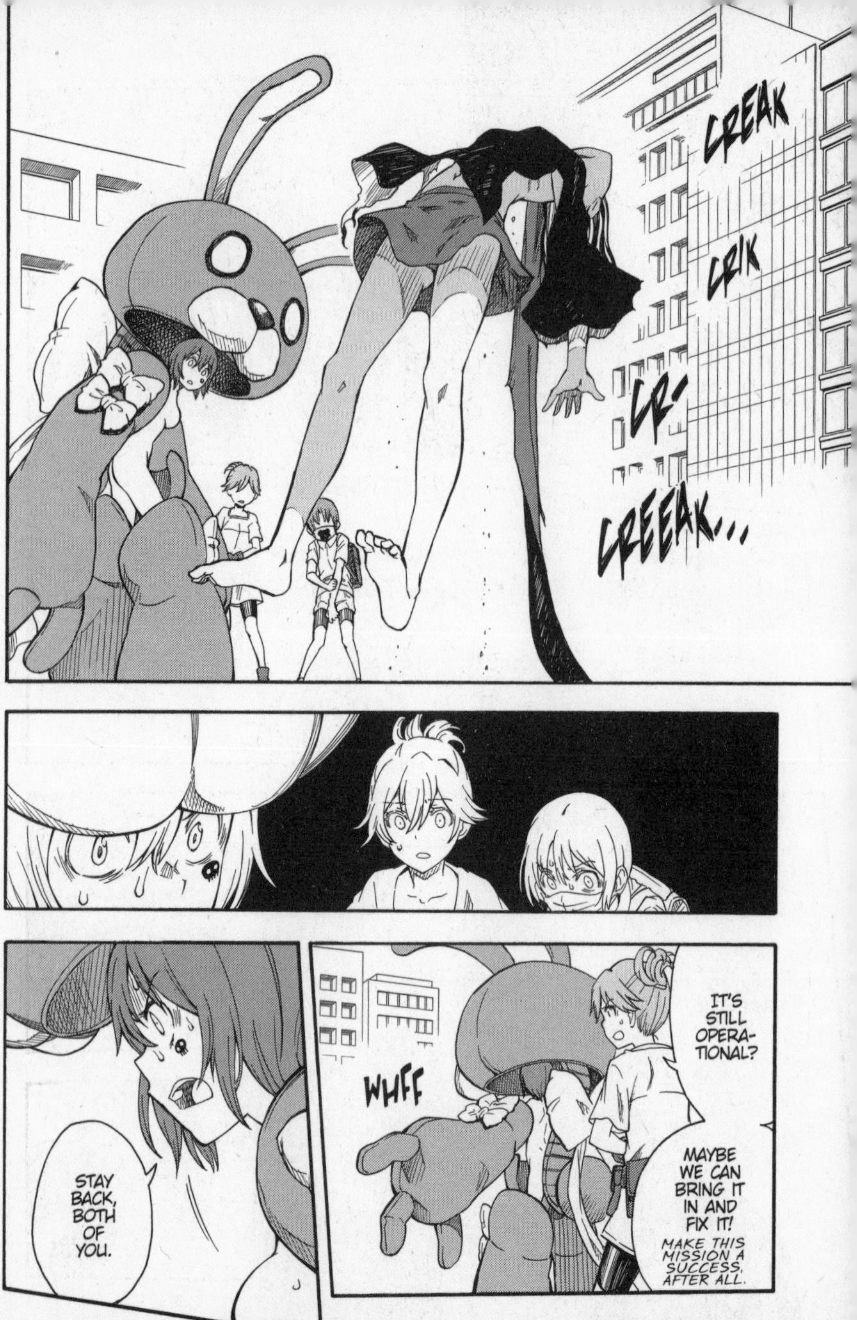
CREAK
CRIK
CR-
CREEAK...
IT'S STILL OPERATIONAL?
WHFF
MAYBE WE CAN BRING IT IN AND FIX IT!
MAKE THIS MISSION A SUCCESS, AFTER ALL.
STAY BACK, BOTH OF YOU.

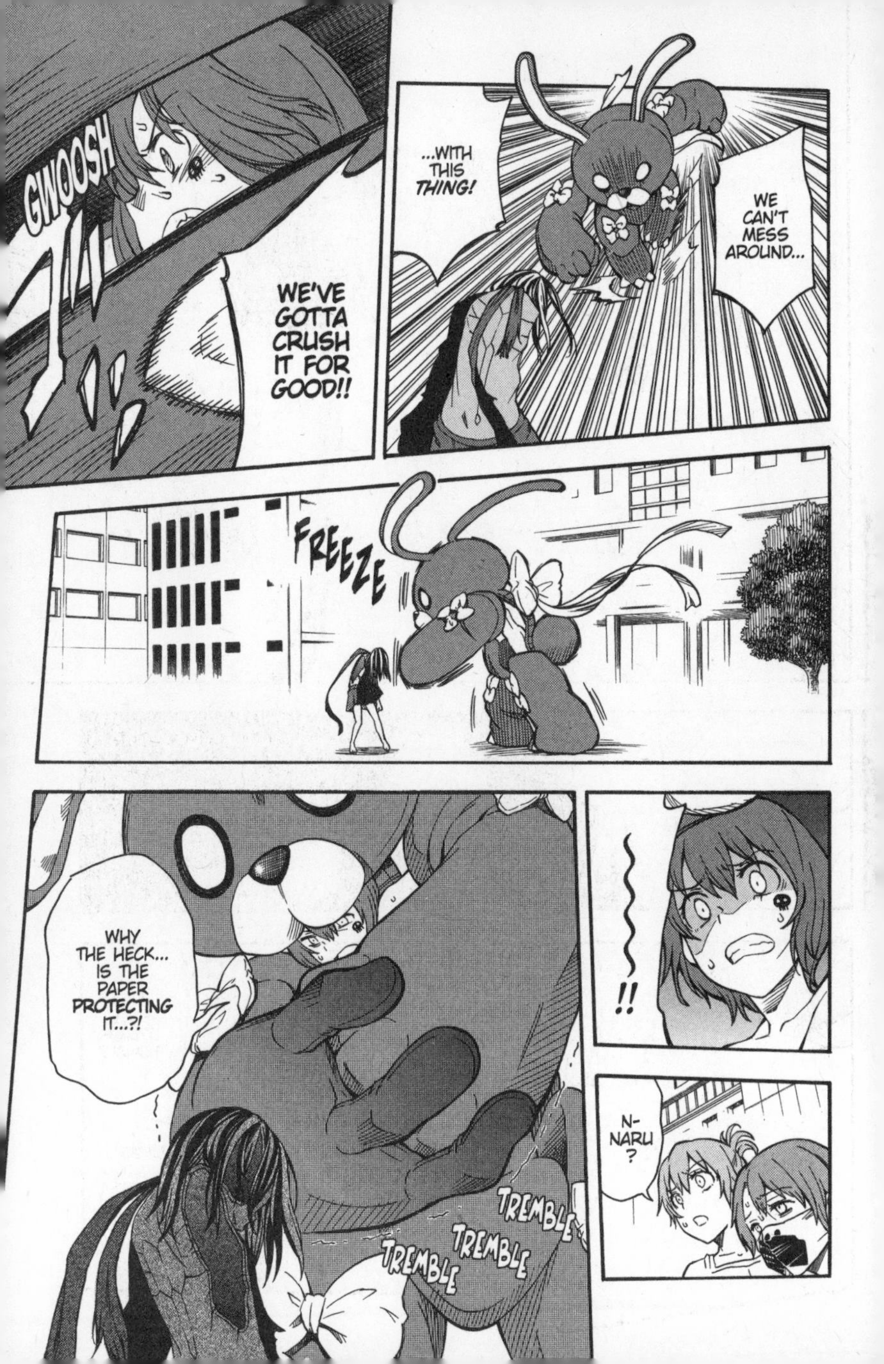
WE CAN'T MESS AROUND...
...WITH THIS THING!
WE'VE GOTTA CRUSH IT FOR GOOD!!
GWOOSH
FREEZE
!!
WHY THE HECK... IS THE PAPER PROTECTING IT...?!
N-NARU?
TREMBLE
TREMBLE
TREMBLE

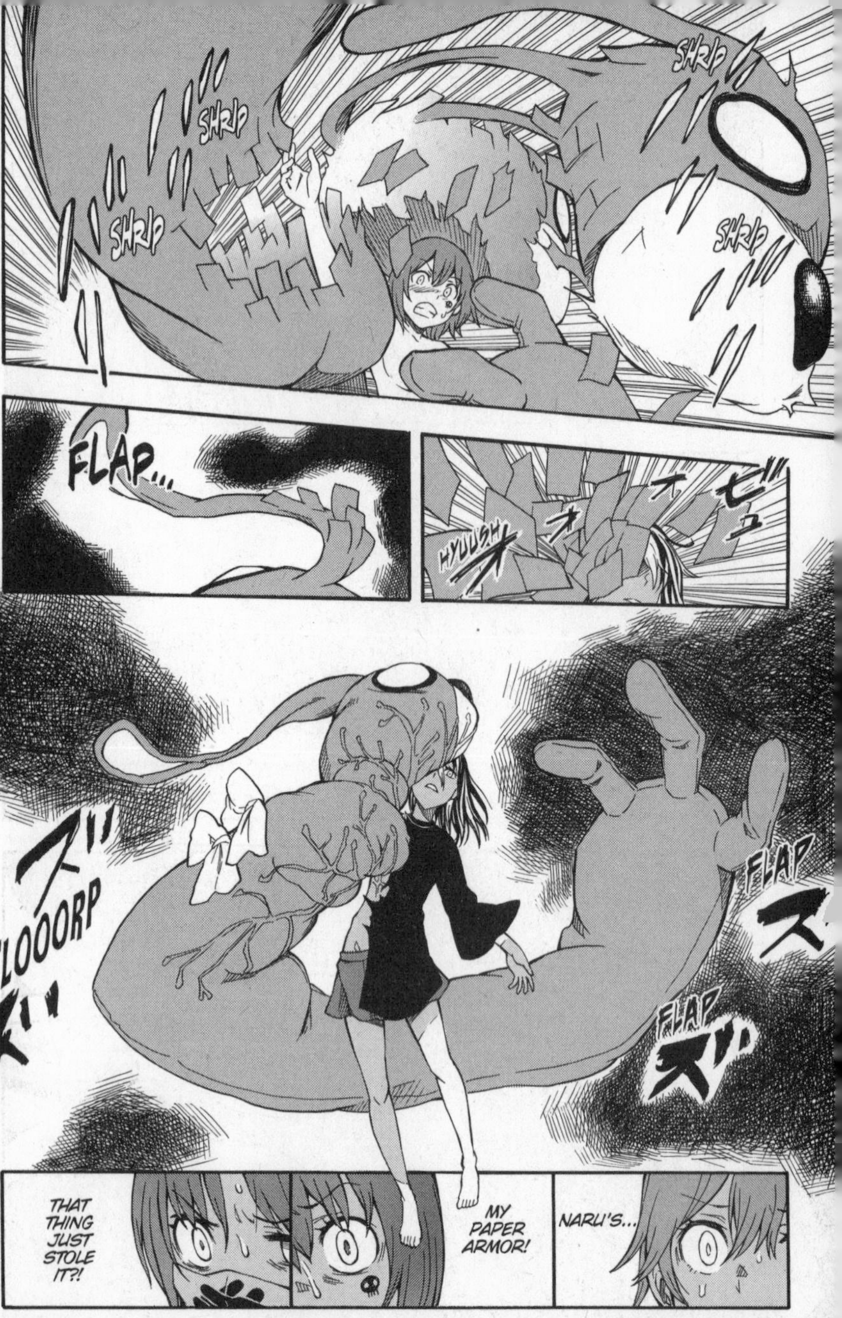
SHRIP
SHRIP
SHRIP
SHRIP
HYUUSH
FLAP...
FLAP
FLAP
FLOOORP
NARU'S...
MY PAPER ARMOR!
THAT THING JUST STOLE IT?!

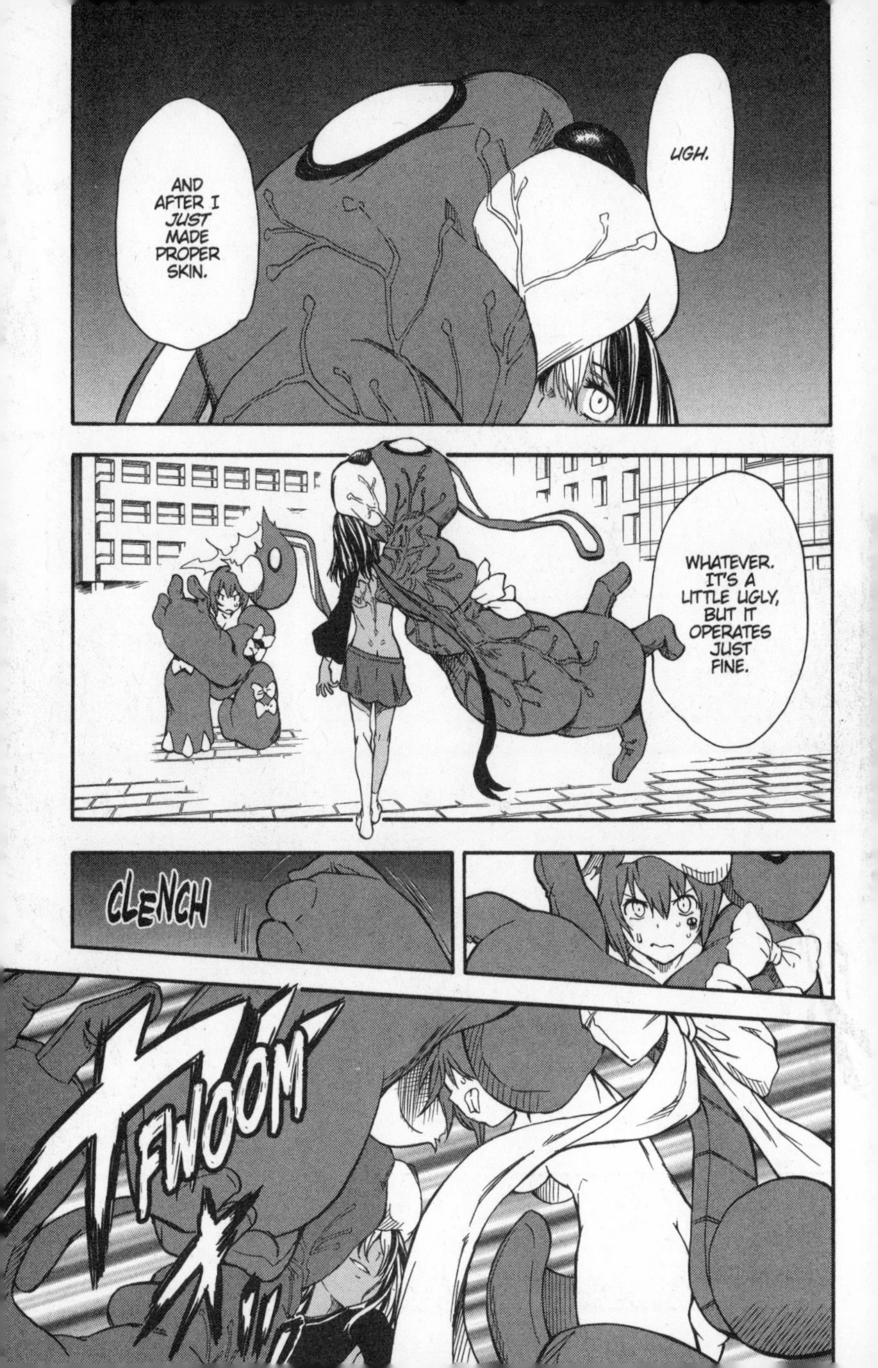
UGH.
AND AFTER I JUST MADE PROPER SKIN.
WHATEVER. IT'S A LITTLE UGLY, BUT IT OPERATES JUST FINE.
CLENCH
FWOOM

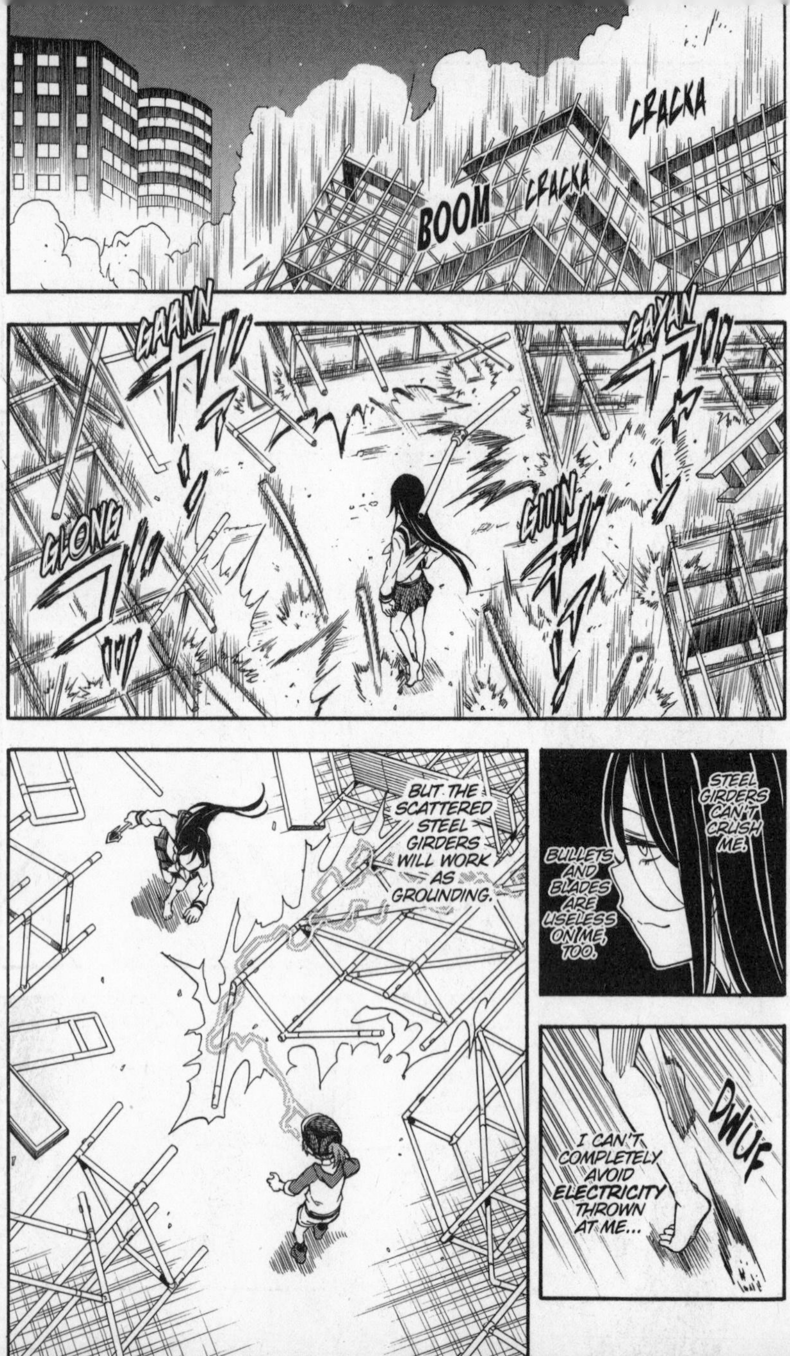
CRACKA
CRACKA
BOOM
GAYAN
GAANN
GUUN
GLONG
STEEL GIRDERS CAN'T CRUSH ME.
BULLETS AND BLADES ARE USELESS ON ME, TOO.
BUT THE SCATTERED STEEL GIRDERS WILL WORK AS GROUNDING.
DWUF
I CAN'T COMPLETELY AVOID ELECTRICITY THROWN AT ME...

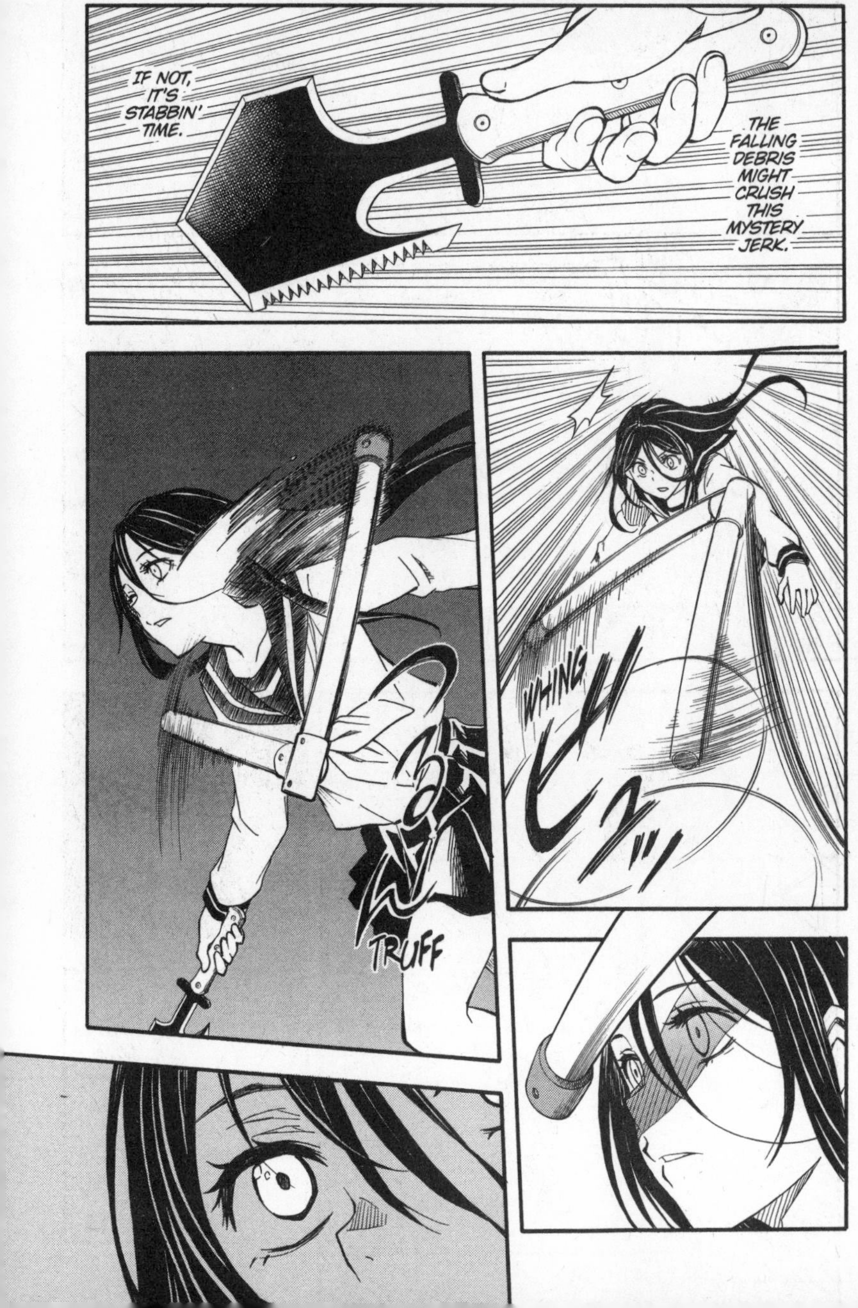
THE FALLING DEBRIS MIGHT CRUSH THIS MYSTERY JERK.
IF NOT, IT'S STABBIN' TIME.
WHING
TRUFF

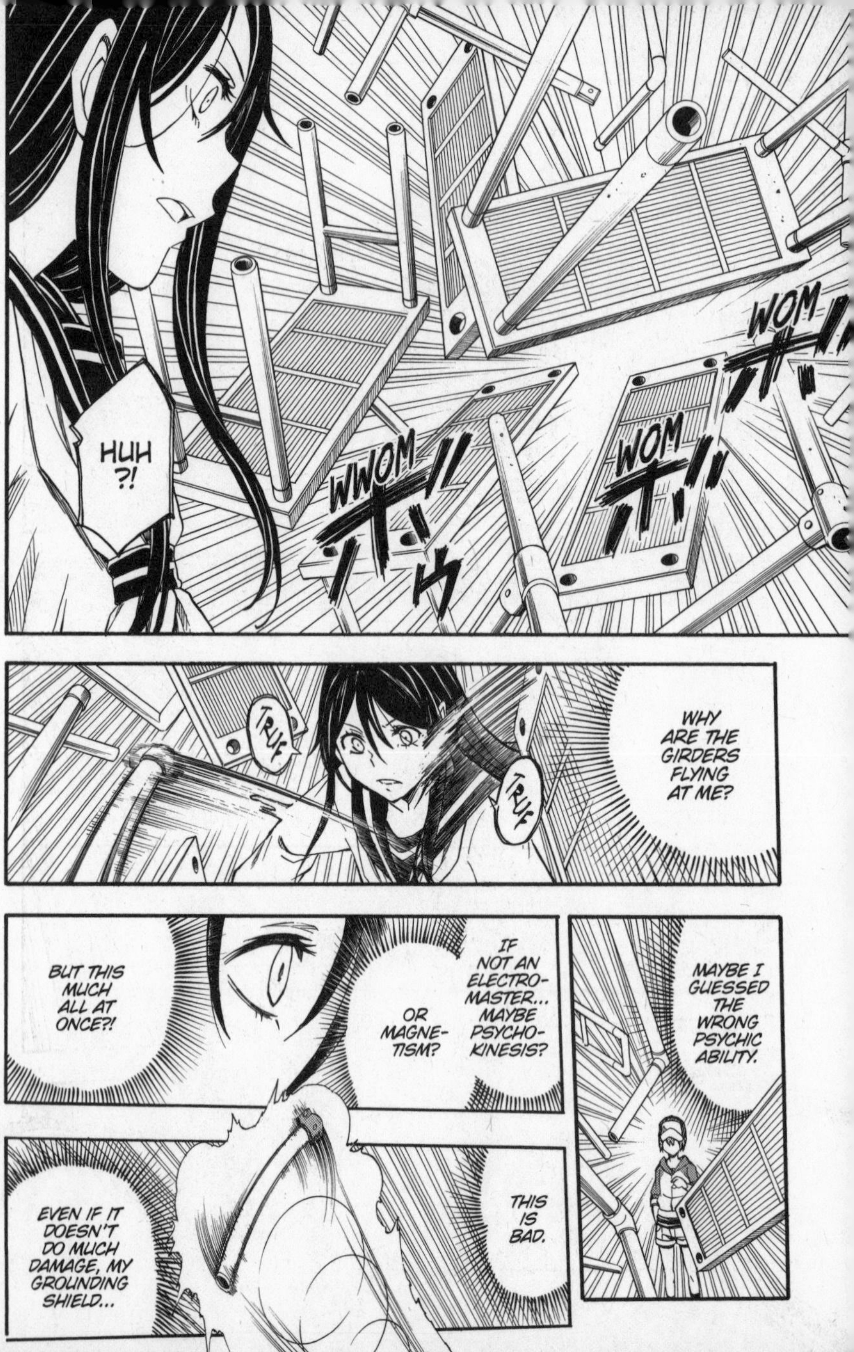
WOM
WOM
WWOM
HUH?!
WHY ARE THE GIRDERS FLYING AT ME?
TRUF
TRUF
MAYBE I GUESSED THE WRONG PSYCHIC ABILITY.
IF NOT AN ELECTRO-MASTER... MAYBE PSYCHO-KINESIS?
OR MAGNE-TISM?
BUT THIS MUCH ALL AT ONCE?!
THIS IS BAD.
EVEN IF IT DOESN'T DO MUCH DAMAGE, MY GROUNDING SHIELD...

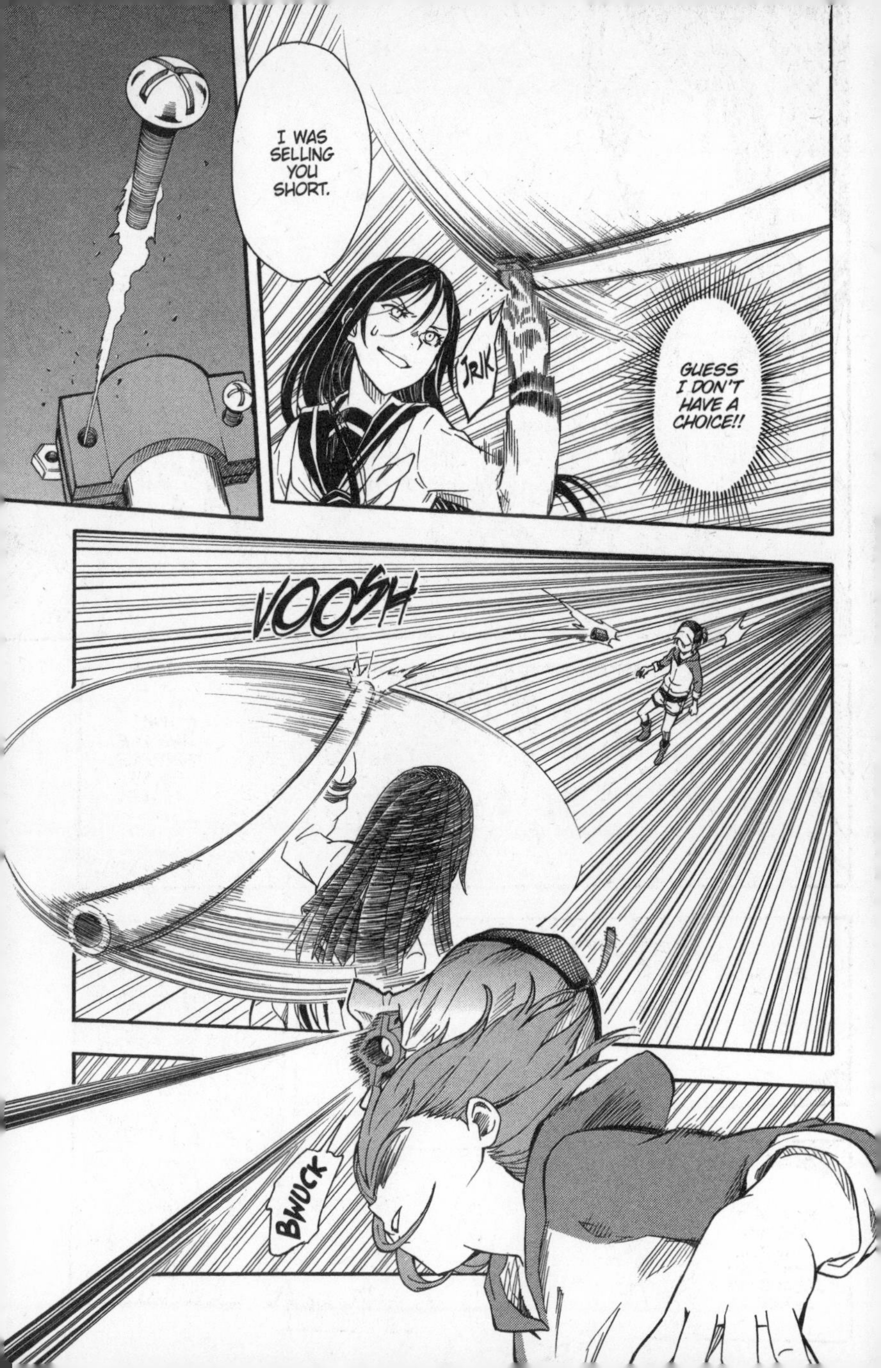
I WAS SELLING YOU SHORT.
JRIK
GUESS I DON'T HAVE A CHOICE!!
VOOSH
BWUCK

I TRADED MY FINGERTIP...

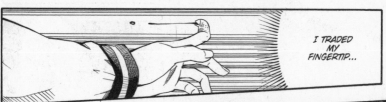

...FOR AN ATTACK YOU CAN'T DODGE!

AND EVEN IF THE ELECTRICITY KNOCKS ME OUT, MY INERTIA WILL STILL THROW ME AT YOU!!

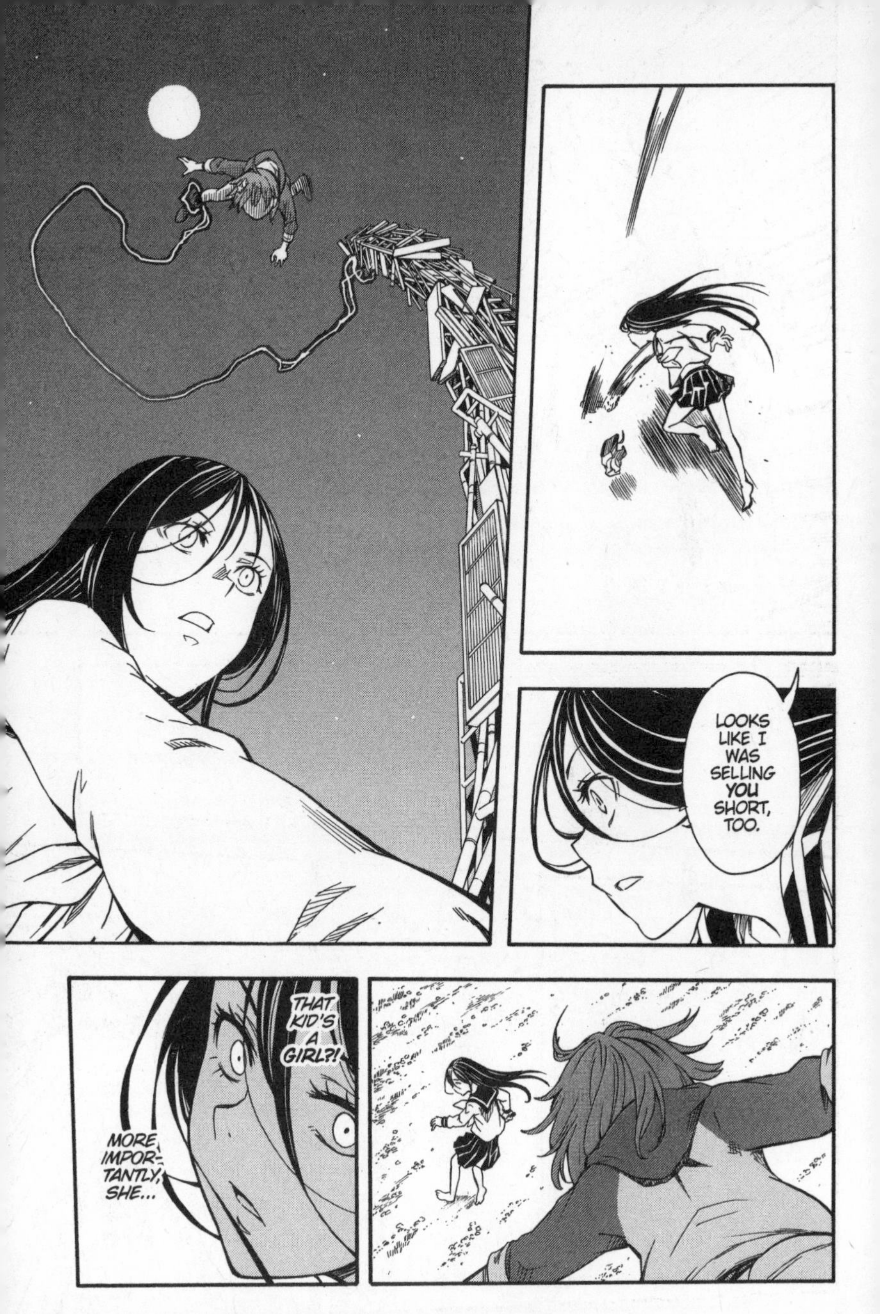
LOOKS LIKE I WAS SELLING YOU SHORT, TOO.
THAT KID'S A GIRL?!
MORE IMPOR-TANTLY, SHE...

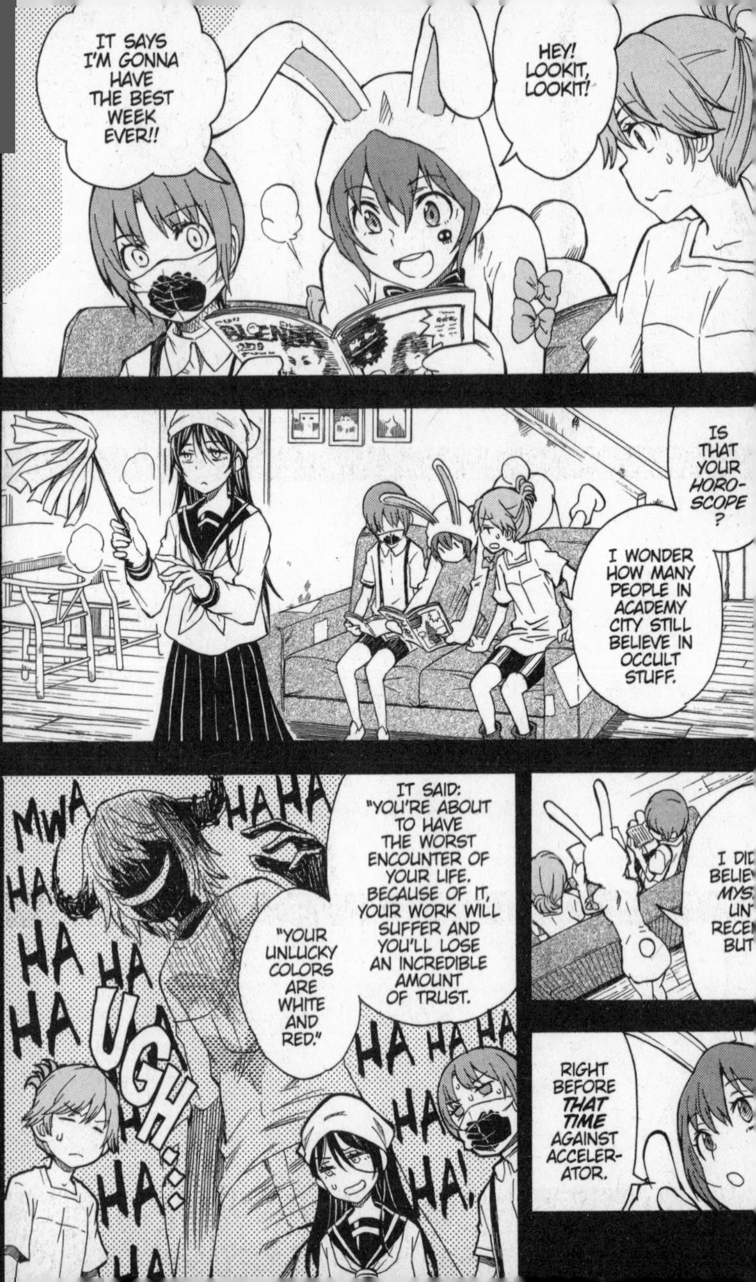
HEY! LOOKIT, LOOKIT!
IT SAYS I'M GONNA HAVE THE BEST WEEK EVER!!
IS THAT YOUR HORO-SCOPE?
I WONDER HOW MANY PEOPLE IN ACADEMY CITY STILL BELIEVE IN OCCULT STUFF.
RIGHT BEFORE THAT TIME AGAINST ACCELER-ATOR.
IT SAID: "YOU'RE ABOUT TO HAVE THE WORST ENCOUNTER OF YOUR LIFE. BECAUSE OF IT, YOUR WORK WILL SUFFER AND YOU'LL LOSE AN INCREDIBLE AMOUNT OF TRUST.
"YOUR UNLUCKY COLORS ARE WHITE AND RED."
MWA HA HA HA HA HA HA HA HA HA HA HA HA HA HA!
UGH..

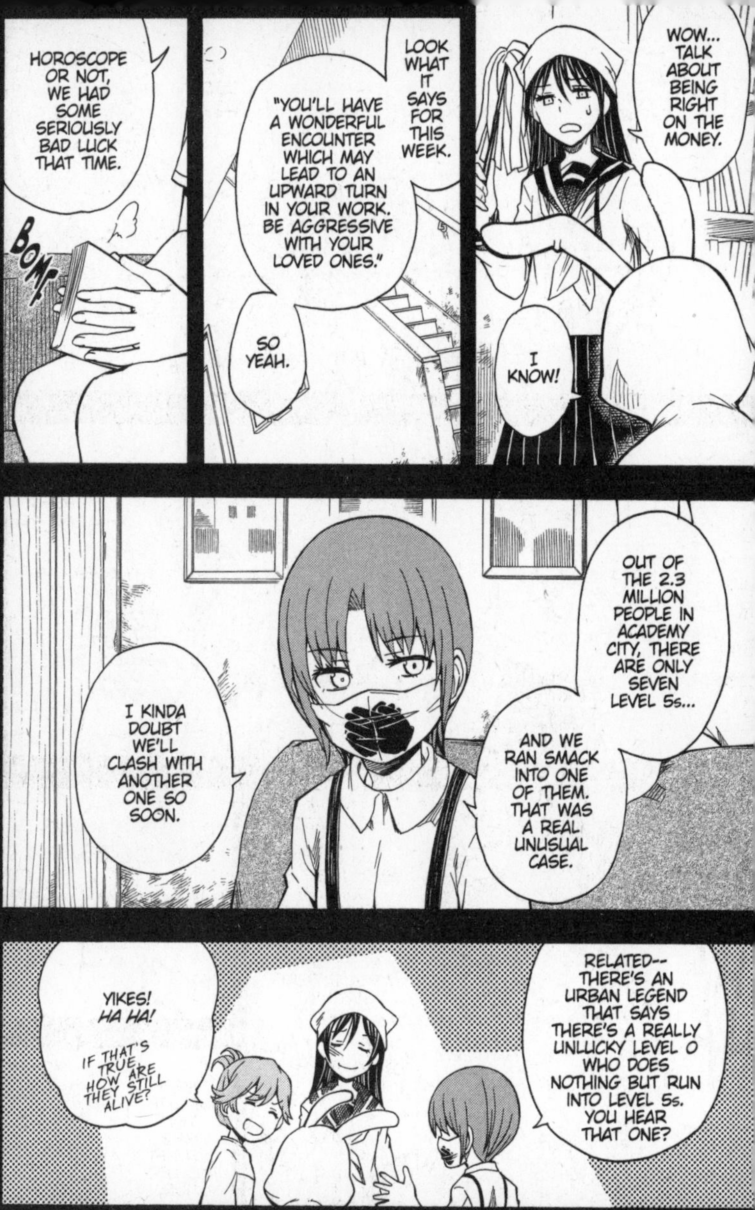
WOW... TALK ABOUT BEING RIGHT ON THE MONEY.
I KNOW!
LOOK WHAT IT SAYS FOR THIS WEEK.
"YOU'LL HAVE A WONDERFUL ENCOUNTER WHICH MAY LEAD TO AN UPWARD TURN IN YOUR WORK. BE AGGRESSIVE WITH YOUR LOVED ONES."
SO YEAH.
HOROSCOPE OR NOT, WE HAD SOME SERIOUSLY BAD LUCK THAT TIME.
BOMF
OUT OF THE 2.3 MILLION PEOPLE IN ACADEMY CITY, THERE ARE ONLY SEVEN LEVEL 5s...
AND WE RAN SMACK INTO ONE OF THEM. THAT WAS A REAL UNUSUAL CASE.
I KINDA DOUBT WE'LL CLASH WITH ANOTHER ONE SO SOON.
RELATED-- THERE'S AN URBAN LEGEND THAT SAYS THERE'S A REALLY UNLUCKY LEVEL 0 WHO DOES NOTHING BUT RUN INTO LEVEL 5s. YOU HEAR THAT ONE?
YIKES! HA HA!
IF THAT'S TRUE, HOW ARE THEY STILL ALIVE?

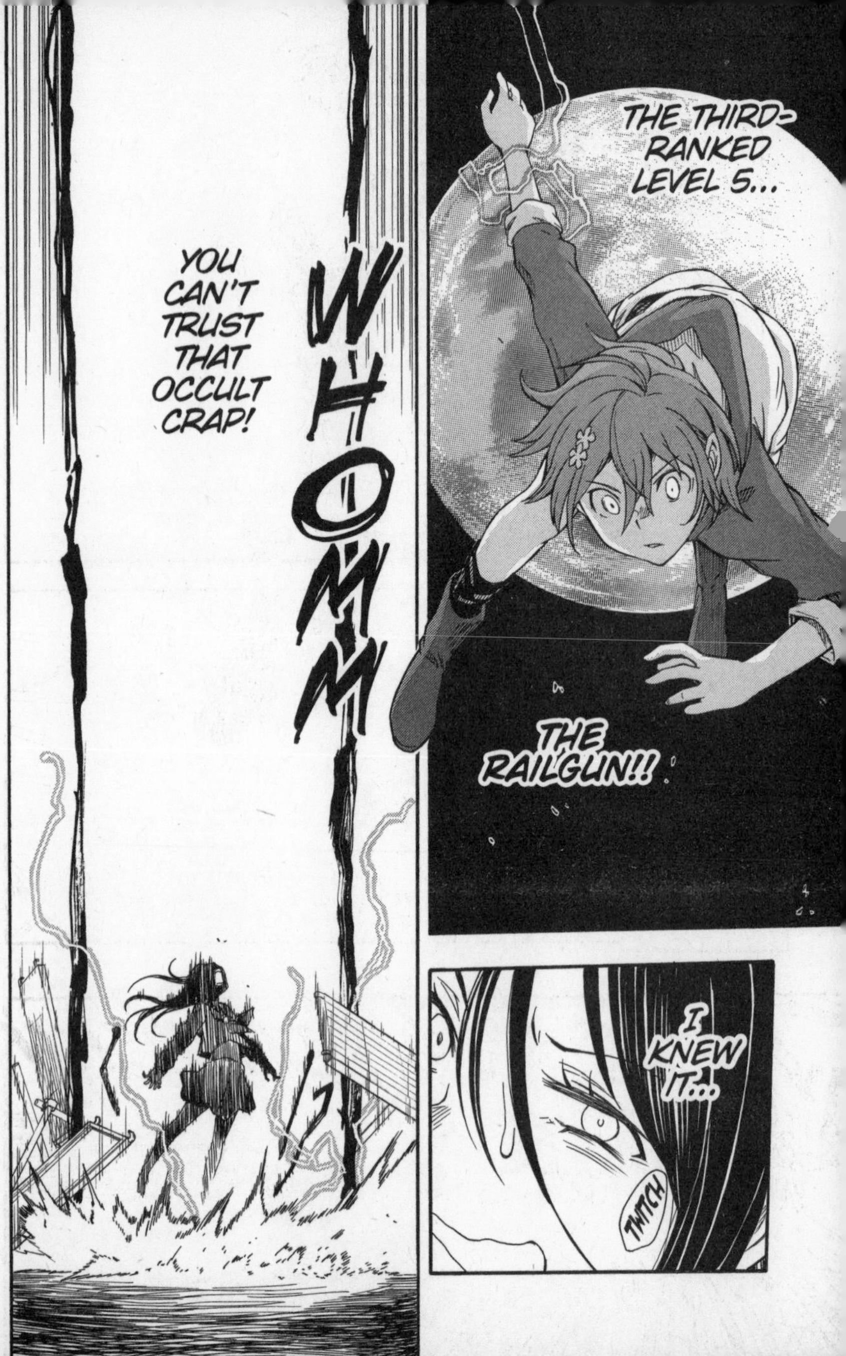
THE THIRD-RANKED LEVEL 5...
THE RAILGUN!!
I KNEW IT...
TWITCH
YOU CAN'T TRUST THAT OCCULT CRAP!
WHOMM

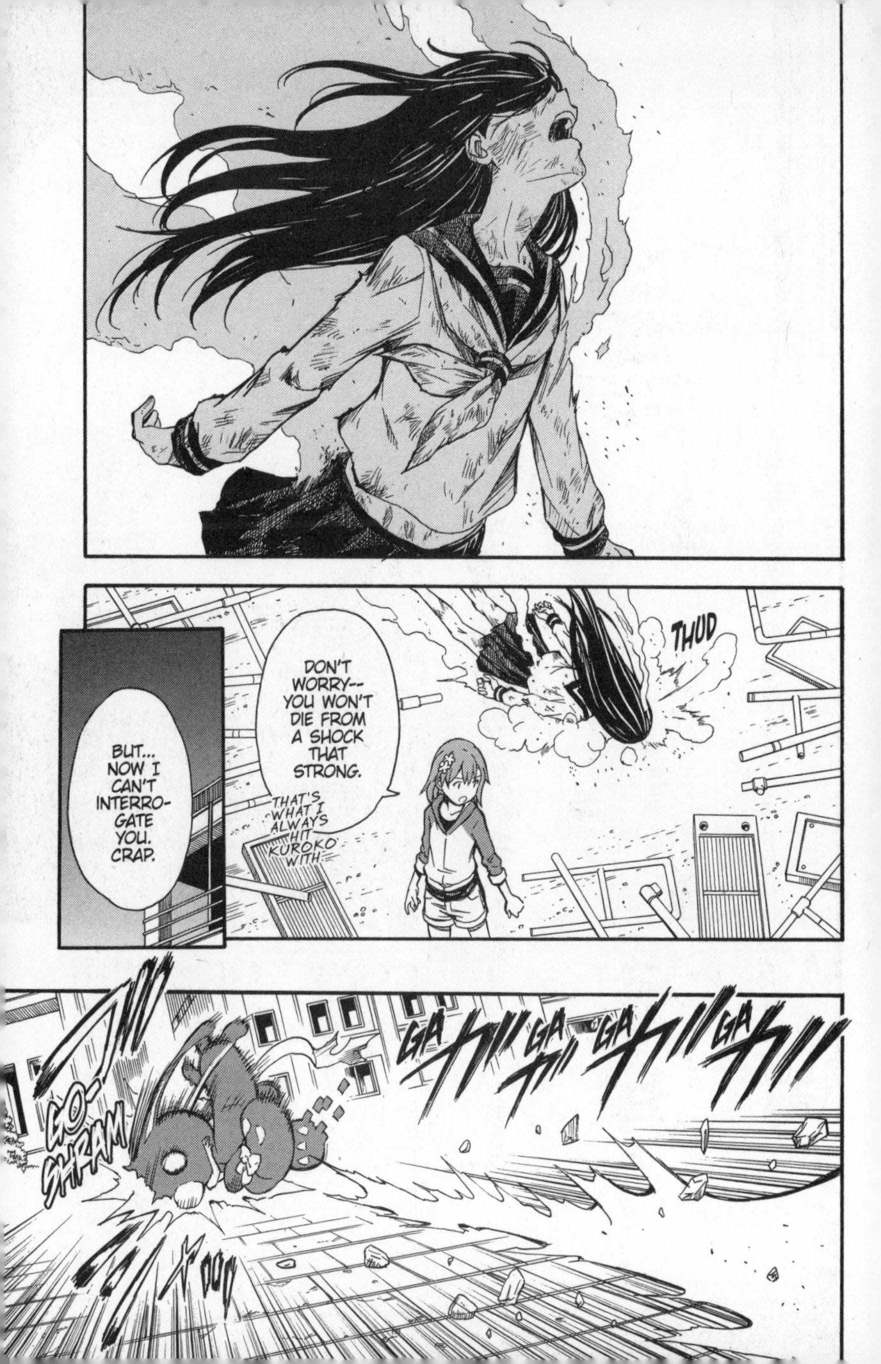

THUD
DON'T WORRY-- YOU WON'T DIE FROM A SHOCK THAT STRONG.
THAT'S WHAT I ALWAYS HIT KUROKO WITH.
BUT... NOW I CAN'T INTERRO-GATE YOU. CRAP.
GA GA GA GA
GO-SHRAM
DOO

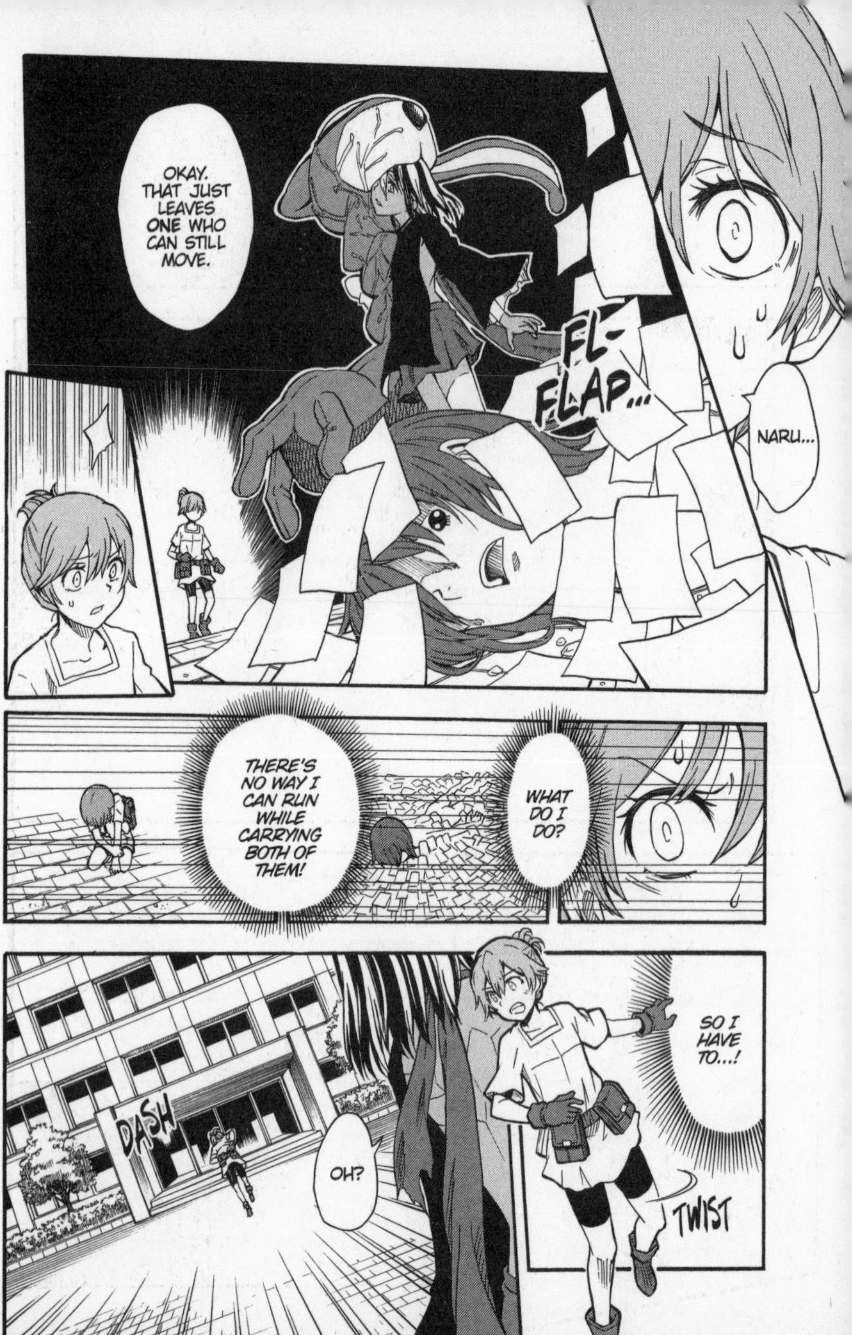
NARU...
OKAY. THAT JUST LEAVES ONE WHO CAN STILL MOVE.
FL-FLAP...
WHAT DO I DO?
THERE'S NO WAY I CAN RUN WHILE CARRYING BOTH OF THEM!
SO I HAVE TO...!
OH?
TWIST
DASH

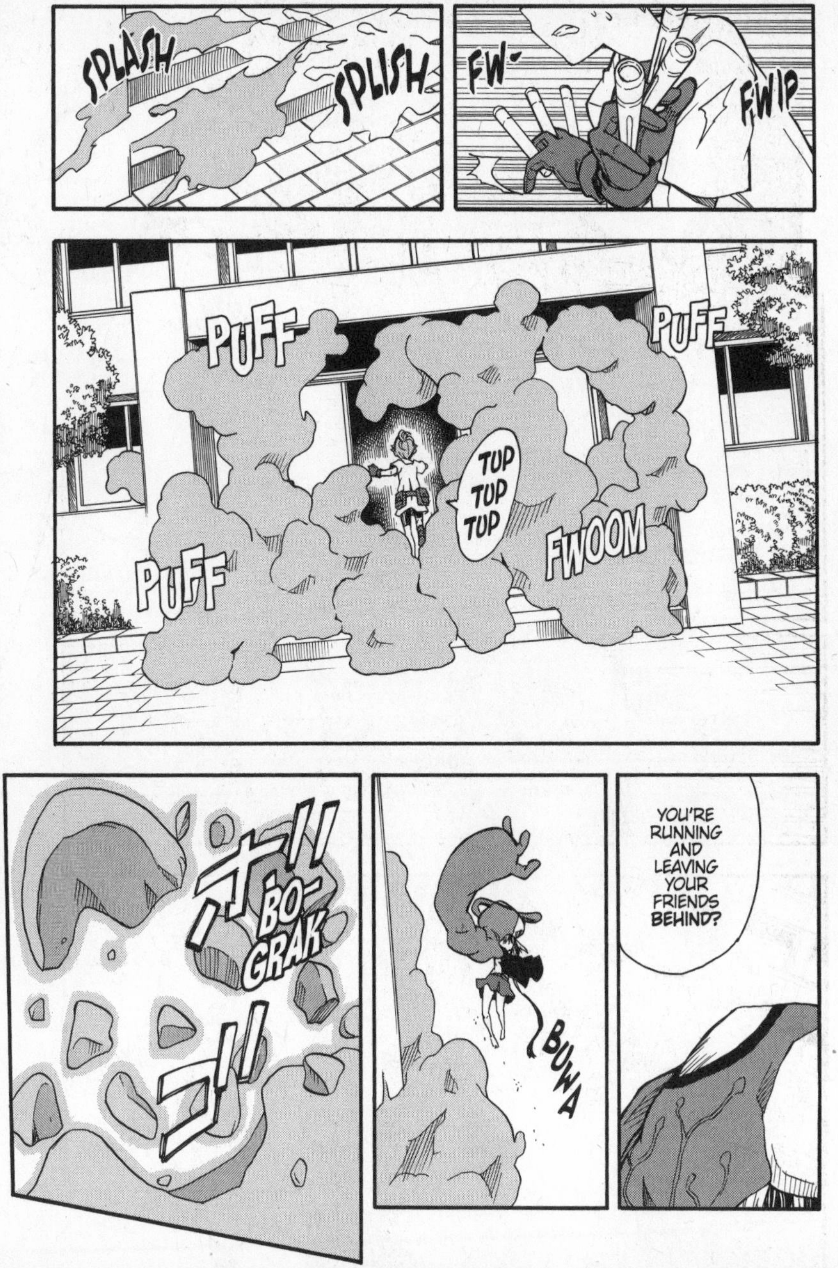
FW-
FWIP
SPLASH
SPLISH
PUFF
PUFF
TUP TUP TUP
FWOOM
PUFF
YOU'RE RUNNING AND LEAVING YOUR FRIENDS BEHIND?
BUWA
BO-GRAK

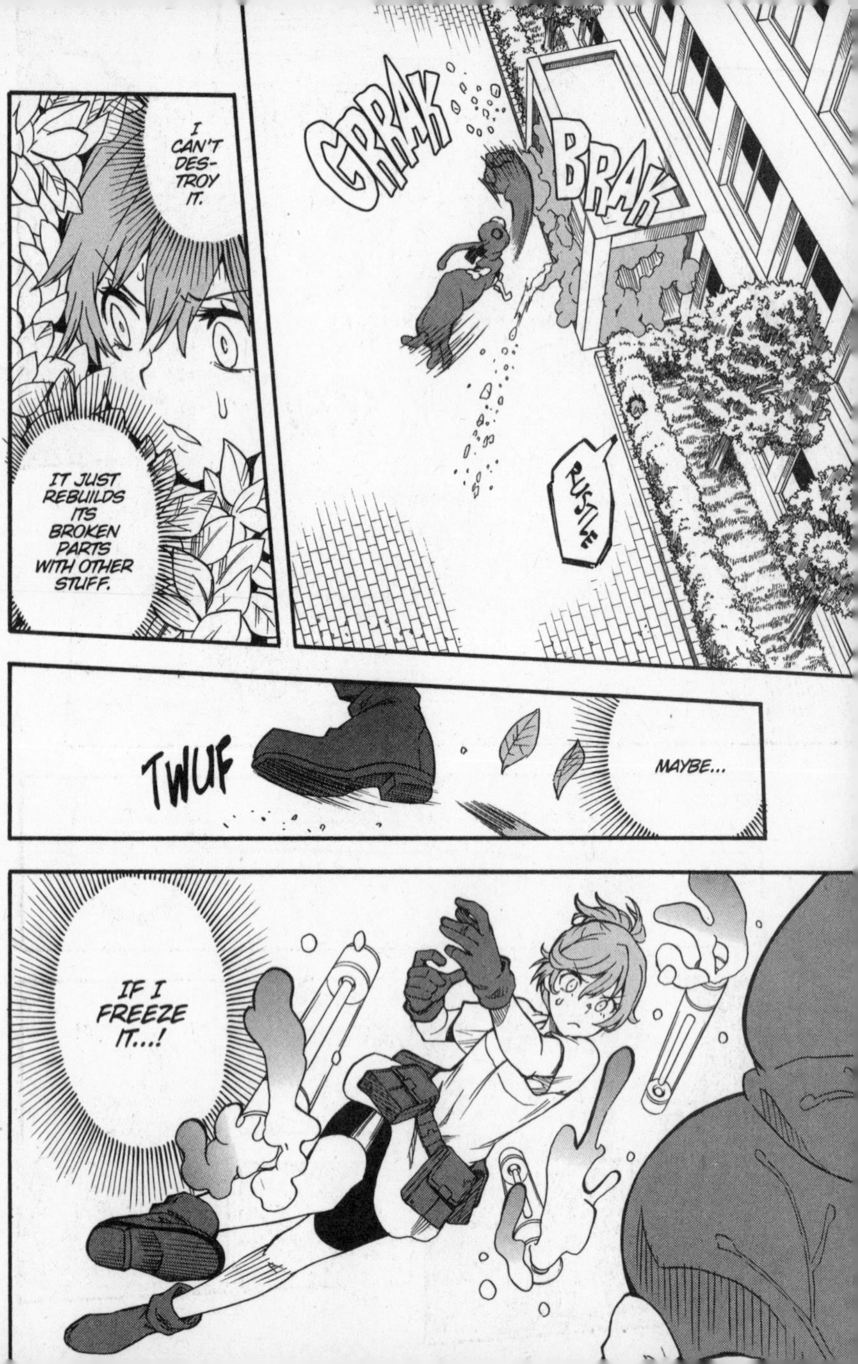
BRAK
CRRAK
RUSTLE
I CAN'T DES-TROY IT.
IT JUST REBUILDS ITS BROKEN PARTS WITH OTHER STUFF.
MAYBE...
TWUF
IF I FREEZE IT...!

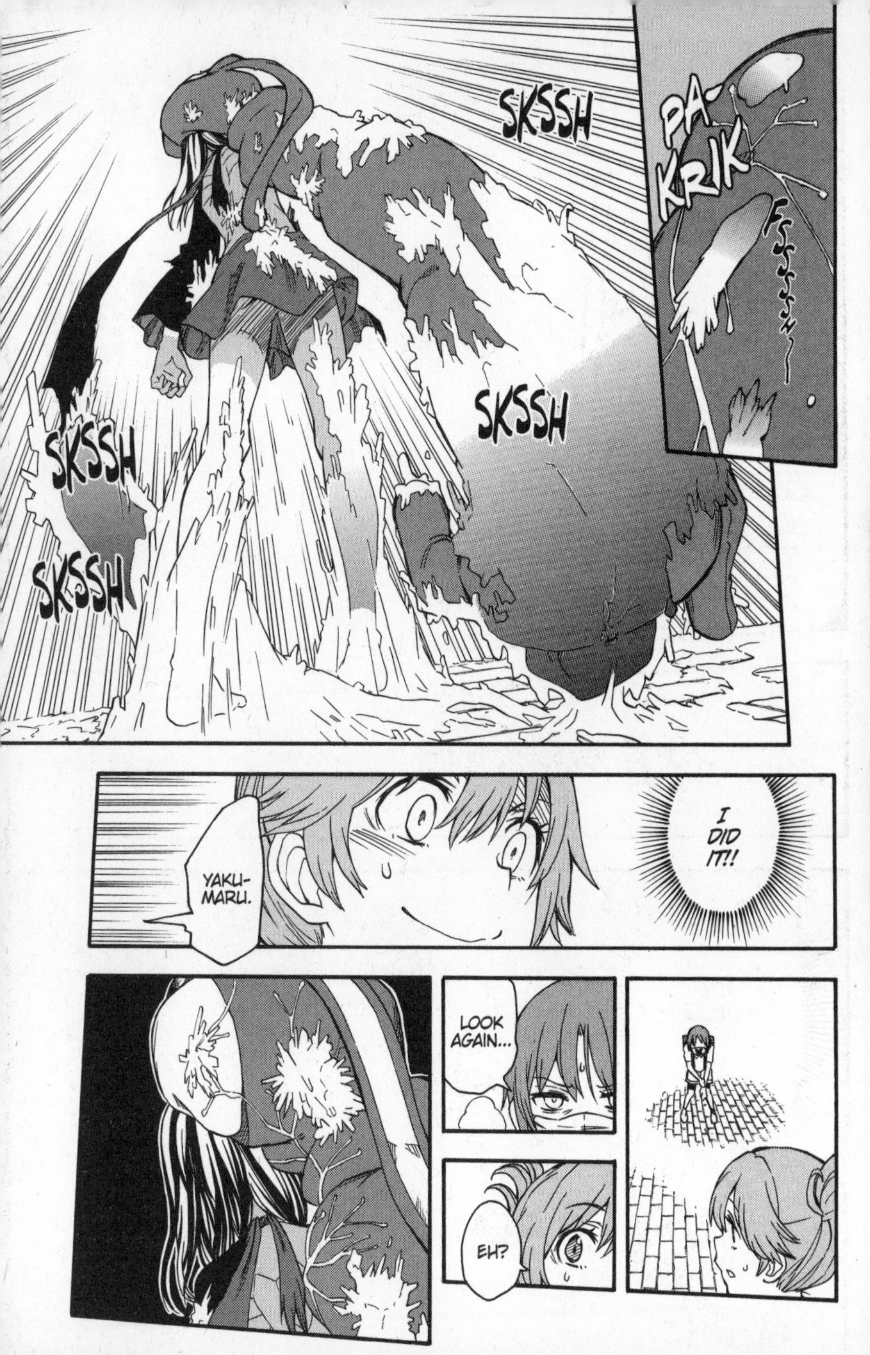
PA-KRIK
FSSSSH~
SKSSH
SKSSH
SKSSH
SKSSH
I DID IT!!
YAKU-MARU.
LOOK AGAIN...
EH?

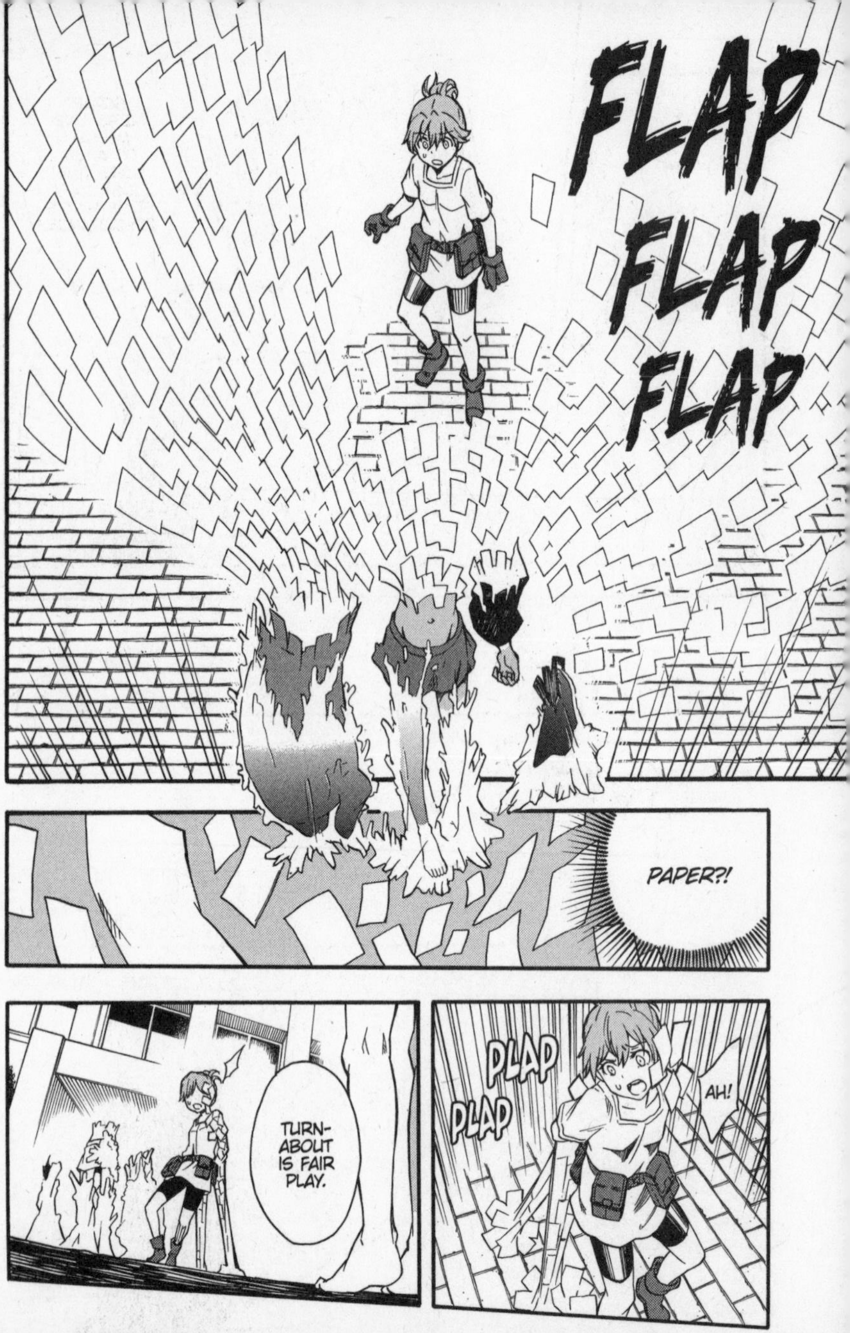
FLAP
FLAP
FLAP
PAPER?!
PLAP
PLAP
AH!
TURN-ABOUT IS FAIR PLAY.

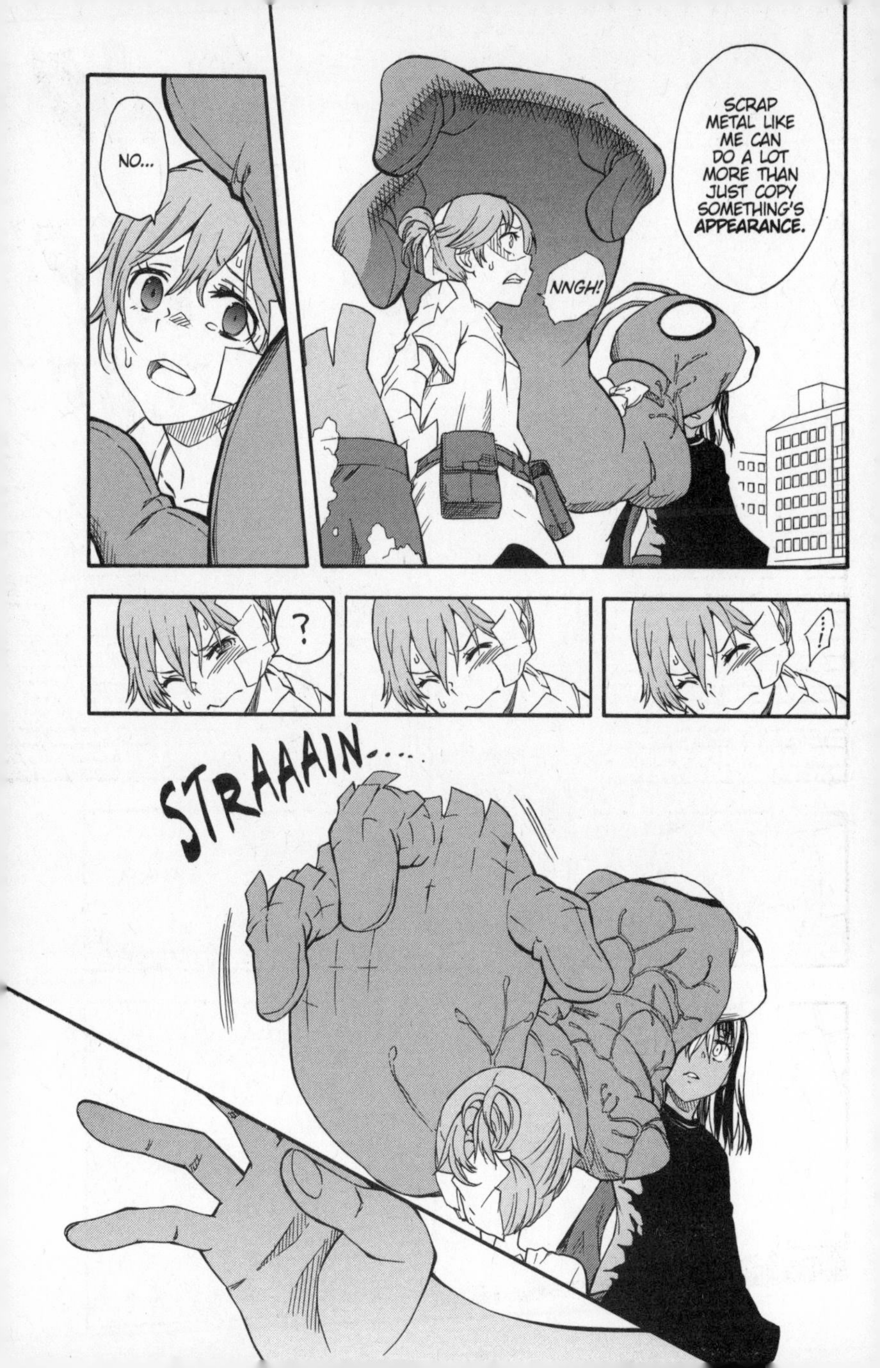

SCRAP METAL LIKE ME CAN DO A LOT MORE THAN JUST COPY SOMETHING'S APPEARANCE.
NNGH!
NO...
...!
?
STRAAAIN....

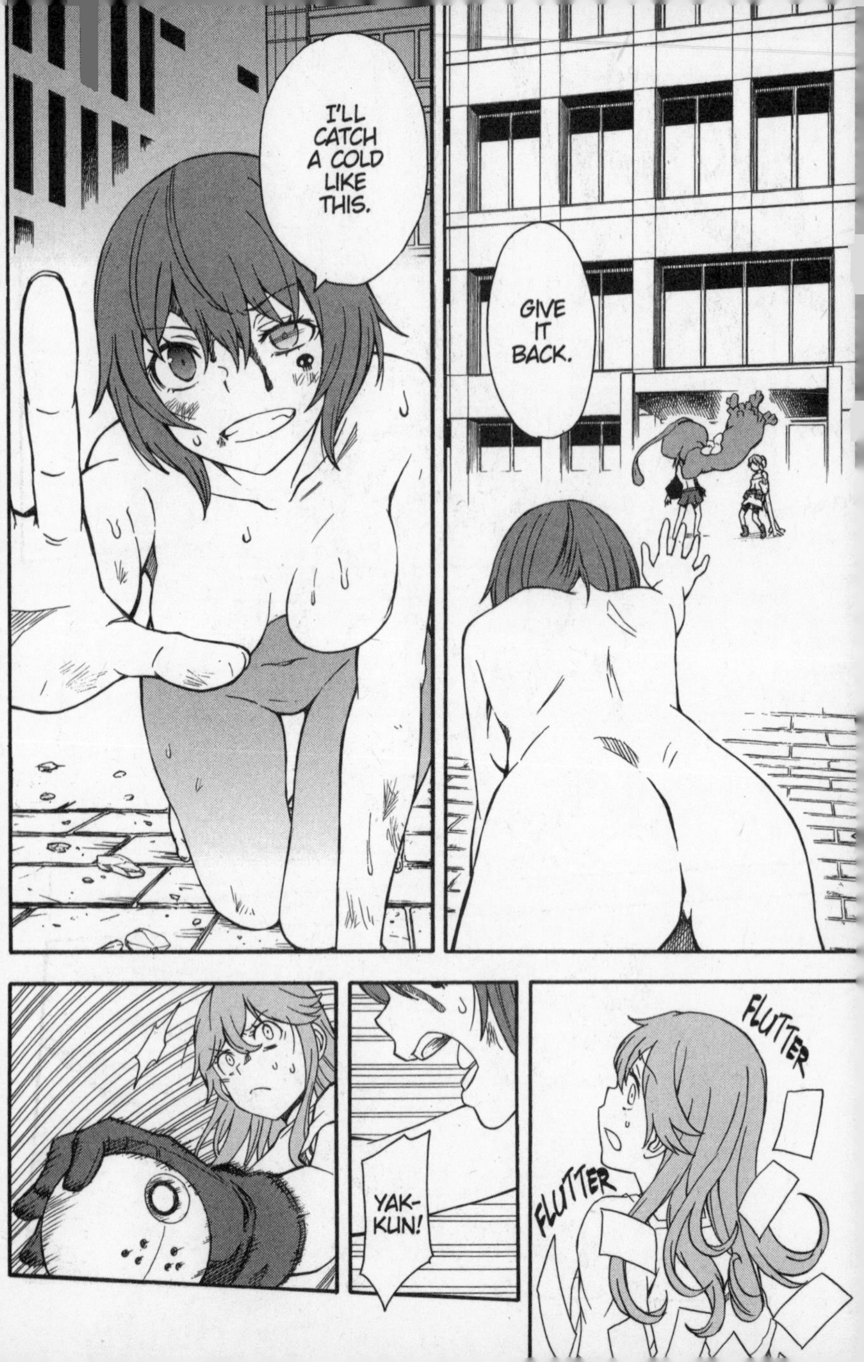
GIVE IT BACK.
I'LL CATCH A COLD LIKE THIS.
FLUTTER
FLUTTER
YAK-KUN!

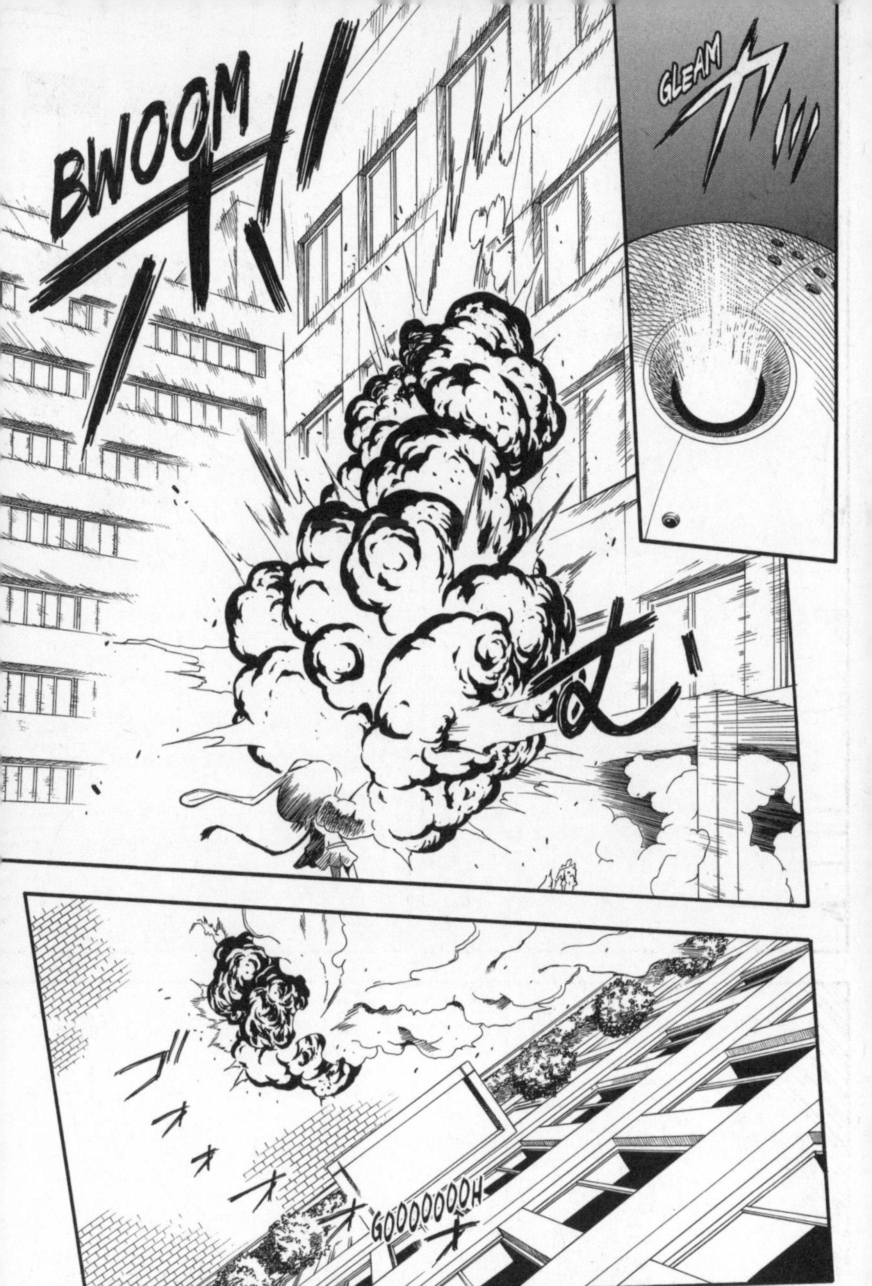
GLEAM
BWOOM
GOOOOOOOH

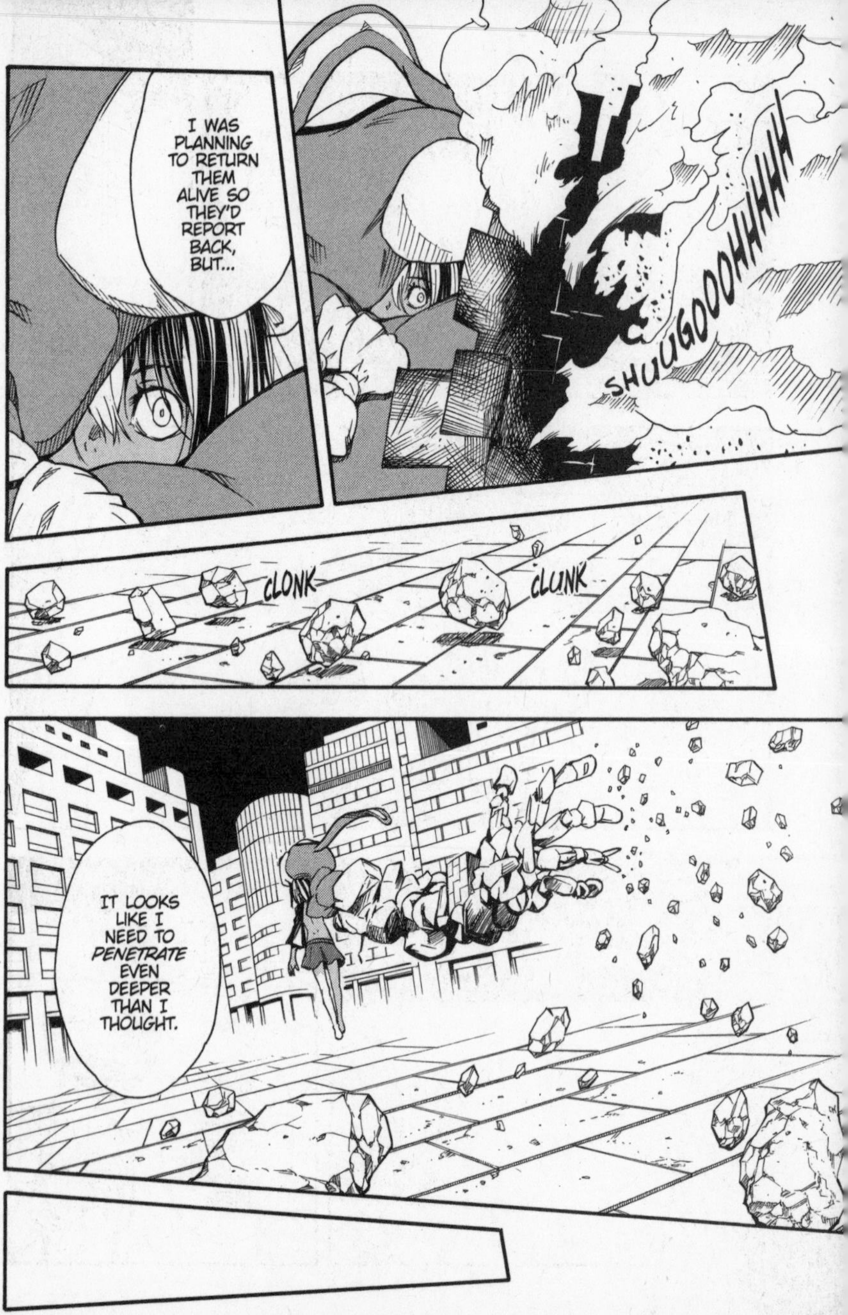
SHUUGOOOHHHHH
I WAS PLANNING TO RETURN THEM ALIVE SO THEY'D REPORT BACK, BUT...
CLUNK
CLONK
IT LOOKS LIKE I NEED TO *PENETRATE* EVEN DEEPER THAN I THOUGHT.

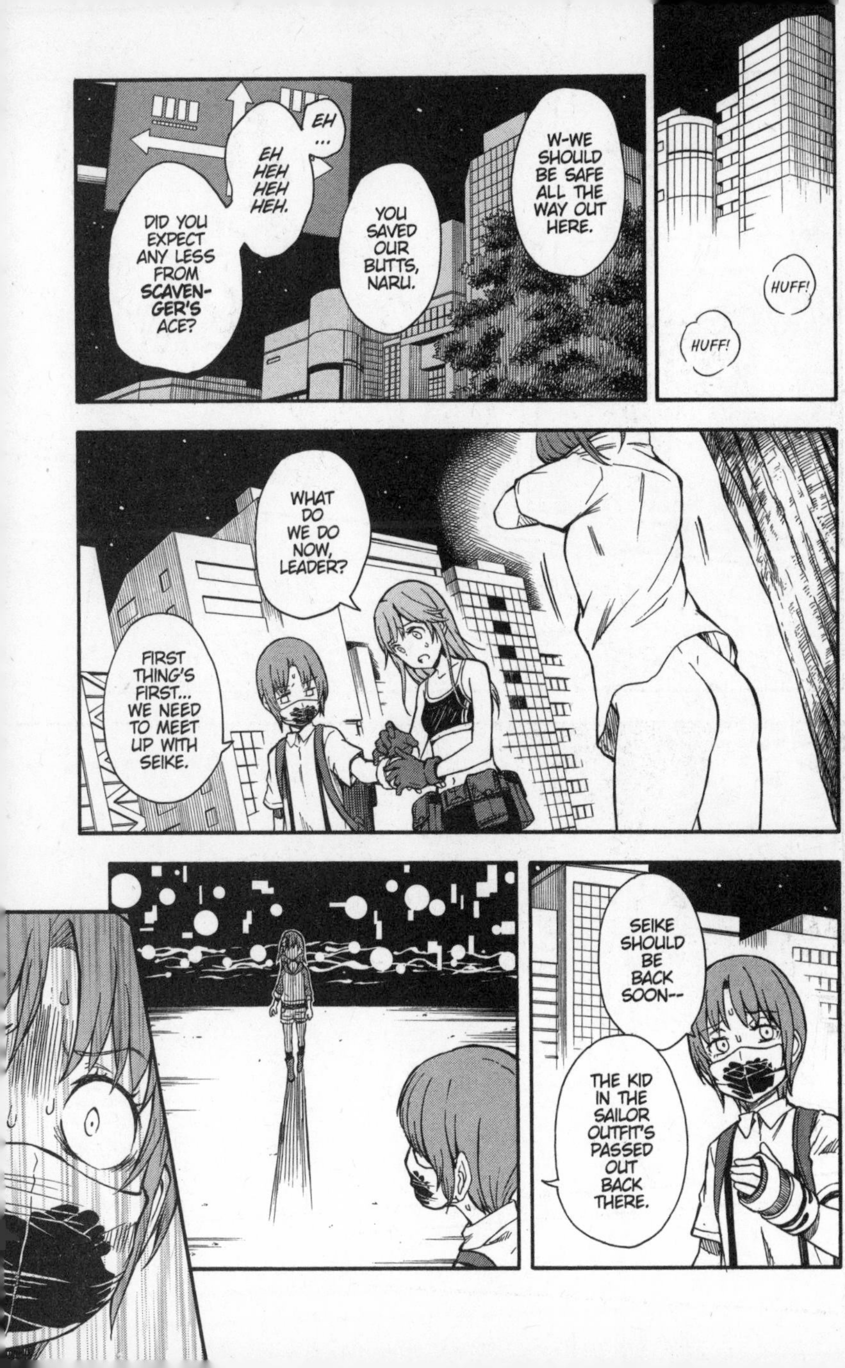
HUFF!
HUFF!
W-WE SHOULD BE SAFE ALL THE WAY OUT HERE.
YOU SAVED OUR BUTTS, NARU.
EH...
EH HEH HEH HEH.
DID YOU EXPECT ANY LESS FROM SCAVENGER'S ACE?
WHAT DO WE DO NOW, LEADER?
FIRST THING'S FIRST... WE NEED TO MEET UP WITH SEIKE.
SEIKE SHOULD BE BACK SOON--
THE KID IN THE SAILOR OUTFIT'S PASSED OUT BACK THERE.

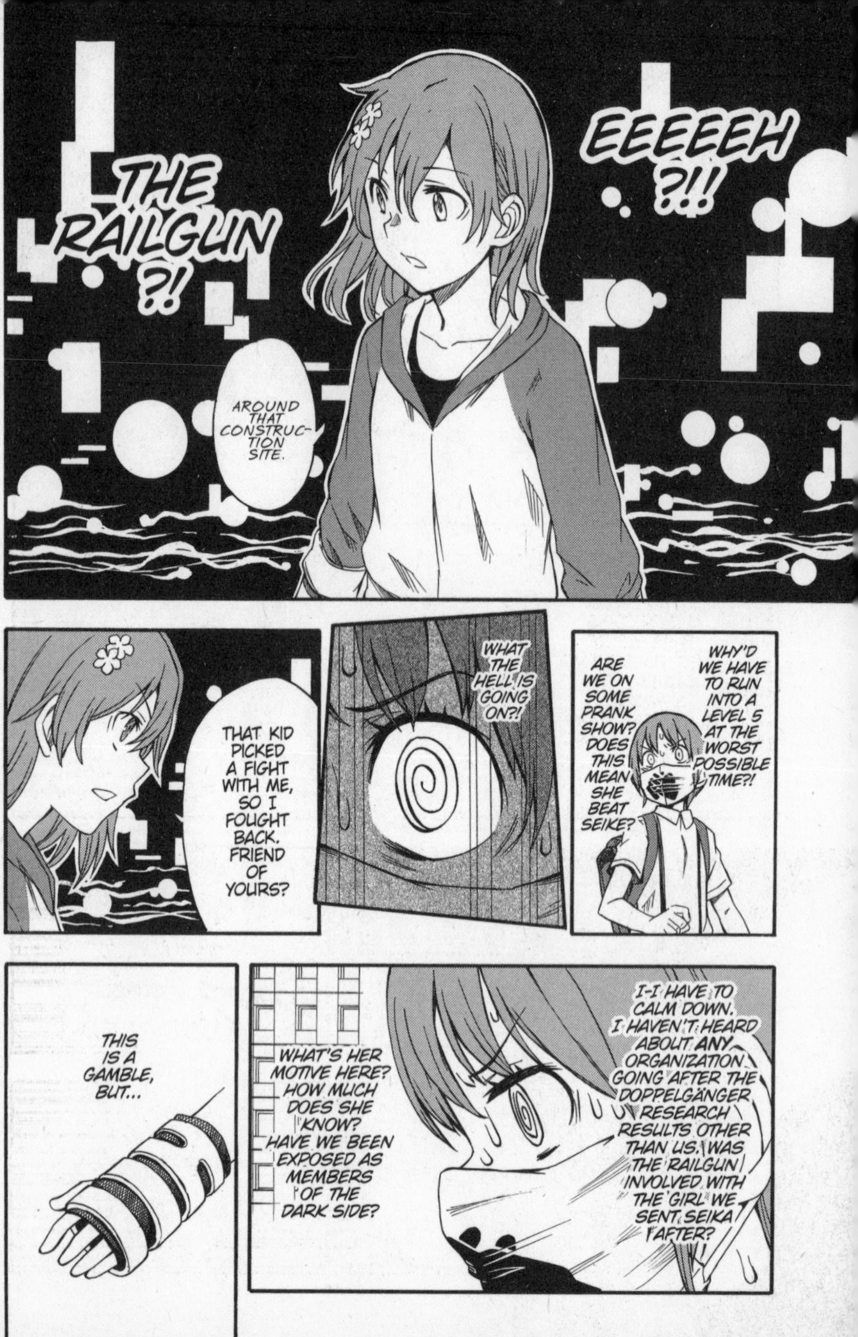

EEEEEEH ?!!
THE RAILGUN ?!
AROUND THAT CONSTRUCTION SITE.
WHY'D WE HAVE TO RUN INTO A LEVEL 5 AT THE WORST POSSIBLE TIME?!
ARE WE ON SOME PRANK SHOW? DOES THIS MEAN SHE BEAT SEIKE?
WHAT THE HELL IS GOING ON?!
THAT KID PICKED A FIGHT WITH ME, SO I FOUGHT BACK. FRIEND OF YOURS?
I-I HAVE TO CALM DOWN. I HAVEN'T HEARD ABOUT ANY ORGANIZATION GOING AFTER THE DOPPELGÄNGER RESEARCH RESULTS OTHER THAN US. WAS THE RAILGUN INVOLVED WITH THE GIRL WE SENT SEIKA AFTER?
WHAT'S HER MOTIVE HERE? HOW MUCH DOES SHE KNOW? HAVE WE BEEN EXPOSED AS MEMBERS OF THE DARK SIDE?
THIS IS A GAMBLE, BUT...

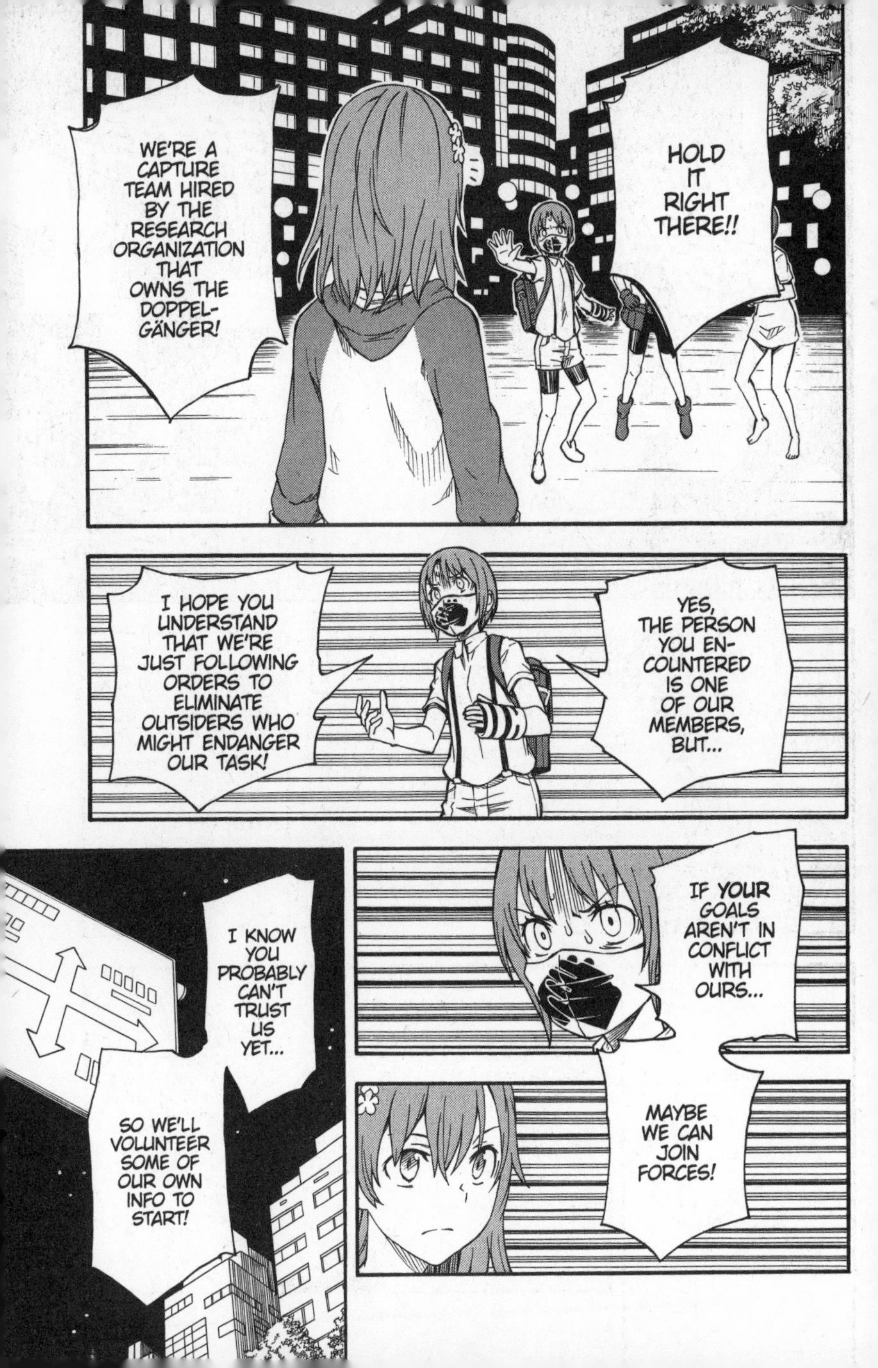
HOLD IT RIGHT THERE!!
WE'RE A CAPTURE TEAM HIRED BY THE RESEARCH ORGANIZATION THAT OWNS THE DOPPEL-GÄNGER!
YES, THE PERSON YOU EN-COUNTERED IS ONE OF OUR MEMBERS, BUT...
I HOPE YOU UNDERSTAND THAT WE'RE JUST FOLLOWING ORDERS TO ELIMINATE OUTSIDERS WHO MIGHT ENDANGER OUR TASK!
IF YOUR GOALS AREN'T IN CONFLICT WITH OURS...
MAYBE WE CAN JOIN FORCES!
I KNOW YOU PROBABLY CAN'T TRUST US YET...
SO WE'LL VOLUNTEER SOME OF OUR OWN INFO TO START!

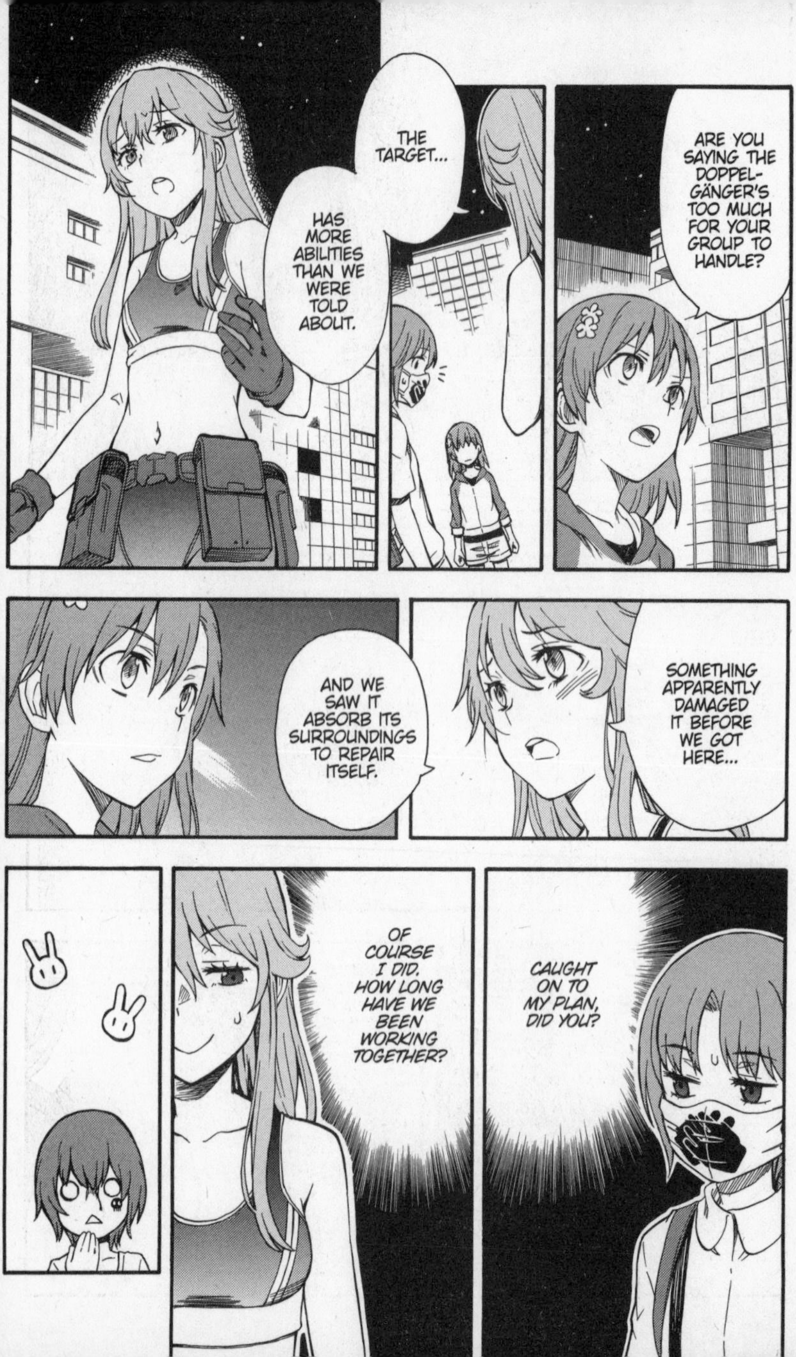
ARE YOU SAYING THE DOPPEL-GÄNGER'S TOO MUCH FOR YOUR GROUP TO HANDLE?
THE TARGET...
HAS MORE ABILITIES THAN WE WERE TOLD ABOUT.
SOMETHING APPARENTLY DAMAGED IT BEFORE WE GOT HERE...
AND WE SAW IT ABSORB ITS SURROUNDINGS TO REPAIR ITSELF.
CAUGHT ON TO MY PLAN, DID YOU?
OF COURSE I DID. HOW LONG HAVE WE BEEN WORKING TOGETHER?

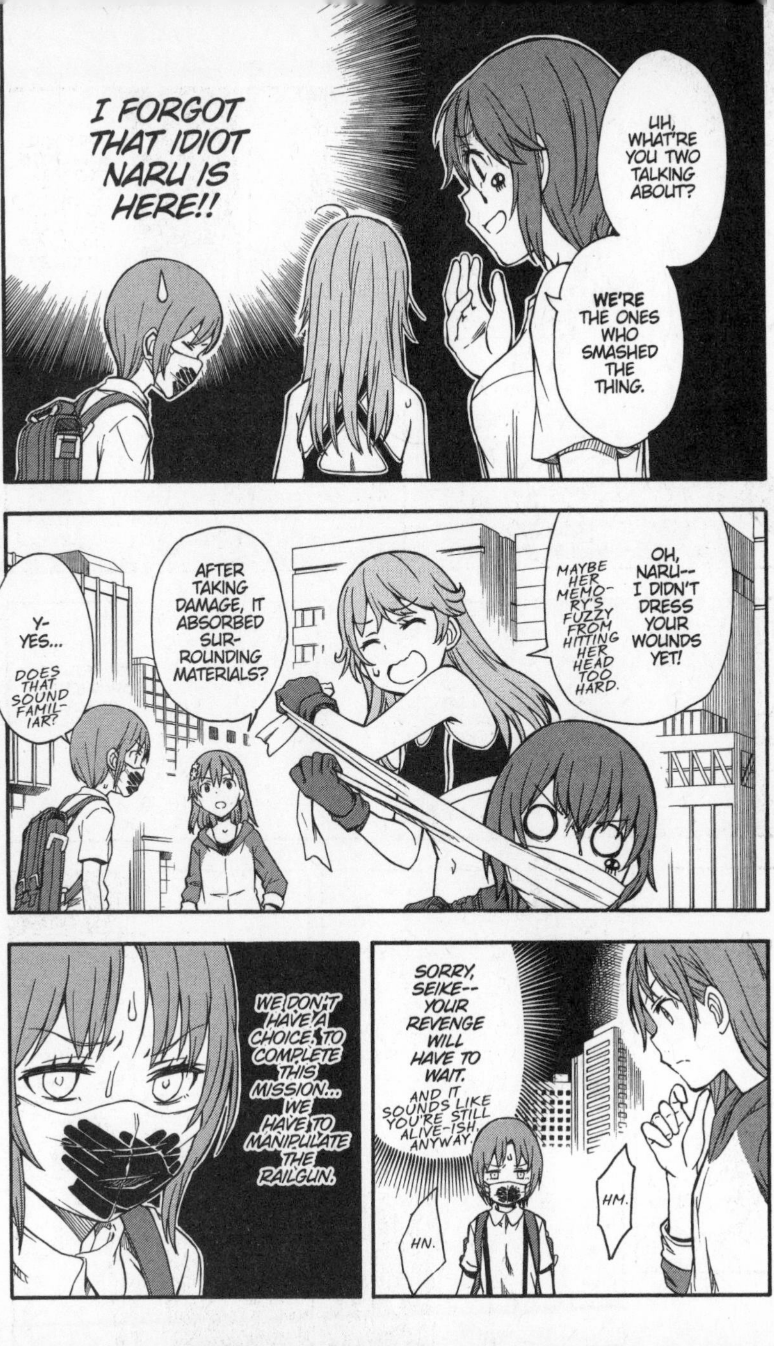
UH, WHAT'RE YOU TWO TALKING ABOUT?
I FORGOT THAT IDIOT NARU IS HERE!!
WE'RE THE ONES WHO SMASHED THE THING.
OH, NARU-- I DIDN'T DRESS YOUR WOUNDS YET!
MAYBE HER MEMORY'S FUZZY FROM HITTING HER HEAD TOO HARD.
AFTER TAKING DAMAGE, IT ABSORBED SURROUNDING MATERIALS?
Y-YES...
DOES THAT SOUND FAMILIAR?
SORRY, SEIKE-- YOUR REVENGE WILL HAVE TO WAIT.
AND IT SOUNDS LIKE YOU'RE STILL ALIVE-ISH, ANYWAY.
HM.
HN.
WE DON'T HAVE A CHOICE. TO COMPLETE THIS MISSION... WE HAVE TO MANIPULATE THE RAILGUN.

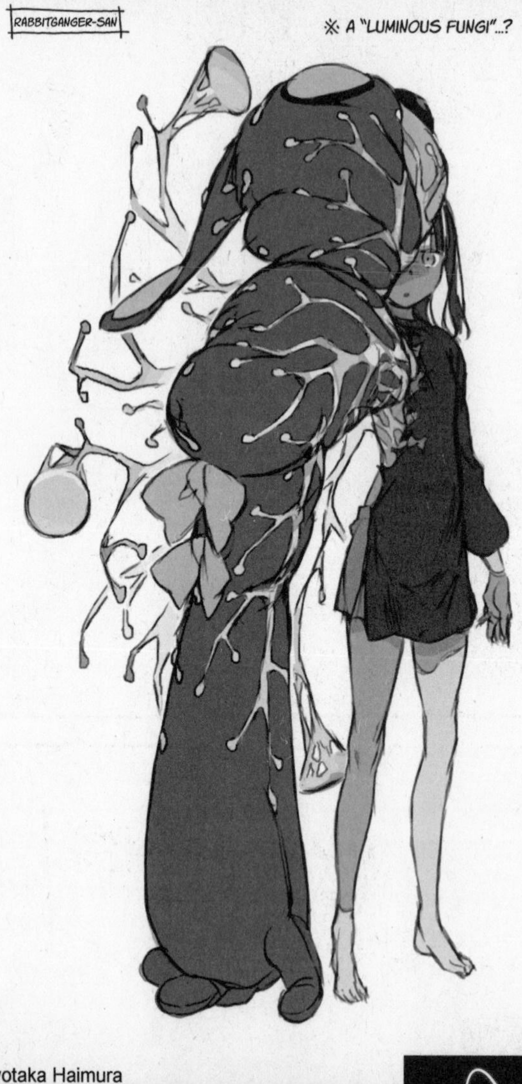
RABBITGANGER-SAN
※ A "LUMINOUS FUNGI"...?
Design/Kiyotaka Haimura

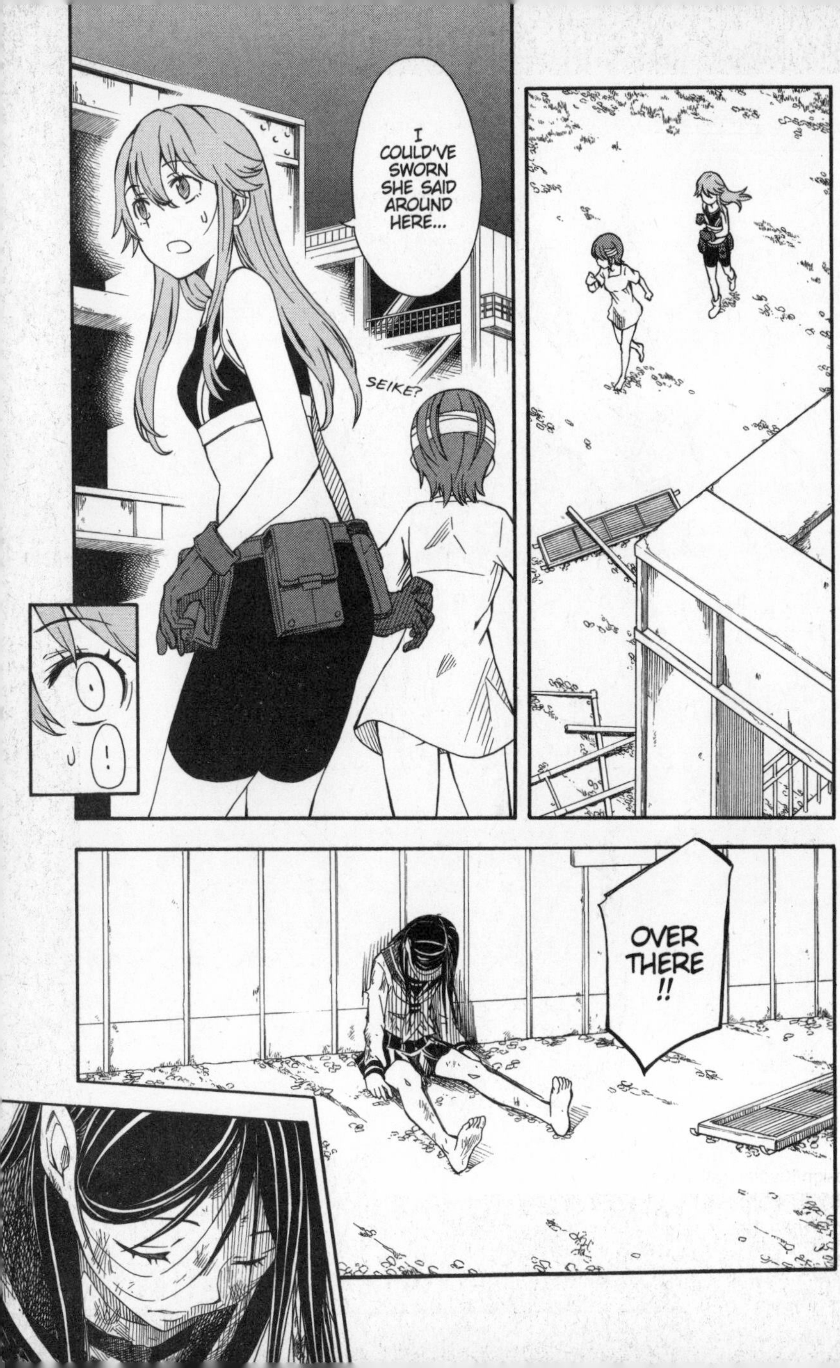
I COULD'VE SWORN SHE SAID AROUND HERE...
SEIKE?
!
OVER THERE!!

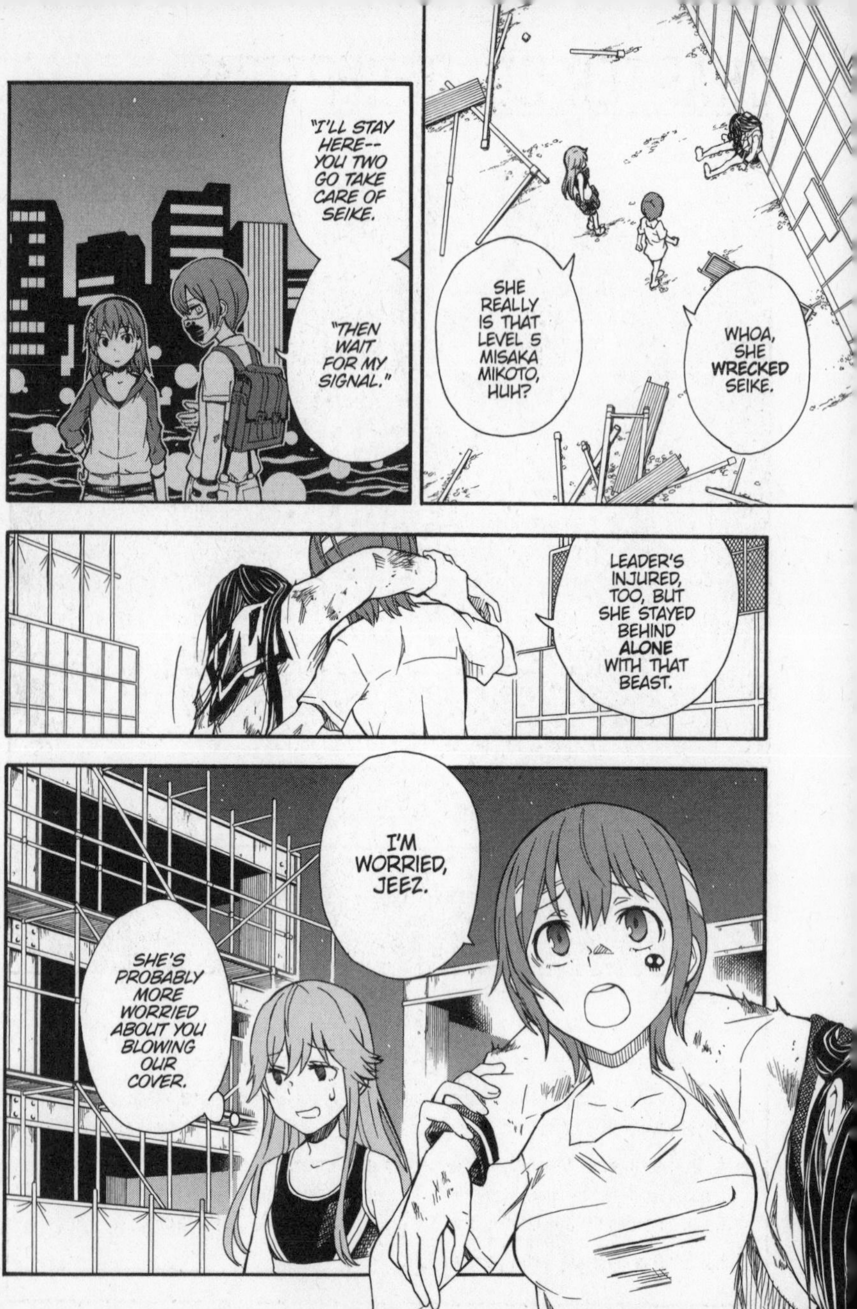
WHOA, SHE WRECKED SEIKE.
SHE REALLY IS THAT LEVEL 5 MISAKA MIKOTO, HUH?
"I'LL STAY HERE-- YOU TWO GO TAKE CARE OF SEIKE.
"THEN WAIT FOR MY SIGNAL."
LEADER'S INJURED, TOO, BUT SHE STAYED BEHIND ALONE WITH THAT BEAST.
I'M WORRIED, JEEZ.
SHE'S PROBABLY MORE WORRIED ABOUT YOU BLOWING OUR COVER.

CHAPTER 90: DECEPTION

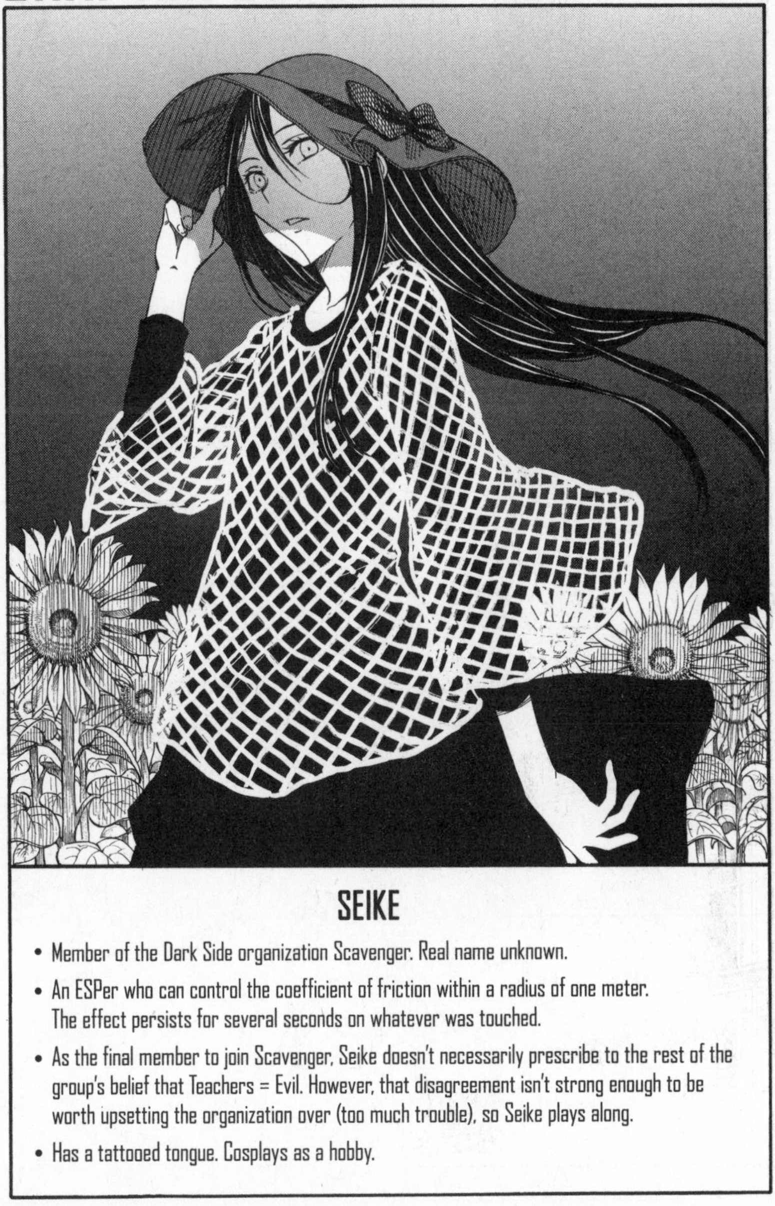

SEIKE

- Member of the Dark Side organization Scavenger. Real name unknown.
- An ESPer who can control the coefficient of friction within a radius of one meter. The effect persists for several seconds on whatever was touched.
- As the final member to join Scavenger, Seike doesn't necessarily prescribe to the rest of the group's belief that Teachers = Evil. However, that disagreement isn't strong enough to be worth upsetting the organization over (too much trouble), so Seike plays along.
- Has a tattooed tongue. Cosplays as a hobby.

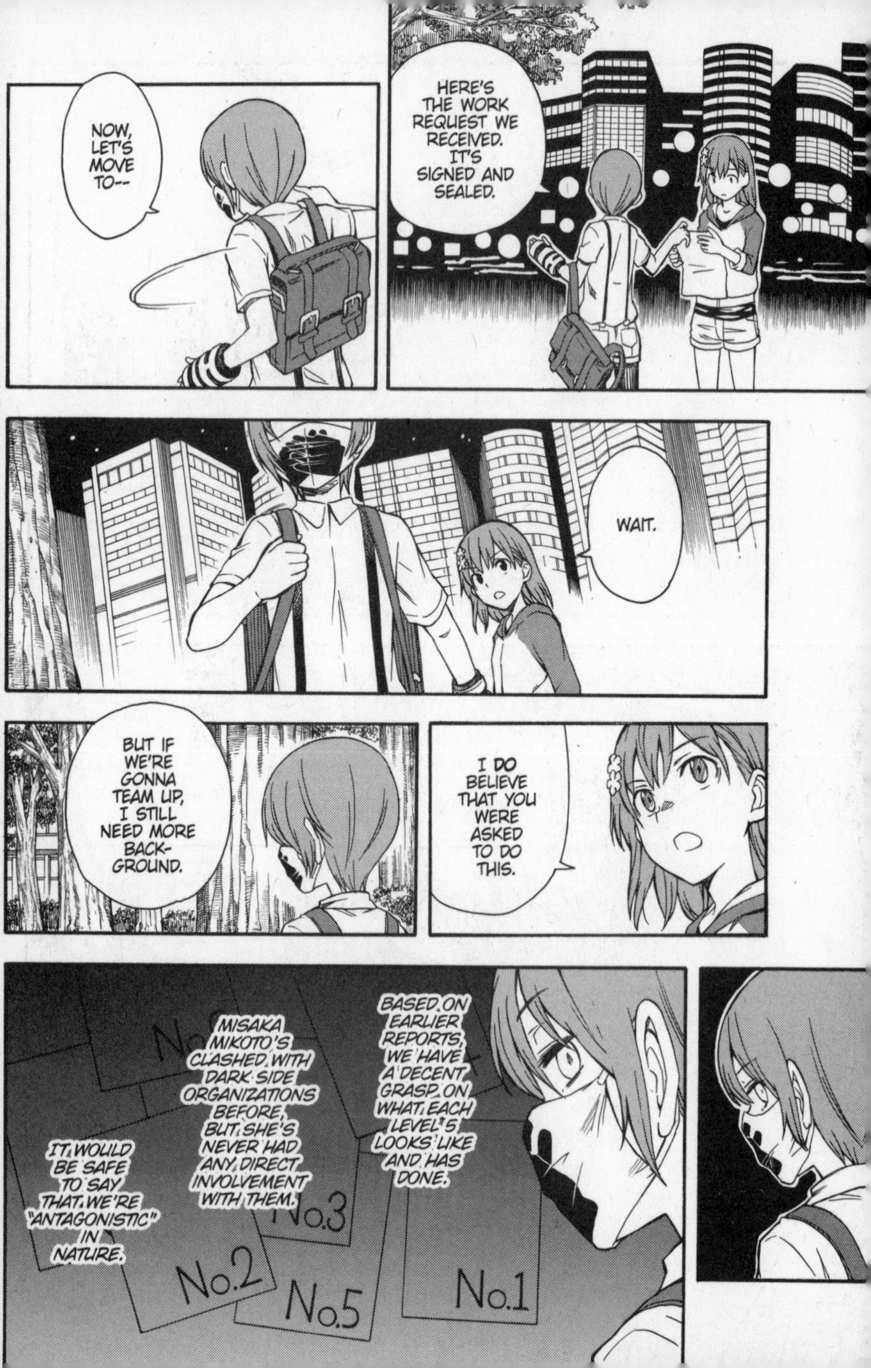
HERE'S THE WORK REQUEST WE RECEIVED. IT'S SIGNED AND SEALED.
NOW, LET'S MOVE TO--
WAIT.
I DO BELIEVE THAT YOU WERE ASKED TO DO THIS.
BUT IF WE'RE GONNA TEAM UP, I STILL NEED MORE BACK-GROUND.
BASED ON EARLIER REPORTS, WE HAVE A DECENT GRASP ON WHAT EACH LEVEL 5 LOOKS LIKE AND HAS DONE.
MISAKA MIKOTO'S CLASHED WITH DARK SIDE ORGANIZATIONS BEFORE, BUT SHE'S NEVER HAD ANY DIRECT INVOLVEMENT WITH THEM.
IT WOULD BE SAFE TO SAY THAT WE'RE "ANTAGONISTIC" IN NATURE.
No.3
No.2
No.5
No.1

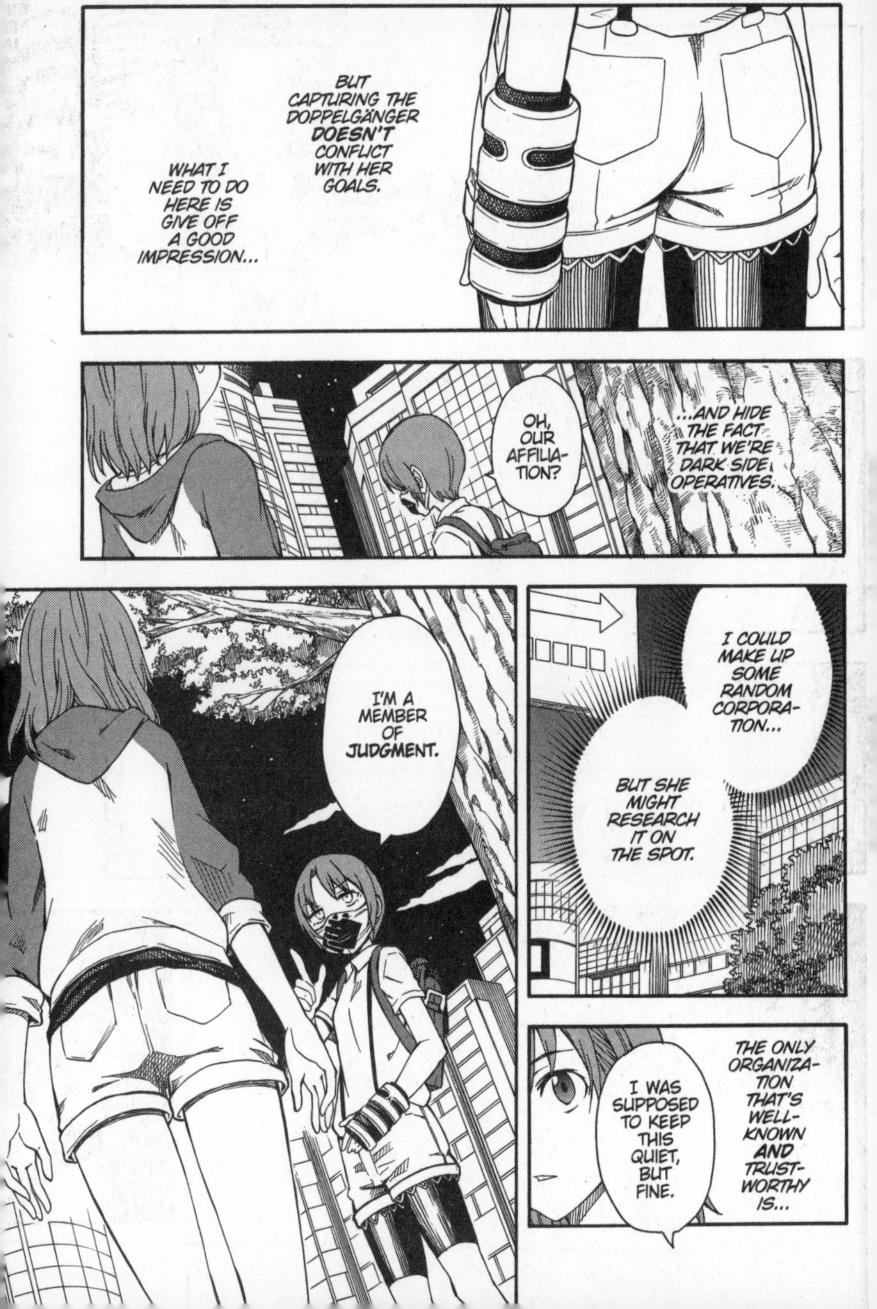
BUT CAPTURING THE DOPPELGÄNGER DOESN'T CONFLICT WITH HER GOALS.
WHAT I NEED TO DO HERE IS GIVE OFF A GOOD IMPRESSION...
...AND HIDE THE FACT THAT WE'RE DARK SIDE OPERATIVES.
OH, OUR AFFILIATION?
I COULD MAKE UP SOME RANDOM CORPORATION...
BUT SHE MIGHT RESEARCH IT ON THE SPOT.
I'M A MEMBER OF JUDGMENT.
THE ONLY ORGANIZATION THAT'S WELL-KNOWN AND TRUSTWORTHY IS...
I WAS SUPPOSED TO KEEP THIS QUIET, BUT FINE.

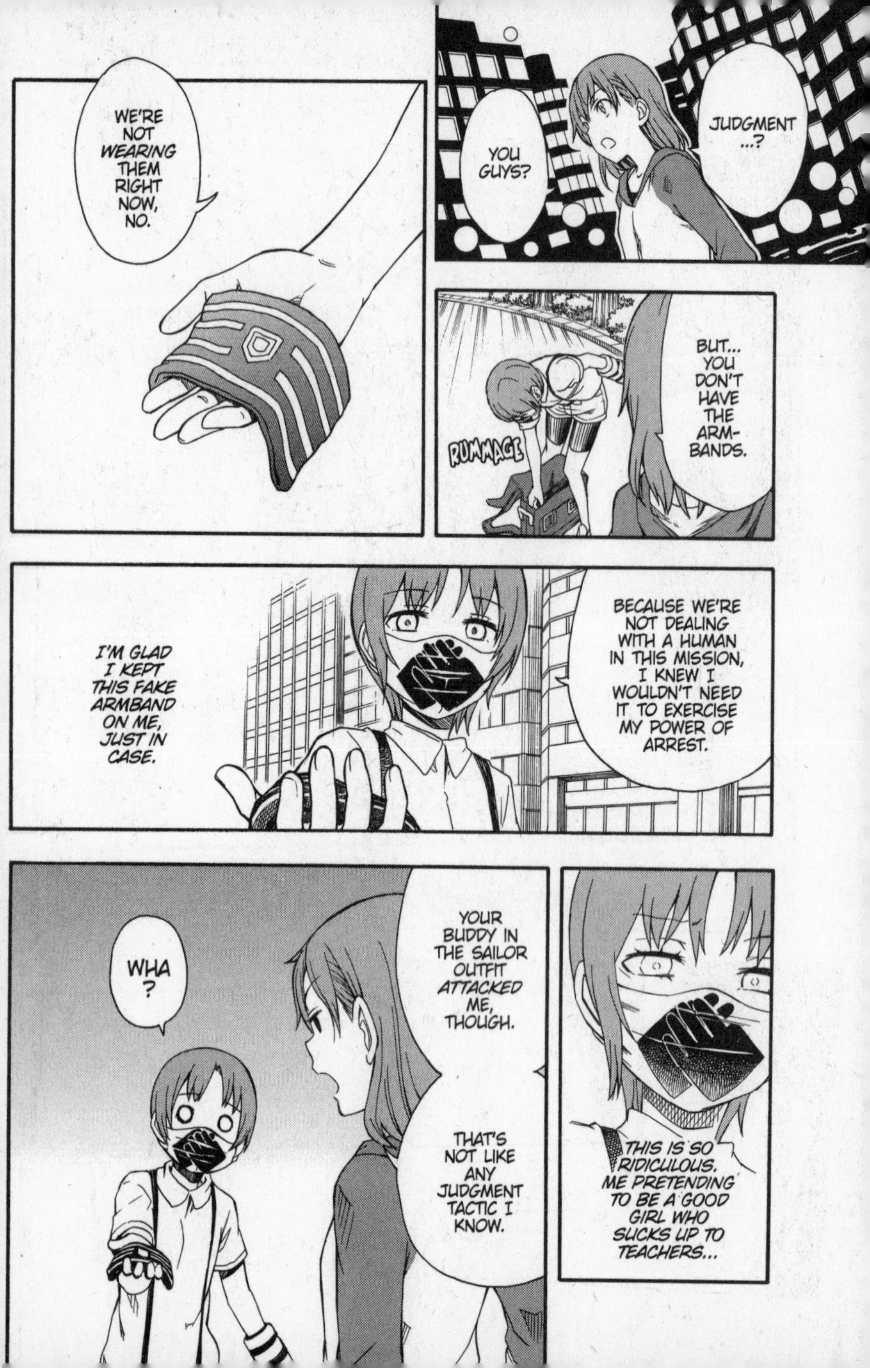
JUDGMENT ...?
YOU GUYS?
BUT... YOU DON'T HAVE THE ARM-BANDS.
RUMMAGE
WE'RE NOT *WEARING* THEM RIGHT NOW, NO.
BECAUSE WE'RE NOT DEALING WITH A HUMAN IN THIS MISSION, I KNEW I WOULDN'T NEED IT TO EXERCISE MY POWER OF ARREST.
I'M GLAD I KEPT THIS FAKE ARMBAND ON ME, JUST IN CASE.
THIS IS SO RIDICULOUS. ME PRETENDING TO BE A GOOD GIRL WHO SUCKS UP TO TEACHERS...
YOUR BUDDY IN THE SAILOR OUTFIT *ATTACKED* ME, THOUGH.
THAT'S NOT LIKE ANY JUDGMENT TACTIC I KNOW.
WHA?

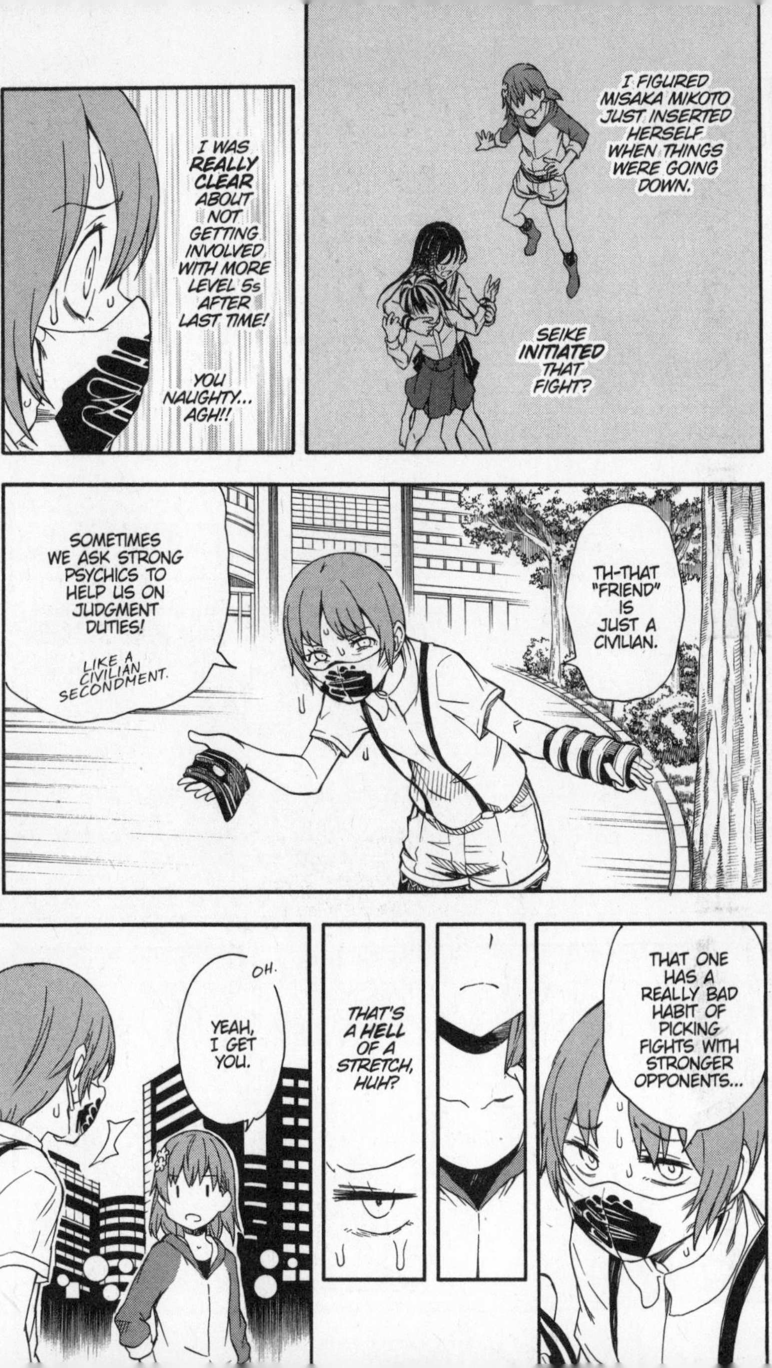

I FIGURED MISAKA MIKOTO JUST INSERTED HERSELF WHEN THINGS WERE GOING DOWN.
SEIKE INITIATED THAT FIGHT?
I WAS REALLY CLEAR ABOUT NOT GETTING INVOLVED WITH MORE LEVEL 5s AFTER LAST TIME!
YOU NAUGHTY... AGH!!
TH-THAT "FRIEND" IS JUST A CIVILIAN.
SOMETIMES WE ASK STRONG PSYCHICS TO HELP US ON JUDGMENT DUTIES!
LIKE A CIVILIAN SECONDMENT.
THAT ONE HAS A REALLY BAD HABIT OF PICKING FIGHTS WITH STRONGER OPPONENTS...
THAT'S A HELL OF A STRETCH, HUH?
OH.
YEAH, I GET YOU.

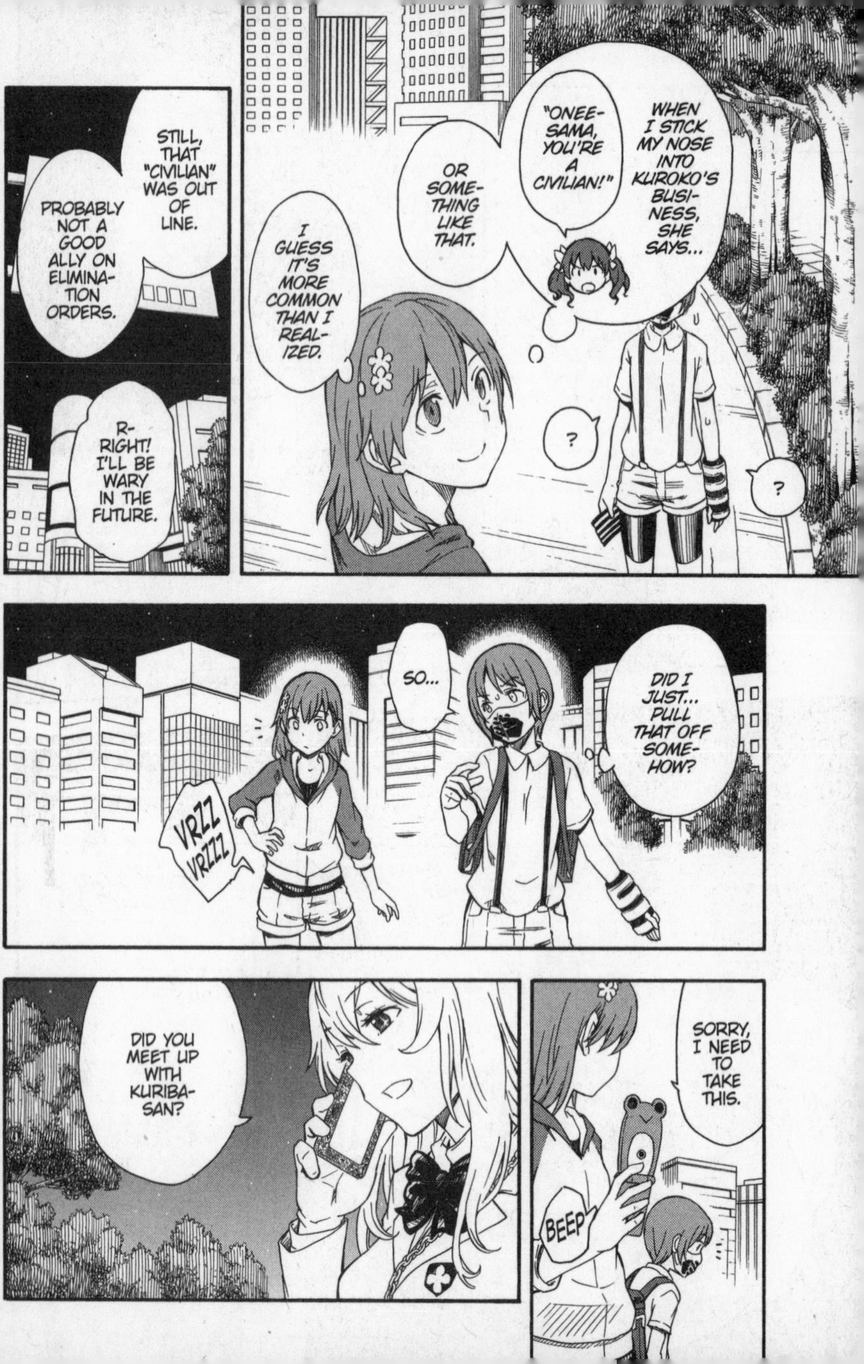
WHEN I STICK MY NOSE INTO KUROKO'S BUSINESS, SHE SAYS...
"ONEE-SAMA, YOU'RE A CIVILIAN!"
OR SOMETHING LIKE THAT.
I GUESS IT'S MORE COMMON THAN I REALIZED.
?
?
STILL, THAT "CIVILIAN" WAS OUT OF LINE.
PROBABLY NOT A GOOD ALLY ON ELIMINATION ORDERS.
R-RIGHT! I'LL BE WARY IN THE FUTURE.
DID I JUST... PULL THAT OFF SOMEHOW?
SO...
VRZZZ VRZZZ
SORRY, I NEED TO TAKE THIS.
BEEP
DID YOU MEET UP WITH KURIBA-SAN?

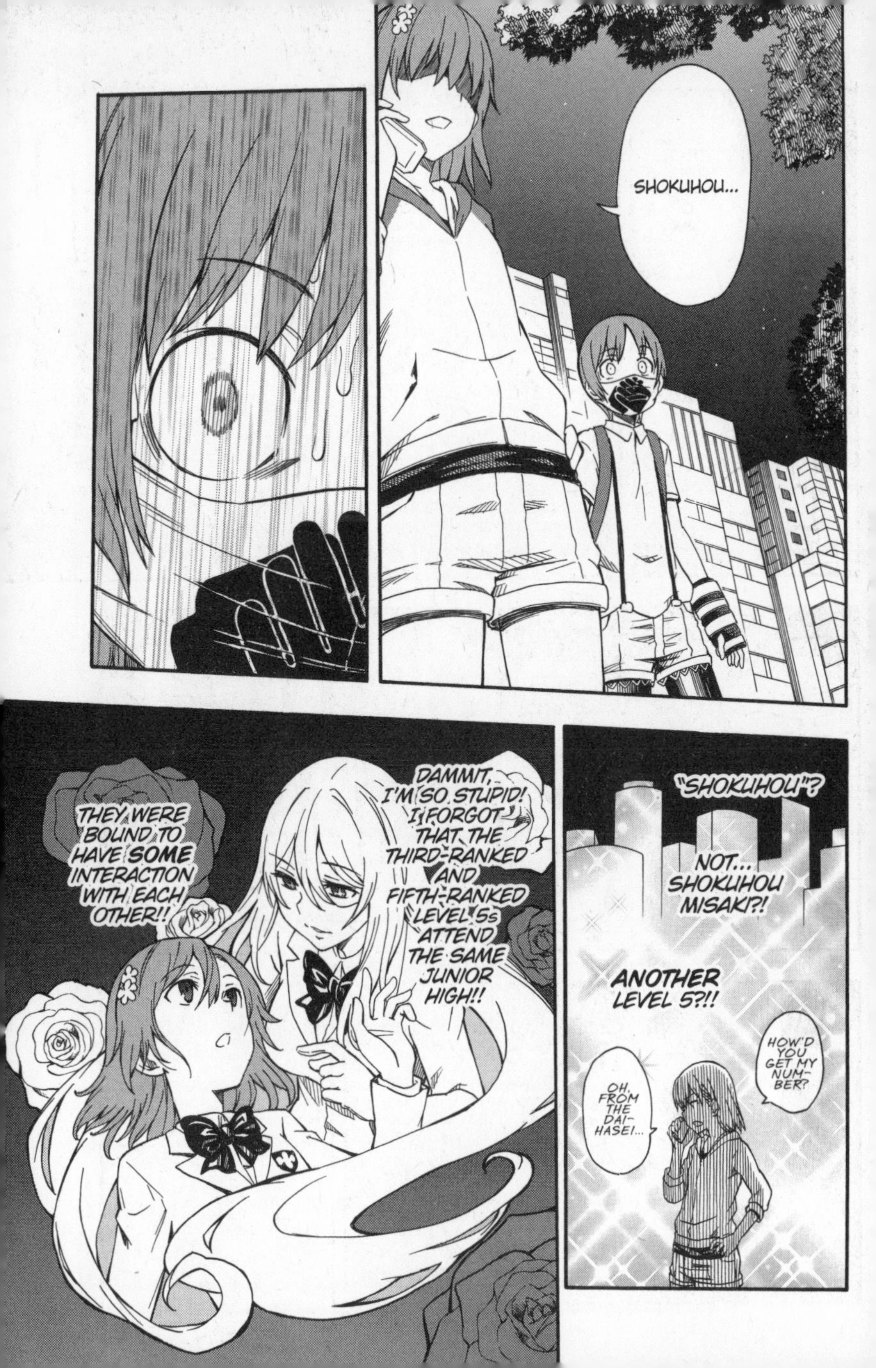
SHOKUHOU...
"SHOKUHOU"?
NOT... SHOKUHOU MISAKI?!
ANOTHER LEVEL 5?!!
HOW'D YOU GET MY NUMBER?
OH, FROM THE DAIHASEI...
DAMMIT, I'M SO STUPID! I FORGOT THAT THE THIRD-RANKED AND FIFTH-RANKED LEVEL 5s ATTEND THE SAME JUNIOR HIGH!!
THEY WERE BOUND TO HAVE SOME INTERACTION WITH EACH OTHER!!

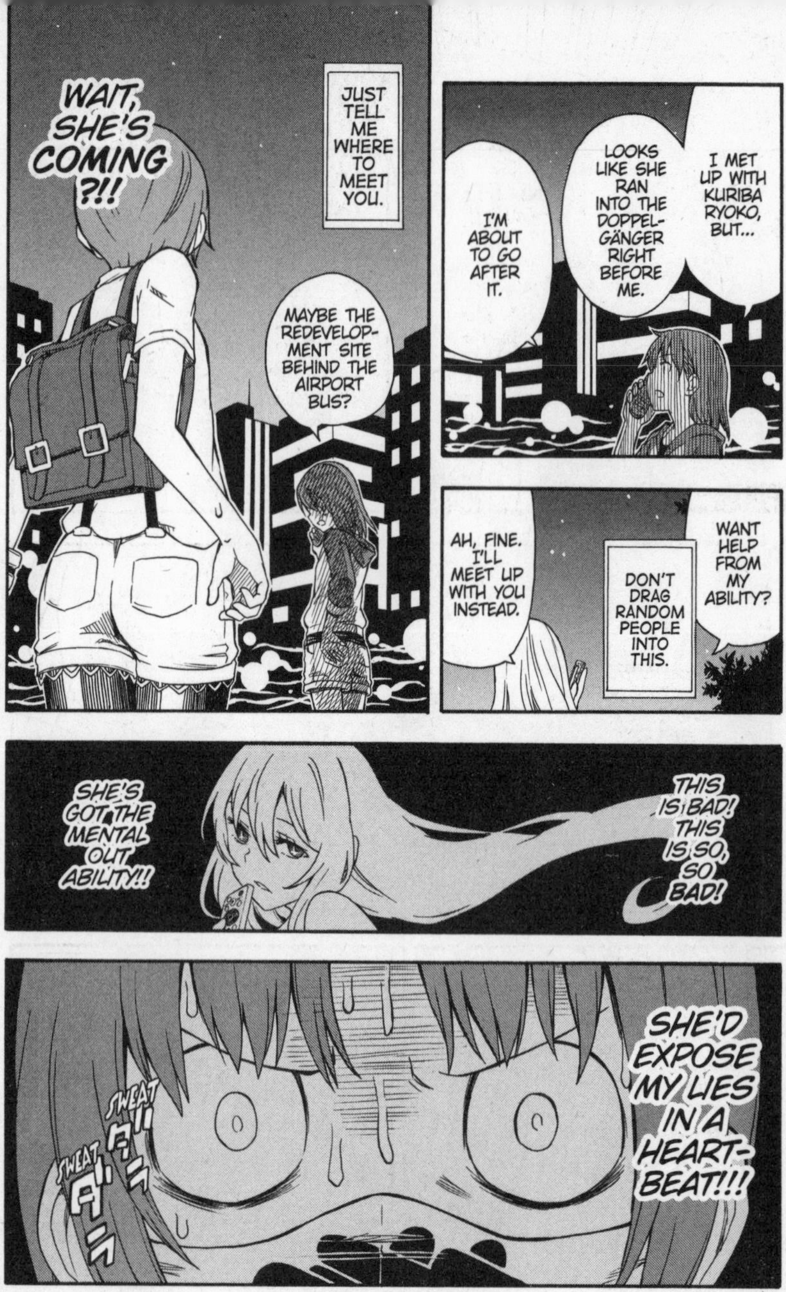
I MET UP WITH KURIBA RYOKO, BUT...
LOOKS LIKE SHE RAN INTO THE DOPPEL-GÄNGER RIGHT BEFORE ME.
I'M ABOUT TO GO AFTER IT.
WANT HELP FROM MY ABILITY?
DON'T DRAG RANDOM PEOPLE INTO THIS.
AH, FINE. I'LL MEET UP WITH YOU INSTEAD.
JUST TELL ME WHERE TO MEET YOU.
MAYBE THE REDEVELOPMENT SITE BEHIND THE AIRPORT BUS?
WAIT, SHE'S COMING?!!
THIS IS BAD! THIS IS SO, SO BAD!
SHE'S GOT THE MENTAL OUT ABILITY!!
SHE'D EXPOSE MY LIES IN A HEART-BEAT!!!
SWEAT
SWEAT

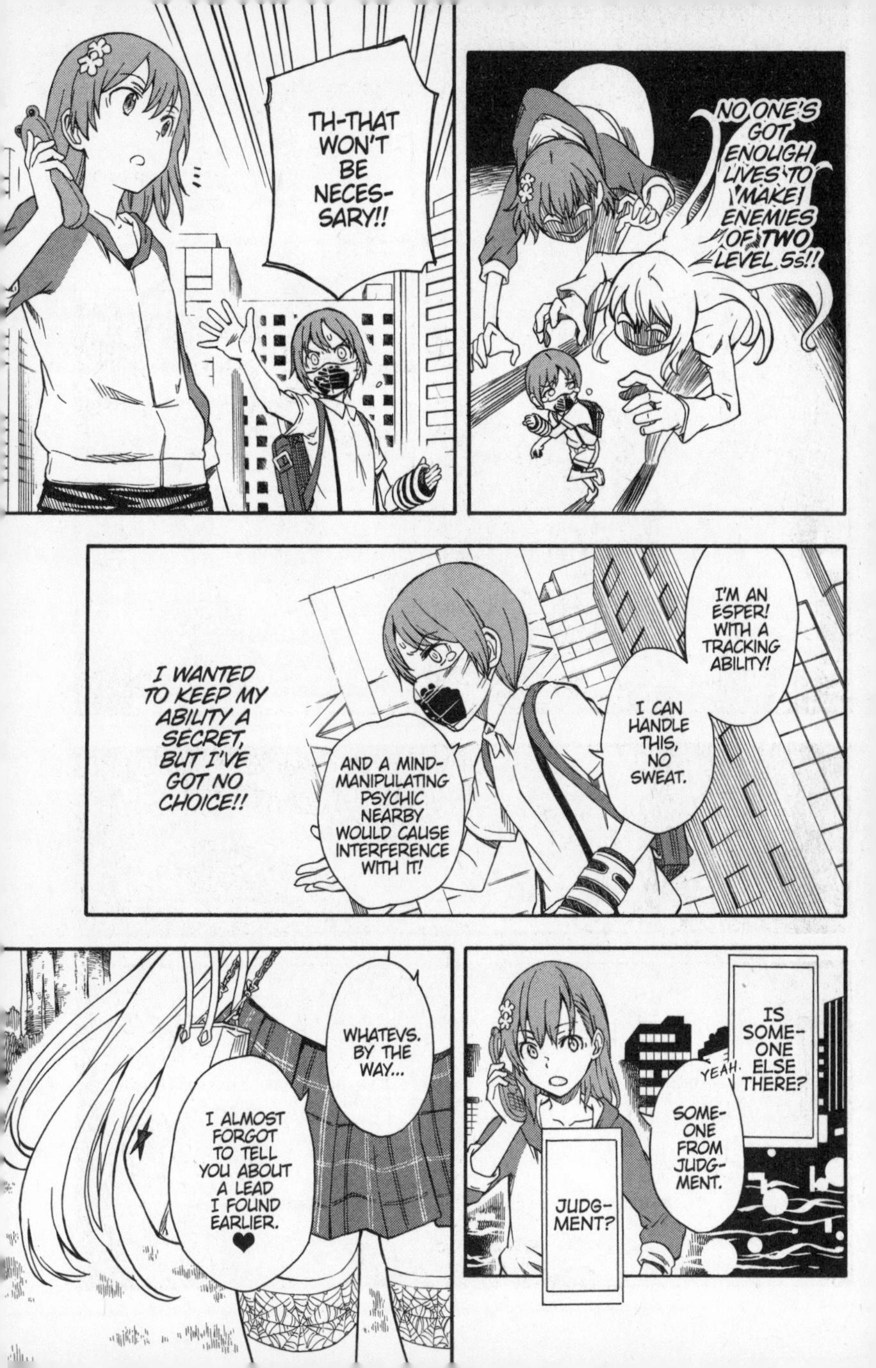
NO ONE'S GOT ENOUGH LIVES TO MAKE ENEMIES OF TWO LEVEL 5s!!
TH-THAT WON'T BE NECES-SARY!!
I'M AN ESPER! WITH A TRACKING ABILITY!
I CAN HANDLE THIS, NO SWEAT.
AND A MIND-MANIPULATING PSYCHIC NEARBY WOULD CAUSE INTERFERENCE WITH IT!
I WANTED TO KEEP MY ABILITY A SECRET, BUT I'VE GOT NO CHOICE!!
IS SOME-ONE ELSE THERE?
YEAH.
SOME-ONE FROM JUDG-MENT.
JUDG-MENT?
WHATEVS. BY THE WAY...
I ALMOST FORGOT TO TELL YOU ABOUT A LEAD I FOUND EARLIER. ♥

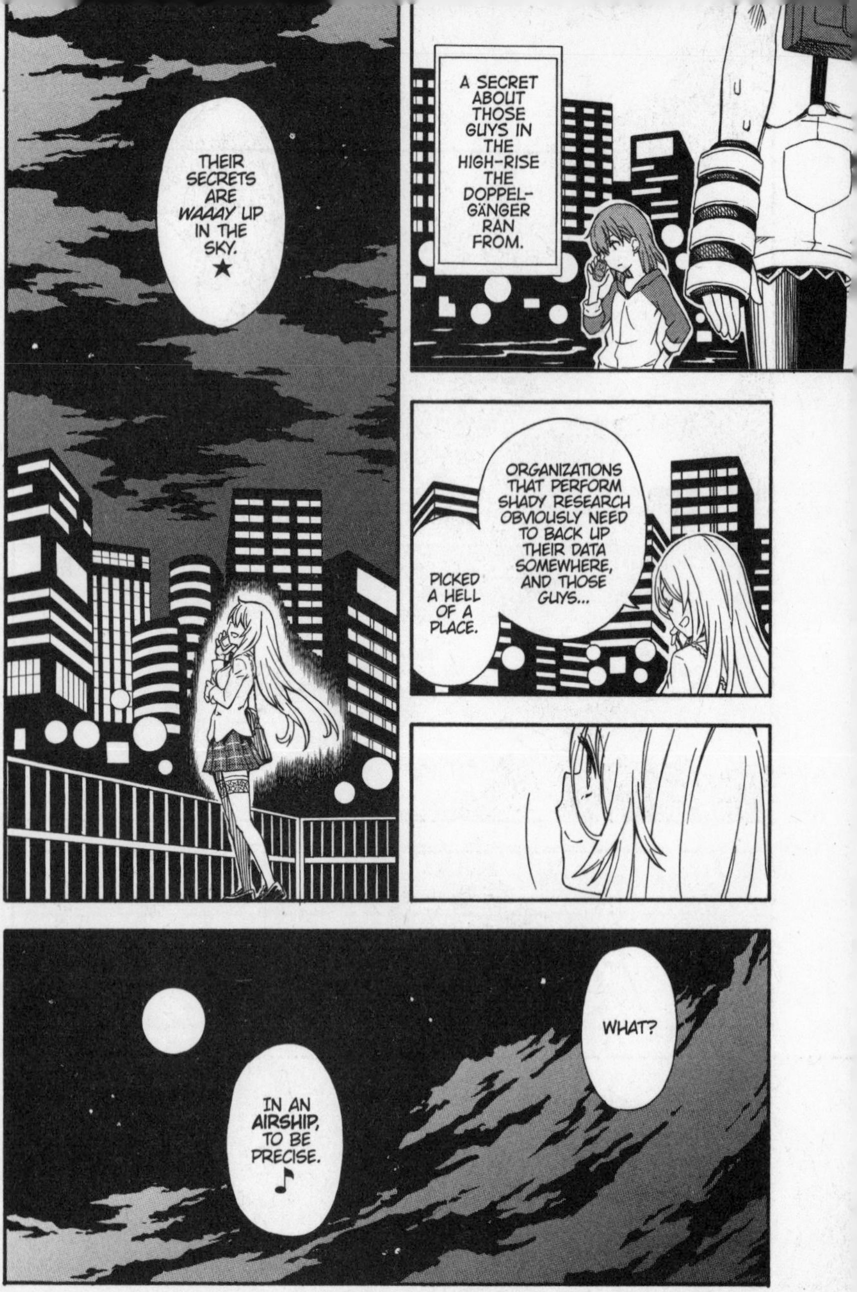
A SECRET ABOUT THOSE GUYS IN THE HIGH-RISE THE DOPPEL-GÄNGER RAN FROM.
ORGANIZATIONS THAT PERFORM SHADY RESEARCH OBVIOUSLY NEED TO BACK UP THEIR DATA SOMEWHERE, AND THOSE GUYS...
PICKED A HELL OF A PLACE.
THEIR SECRETS ARE *WAAAY* UP IN THE SKY. ★
WHAT?
IN AN **AIRSHIP**, TO BE PRECISE. ♪

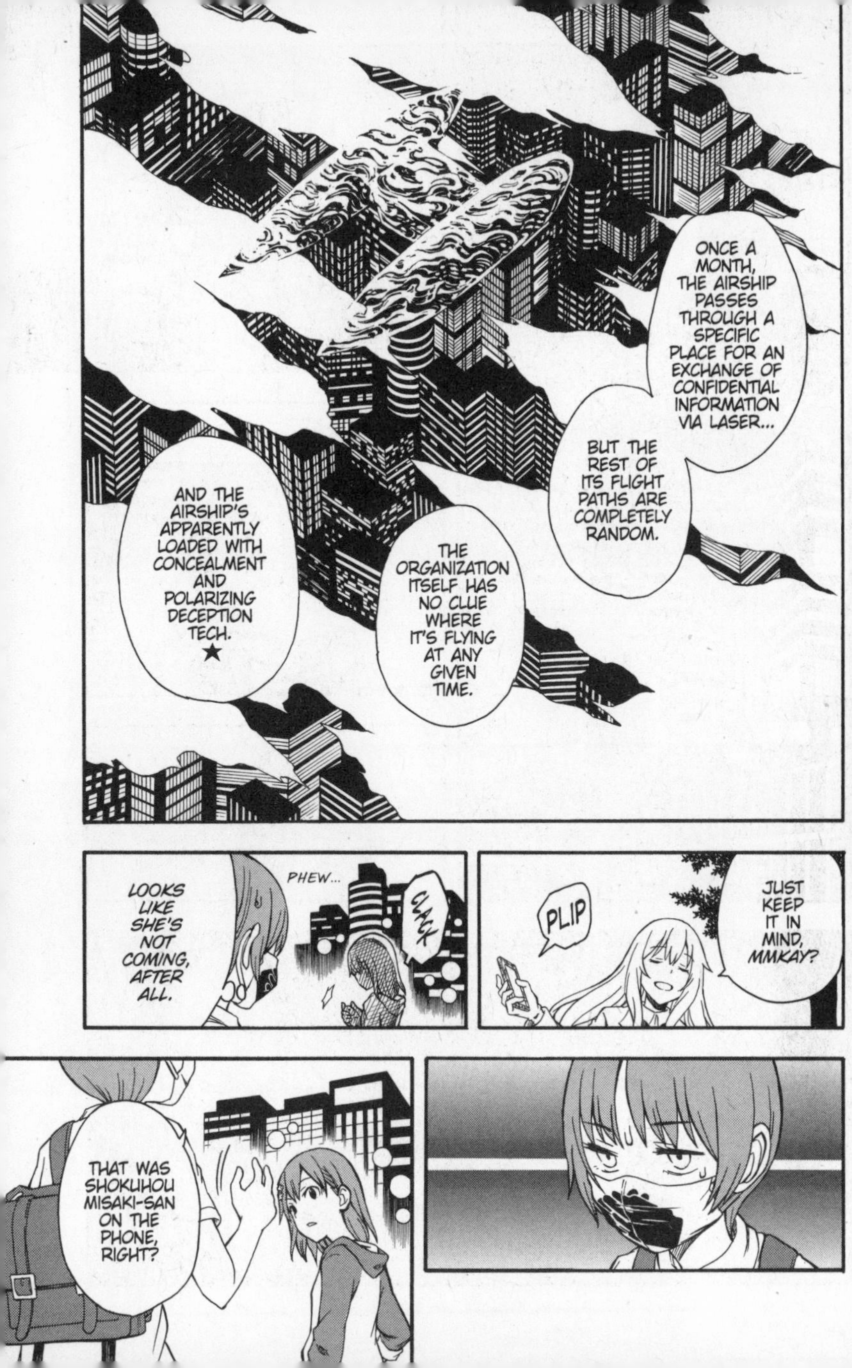
ONCE A MONTH, THE AIRSHIP PASSES THROUGH A SPECIFIC PLACE FOR AN EXCHANGE OF CONFIDENTIAL INFORMATION VIA LASER...
BUT THE REST OF ITS FLIGHT PATHS ARE COMPLETELY RANDOM.
THE ORGANIZATION ITSELF HAS NO CLUE WHERE IT'S FLYING AT ANY GIVEN TIME.
AND THE AIRSHIP'S APPARENTLY LOADED WITH CONCEALMENT AND POLARIZING DECEPTION TECH. ★
JUST KEEP IT IN MIND, MMKAY?
PLIP
CLACK
PHEW...
LOOKS LIKE SHE'S NOT COMING, AFTER ALL.
THAT WAS SHOKUHOU MISAKI-SAN ON THE PHONE, RIGHT?

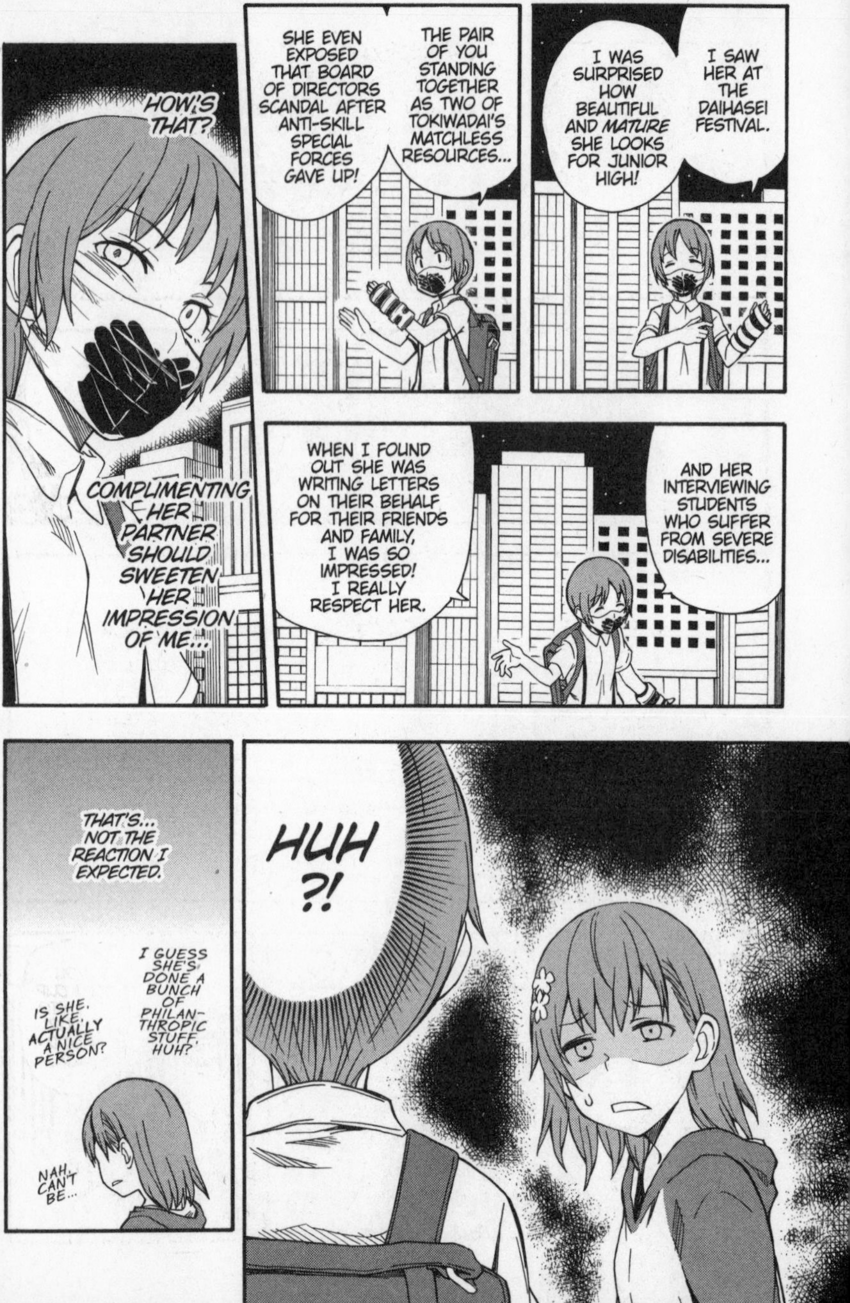
I SAW HER AT THE DAIHASEI FESTIVAL.
I WAS SURPRISED HOW BEAUTIFUL AND MATURE SHE LOOKS FOR JUNIOR HIGH!
THE PAIR OF YOU STANDING TOGETHER AS TWO OF TOKIWADAI'S MATCHLESS RESOURCES...
SHE EVEN EXPOSED THAT BOARD OF DIRECTORS SCANDAL AFTER ANTI-SKILL SPECIAL FORCES GAVE UP!
AND HER INTERVIEWING STUDENTS WHO SUFFER FROM SEVERE DISABILITIES...
WHEN I FOUND OUT SHE WAS WRITING LETTERS ON THEIR BEHALF FOR THEIR FRIENDS AND FAMILY, I WAS SO IMPRESSED! I REALLY RESPECT HER.
HOW'S THAT?
COMPLIMENTING HER PARTNER SHOULD SWEETEN HER IMPRESSION OF ME...
HUH ?!
THAT'S... NOT THE REACTION I EXPECTED.
I GUESS SHE'S DONE A BUNCH OF PHILAN-THROPIC STUFF, HUH?
IS SHE, LIKE, ACTUALLY A NICE PERSON?
NAH, CAN'T BE...

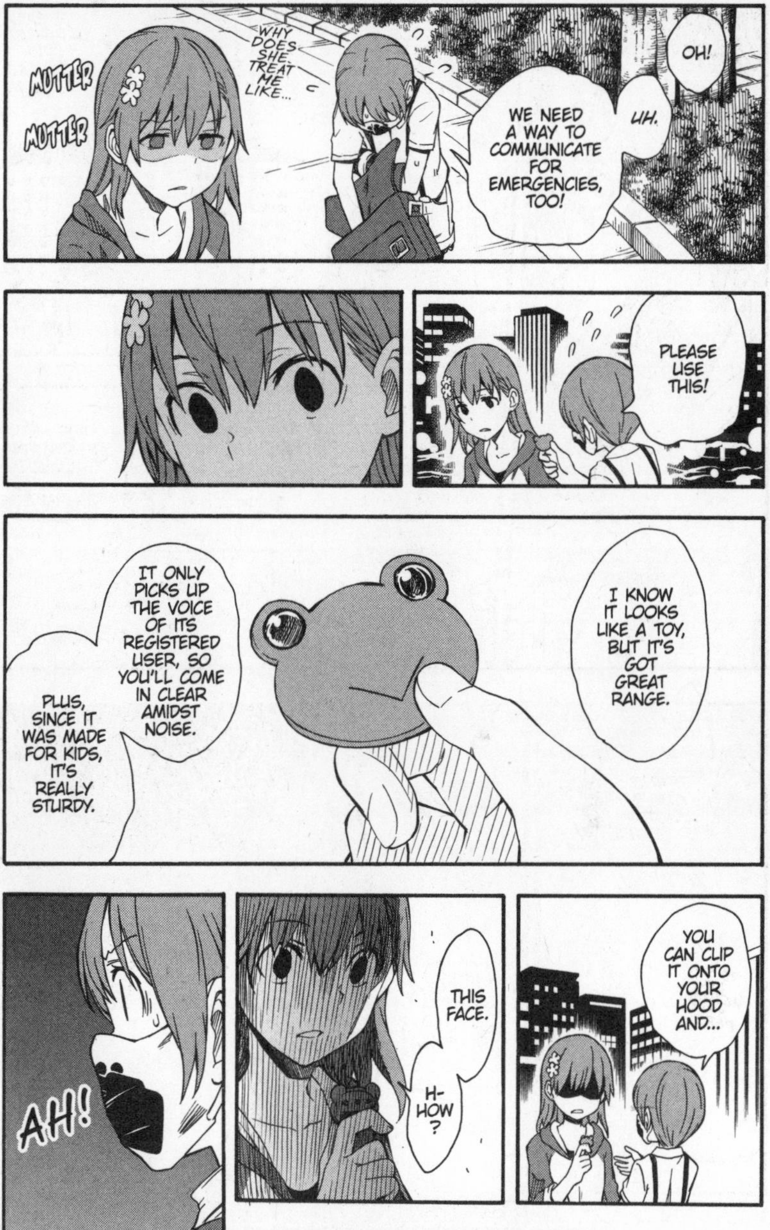
OH!
UH.
WE NEED A WAY TO COMMUNICATE FOR EMERGENCIES, TOO!
WHY DOES SHE TREAT ME LIKE...
MUTTER
MUTTER
PLEASE USE THIS!
I KNOW IT LOOKS LIKE A TOY, BUT IT'S GOT GREAT RANGE.
IT ONLY PICKS UP THE VOICE OF ITS REGISTERED USER, SO YOU'LL COME IN CLEAR AMIDST NOISE.
PLUS, SINCE IT WAS MADE FOR KIDS, IT'S REALLY STURDY.
YOU CAN CLIP IT ONTO YOUR HOOD AND...
THIS FACE.
H-HOW?
AH!

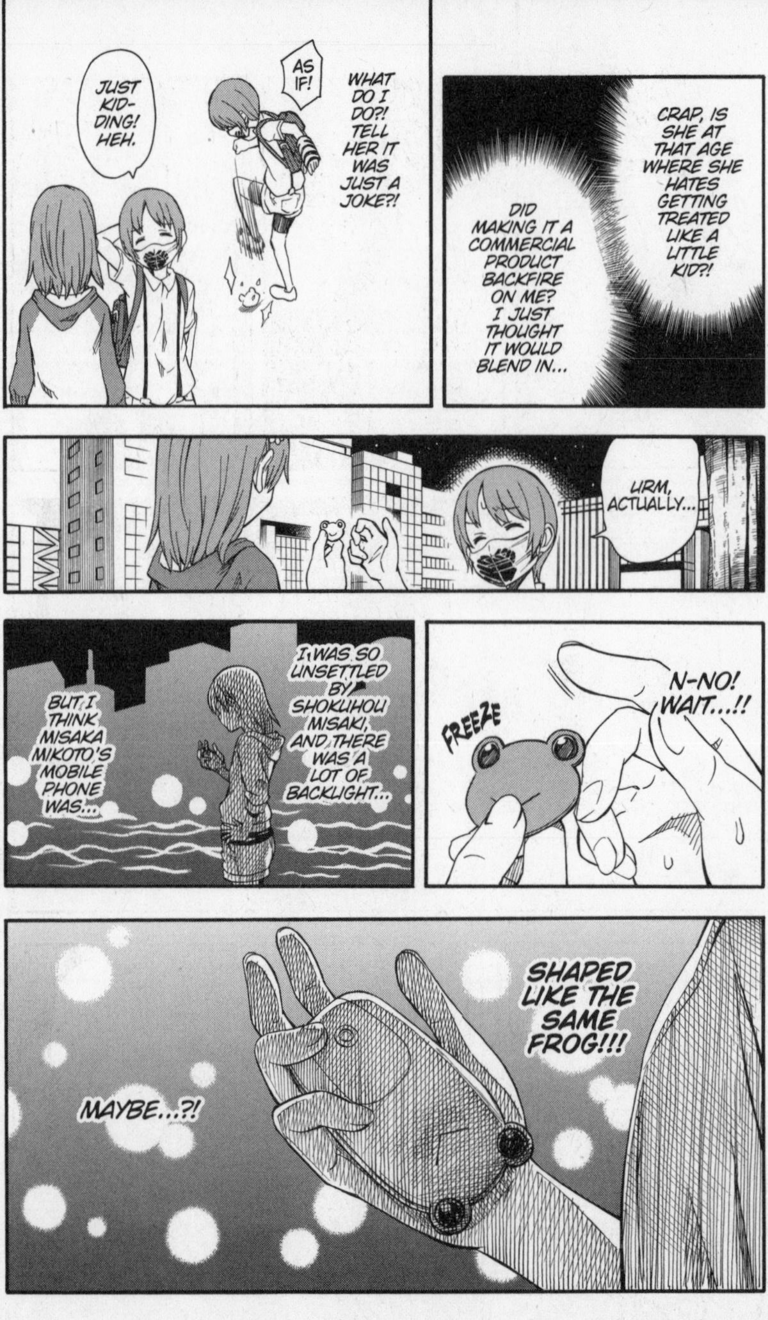
CRAP, IS SHE AT THAT AGE WHERE SHE HATES GETTING TREATED LIKE A LITTLE KID?!
DID MAKING IT A COMMERCIAL PRODUCT BACKFIRE ON ME? I JUST THOUGHT IT WOULD BLEND IN...
WHAT DO I DO?! TELL HER IT WAS JUST A JOKE?!
AS IF!
JUST KID-DING! HEH.
URM, ACTUALLY...
N-NO! WAIT...!!
FREEZE
I WAS SO UNSETTLED BY SHOKUHOU MISAKI, AND THERE WAS A LOT OF BACKLIGHT...
BUT I THINK MISAKA MIKOTO'S MOBILE PHONE WAS...
SHAPED LIKE THE SAME FROG!!!
MAYBE...?!

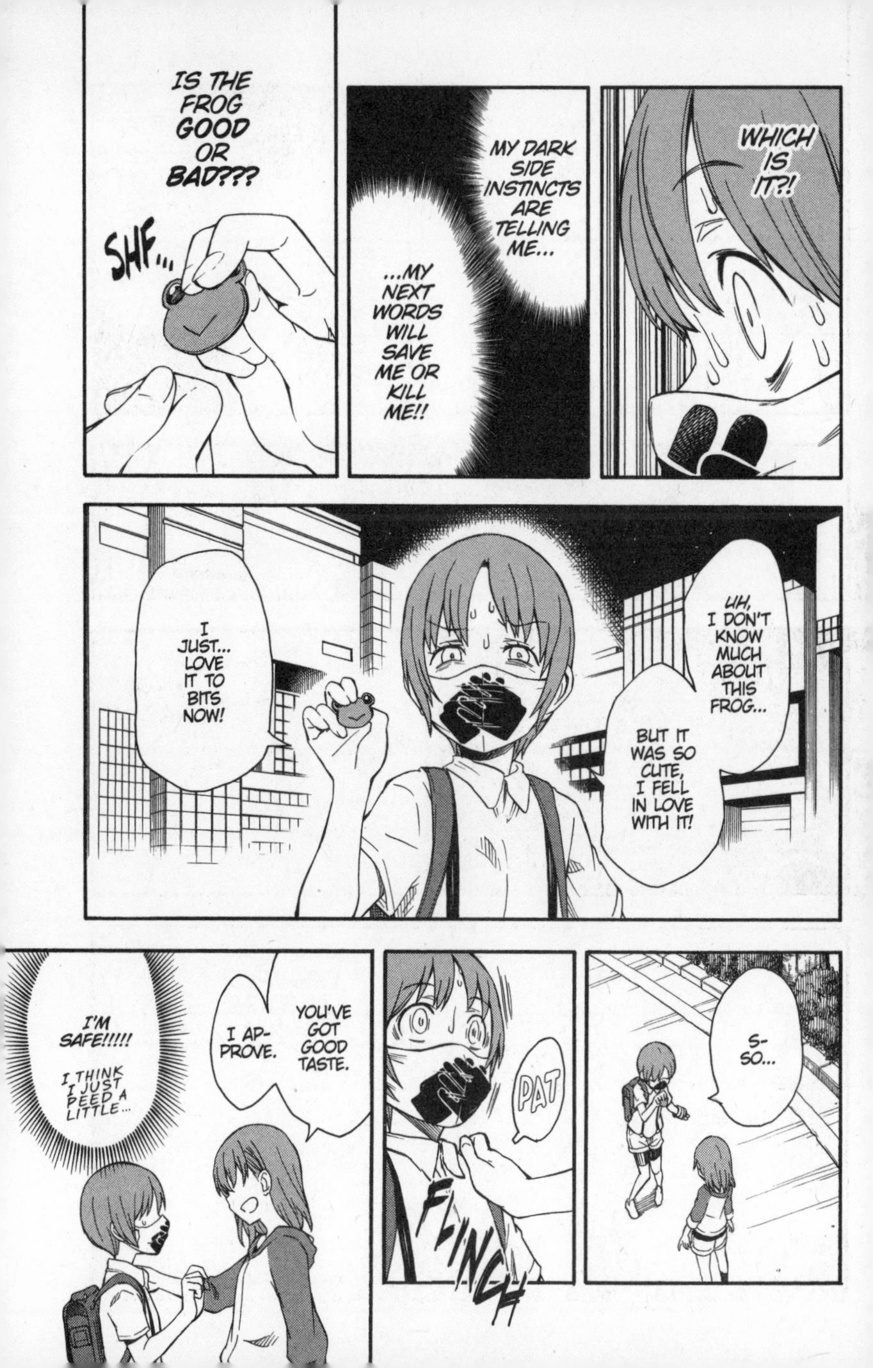
WHICH IS IT?!
MY DARK SIDE INSTINCTS ARE TELLING ME...
...MY NEXT WORDS WILL SAVE ME OR KILL ME!!
IS THE FROG GOOD OR BAD???
SHF...
UH, I DON'T KNOW MUCH ABOUT THIS FROG...
BUT IT WAS SO CUTE, I FELL IN LOVE WITH IT!
I JUST... LOVE IT TO BITS NOW!
S-SO...
PAT
FLINCH
YOU'VE GOT GOOD TASTE.
I APPROVE.
I'M SAFE!!!!!
I THINK I JUST PEED A LITTLE...

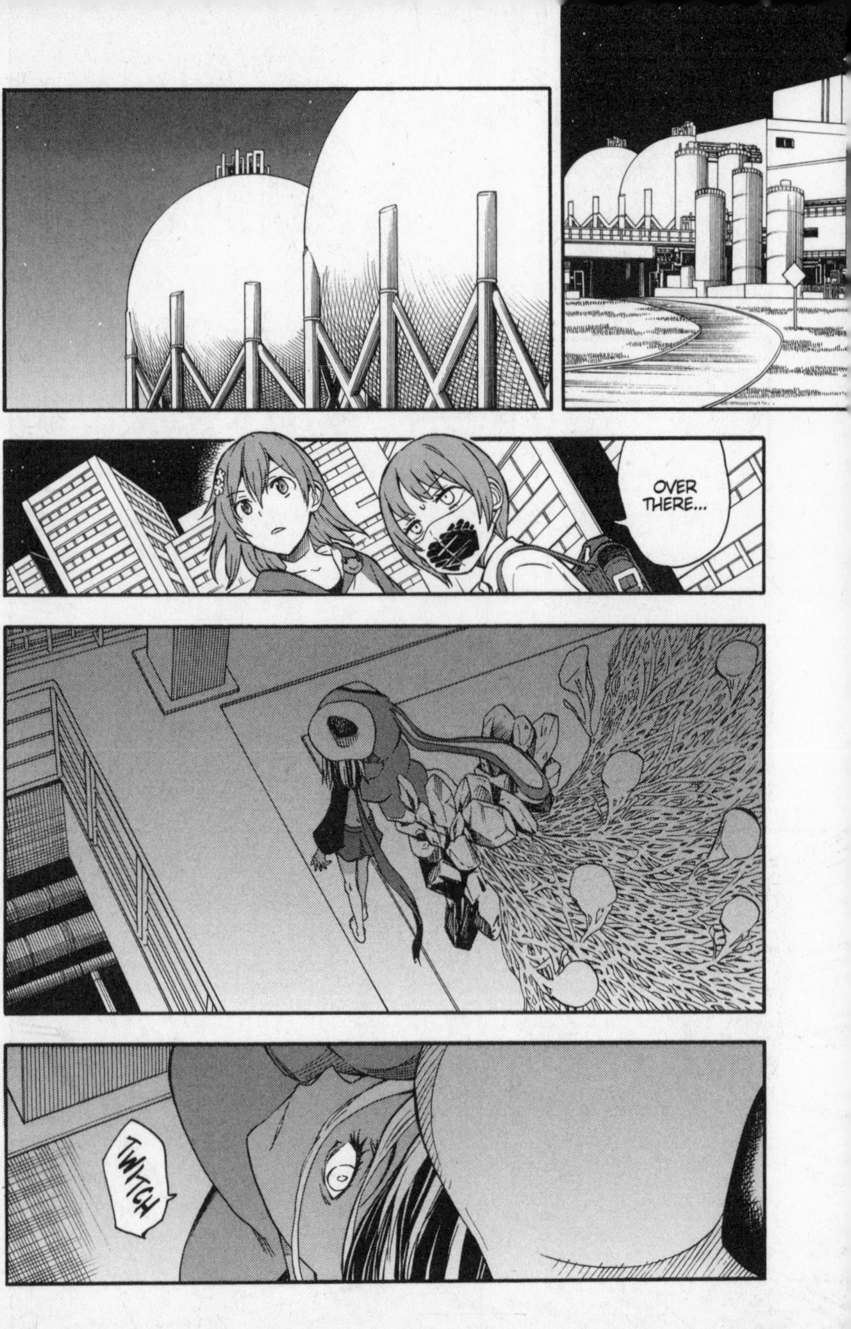
OVER THERE...
TWITCH

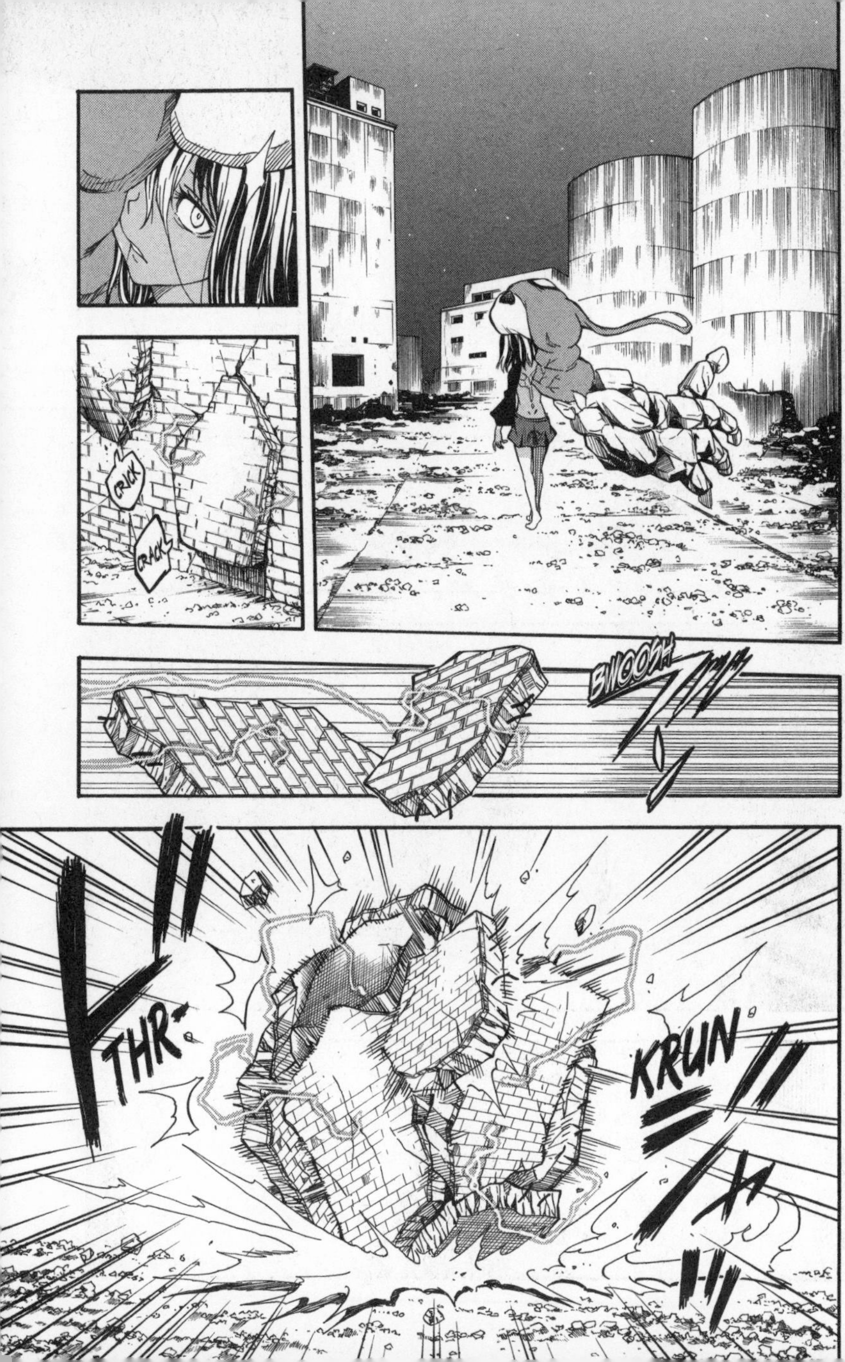
CRICK
CRACK
BWOOSH
THR
KRUN

CHAPTER 91: NEGOTIATION

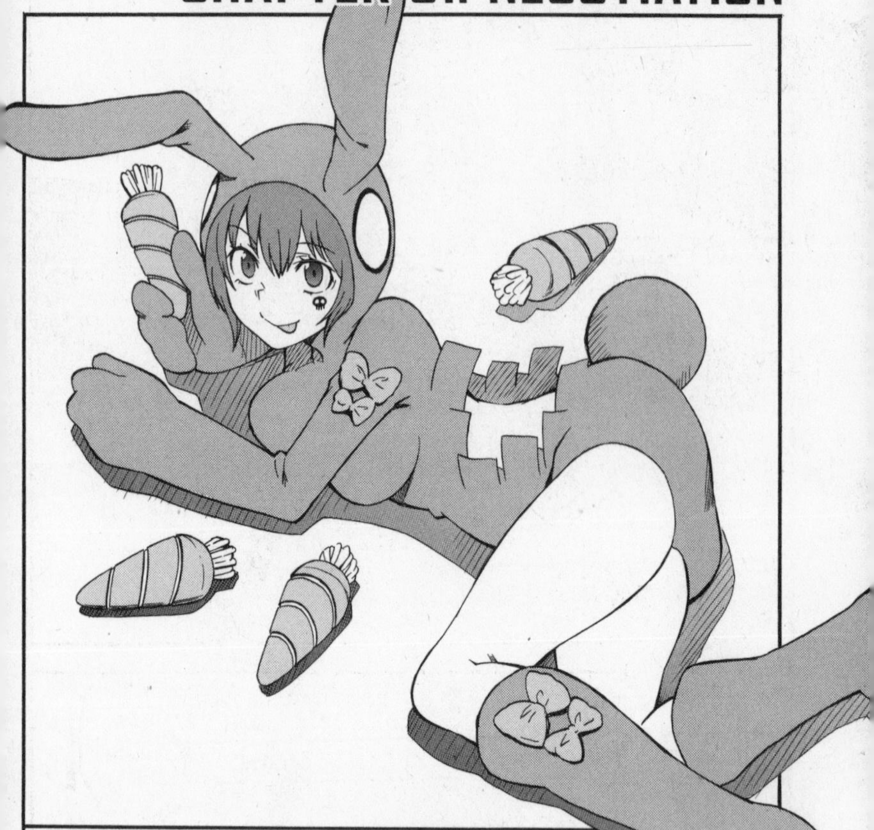

NARU (PSYCHOKINETIC)

- Member of the Dark Side organization Scavenger. Her real name is unknown.
- A psychokinetic ESPer who uses paper as her medium. Paper infused with her psychokinesis has the hardness of an alloy but cloth-like flexibility.
- Since she wears clothes made of paper, when she uses it as a weapon, her clothing shrinks. Although she has no problem showing skin to people, she's not an exhibitionist, either. It may not match her appearance, but she acts like a naughty grade school kid who dives into rivers.
- The other members seem to think of her as a troublesome brat, but she believes herself to be Scavenger's Ace.
- Her hobby is going to art museums. She prefers three-dimensional art.

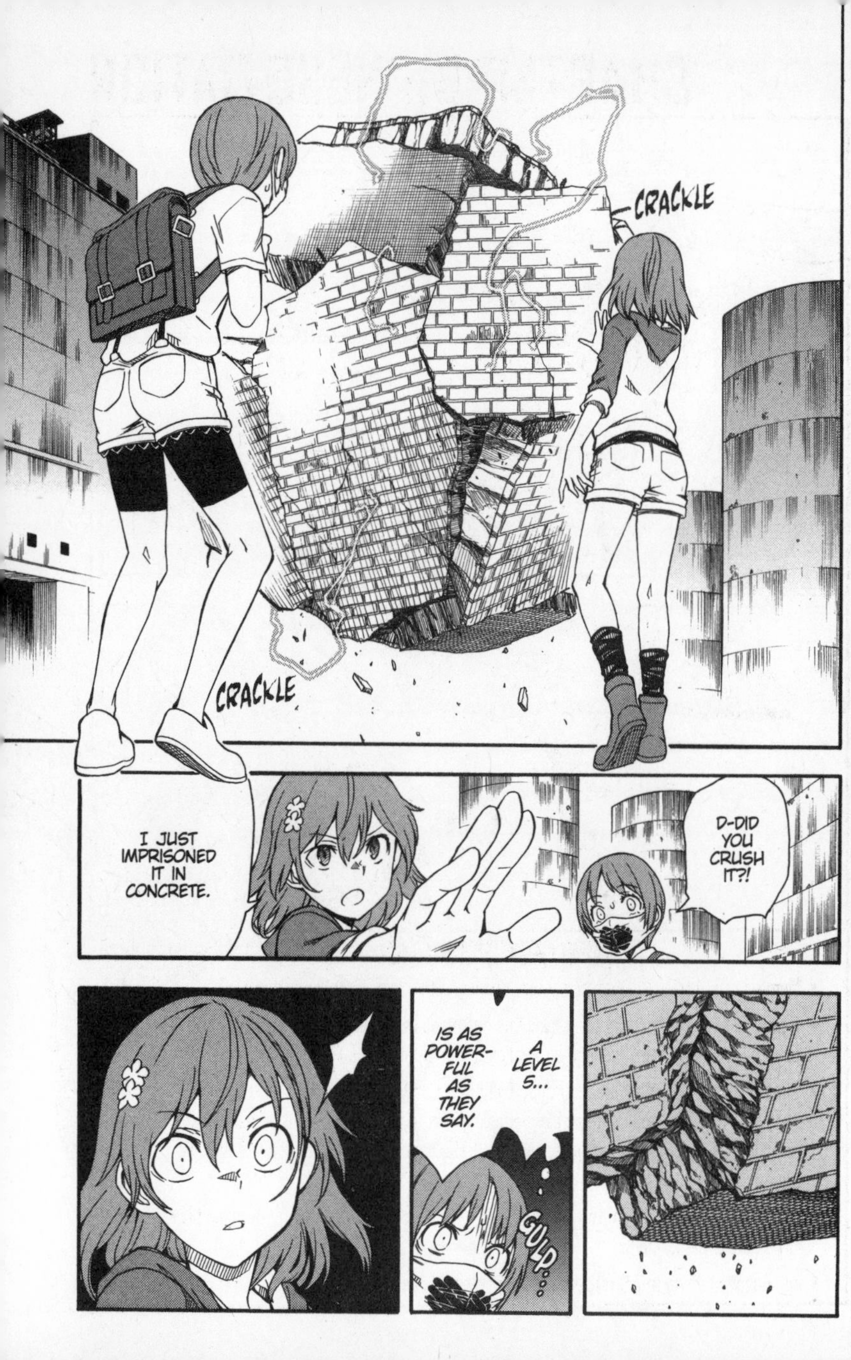
CRACKLE
CRACKLE
D-DID YOU CRUSH IT?!
I JUST IMPRISONED IT IN CONCRETE.
A LEVEL 5...
IS AS POWERFUL AS THEY SAY.
GULP...

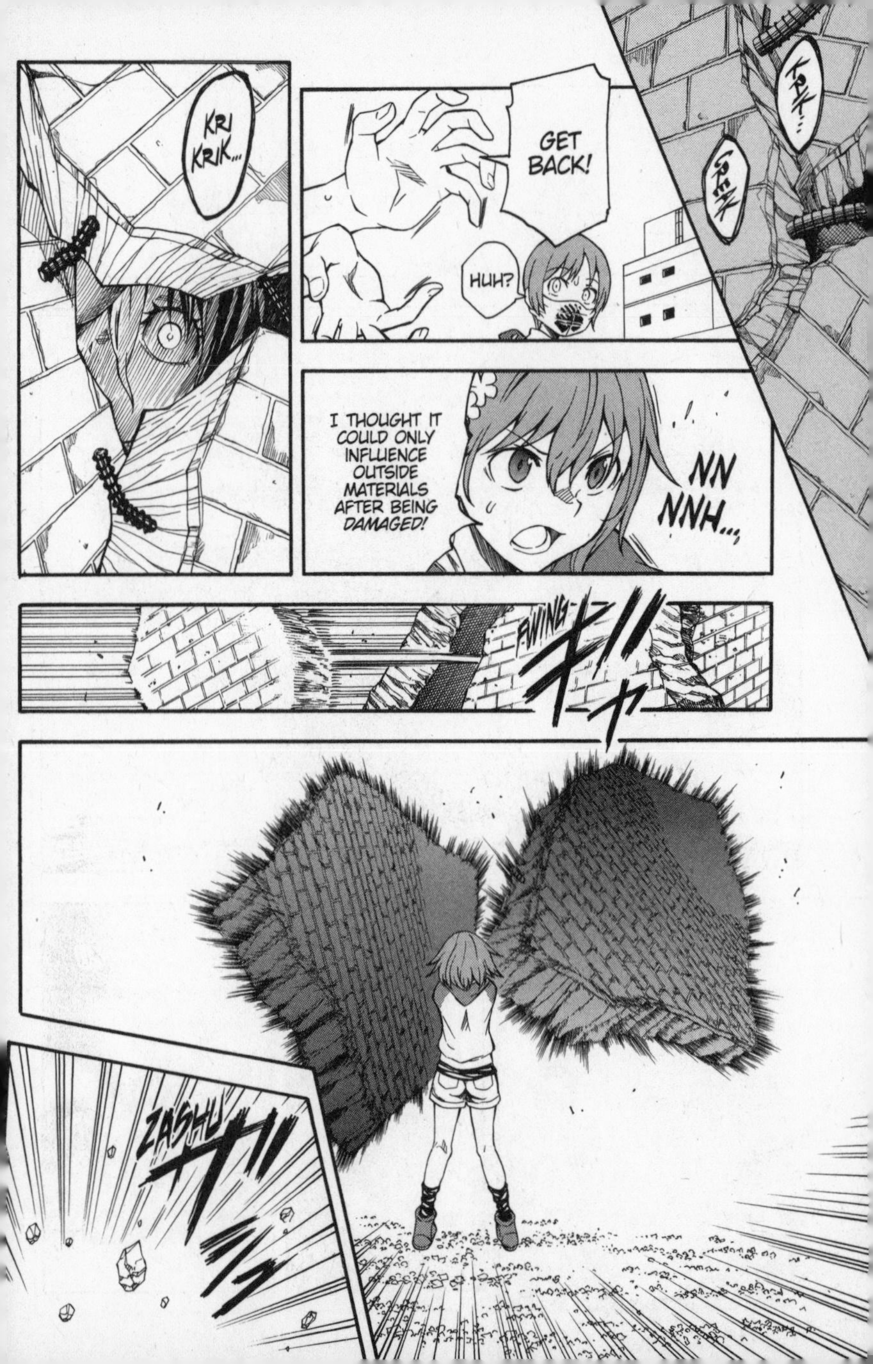
KRIK...
CREAK
GET BACK!
HUH?
KRI KRIK...
NN NNH...
I THOUGHT IT COULD ONLY INFLUENCE OUTSIDE MATERIALS AFTER BEING DAMAGED!
FWING
ZASHU

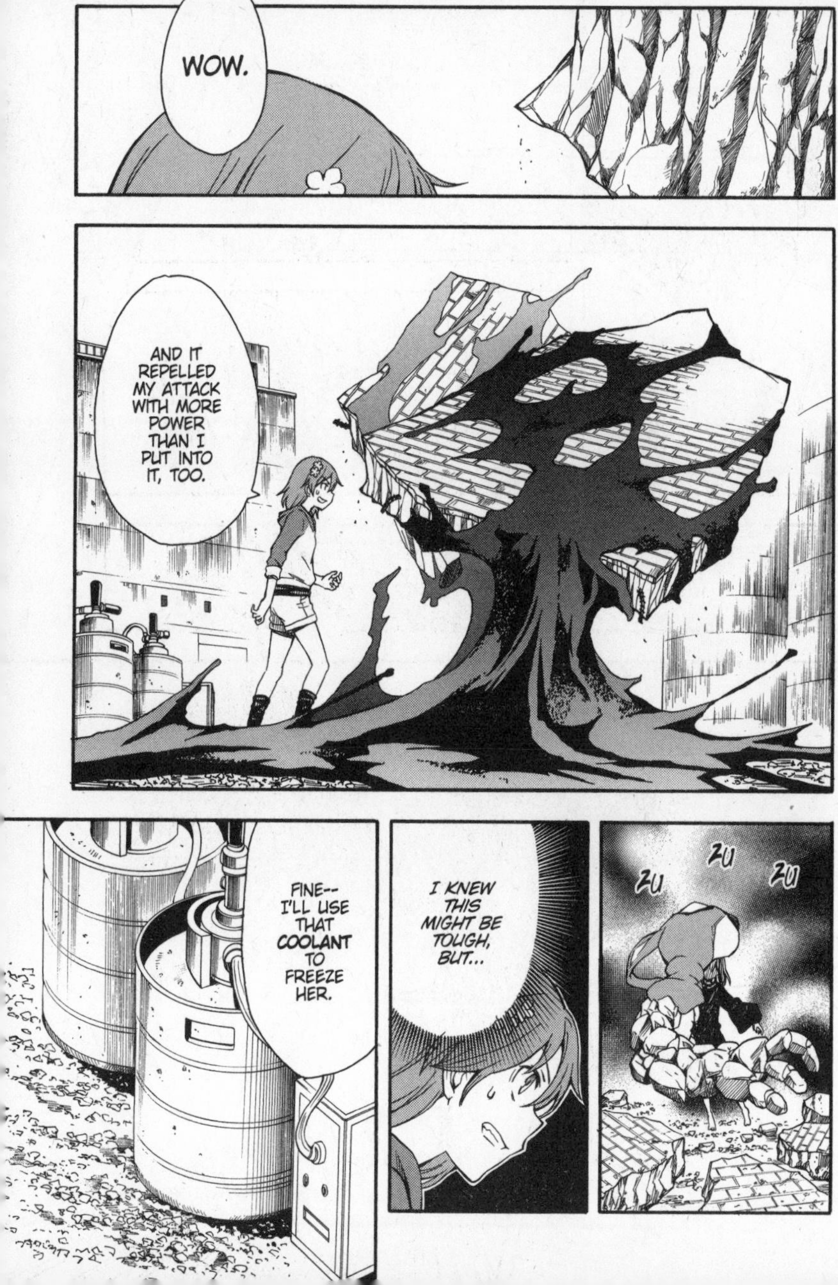
WOW.
AND IT REPELLED MY ATTACK WITH MORE POWER THAN I PUT INTO IT, TOO.
ZU
ZU
ZU
I KNEW THIS MIGHT BE TOUGH, BUT...
FINE-- I'LL USE THAT COOLANT TO FREEZE HER.

CRACK
CRACK
CRACK
GOUUN
WHA ?!

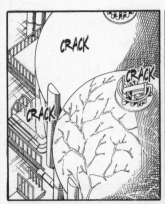

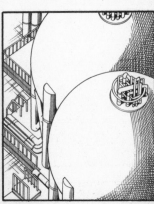

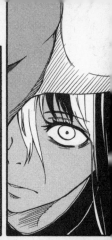

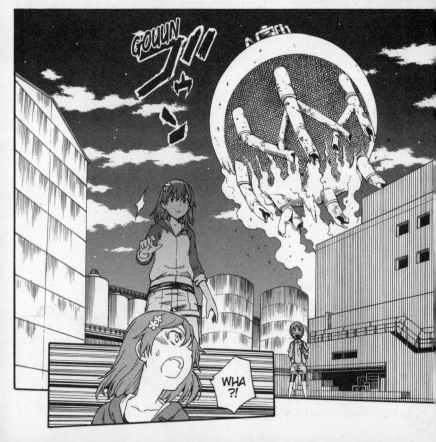

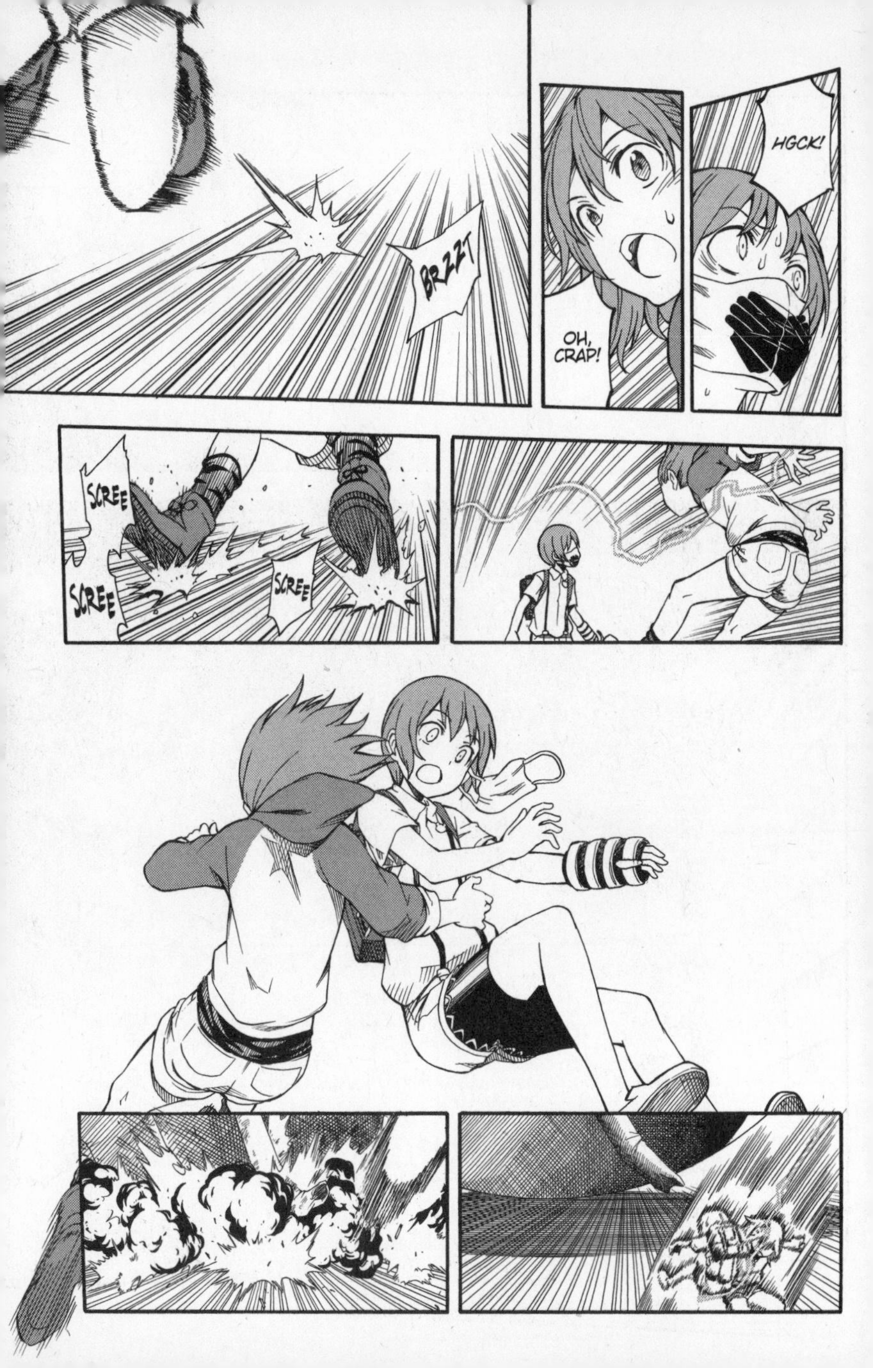
HGCK!
OH, CRAP!
BRZZT
SCREE
SCREE
SCREE

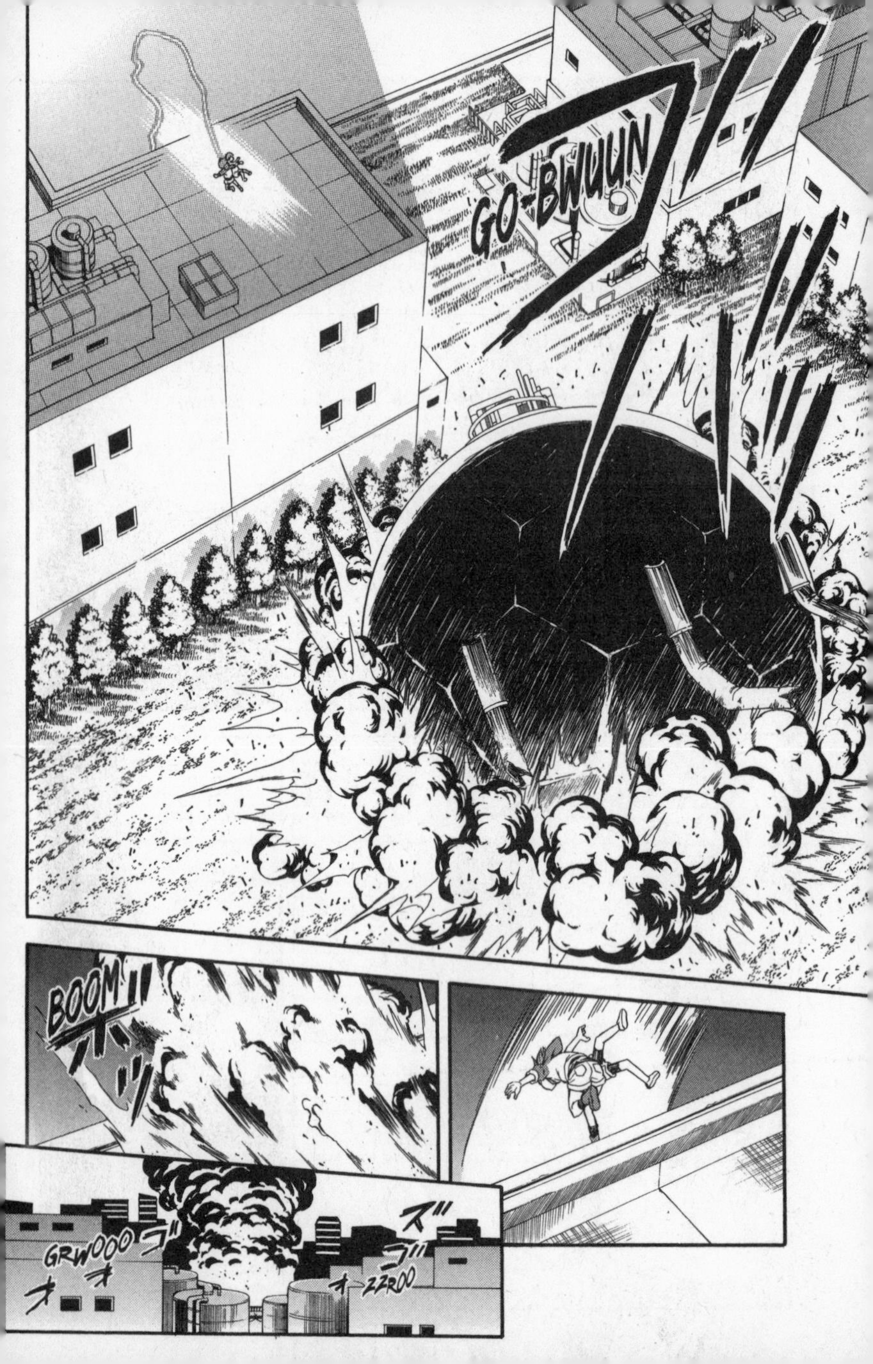
GO-BWUUN
BOOM
GRWOOO
ZZROO

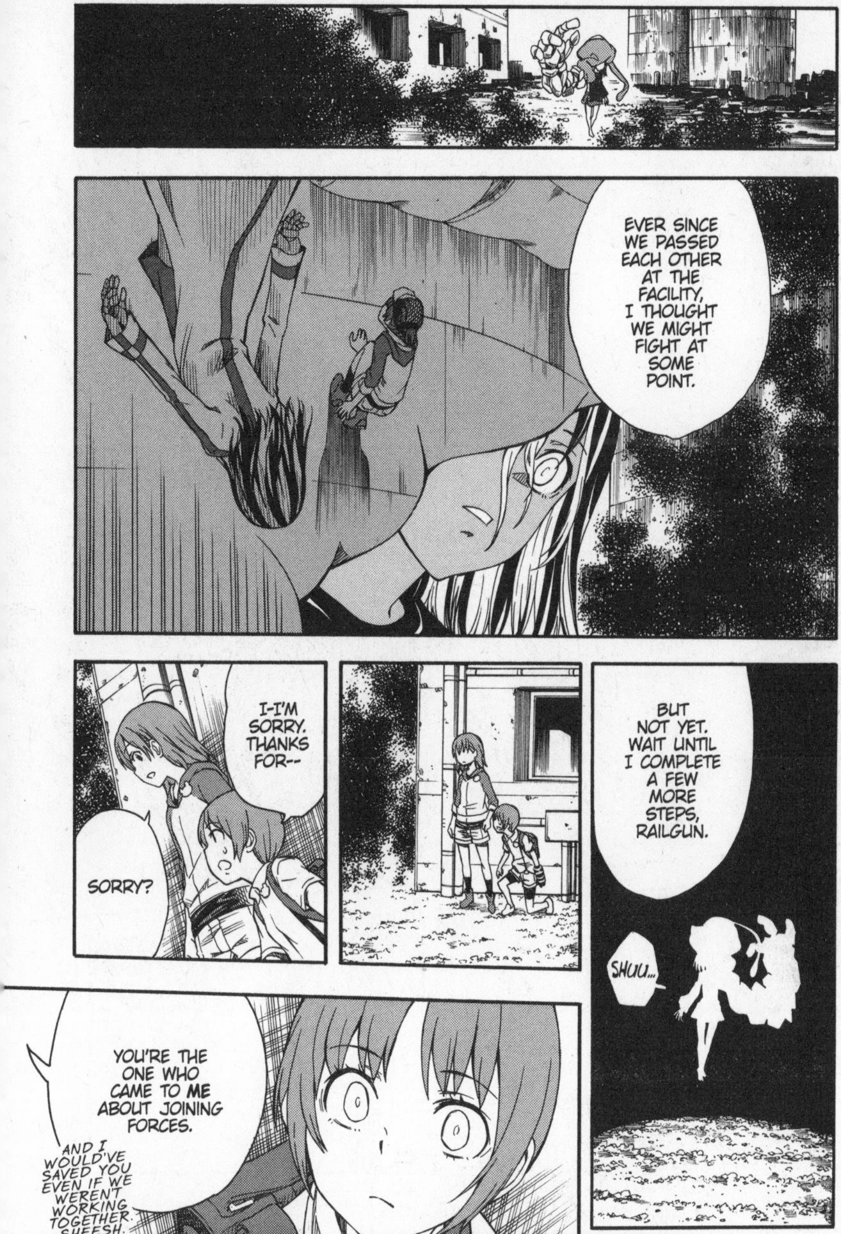
EVER SINCE WE PASSED EACH OTHER AT THE FACILITY, I THOUGHT WE MIGHT FIGHT AT SOME POINT.
BUT NOT YET. WAIT UNTIL I COMPLETE A FEW MORE STEPS, RAILGUN.
SHUU...
I-I'M SORRY. THANKS FOR--
SORRY?
YOU'RE THE ONE WHO CAME TO ME ABOUT JOINING FORCES.
AND I WOULD'VE SAVED YOU EVEN IF WE WERENT WORKING TOGETHER. SHEESH.

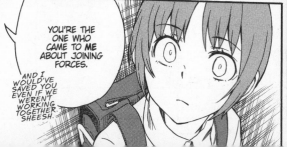

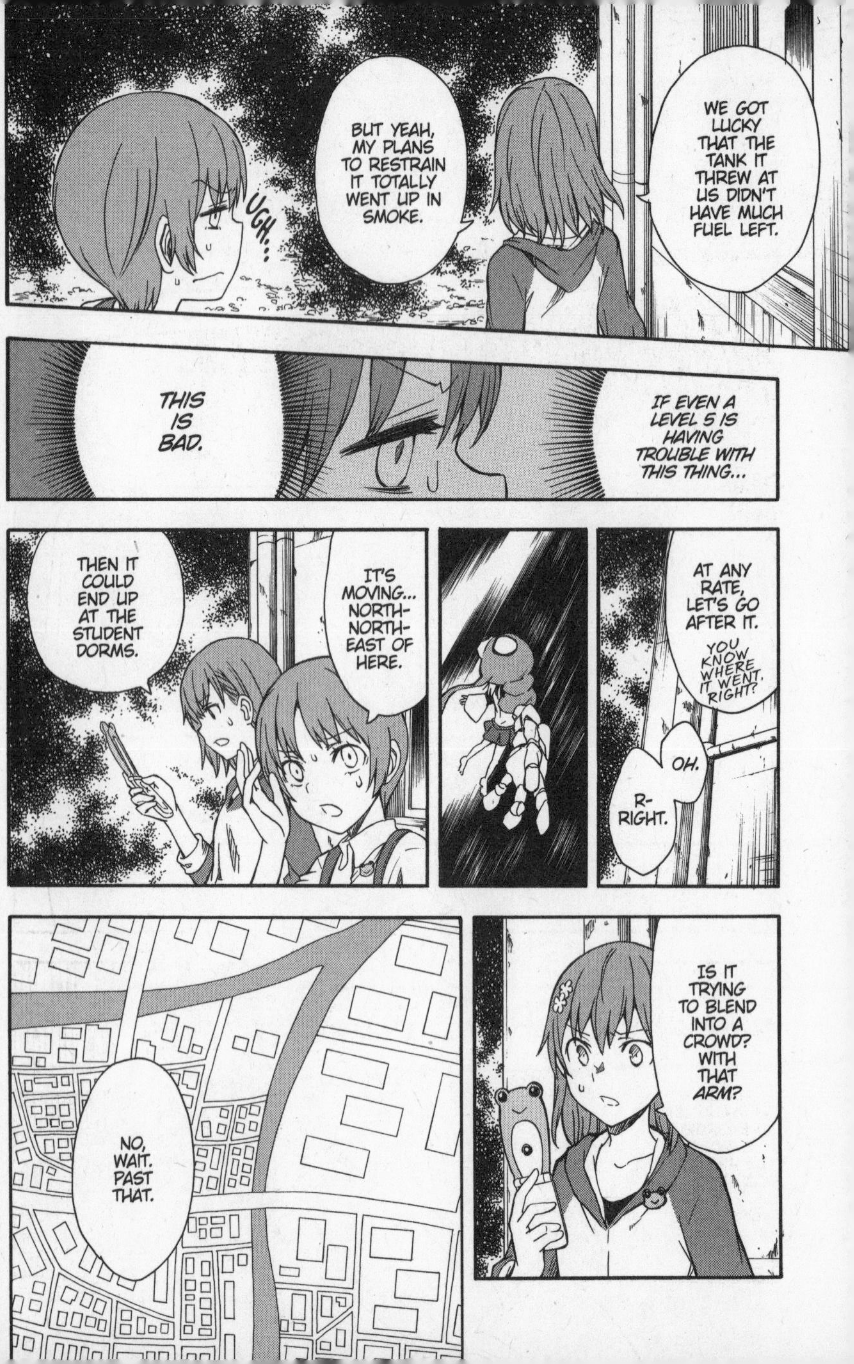
WE GOT LUCKY THAT THE TANK IT THREW AT US DIDN'T HAVE MUCH FUEL LEFT.
BUT YEAH, MY PLANS TO RESTRAIN IT TOTALLY WENT UP IN SMOKE.
UGH...
IF EVEN A LEVEL 5 IS HAVING TROUBLE WITH THIS THING...
THIS IS BAD.
AT ANY RATE, LET'S GO AFTER IT.
YOU KNOW WHERE IT WENT, RIGHT?
OH.
R-RIGHT.
IT'S MOVING... NORTH-NORTHEAST OF HERE.
THEN IT COULD END UP AT THE STUDENT DORMS.
IS IT TRYING TO BLEND INTO A CROWD? WITH THAT ARM?
NO, WAIT. PAST THAT.

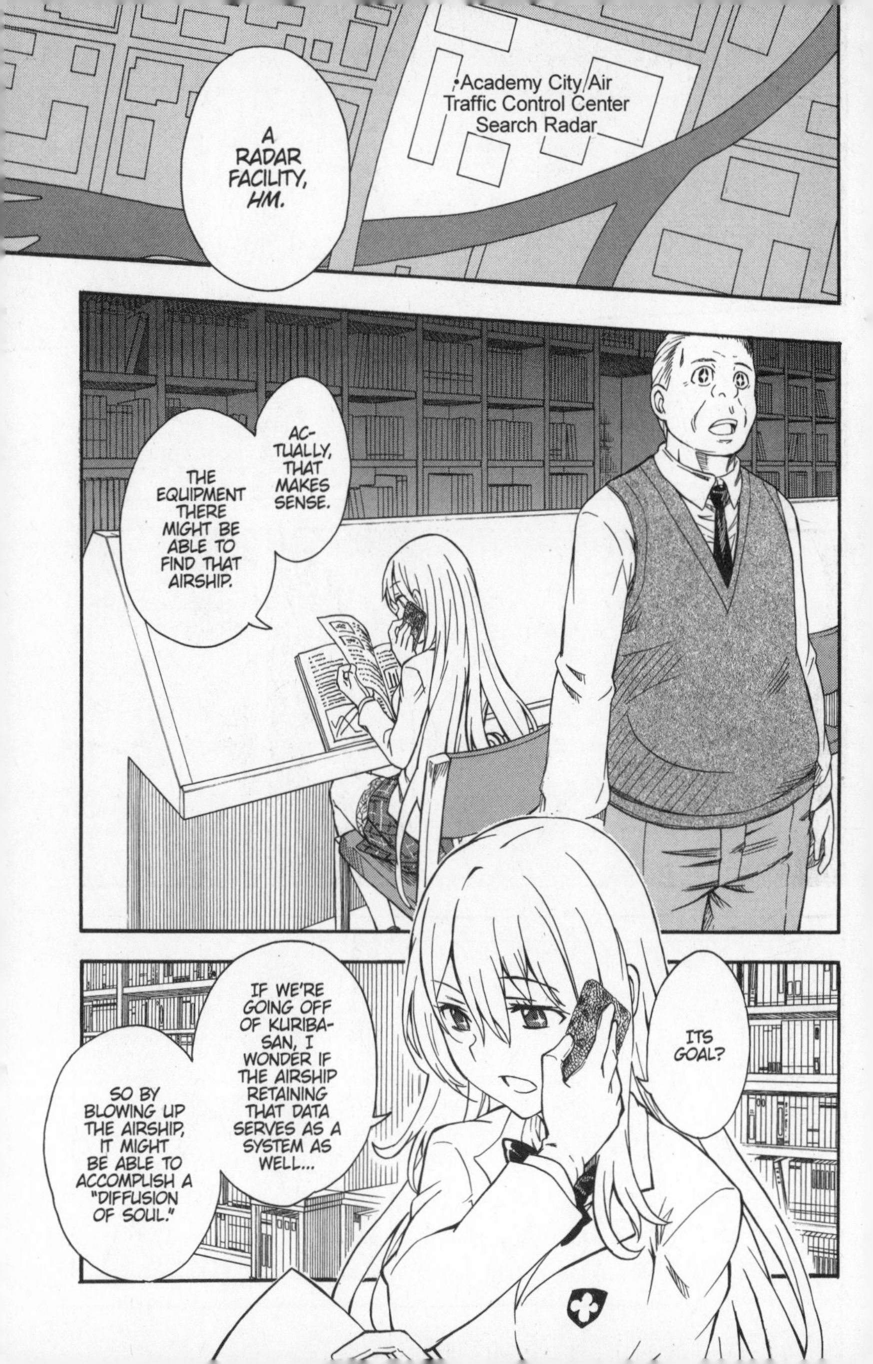
Academy City Air
Traffic Control Center
Search Radar
A RADAR FACILITY, HM.
ACTUALLY, THAT MAKES SENSE.
THE EQUIPMENT THERE MIGHT BE ABLE TO FIND THAT AIRSHIP.
ITS GOAL?
IF WE'RE GOING OFF OF KURIBA-SAN, I WONDER IF THE AIRSHIP RETAINING THAT DATA SERVES AS A SYSTEM AS WELL...
SO BY BLOWING UP THE AIRSHIP, IT MIGHT BE ABLE TO ACCOMPLISH A "DIFFUSION OF SOUL."

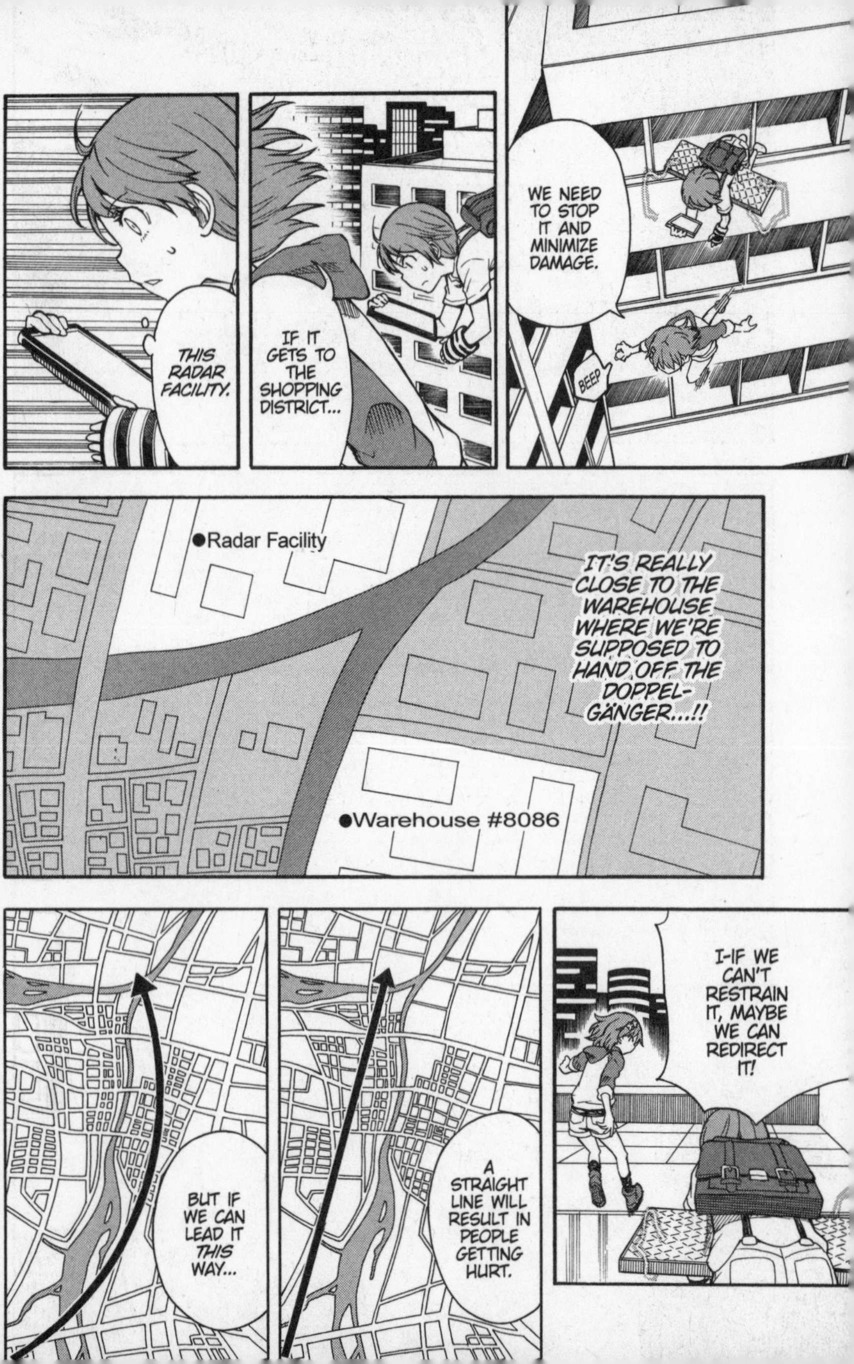
WE NEED TO STOP IT AND MINIMIZE DAMAGE.
BEEP
IF IT GETS TO THE SHOPPING DISTRICT...
THIS RADAR FACILITY.
●Radar Facility
●Warehouse #8086
IT'S REALLY CLOSE TO THE WAREHOUSE WHERE WE'RE SUPPOSED TO HAND OFF THE DOPPEL-GÄNGER...!!
I-IF WE CAN'T RESTRAIN IT, MAYBE WE CAN REDIRECT IT!
A STRAIGHT LINE WILL RESULT IN PEOPLE GETTING HURT.
BUT IF WE CAN LEAD IT *THIS* WAY...

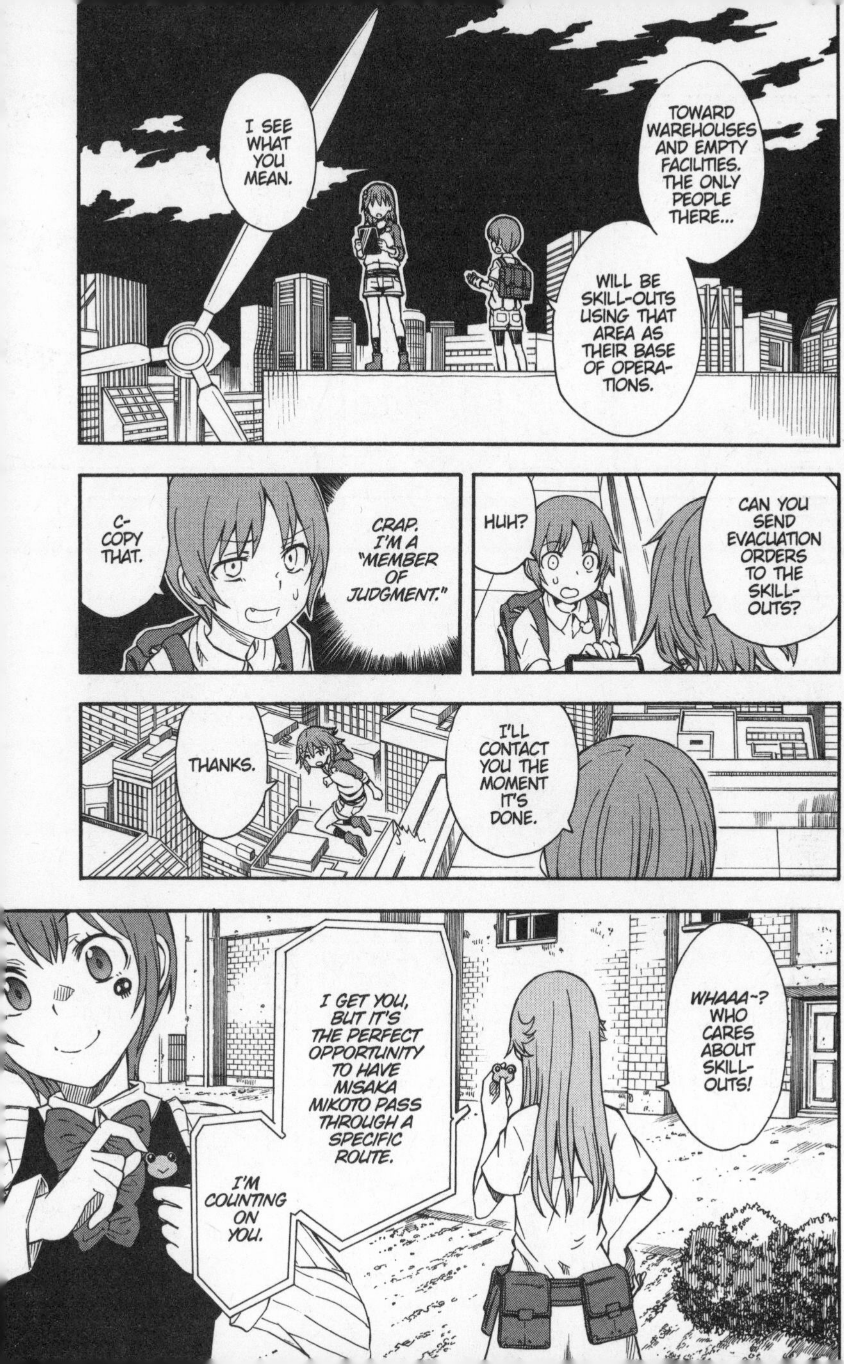
TOWARD WAREHOUSES AND EMPTY FACILITIES. THE ONLY PEOPLE THERE...
WILL BE SKILL-OUTS USING THAT AREA AS THEIR BASE OF OPERA-TIONS.
I SEE WHAT YOU MEAN.
CAN YOU SEND EVACUATION ORDERS TO THE SKILL-OUTS?
HUH?
CRAP. I'M A "MEMBER OF JUDGMENT."
C-COPY THAT.
I'LL CONTACT YOU THE MOMENT IT'S DONE.
THANKS.
WHAAA~? WHO CARES ABOUT SKILL-OUTS!
I GET YOU, BUT IT'S THE PERFECT OPPORTUNITY TO HAVE MISAKA MIKOTO PASS THROUGH A SPECIFIC ROUTE.
I'M COUNTING ON YOU.

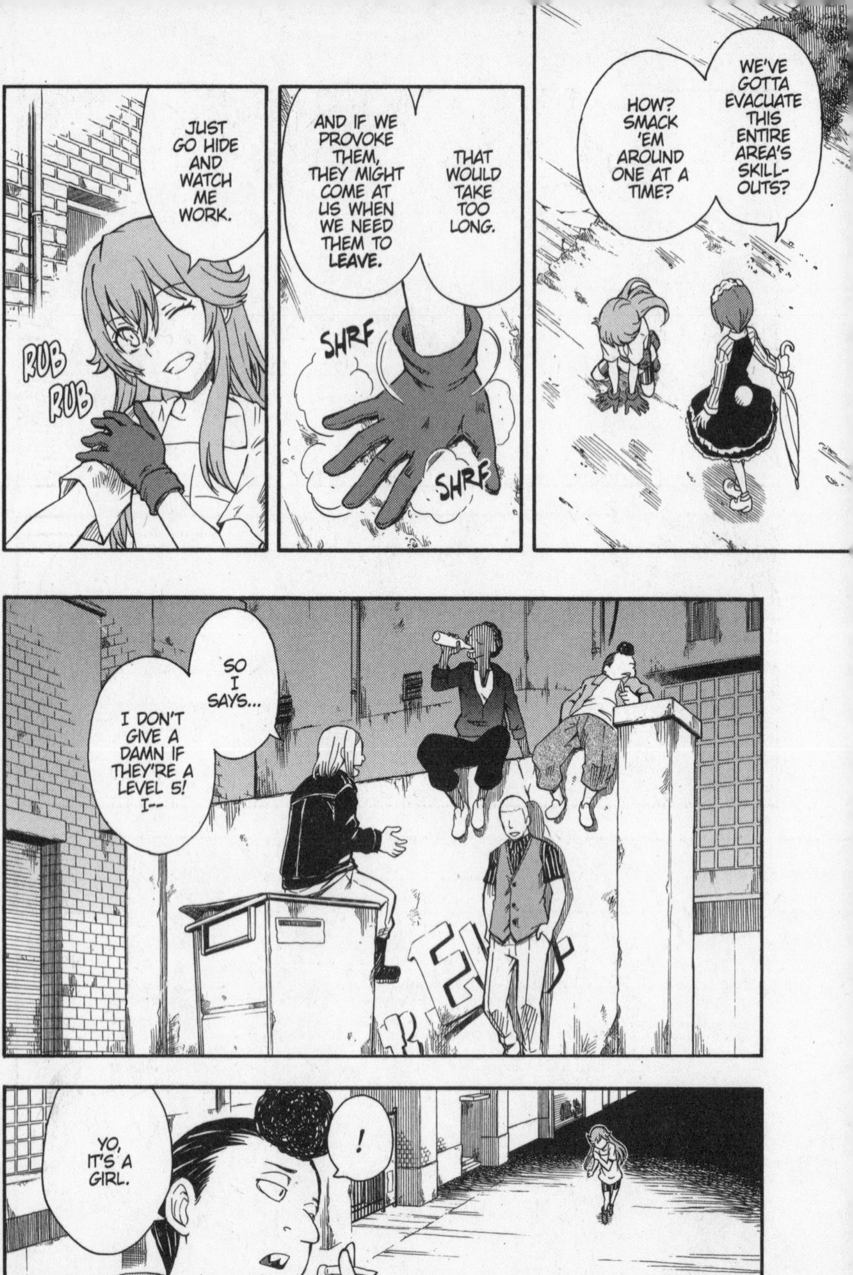
WE'VE GOTTA EVACUATE THIS ENTIRE AREA'S SKILL-OUTS?
HOW? SMACK 'EM AROUND ONE AT A TIME?
THAT WOULD TAKE TOO LONG.
AND IF WE PROVOKE THEM, THEY MIGHT COME AT US WHEN WE NEED THEM TO LEAVE.
SHRF
SHRF
JUST GO HIDE AND WATCH ME WORK.
RUB RUB
SO I SAYS...
I DON'T GIVE A DAMN IF THEY'RE A LEVEL 5! I--
!
YO, IT'S A GIRL.

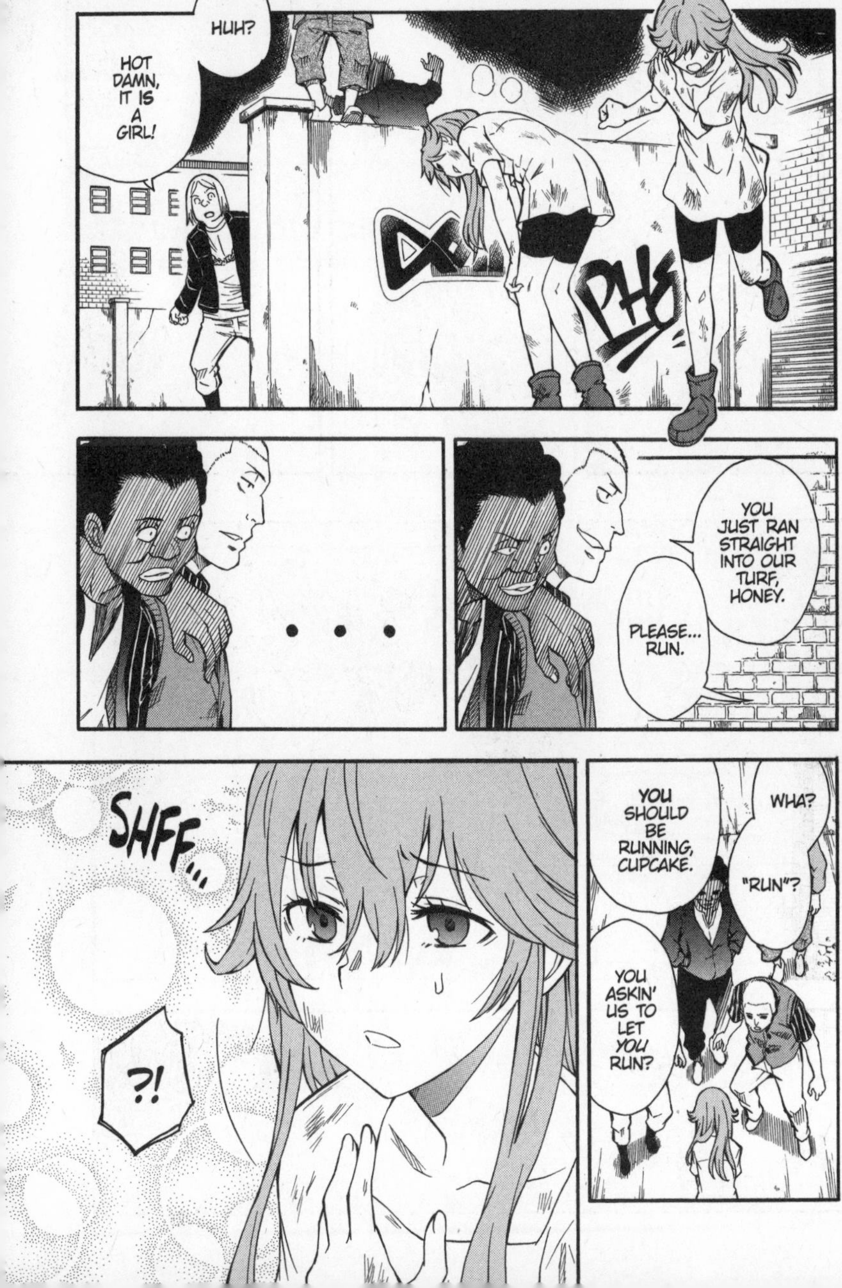
HUH?
HOT DAMN, IT IS A GIRL!
PHS
...
YOU JUST RAN STRAIGHT INTO OUR TURF, HONEY.
PLEASE... RUN.
WHA? "RUN"?
YOU SHOULD BE RUNNING, CUPCAKE.
YOU ASKIN' US TO LET YOU RUN?
SHFF...
?!

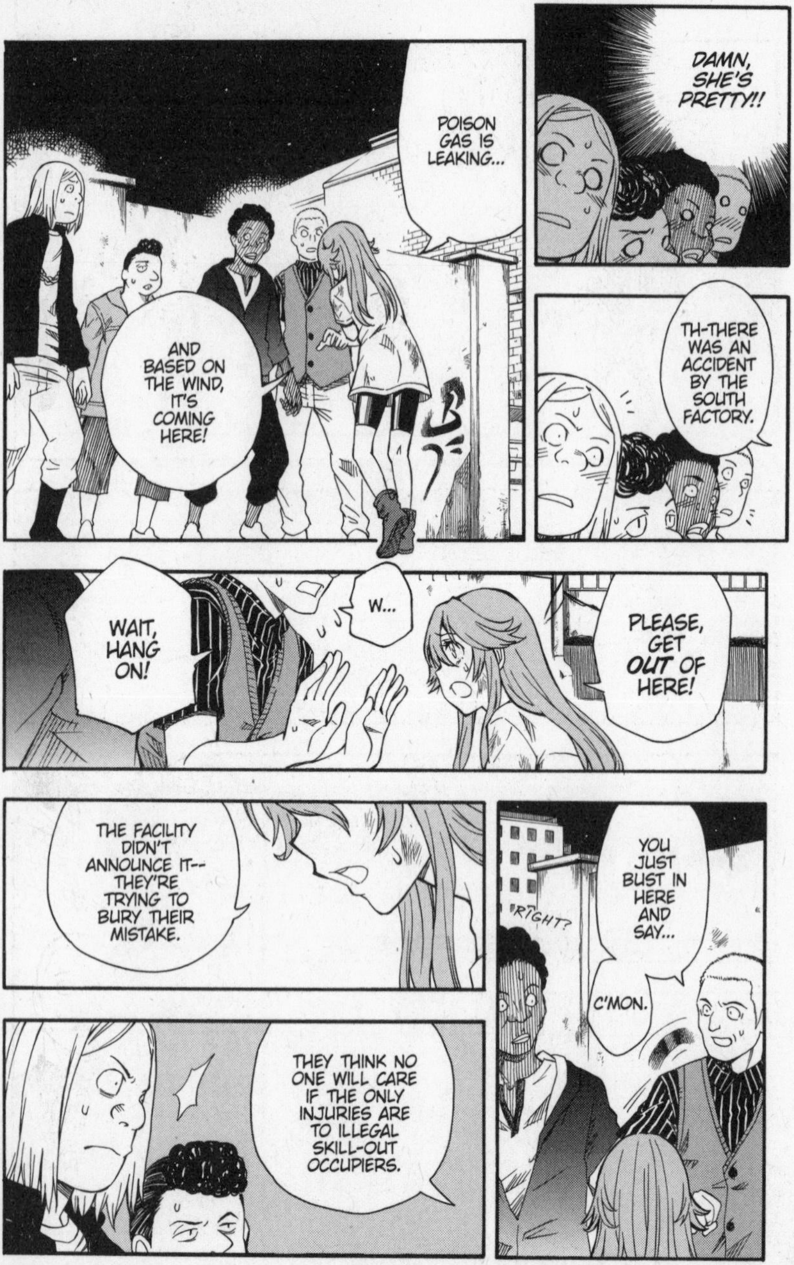
DAMN, SHE'S PRETTY!!
TH-THERE WAS AN ACCIDENT BY THE SOUTH FACTORY.
POISON GAS IS LEAKING...
AND BASED ON THE WIND, IT'S COMING HERE!
PLEASE, GET OUT OF HERE!
W...
WAIT, HANG ON!
YOU JUST BUST IN HERE AND SAY...
RIGHT?
C'MON.
THE FACILITY DIDN'T ANNOUNCE IT-- THEY'RE TRYING TO BURY THEIR MISTAKE.
THEY THINK NO ONE WILL CARE IF THE ONLY INJURIES ARE TO ILLEGAL SKILL-OUT OCCUPIERS.

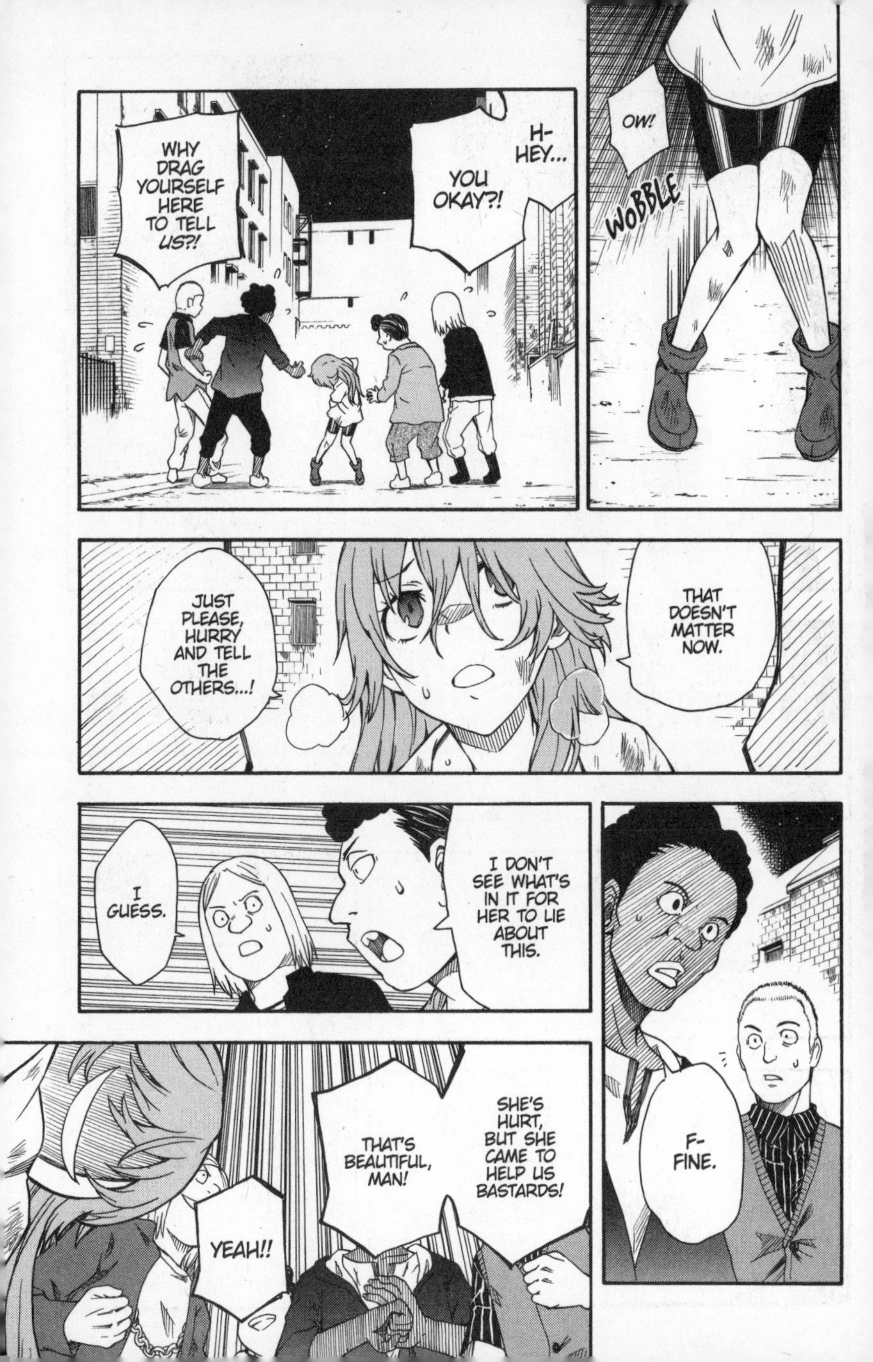
OW!
WOBBLE
H-HEY...
YOU OKAY?!
WHY DRAG YOURSELF HERE TO TELL US?!
THAT DOESN'T MATTER NOW.
JUST PLEASE, HURRY AND TELL THE OTHERS...!
I DON'T SEE WHAT'S IN IT FOR HER TO LIE ABOUT THIS.
I GUESS.
F-FINE.
SHE'S HURT, BUT SHE CAME TO HELP US BASTARDS!
THAT'S BEAUTIFUL, MAN!
YEAH!!

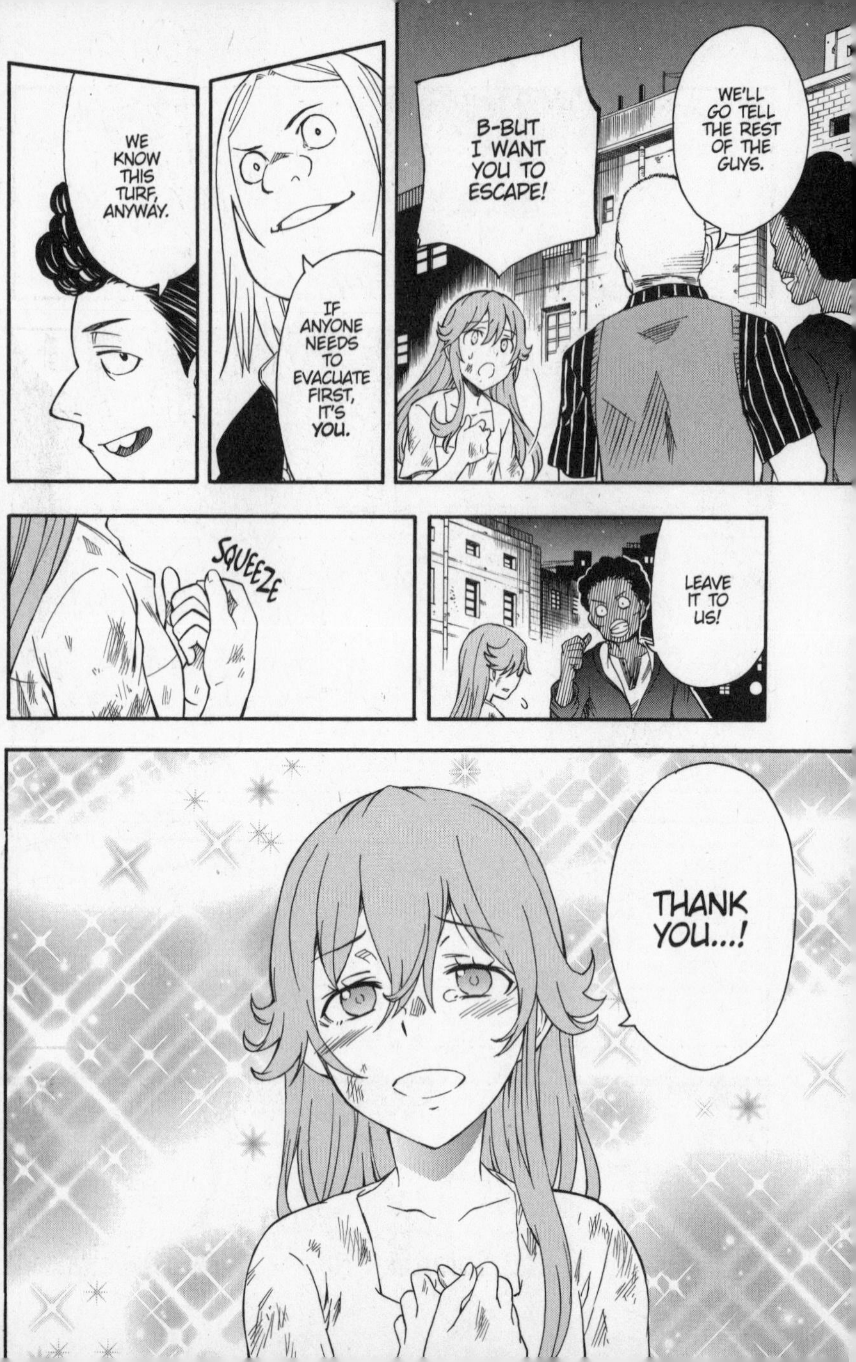

WE'LL GO TELL THE REST OF THE GUYS.
B-BUT I WANT YOU TO ESCAPE!
IF ANYONE NEEDS TO EVACUATE FIRST, IT'S YOU.
WE KNOW THIS TURF, ANYWAY.
LEAVE IT TO US!
SQUEEZE
THANK YOU...!

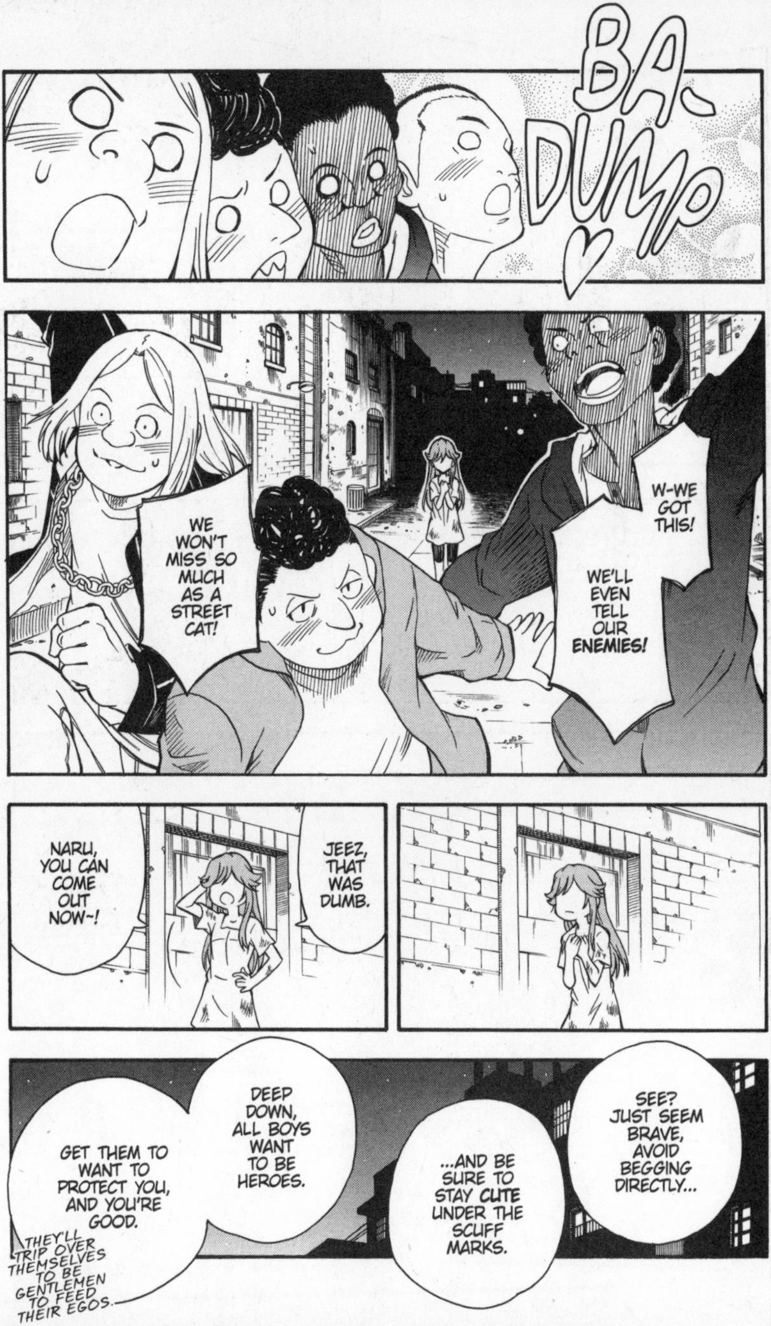

BA-DUMP
W-WE GOT THIS!
WE'LL EVEN TELL OUR ENEMIES!
WE WON'T MISS SO MUCH AS A STREET CAT!
JEEZ, THAT WAS DUMB.
NARU, YOU CAN COME OUT NOW~!
SEE? JUST SEEM BRAVE, AVOID BEGGING DIRECTLY...
...AND BE SURE TO STAY CUTE UNDER THE SCUFF MARKS.
DEEP DOWN, ALL BOYS WANT TO BE HEROES.
GET THEM TO WANT TO PROTECT YOU, AND YOU'RE GOOD.
THEY'LL TRIP OVER THEMSELVES TO BE GENTLEMEN TO FEED THEIR EGOS.

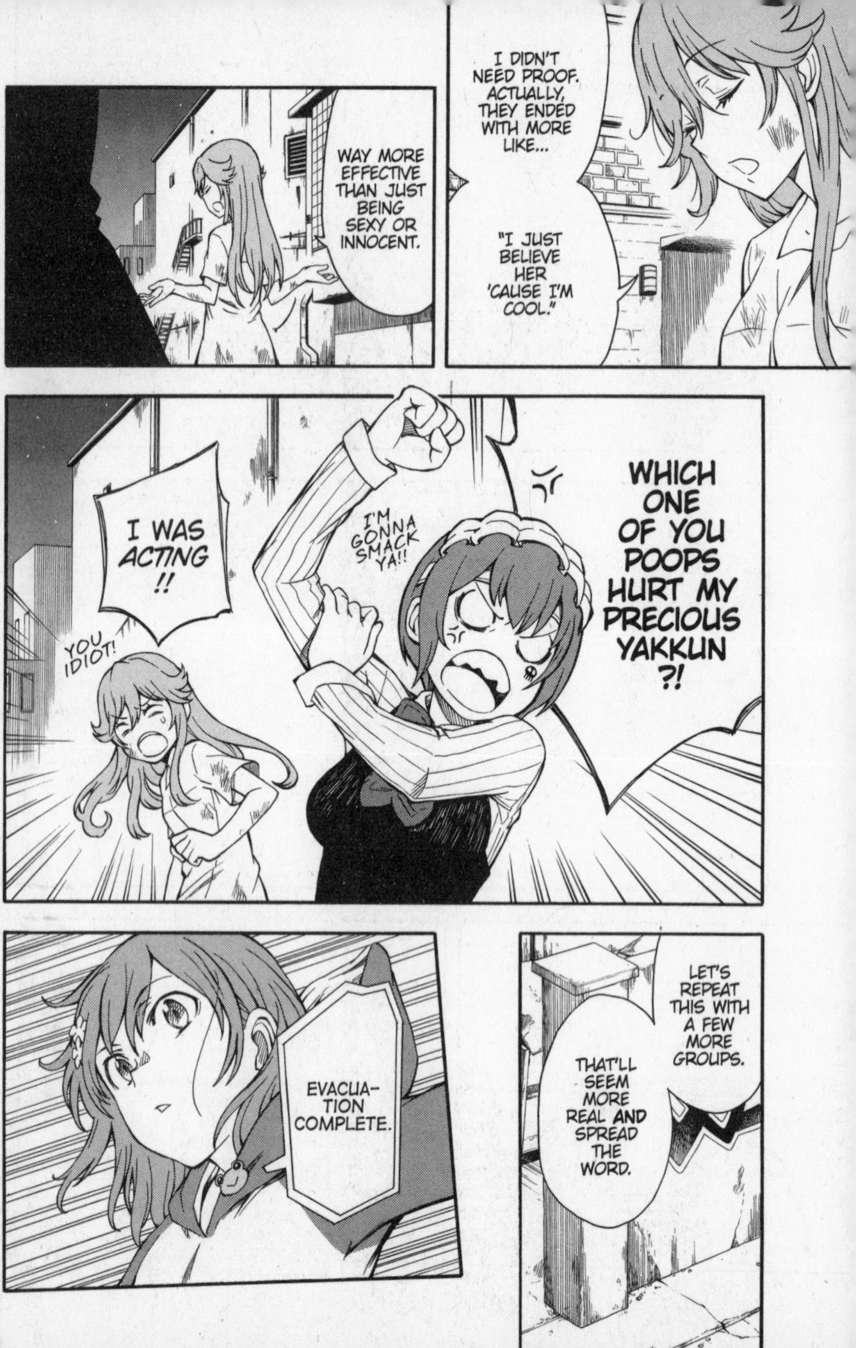

I DIDN'T NEED PROOF. ACTUALLY, THEY ENDED WITH MORE LIKE...
"I JUST BELIEVE HER 'CAUSE I'M COOL."
WAY MORE EFFECTIVE THAN JUST BEING SEXY OR INNOCENT.
WHICH ONE OF YOU POOPS HURT MY PRECIOUS YAKKUN ?!
I'M GONNA SMACK YA!!
I WAS ACTING !!
YOU IDIOT!
LET'S REPEAT THIS WITH A FEW MORE GROUPS.
THAT'LL SEEM MORE REAL AND SPREAD THE WORD.
EVACUA-TION COMPLETE.

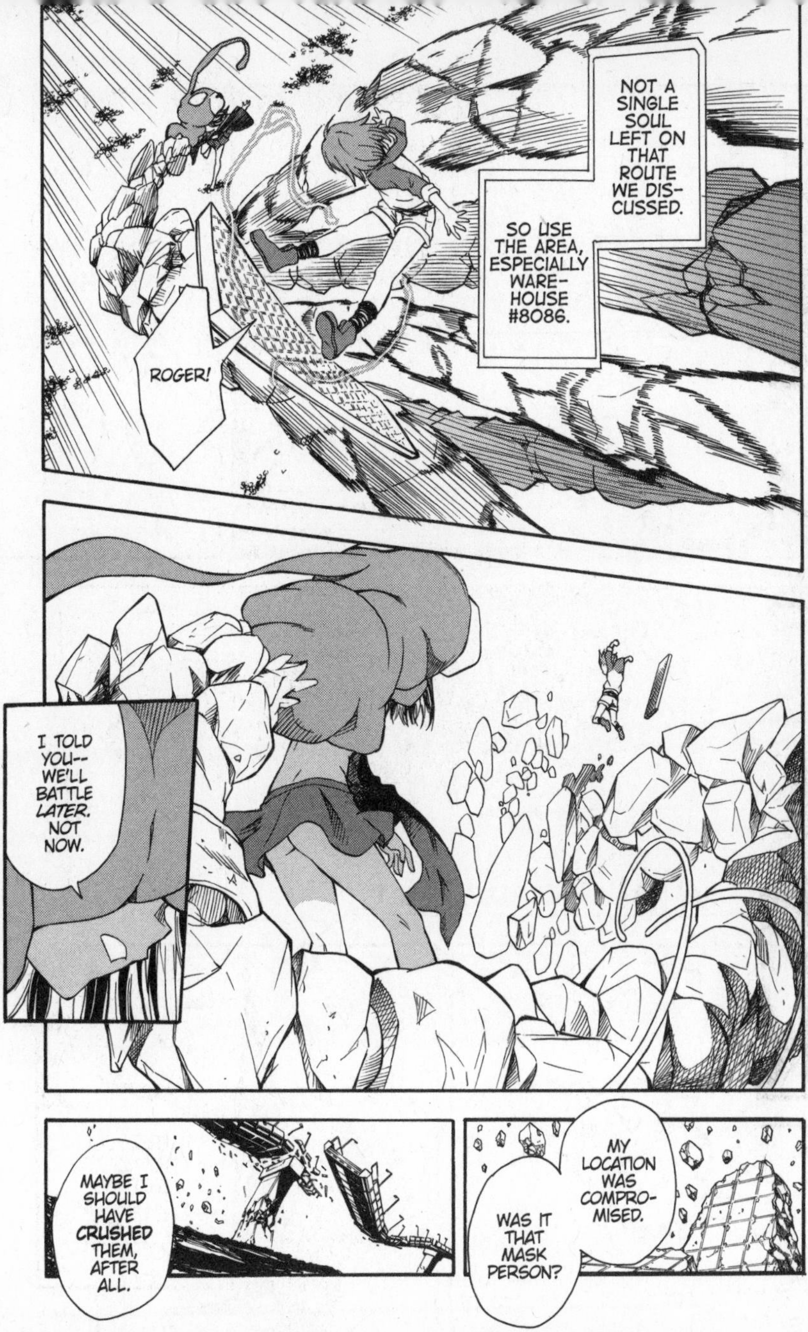
NOT A SINGLE SOUL LEFT ON THAT ROUTE WE DISCUSSED.
SO USE THE AREA, ESPECIALLY WARE-HOUSE #8086.
ROGER!
I TOLD YOU-- WE'LL BATTLE *LATER*. NOT NOW.
MY LOCATION WAS COMPRO-MISED.
WAS IT THAT MASK PERSON?
MAYBE I SHOULD HAVE **CRUSHED** THEM, AFTER ALL.

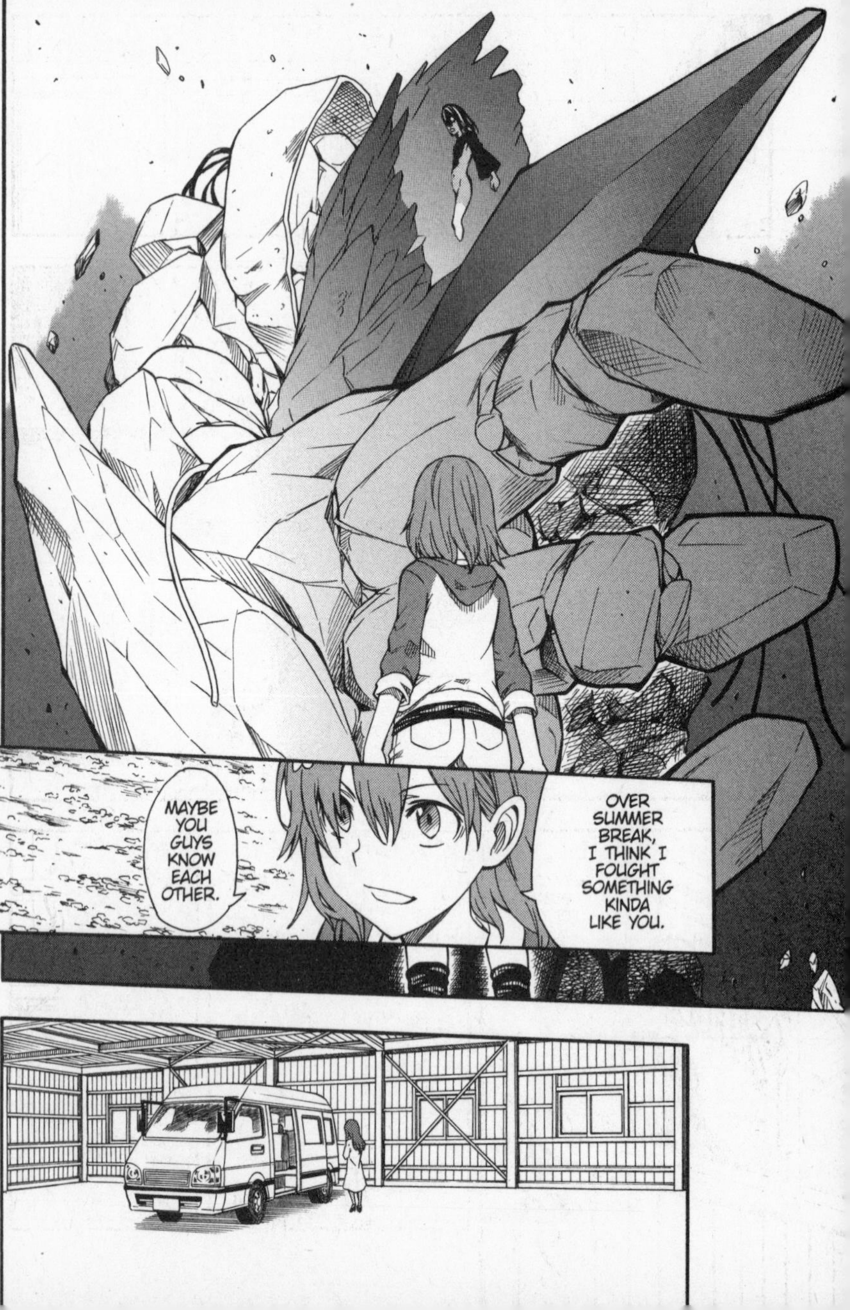
OVER SUMMER BREAK, I THINK I FOUGHT SOMETHING KINDA LIKE YOU.
MAYBE YOU GUYS KNOW EACH OTHER.

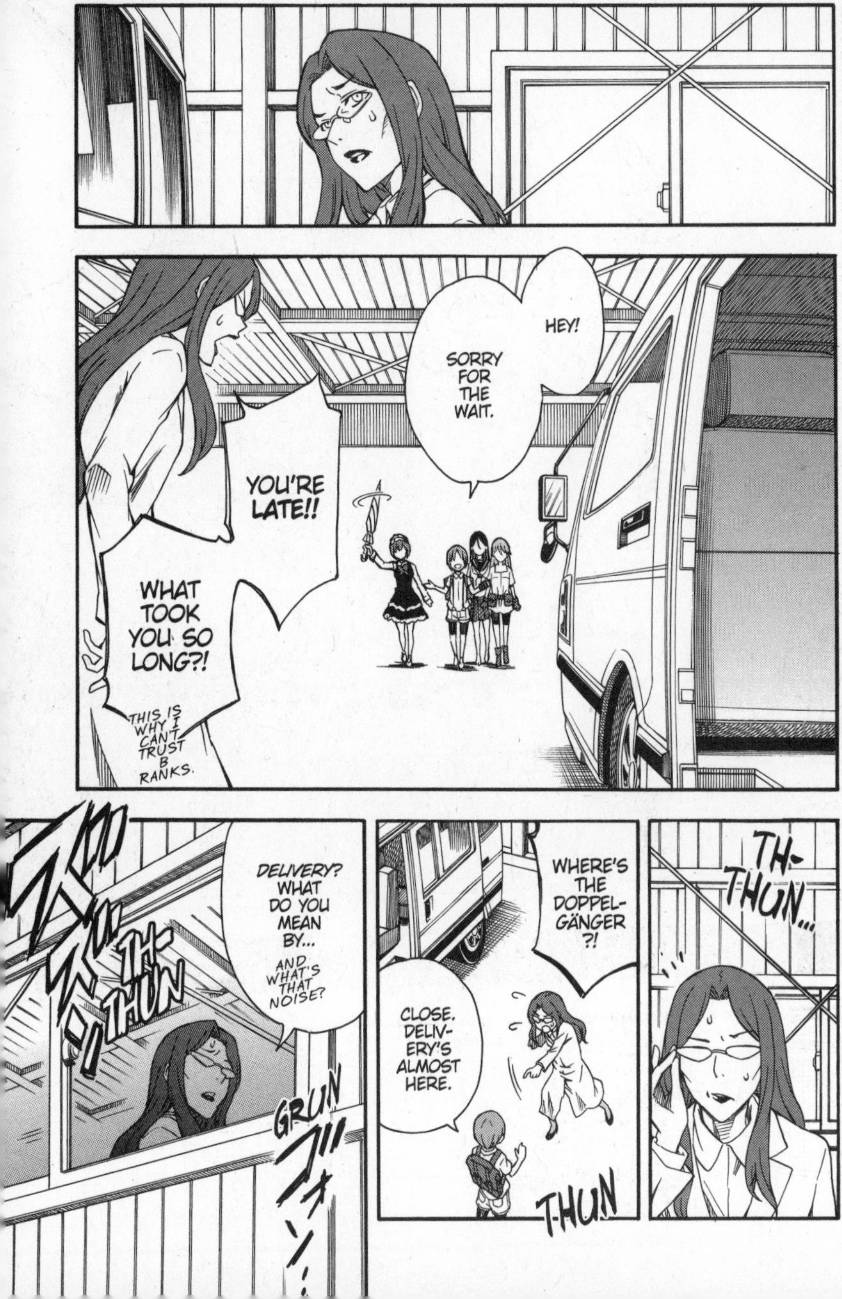
HEY!
SORRY FOR THE WAIT.
YOU'RE LATE!!
WHAT TOOK YOU SO LONG?!
THIS IS WHY I CAN'T TRUST B RANKS.
TH-THUN...
WHERE'S THE DOPPEL-GÄNGER?!
CLOSE. DELIV-ERY'S ALMOST HERE.
THUN
DELIVERY? WHAT DO YOU MEAN BY...
AND WHAT'S THAT NOISE?
TH-THUN
GRUN

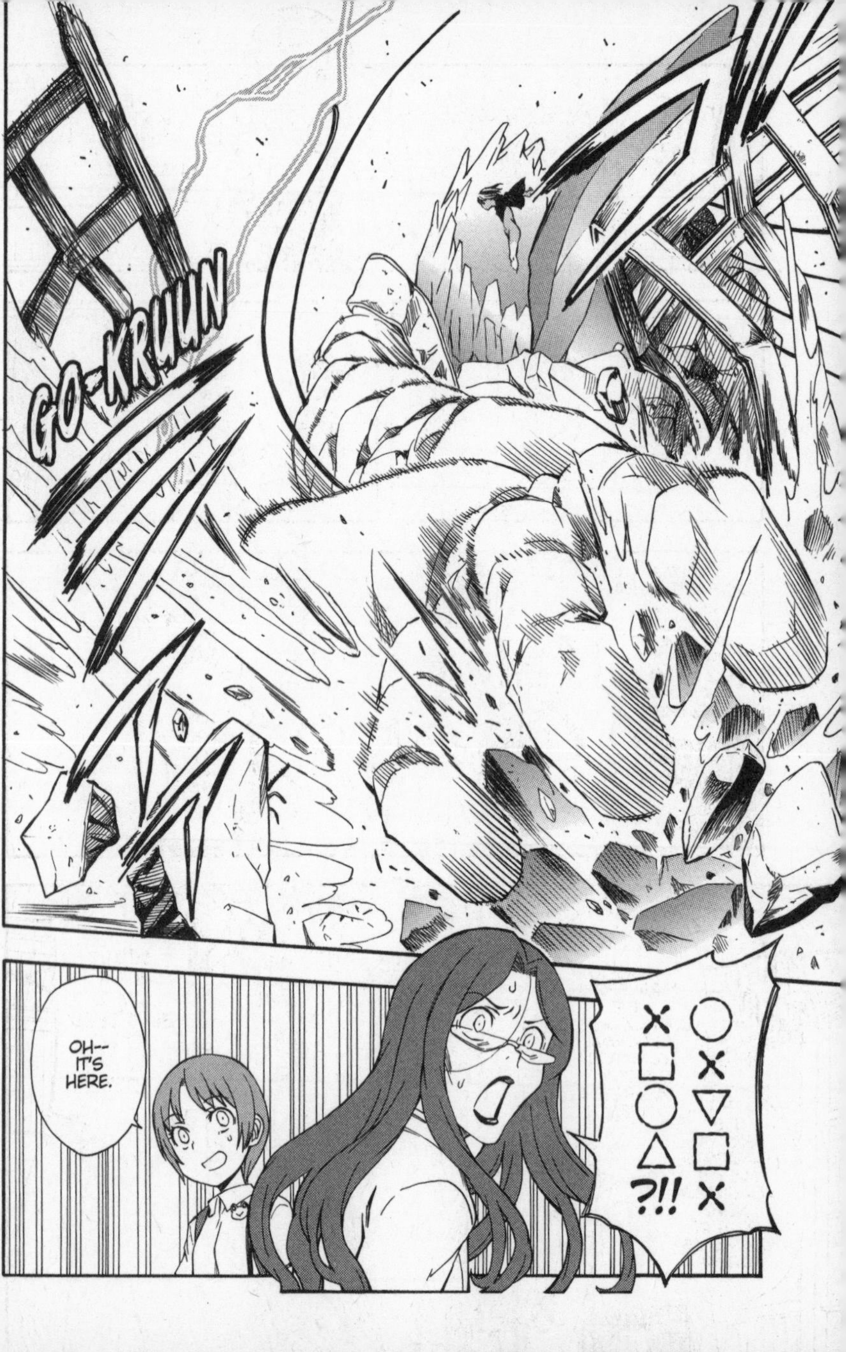
GO-KRUUN
× ○
□ ×
○ ▽
△ □
?!! ×
OH-- IT'S HERE.

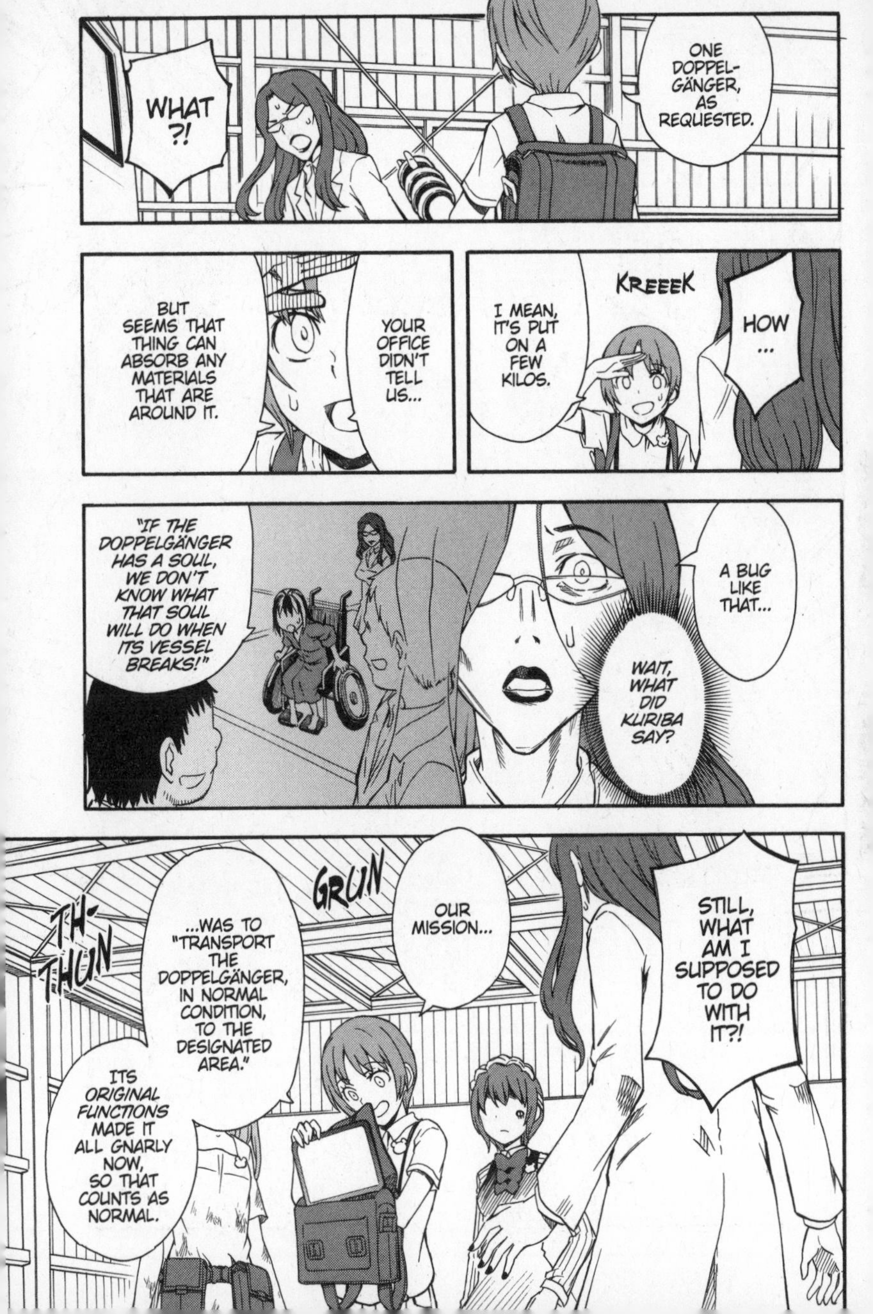
ONE DOPPEL-GÄNGER, AS REQUESTED.
WHAT ?!
HOW ...
KREEEK
I MEAN, IT'S PUT ON A FEW KILOS.
YOUR OFFICE DIDN'T TELL US...
BUT SEEMS THAT THING CAN ABSORB ANY MATERIALS THAT ARE AROUND IT.
A BUG LIKE THAT...
WAIT, WHAT DID KURIBA SAY?
"IF THE DOPPELGÄNGER HAS A SOUL, WE DON'T KNOW WHAT THAT SOUL WILL DO WHEN ITS VESSEL BREAKS!"
STILL, WHAT AM I SUPPOSED TO DO WITH IT?!
GRUN
OUR MISSION...
...WAS TO "TRANSPORT THE DOPPELGÄNGER, IN NORMAL CONDITION, TO THE DESIGNATED AREA."
TH-THUN
ITS ORIGINAL FUNCTIONS MADE IT ALL GNARLY NOW, SO THAT COUNTS AS NORMAL.

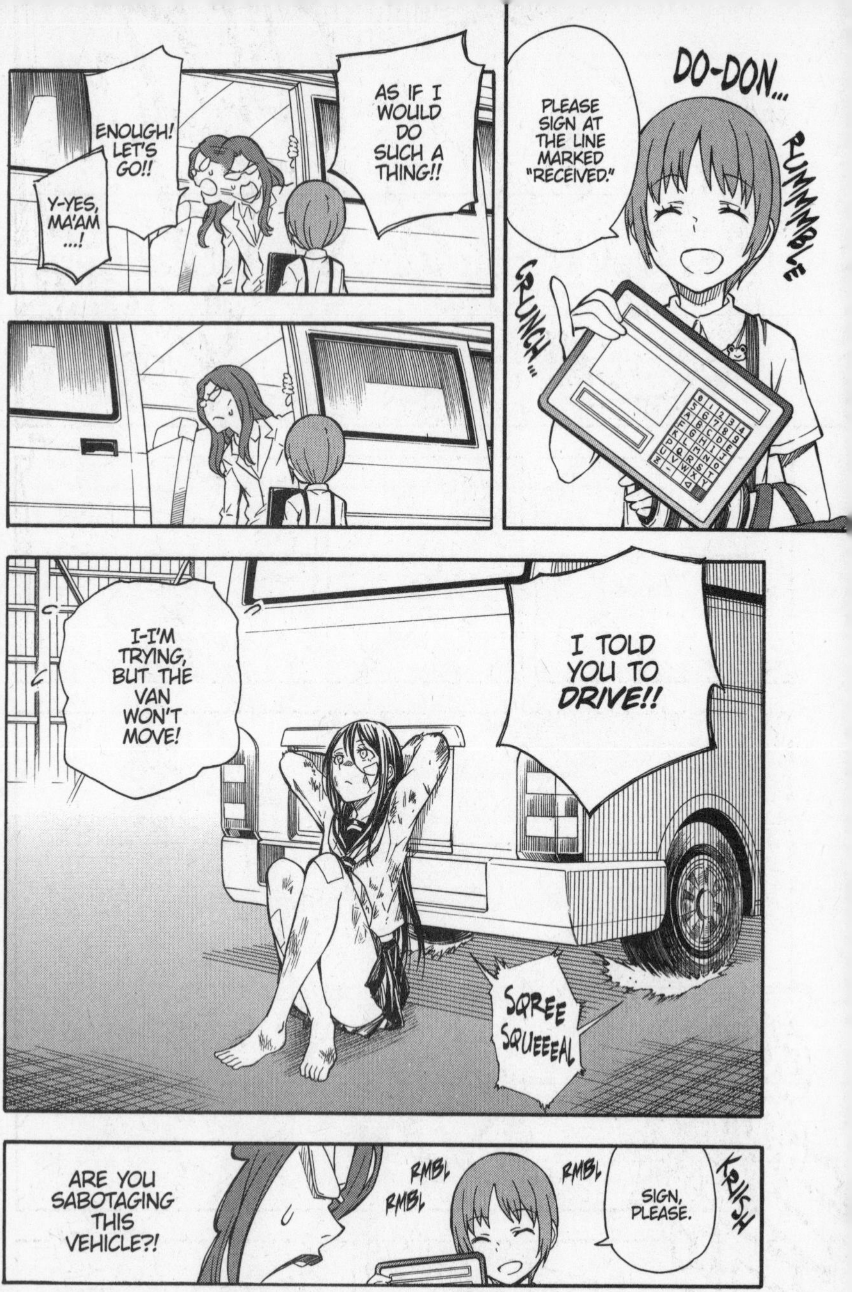
DO-DON...
RUMMMBLE
PLEASE SIGN AT THE LINE MARKED "RECEIVED."
CRUNCH...
AS IF I WOULD DO SUCH A THING!!
ENOUGH! LET'S GO!!
Y-YES, MA'AM ...!
I TOLD YOU TO *DRIVE!!*
I-I'M TRYING, BUT THE VAN WON'T MOVE!
SQREE SQUEEEAL
KRUSH
SIGN, PLEASE.
RMBL
RMBL
RMBL
ARE YOU SABOTAGING THIS VEHICLE?!

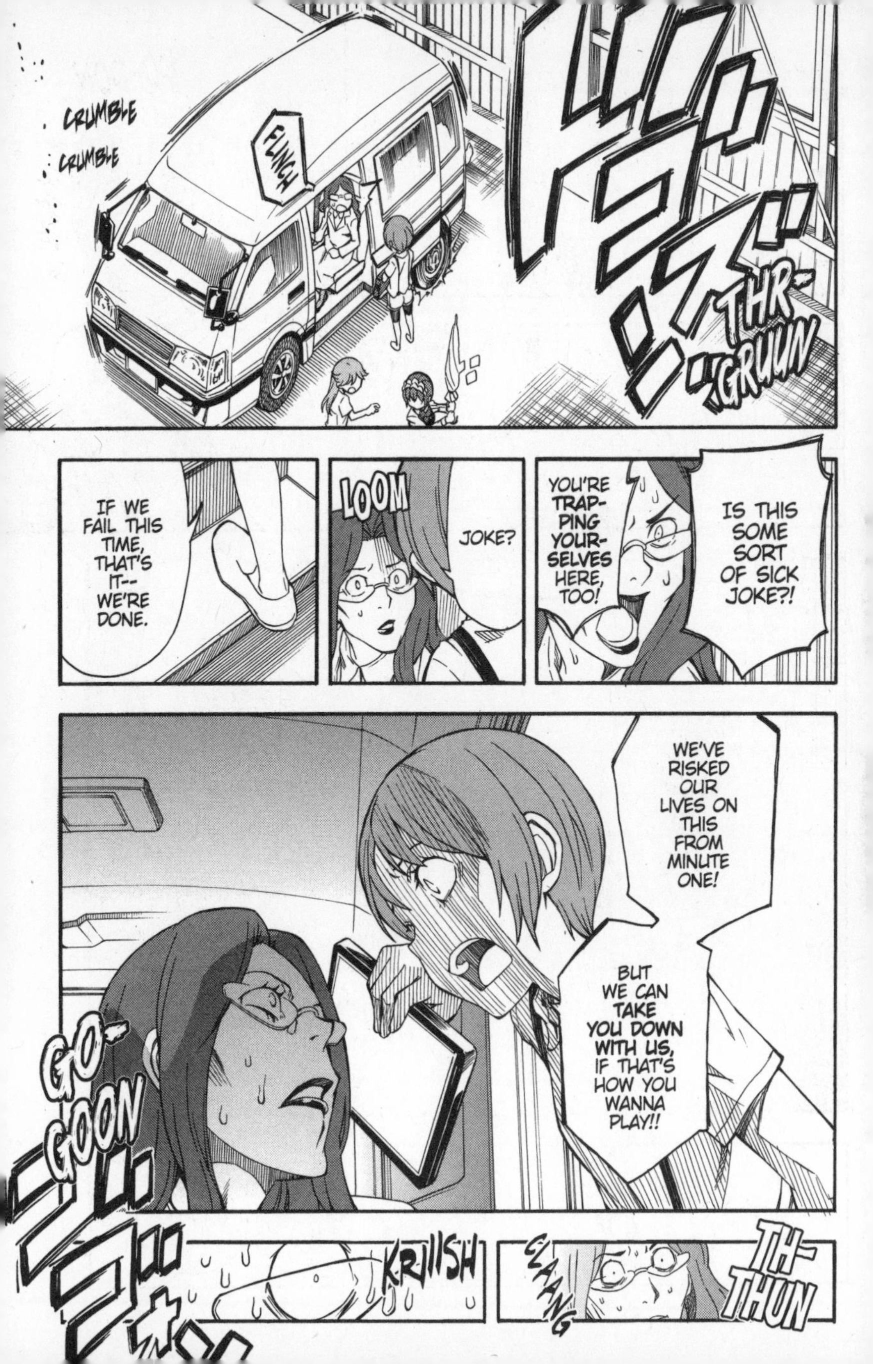

THR-
GRUUN
FLINCH
CRUMBLE
CRUMBLE
IS THIS SOME SORT OF SICK JOKE?!
YOU'RE TRAP-PING YOUR-SELVES HERE, TOO!
JOKE?
LOOM
IF WE FAIL THIS TIME, THAT'S IT-- WE'RE DONE.
WE'VE RISKED OUR LIVES ON THIS FROM MINUTE ONE!
BUT WE CAN TAKE YOU DOWN WITH US, IF THAT'S HOW YOU WANNA PLAY!!
GO-GOON
TH-THUN
CLANG
KRIIISH

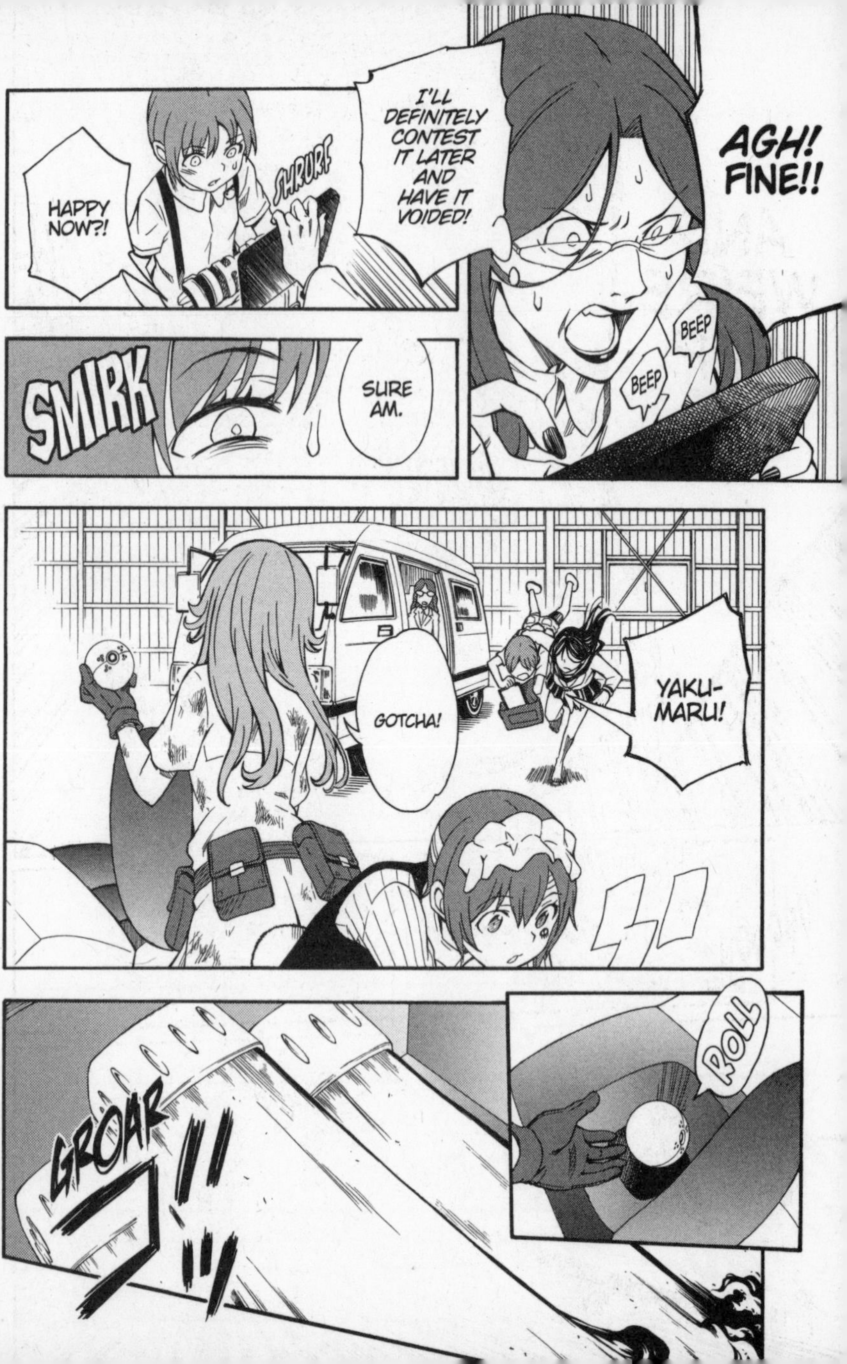
AGH! FINE!!
BEEP
BEEP
I'LL DEFINITELY CONTEST IT LATER AND HAVE IT VOIDED!
SHURF
HAPPY NOW?!
SURE AM.
SMIRK
YAKU-MARU!
GOTCHA!
ROLL
GROAR

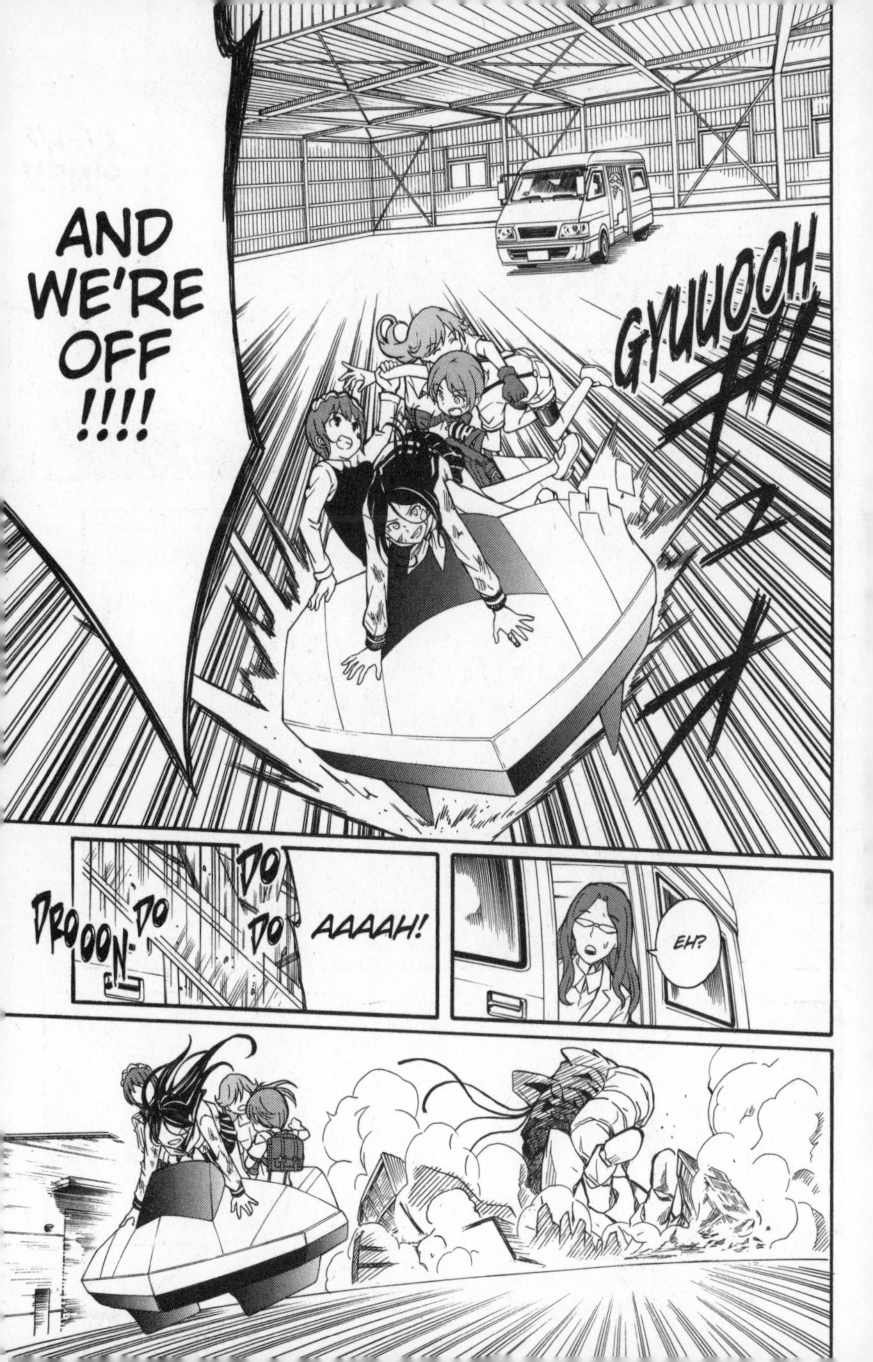
AND WE'RE OFF !!!!
GYUUOOH
DO
DO
DO
DROOON
AAAAH!
EH?

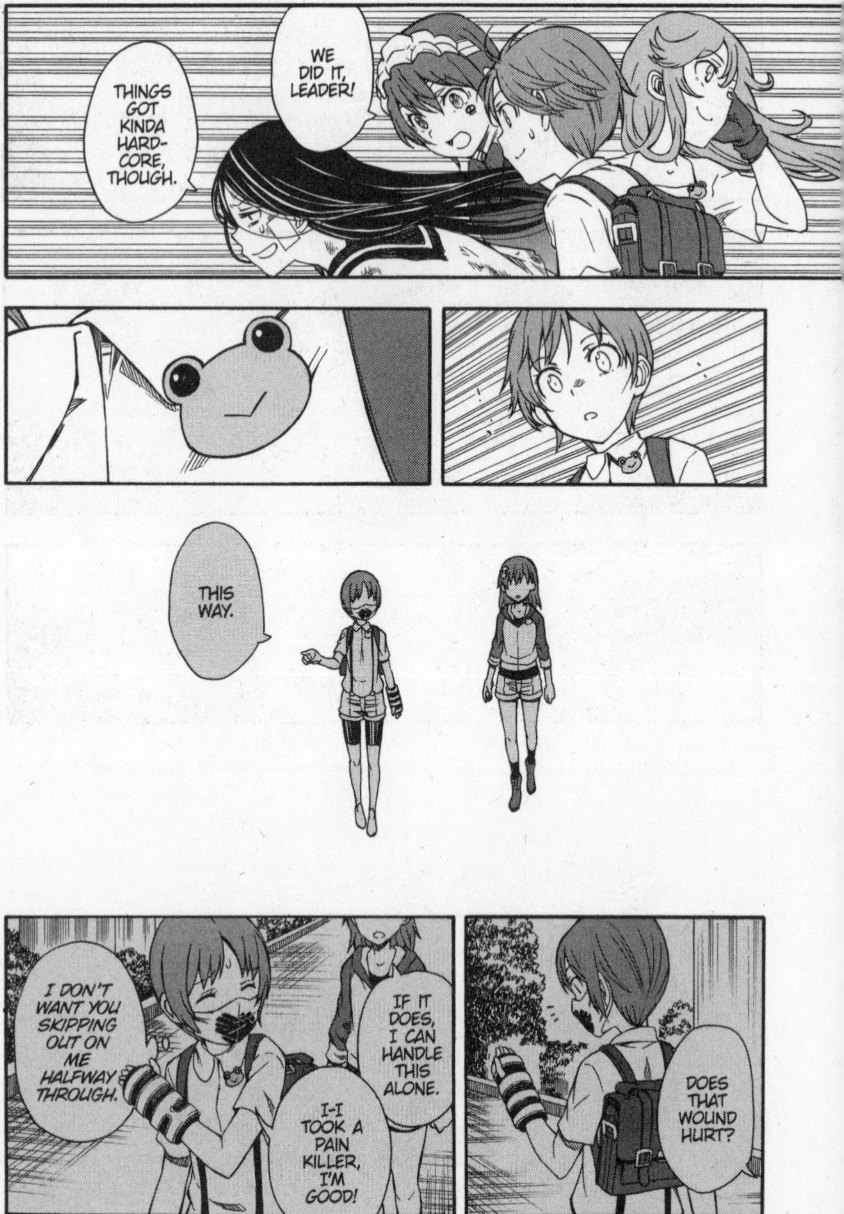
WE DID IT, LEADER!
THINGS GOT KINDA HARD-CORE, THOUGH.
THIS WAY.
DOES THAT WOUND HURT?
I-I TOOK A PAIN KILLER, I'M GOOD!
IF IT DOES, I CAN HANDLE THIS ALONE.
I DON'T WANT YOU SKIPPING OUT ON ME HALFWAY THROUGH.

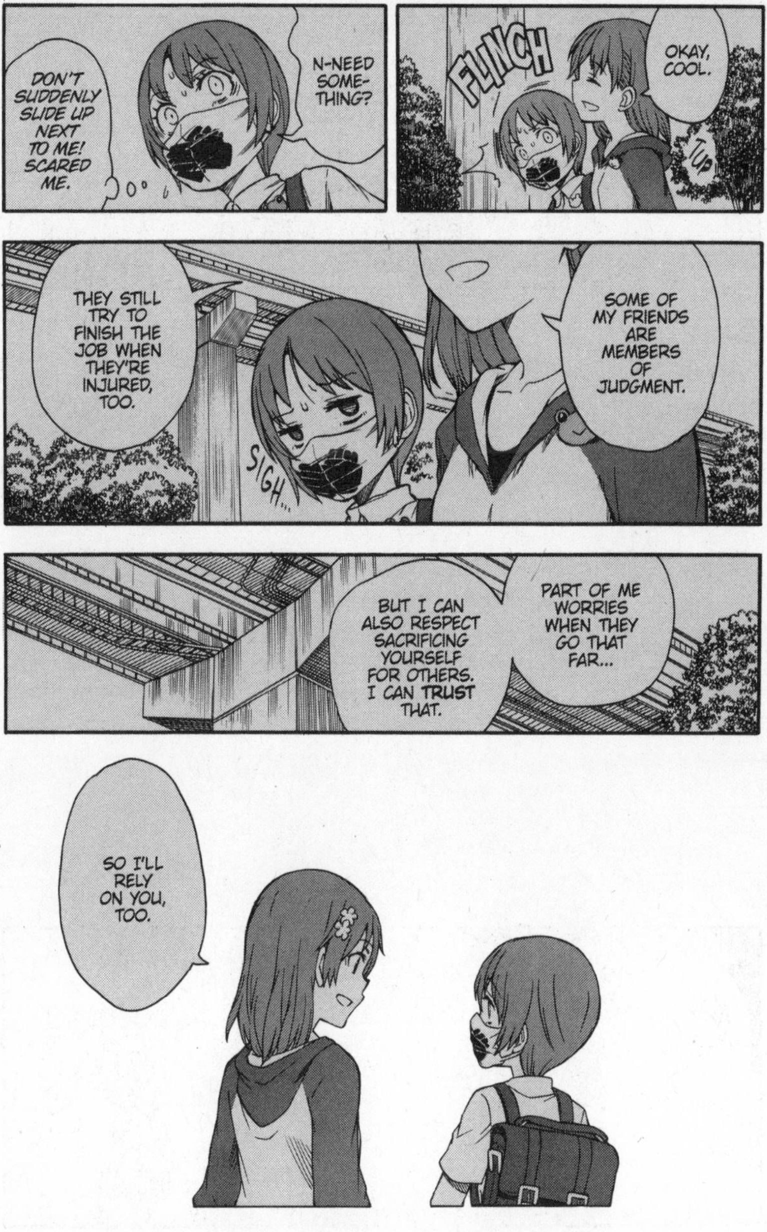
OKAY, COOL.
FLINCH
TUP
N-NEED SOMETHING?
DON'T SUDDENLY SLIDE UP NEXT TO ME! SCARED ME.
SOME OF MY FRIENDS ARE MEMBERS OF JUDGMENT.
THEY STILL TRY TO FINISH THE JOB WHEN THEY'RE INJURED, TOO.
SIGH...
PART OF ME WORRIES WHEN THEY GO THAT FAR...
BUT I CAN ALSO RESPECT SACRIFICING YOURSELF FOR OTHERS. I CAN TRUST THAT.
SO I'LL RELY ON YOU, TOO.

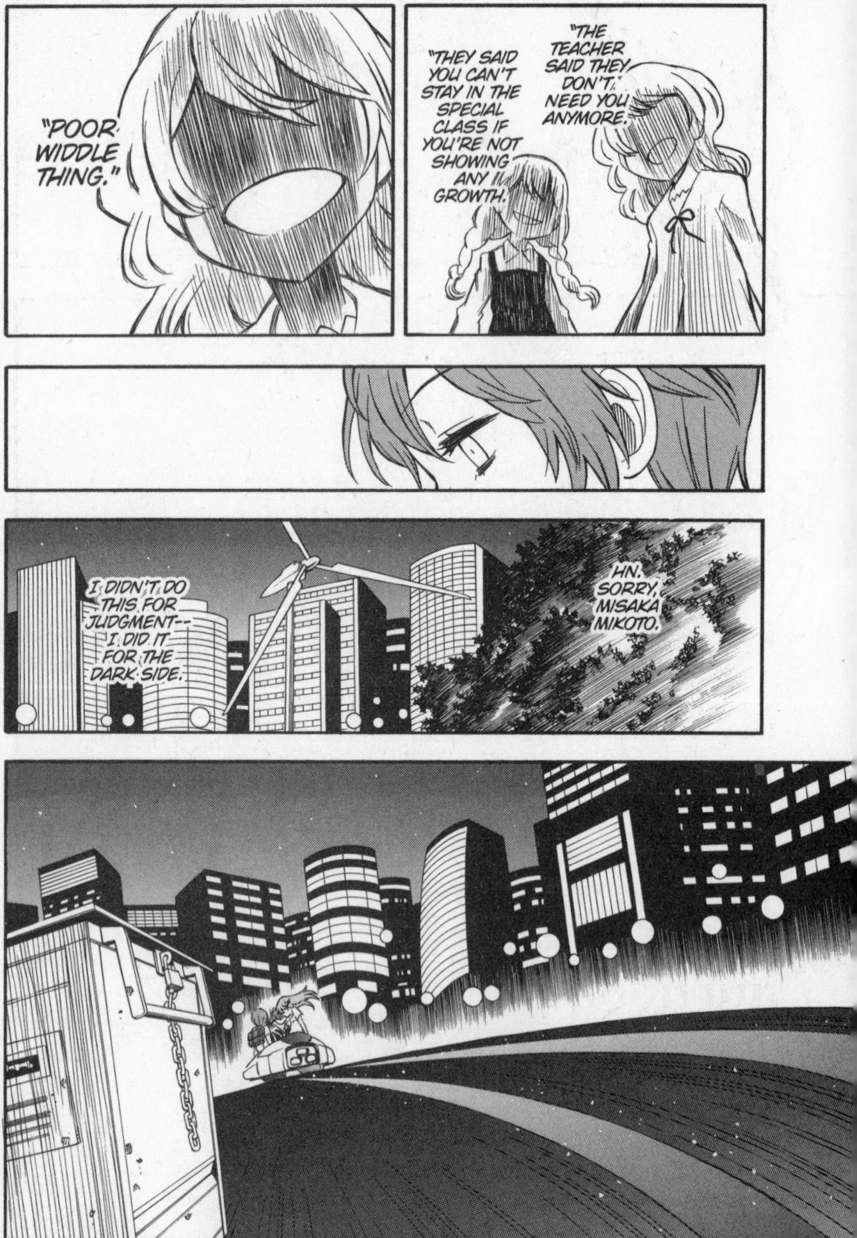
"THE TEACHER SAID THEY DON'T NEED YOU ANYMORE."
"THEY SAID YOU CAN'T STAY IN THE SPECIAL CLASS IF YOU'RE NOT SHOWING ANY GROWTH."
"POOR WIDDLE THING."
HN. SORRY, MISAKA MIKOTO.
I DIDN'T DO THIS FOR JUDGMENT-- I DID IT FOR THE DARK SIDE.

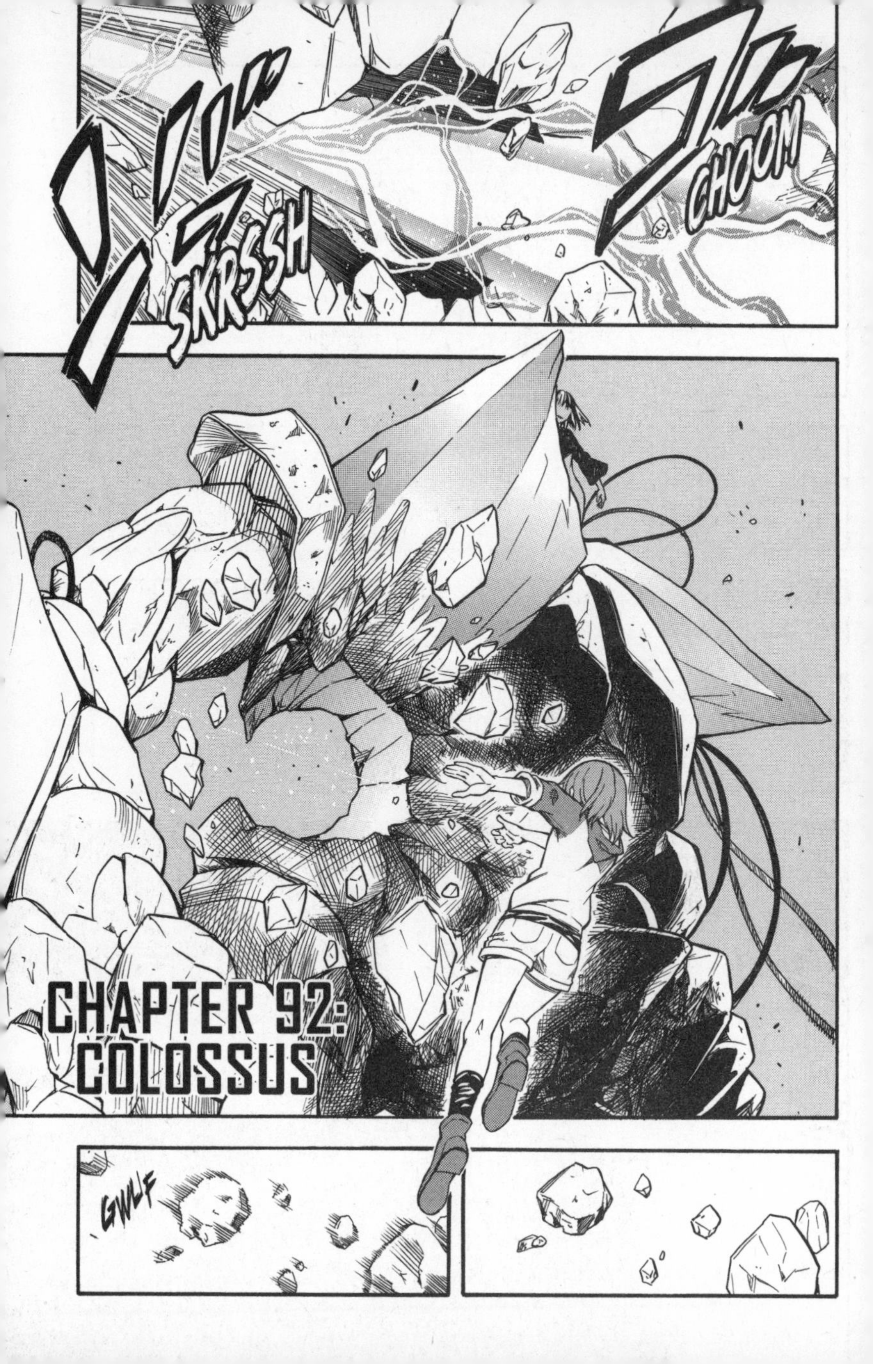
SKRSSH
CHOOM
CHAPTER 92:
COLOSSUS
GWLF

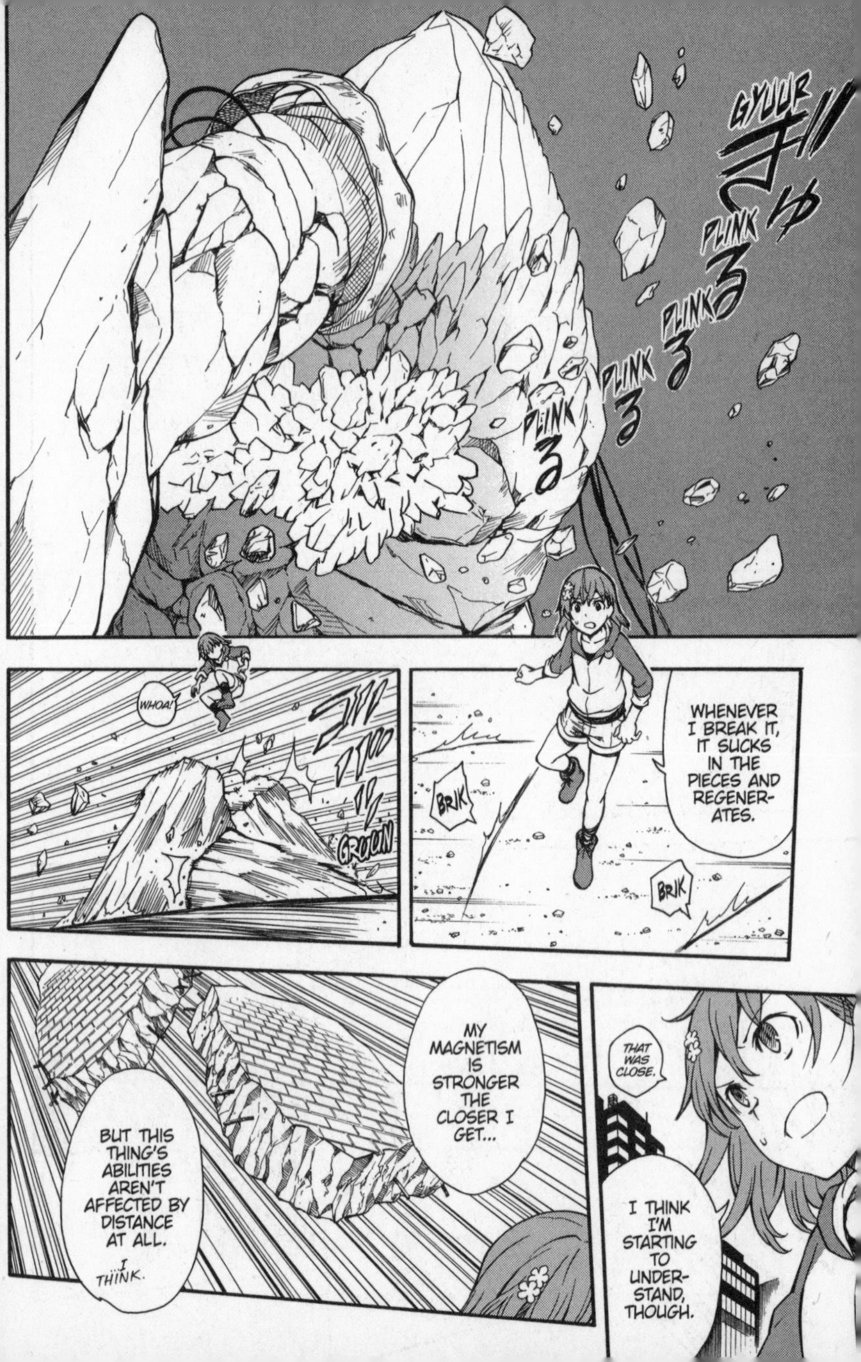
GYUUR
PLINK
PLINK
PLINK
PLINK
WHOA!
GRUUN
WHENEVER I BREAK IT, IT SUCKS IN THE PIECES AND REGENER-ATES.
BRIK
BRIK
THAT WAS CLOSE.
I THINK I'M STARTING TO UNDER-STAND, THOUGH.
MY MAGNETISM IS STRONGER THE CLOSER I GET...
BUT THIS THING'S ABILITIES AREN'T AFFECTED BY DISTANCE AT ALL.
...I THINK.

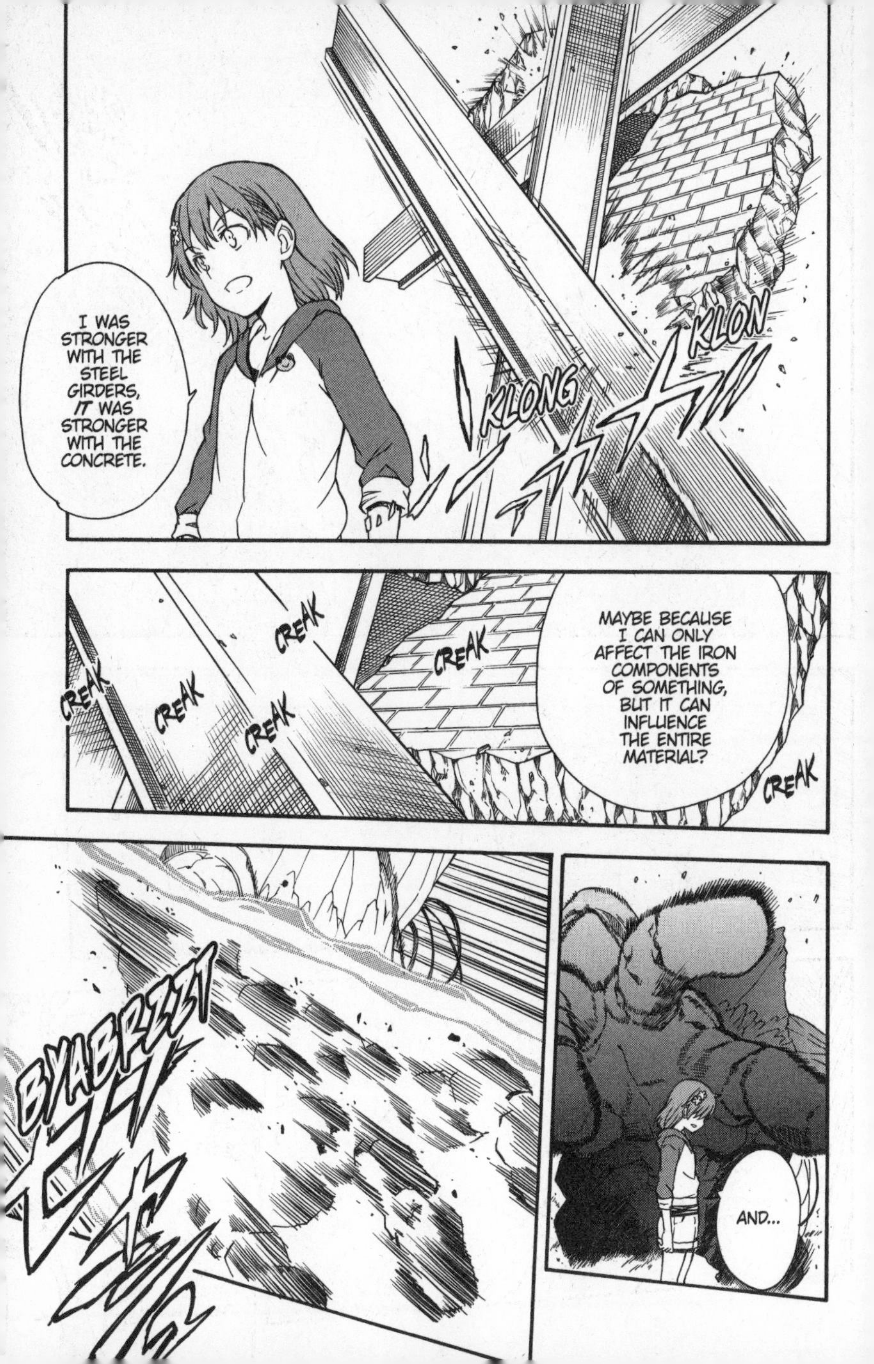
KLON
KLONG
I WAS STRONGER WITH THE STEEL GIRDERS, IT WAS STRONGER WITH THE CONCRETE.
CREAK
MAYBE BECAUSE I CAN ONLY AFFECT THE IRON COMPONENTS OF SOMETHING, BUT IT CAN INFLUENCE THE ENTIRE MATERIAL?
CREAK
CREAK
CREAK
CREAK
CREAK
AND...
BYABRZZZT

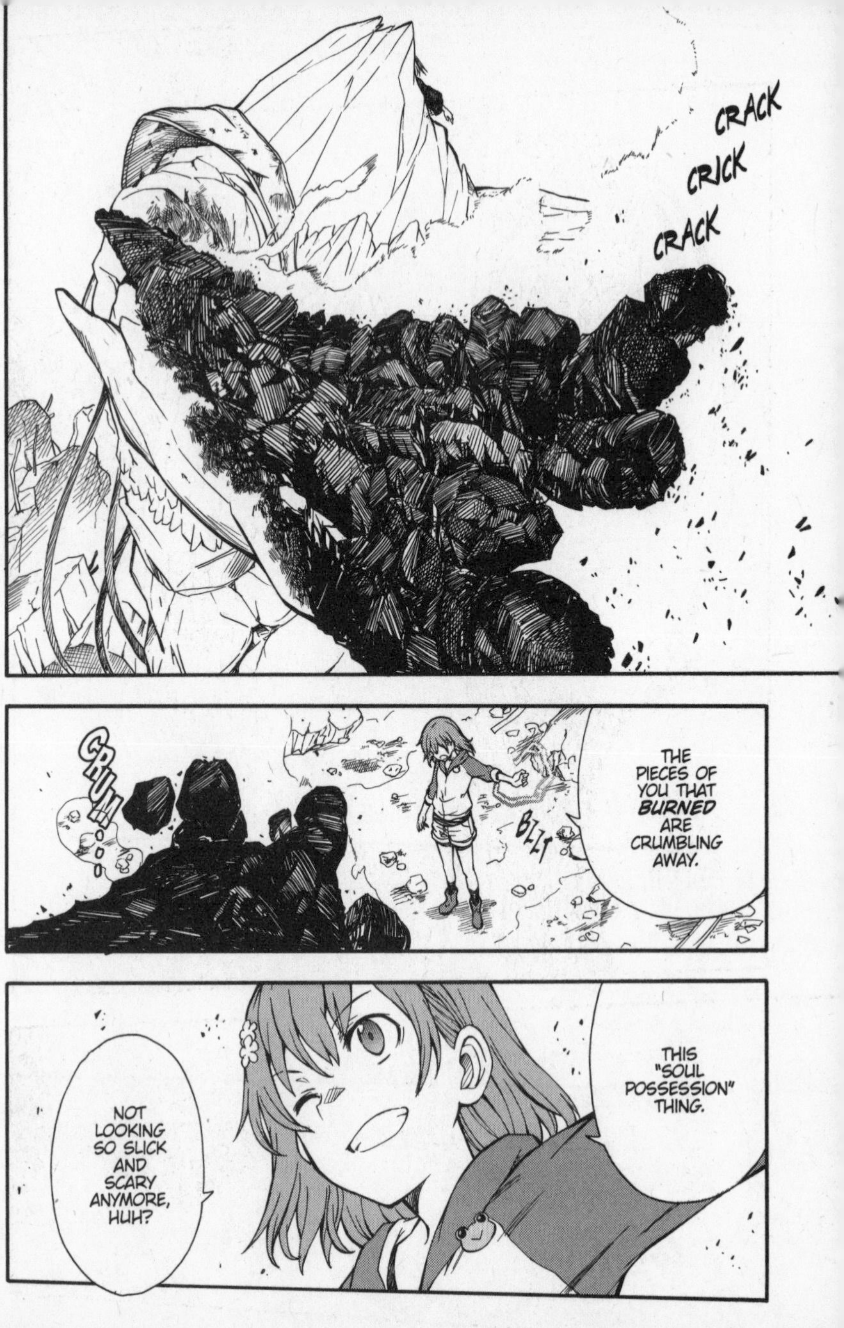
CRACK
CRICK
CRACK
THE PIECES OF YOU THAT BURNED ARE CRUMBLING AWAY.
BZZT
CRUMMM
THIS "SOUL POSSESSION" THING.
NOT LOOKING SO SLICK AND SCARY ANYMORE, HUH?

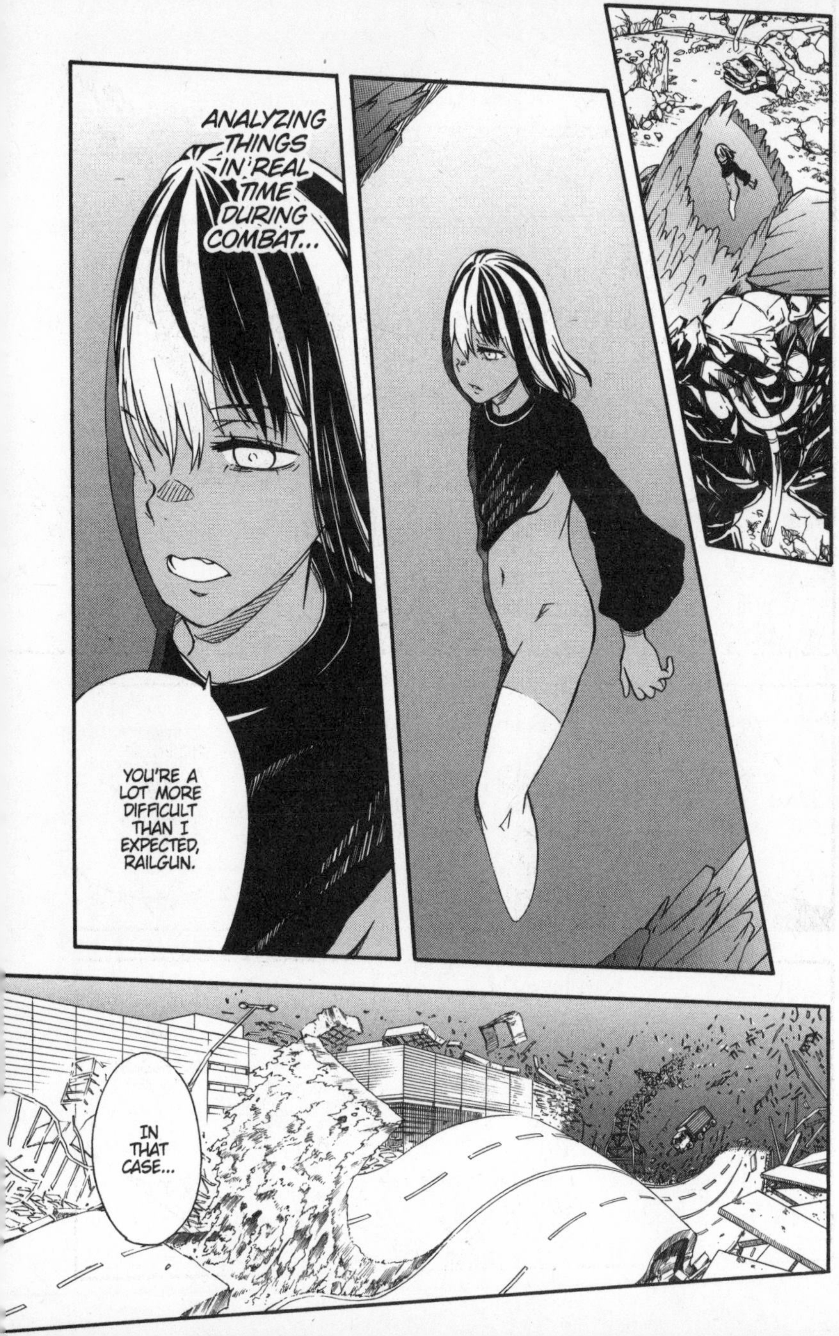
ANALYZING THINGS IN REAL TIME DURING COMBAT...
YOU'RE A LOT MORE DIFFICULT THAN I EXPECTED, RAILGUN.
IN THAT CASE...

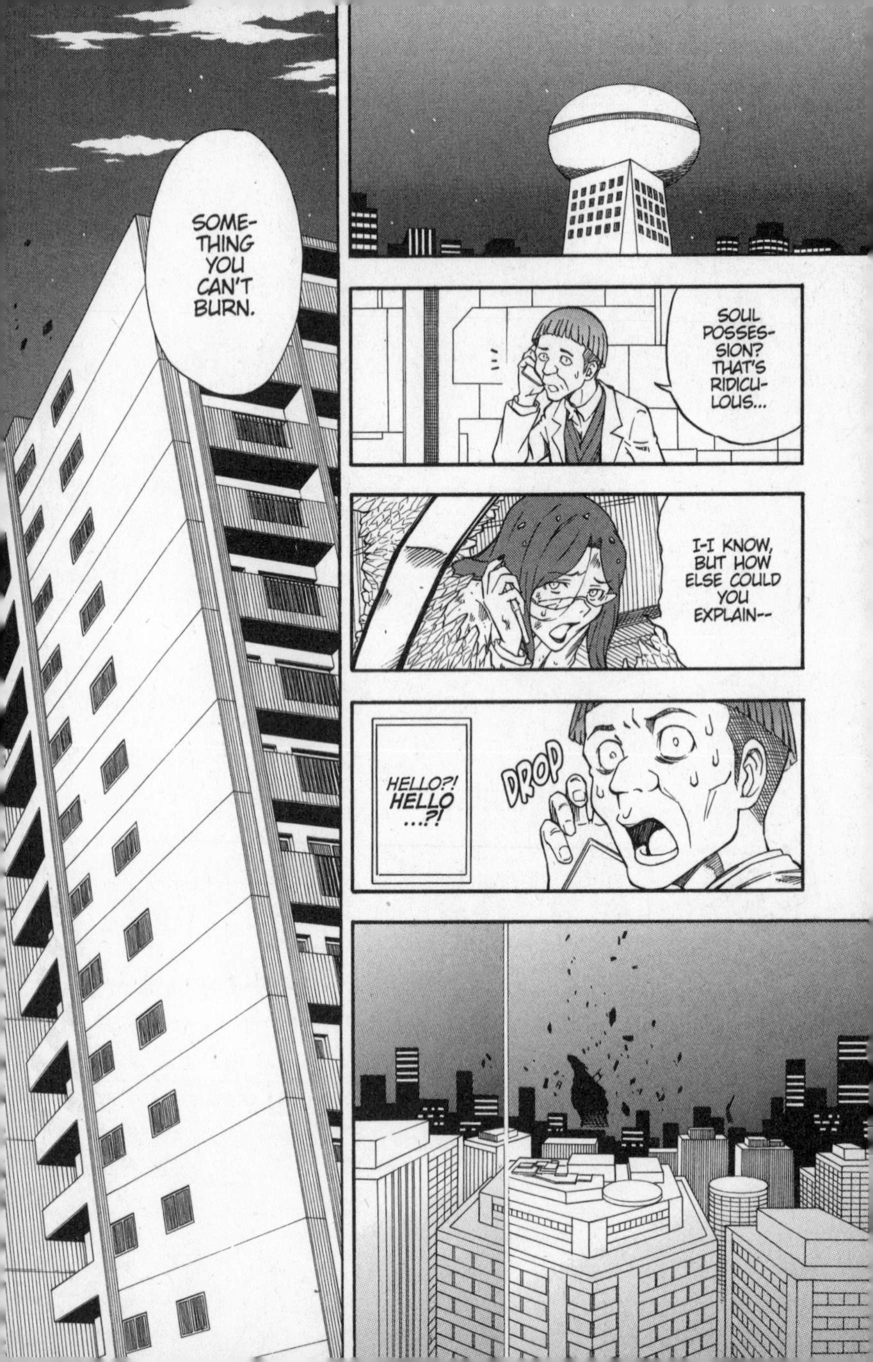
SOME-THING YOU CAN'T BURN.
SOUL POSSES-SION? THAT'S RIDICU-LOUS...
I-I KNOW, BUT HOW ELSE COULD YOU EXPLAIN--
DROP
HELLO?! HELLO ...?!

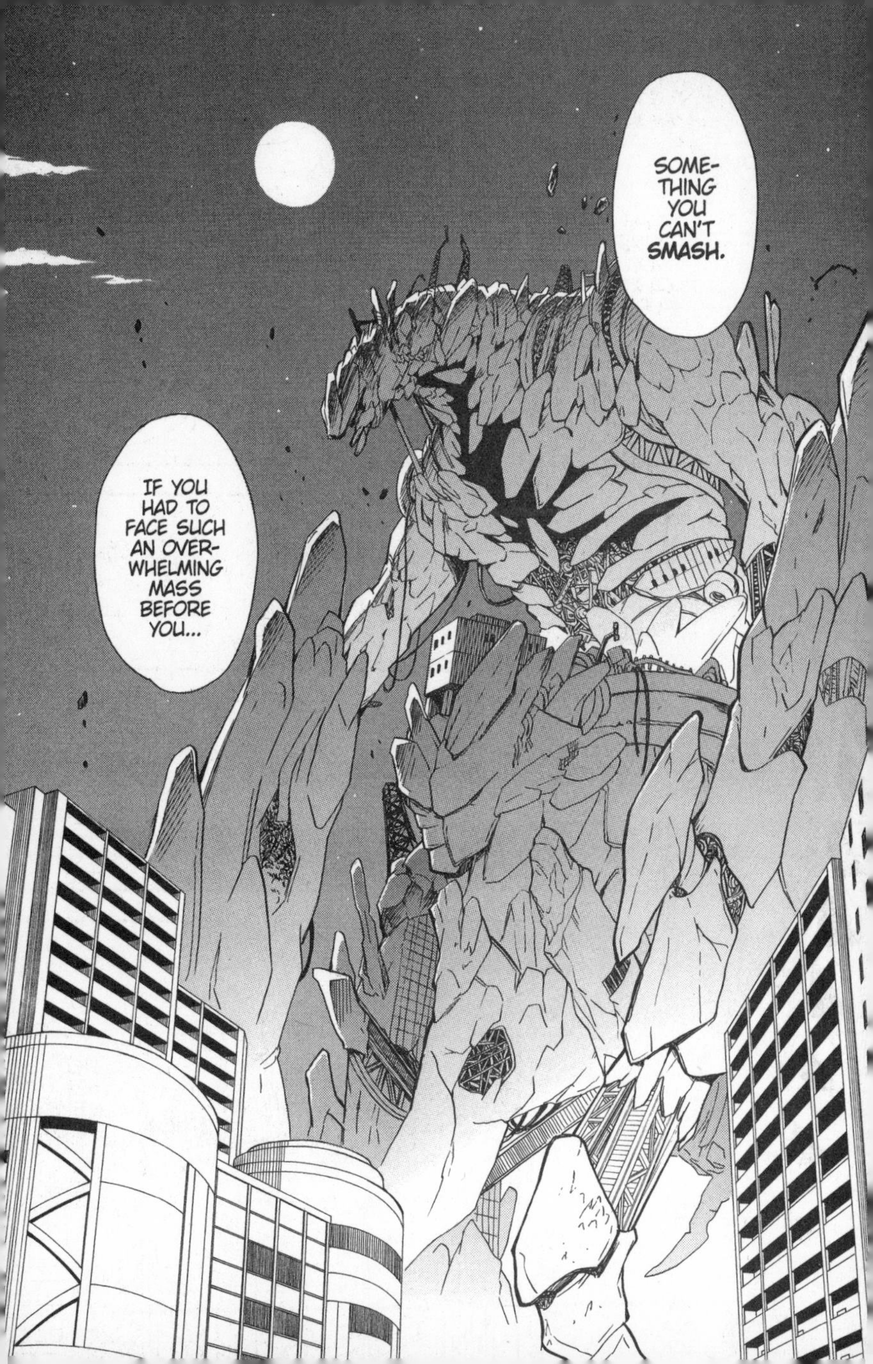
SOME-THING YOU CAN'T SMASH.
IF YOU HAD TO FACE SUCH AN OVER-WHELMING MASS BEFORE YOU...

THUD
THUD
O KAY
THUD
THUD
THUD
...WHAT WOULD YOU DO, RAILGUN?
CREEEEAK

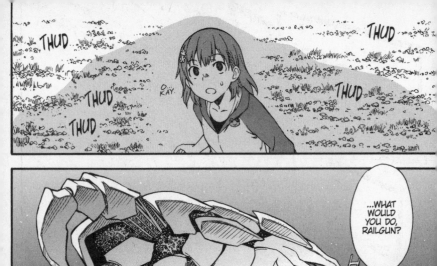

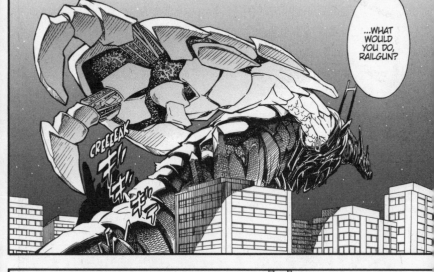

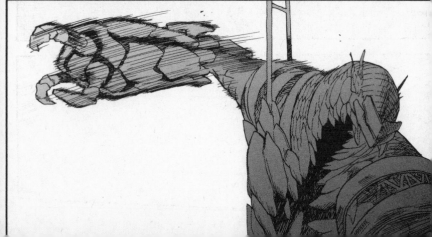

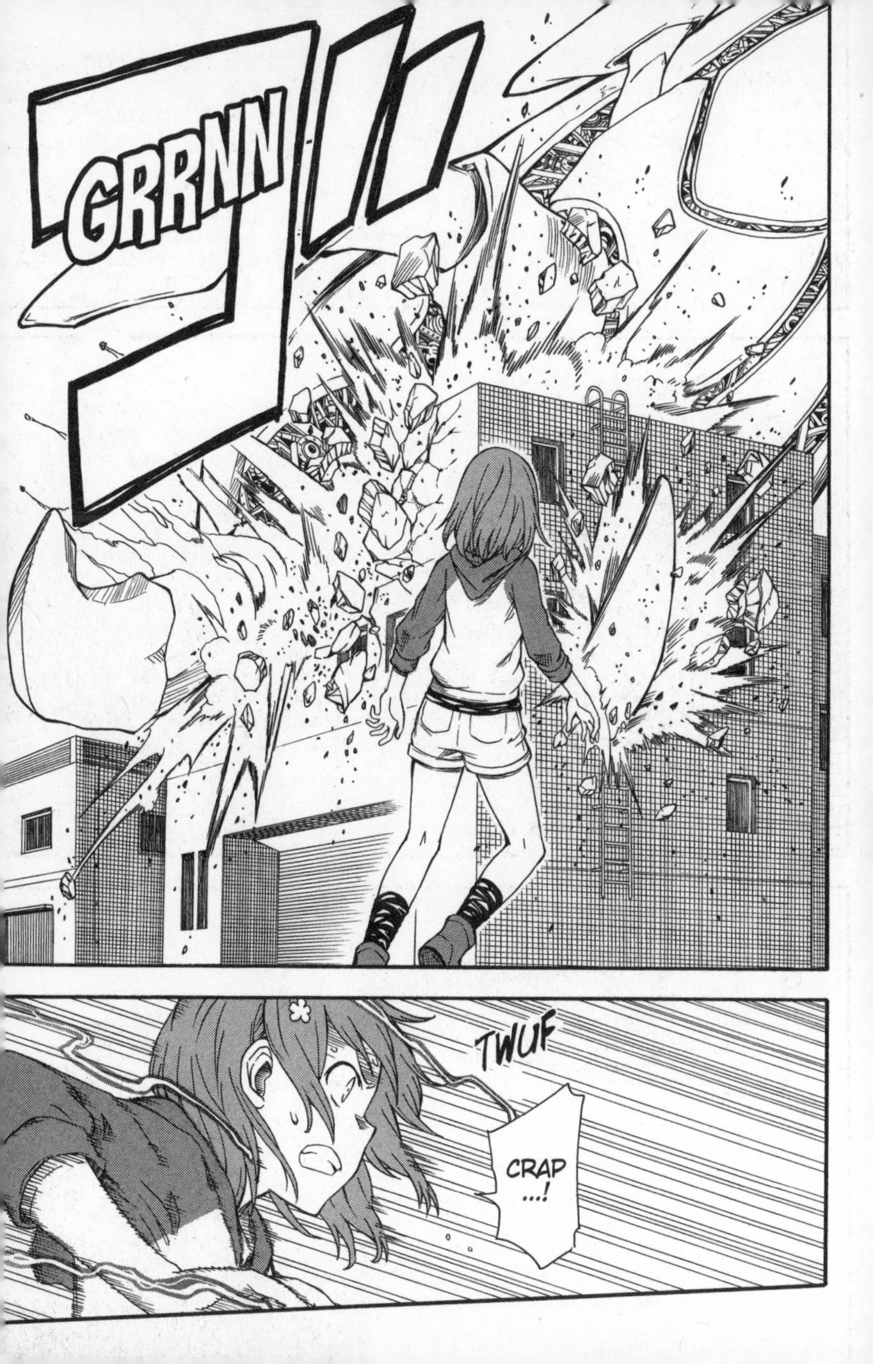
GRRNN
TWUF
CRAP ...!

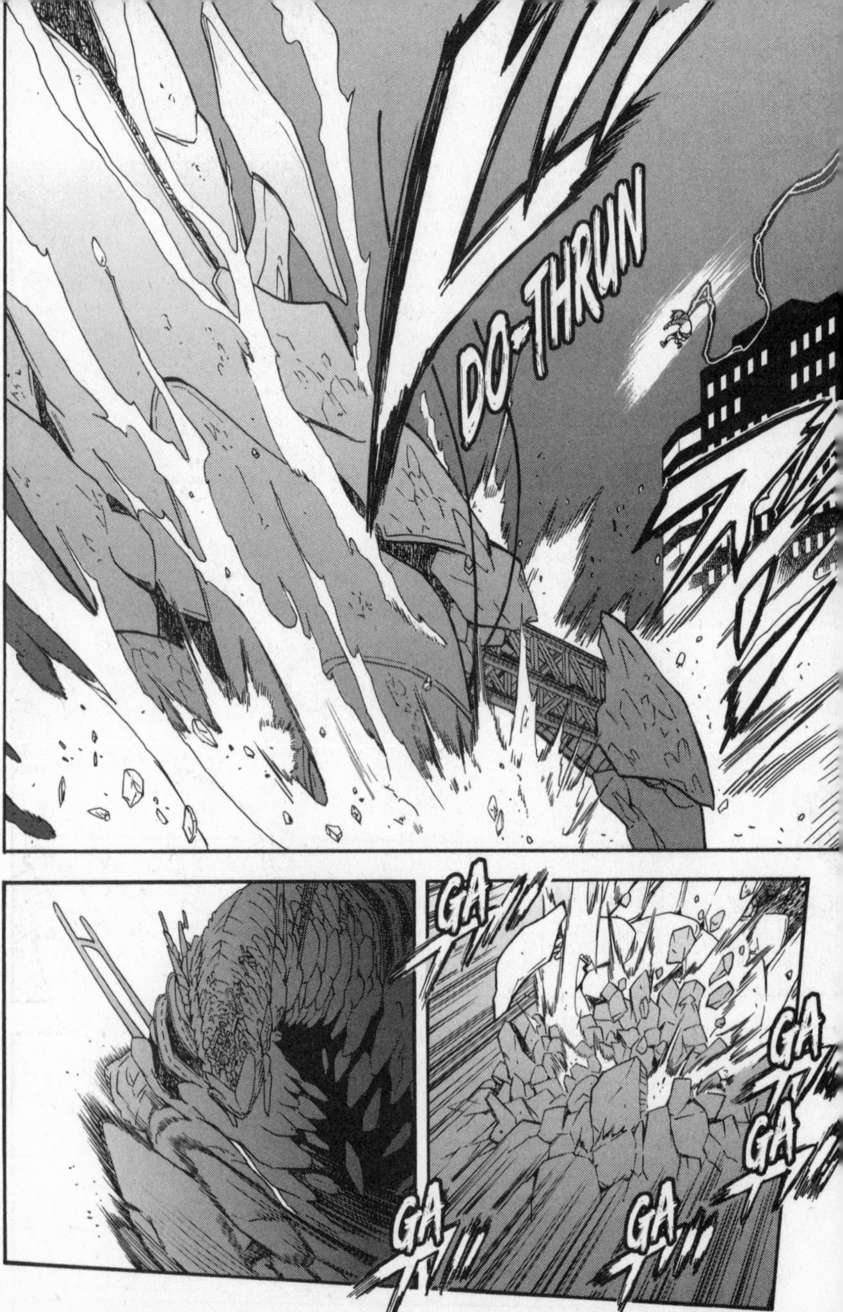
DO-THRUN
GA
GA
GA
GA
GA

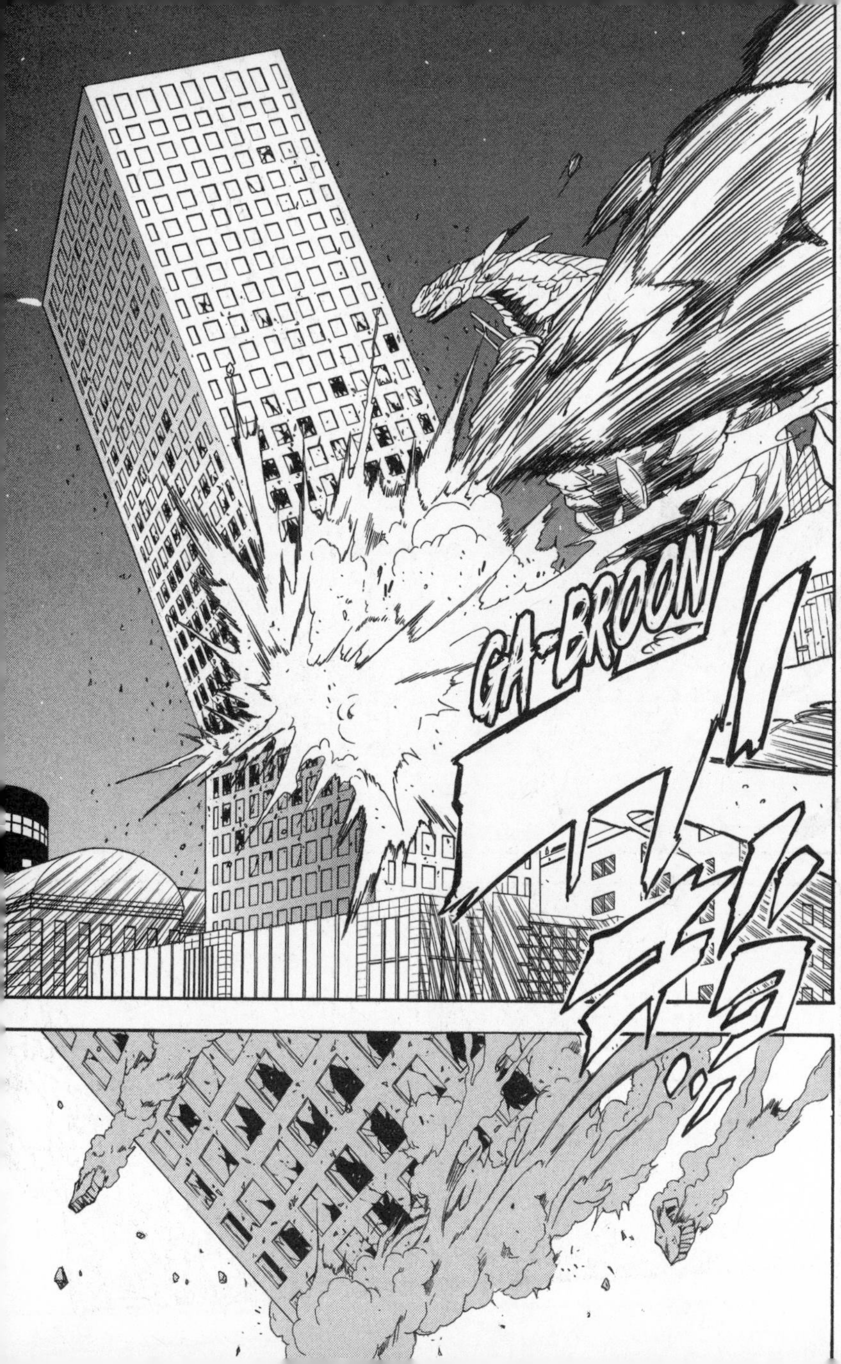
GA-BROON

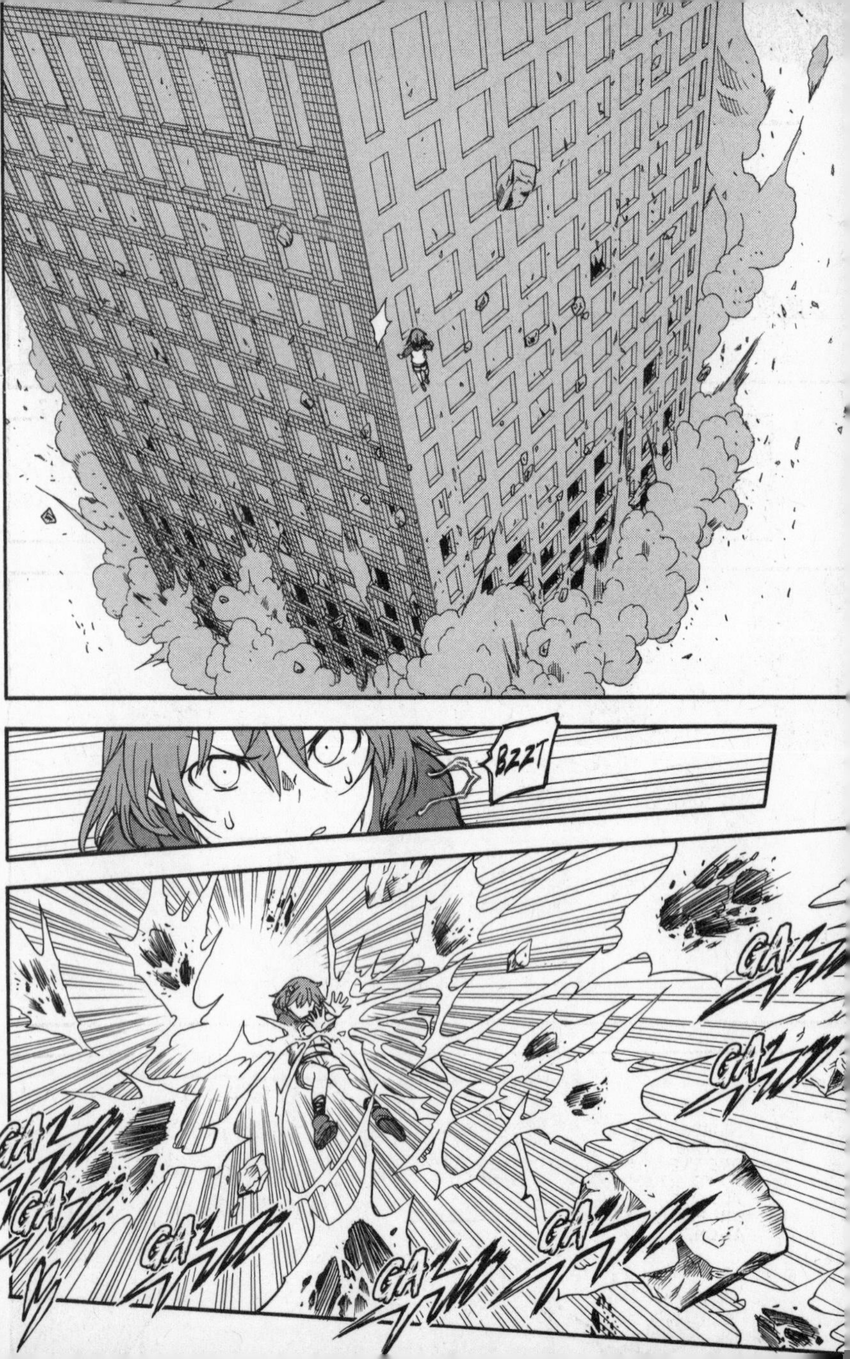
BZZT
GA
GA
GA
GA
GA
GA
GA

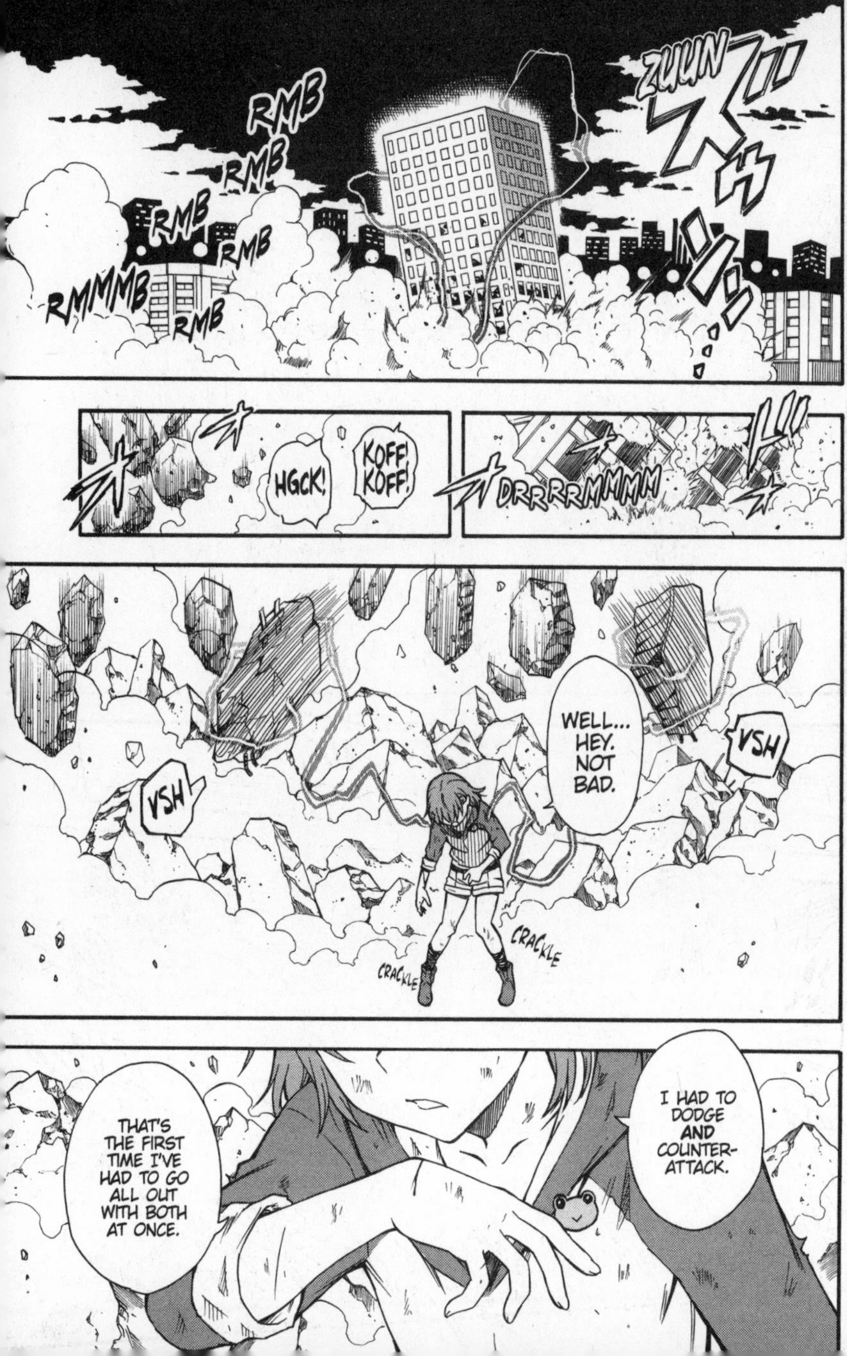

ZUUN
RMB
RMB
RMB
RMB
RMMMB
RMB
KOFF! KOFF!
HGCK!
DRRRRMMMM
WELL... HEY. NOT BAD.
VSH
VSH
CRACKLE
CRACKLE
I HAD TO DODGE AND COUNTER-ATTACK.
THAT'S THE FIRST TIME I'VE HAD TO GO ALL OUT WITH BOTH AT ONCE.

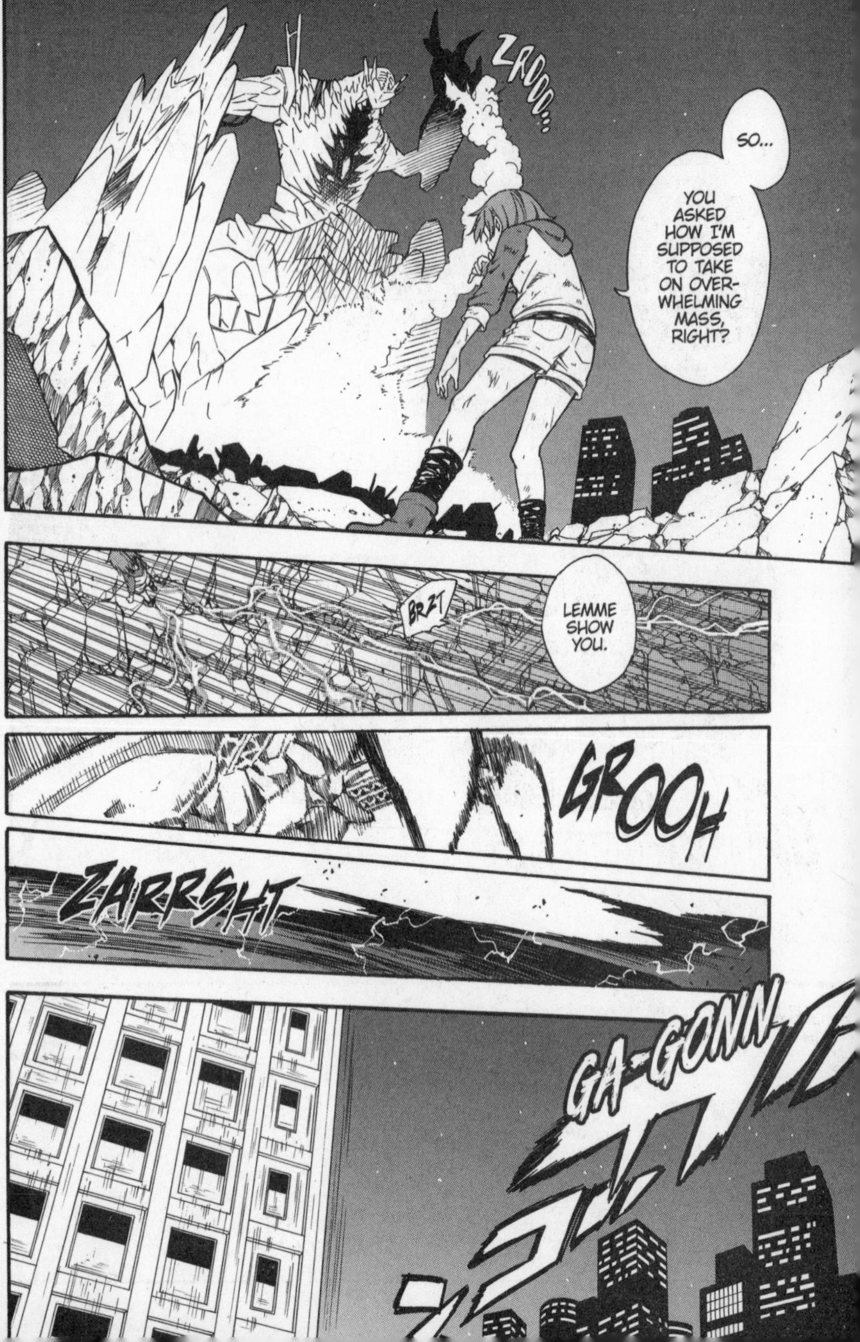
ZROOO...
SO...
YOU ASKED HOW I'M SUPPOSED TO TAKE ON OVER-WHELMING MASS, RIGHT?
BRZT
LEMME SHOW YOU.
GROOOH
ZARRSHT
GA-GONN

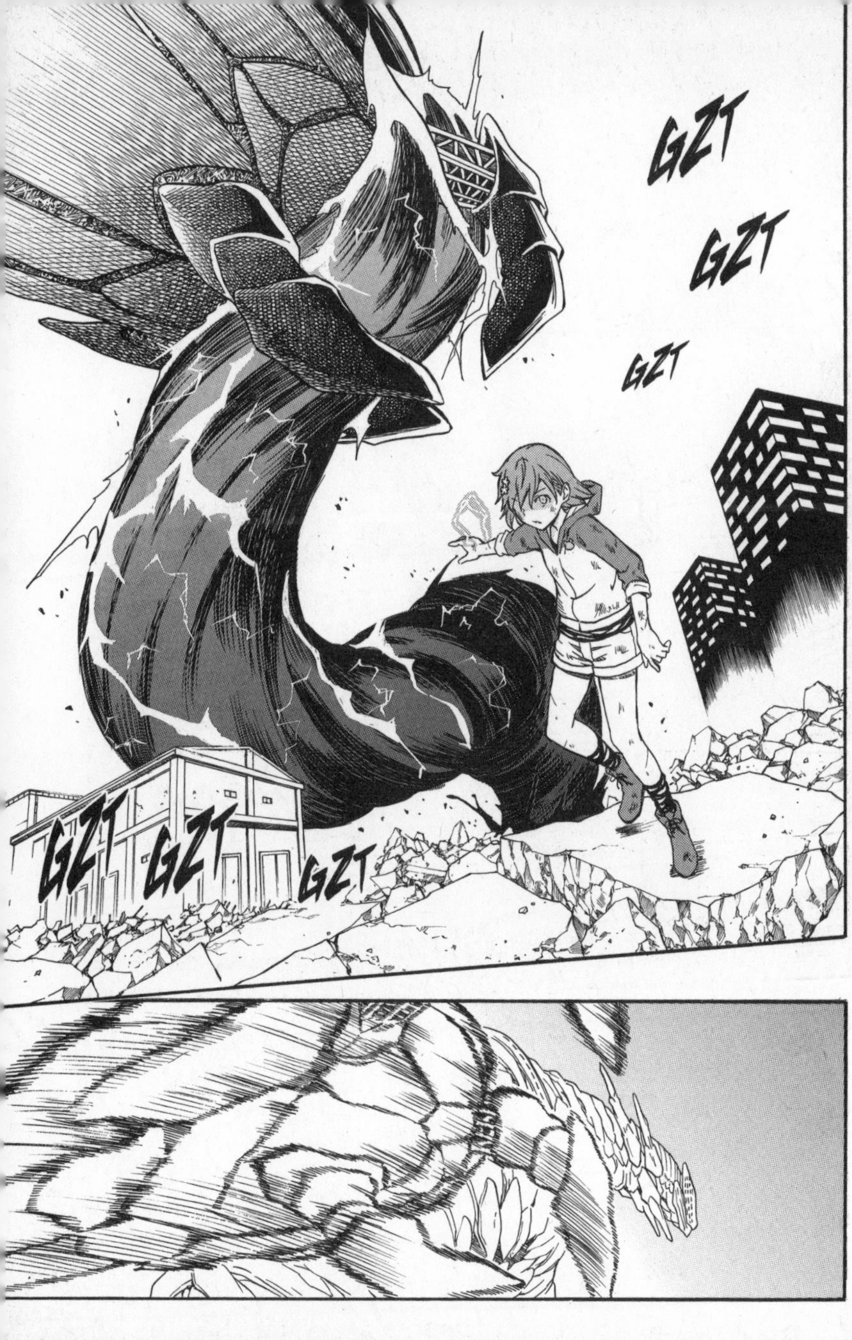
GZT
GZT
GZT
GZT
GZT
GZT

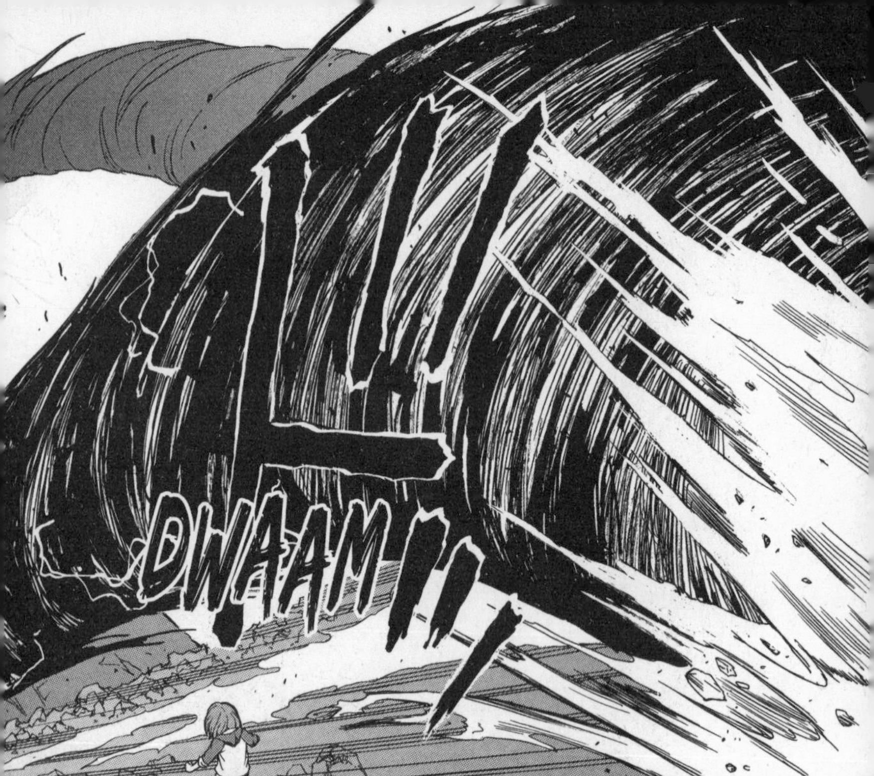
DWAAM!!

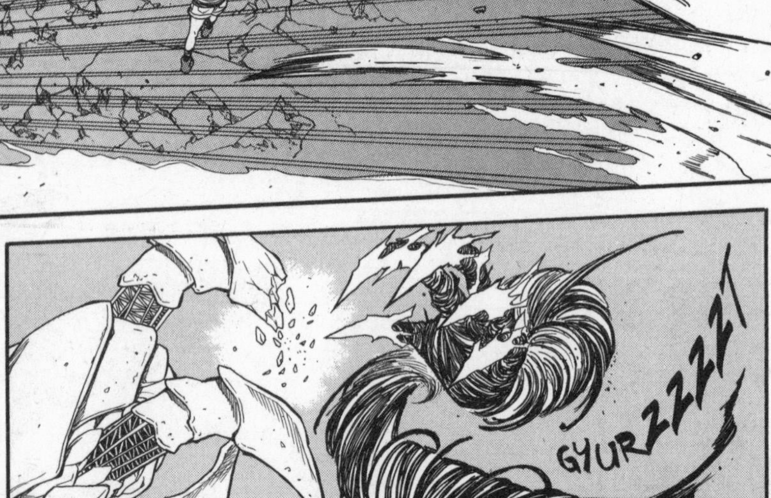
GYURZZZZZ

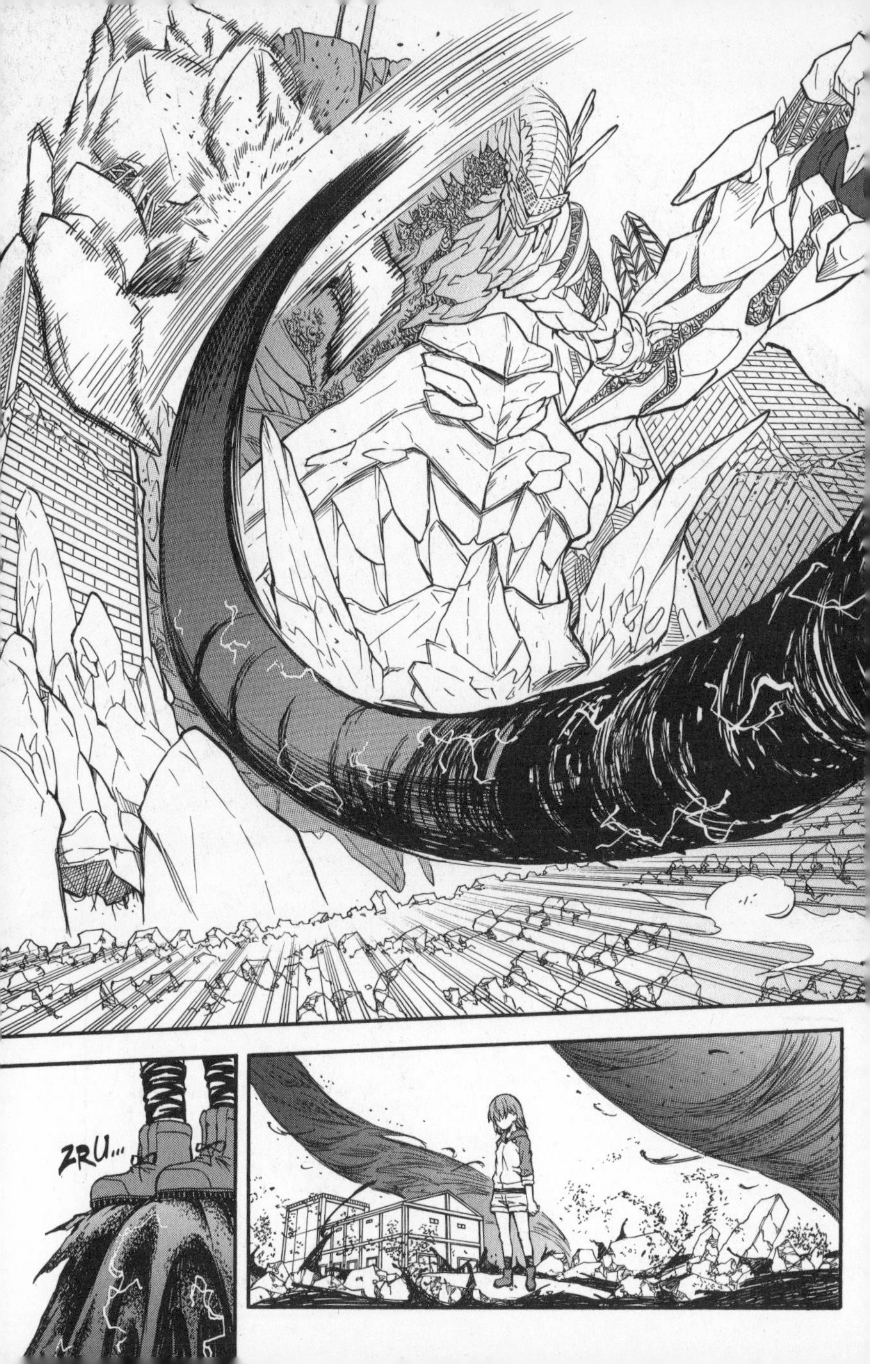
ZRU...

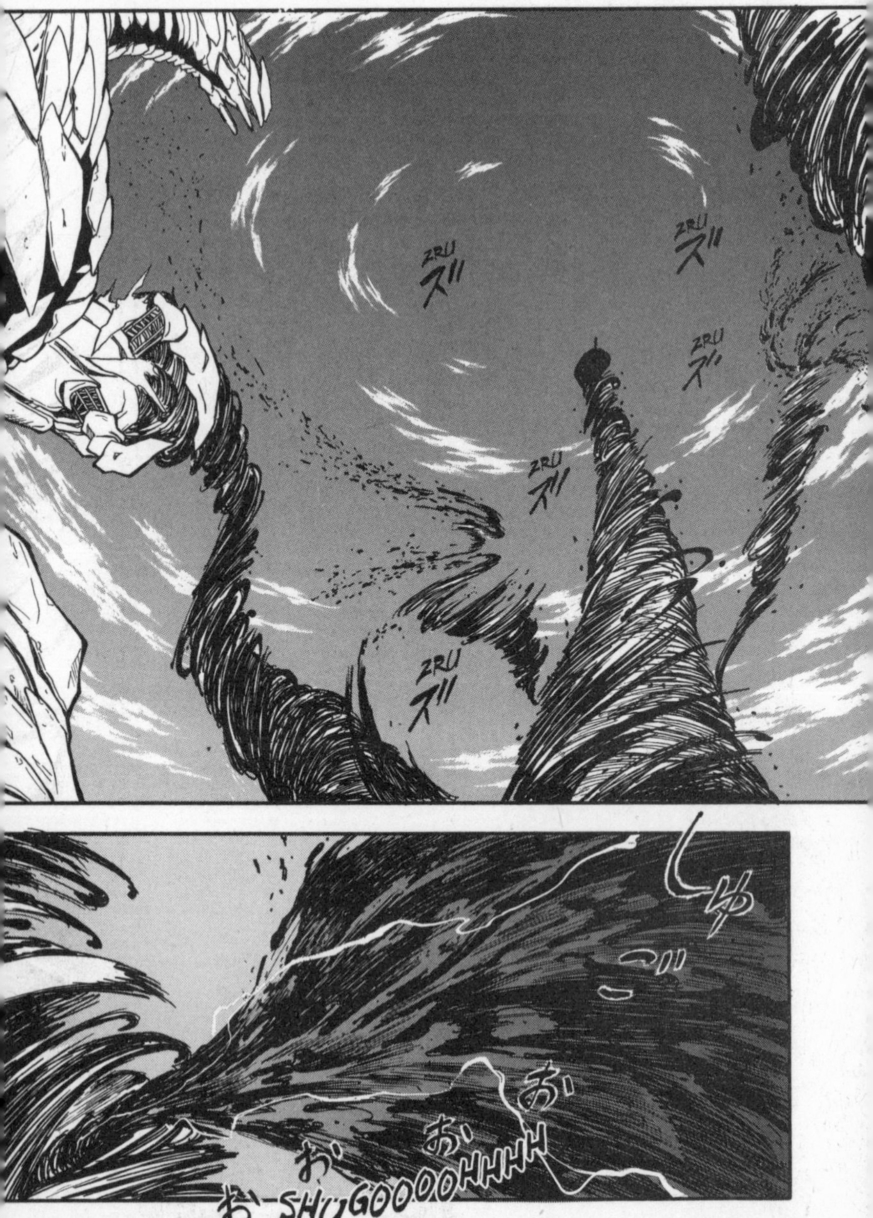

ZRU ズ
ZRU ズ
ZRU ズ
ZRU ズ
ZRU ズ
しゅごご
おおおお
SHUGOOOOHHHH

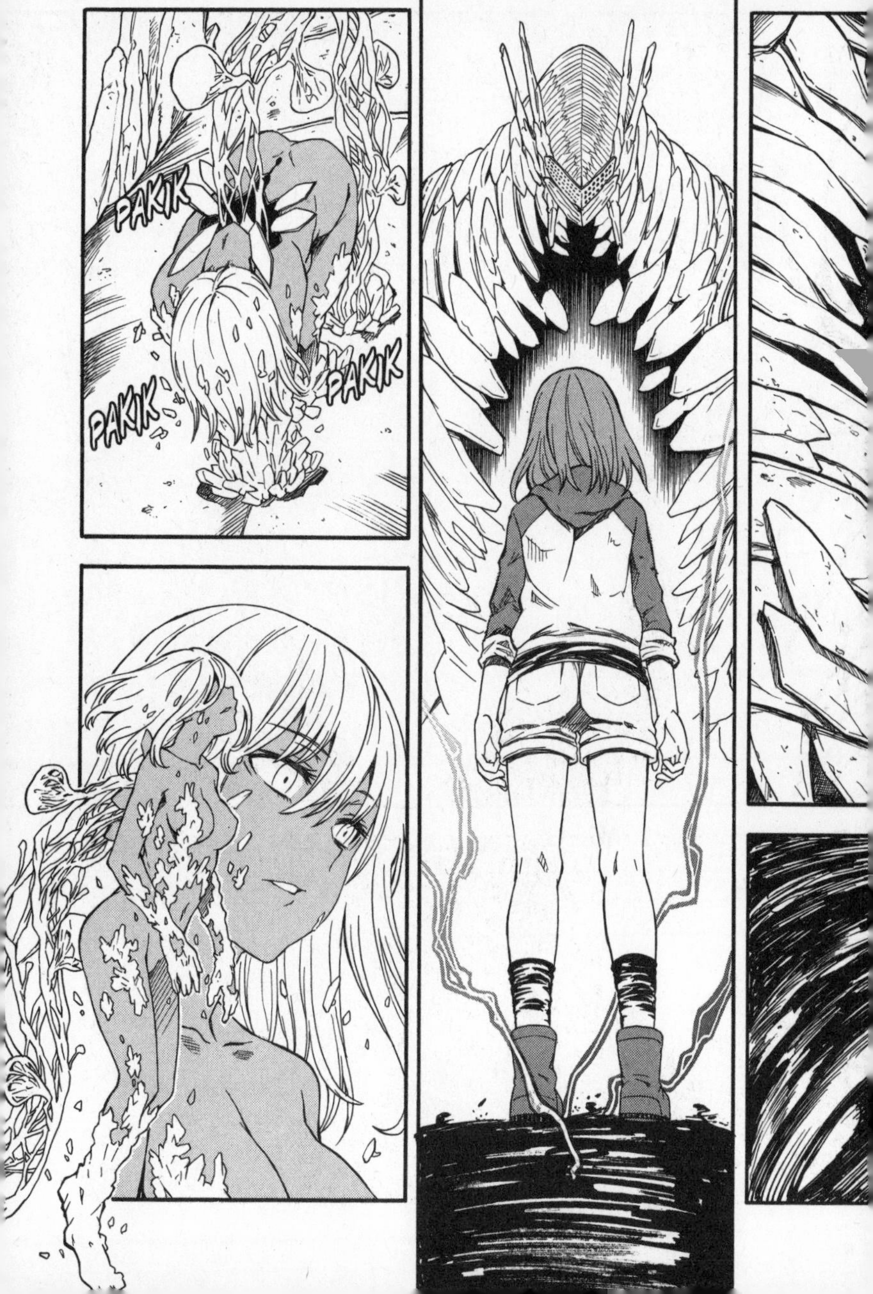
PAKIK
PAKIK
PAKIK

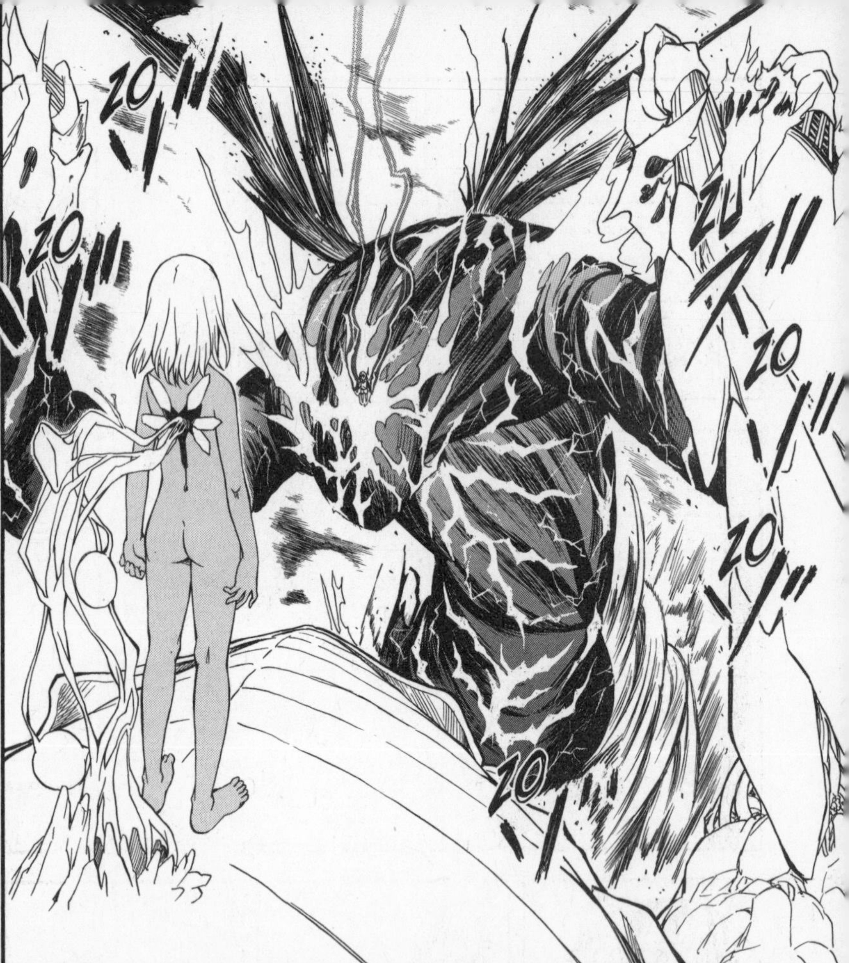
ZU
ZO
ZO
ZO
ZO
ZO
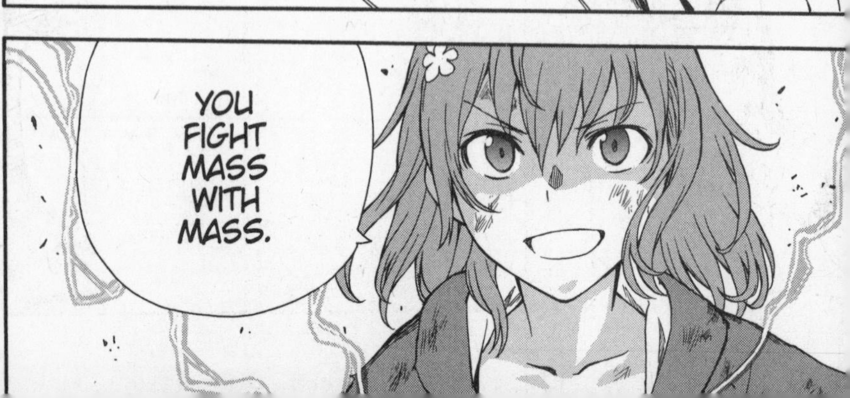
YOU FIGHT MASS WITH MASS.

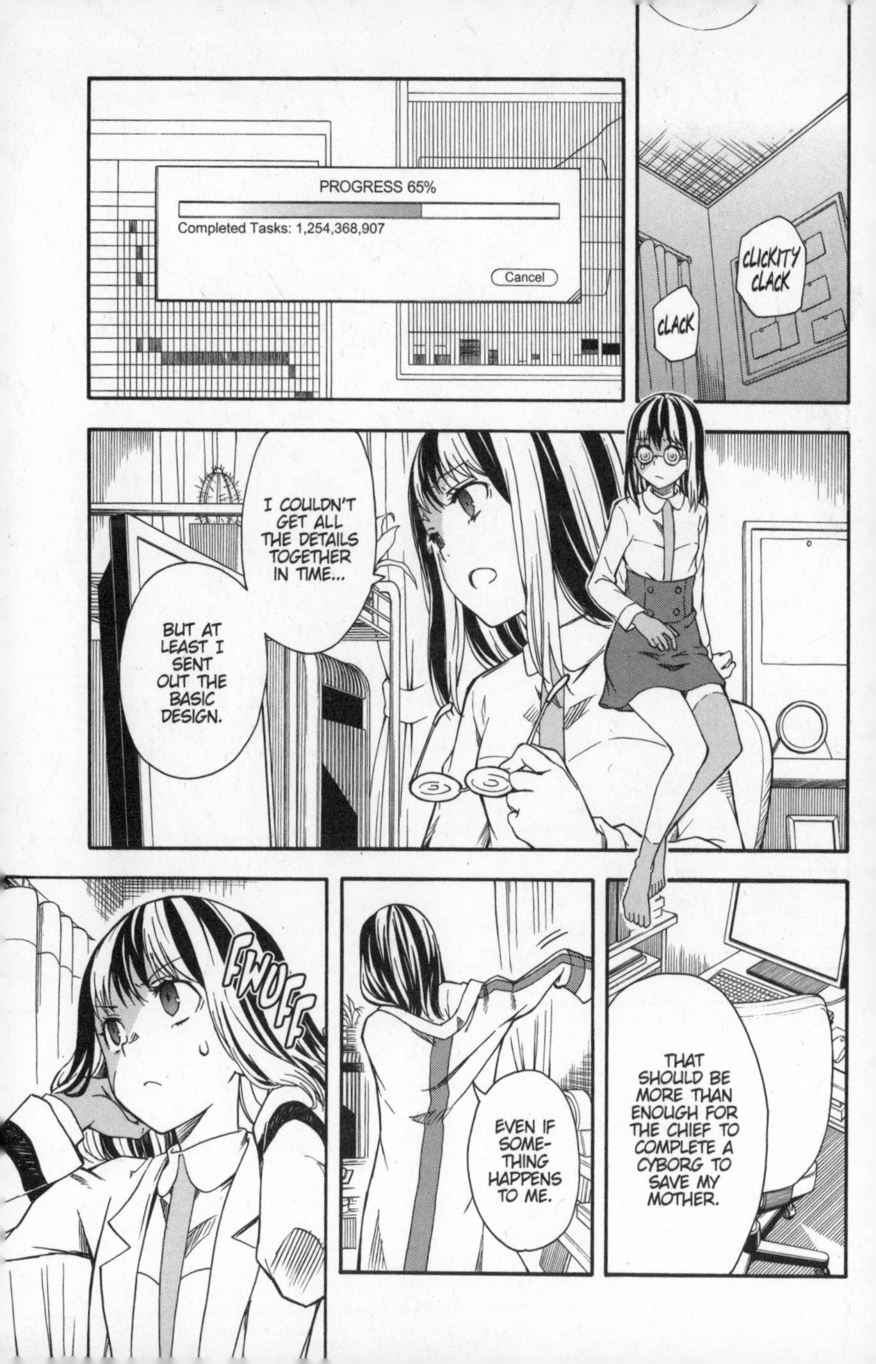
CLICKITY CLACK
CLACK
PROGRESS 65%
Completed Tasks: 1,254,368,907
Cancel
I COULDN'T GET ALL THE DETAILS TOGETHER IN TIME...
BUT AT LEAST I SENT OUT THE BASIC DESIGN.
THAT SHOULD BE MORE THAN ENOUGH FOR THE CHIEF TO COMPLETE A CYBORG TO SAVE MY MOTHER.
EVEN IF SOME-THING HAPPENS TO ME.
FWUFF

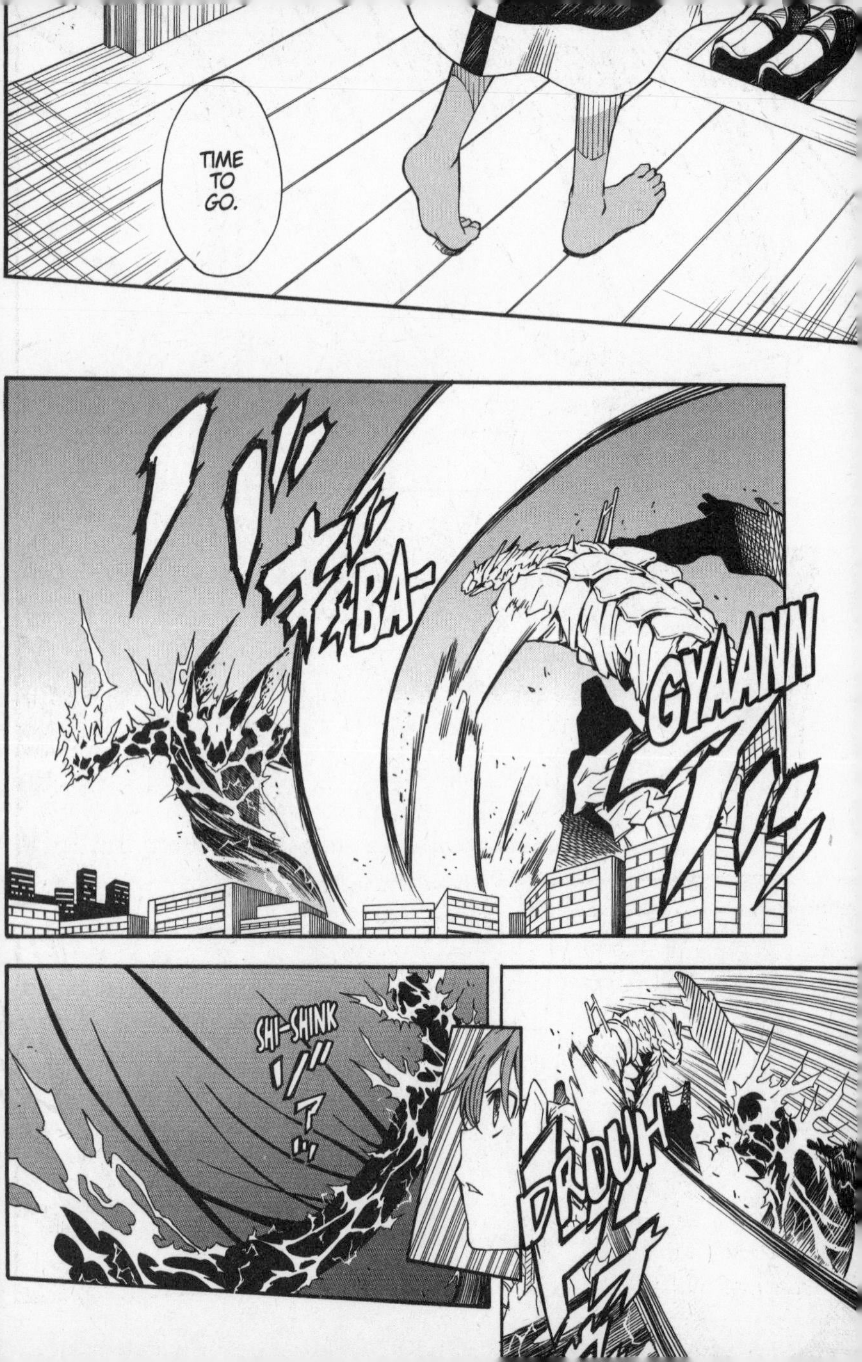

TIME TO GO.
BA-
GYAANN
SHI-SHINK
DRDUH

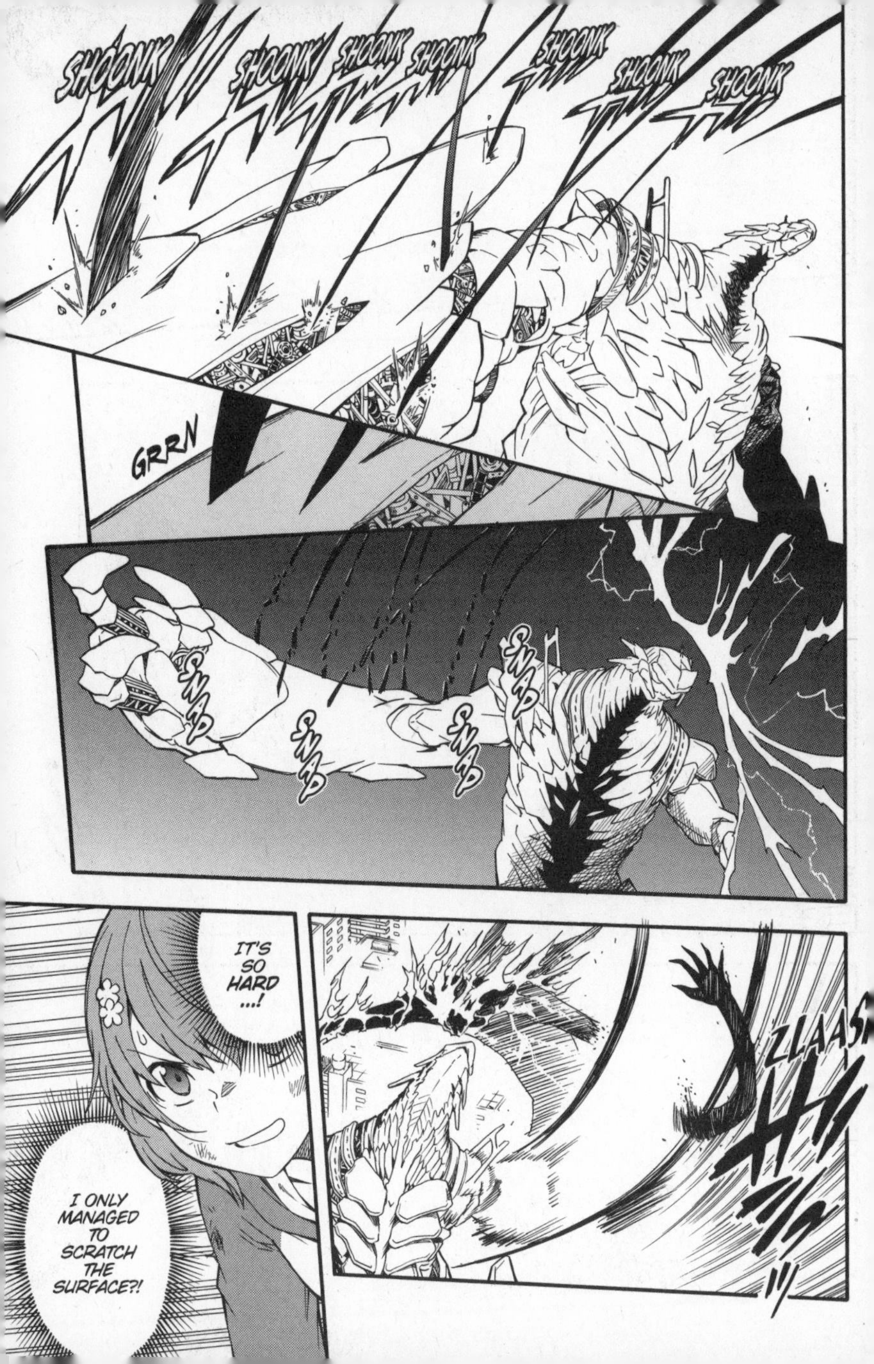
SHOONK
SHOONK
SHOONK
SHOONK
SHOONK
SHOONK
SHOONK
GRRN
SNAP
SNAP
SNAP
SNAP
ZZAASH!!
IT'S SO HARD ...!
I ONLY MANAGED TO SCRATCH THE SURFACE?!

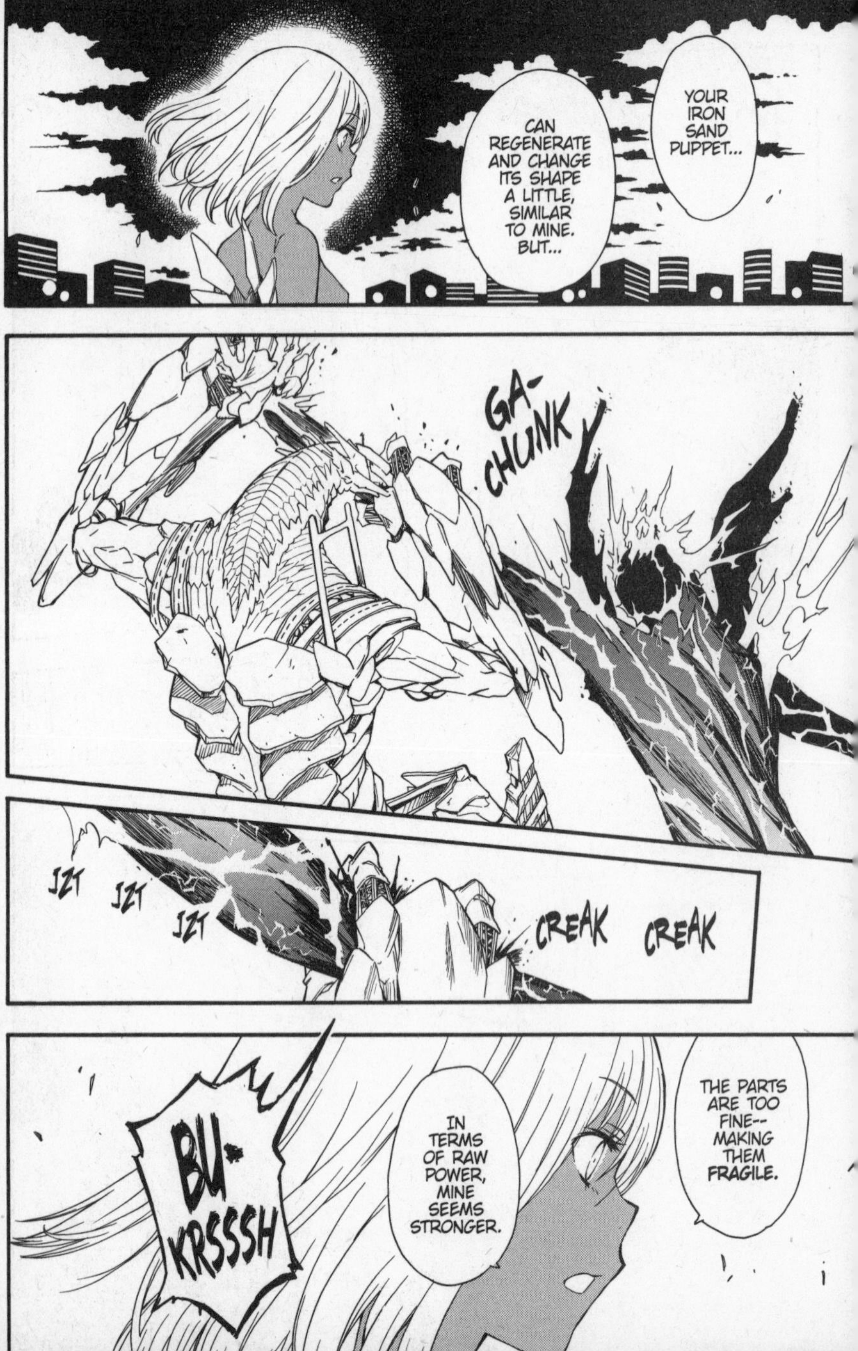
YOUR IRON SAND PUPPET...
CAN REGENERATE AND CHANGE ITS SHAPE A LITTLE, SIMILAR TO MINE. BUT...
GA-CHUNK
CREAK
CREAK
JZT
JZT
JZT
THE PARTS ARE TOO FINE--MAKING THEM FRAGILE.
IN TERMS OF RAW POWER, MINE SEEMS STRONGER.
BU-KRSSSH

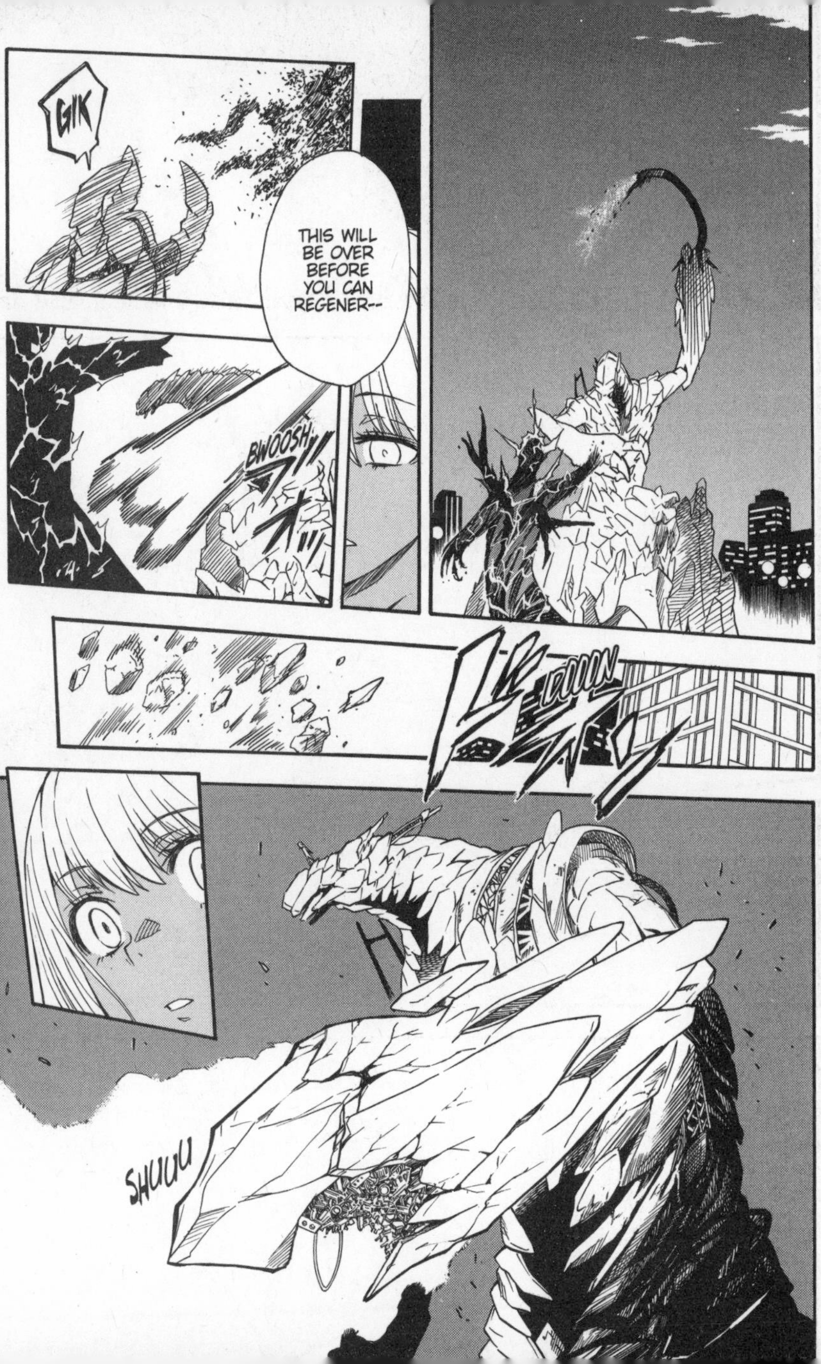
GIK
THIS WILL BE OVER BEFORE YOU CAN REGENER--
BWOOSH
SHUUU

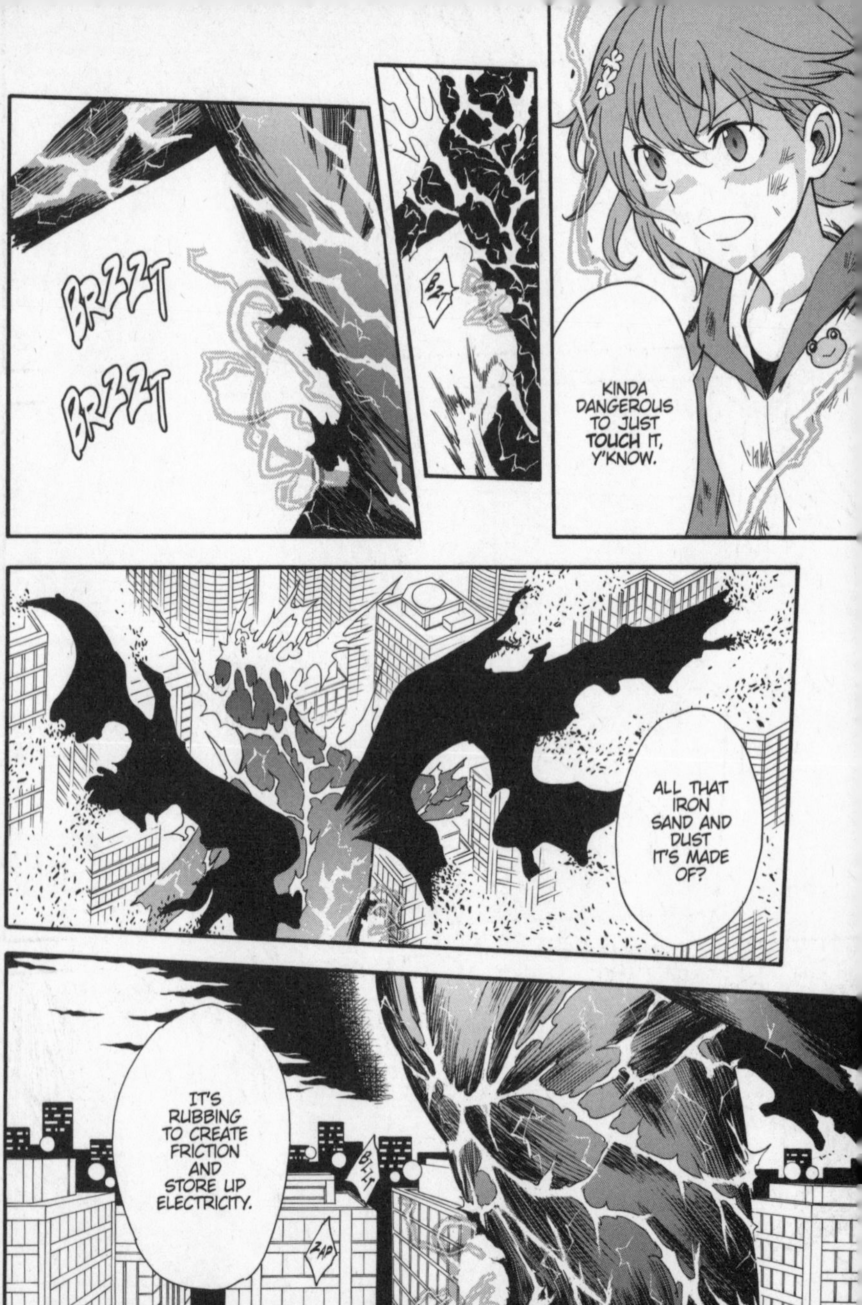
KINDA DANGEROUS TO JUST TOUCH IT, Y'KNOW.
BRZZT
BRZZT
ALL THAT IRON SAND AND DUST IT'S MADE OF?
IT'S RUBBING TO CREATE FRICTION AND STORE UP ELECTRICITY.
ZAP

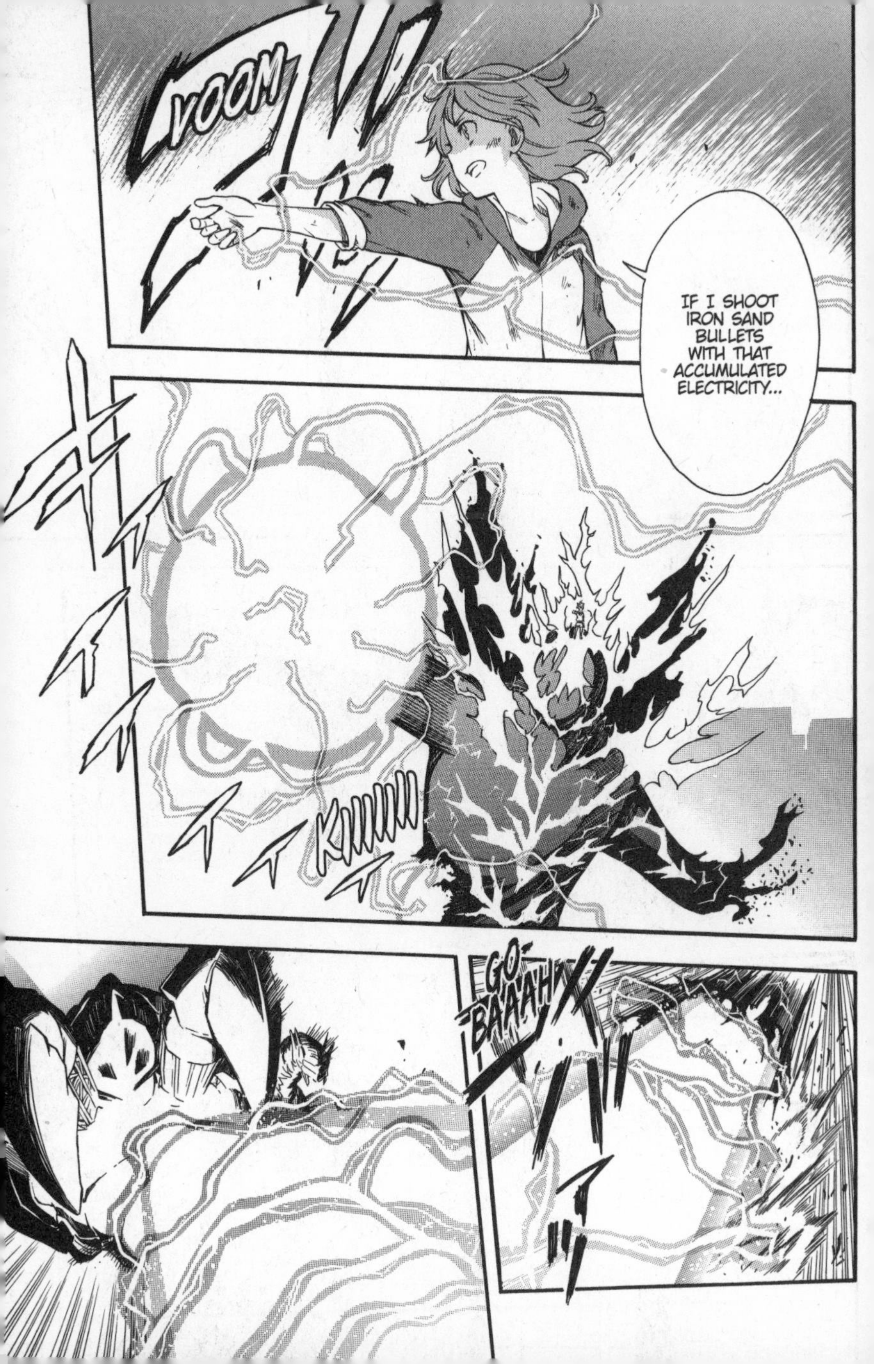
VOOM
IF I SHOOT IRON SAND BULLETS WITH THAT ACCUMULATED ELECTRICITY...
KIIIIIII
GO-BAAAHH

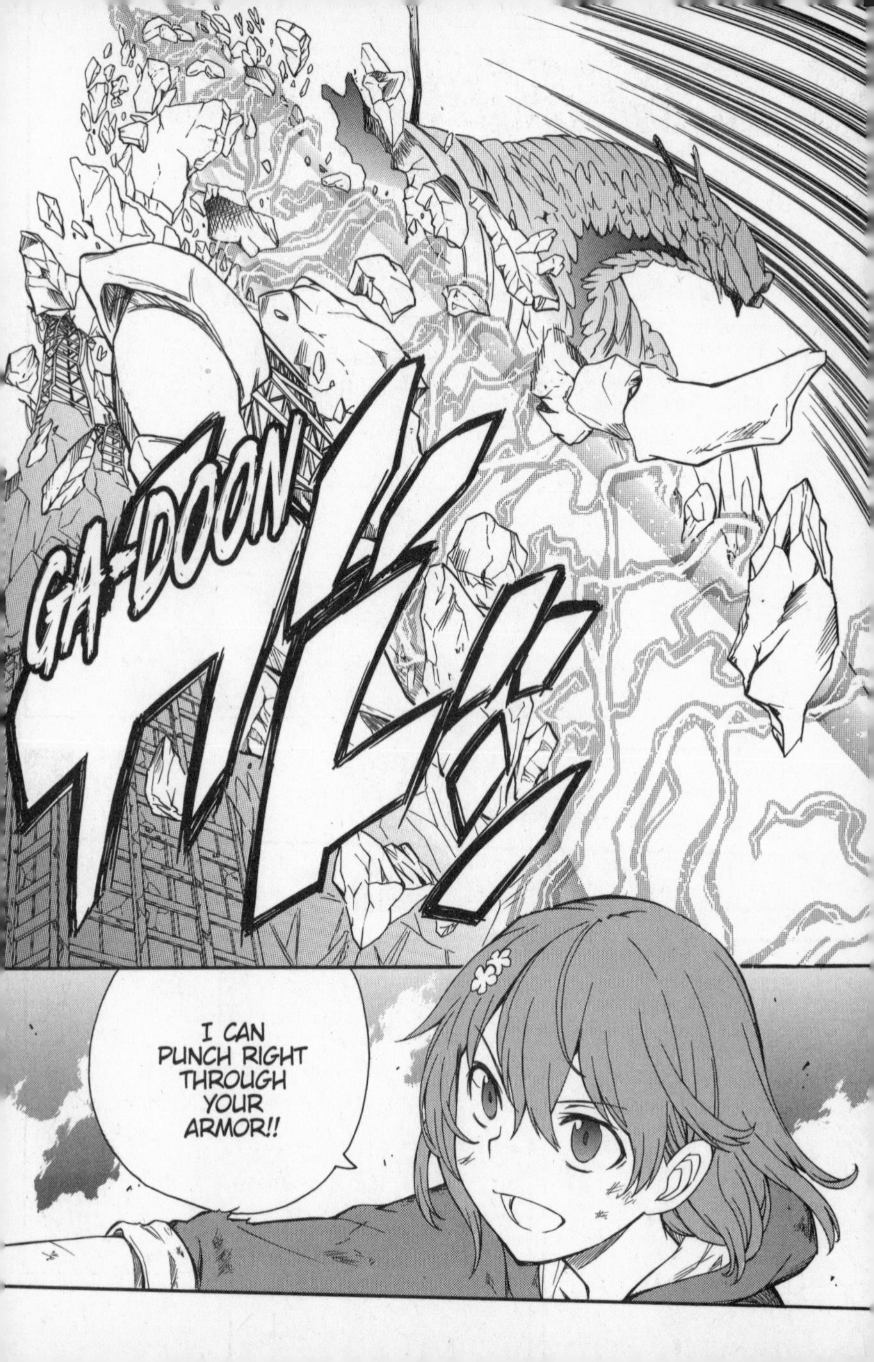
GA-DOON
I CAN PUNCH RIGHT THROUGH YOUR ARMOR!!

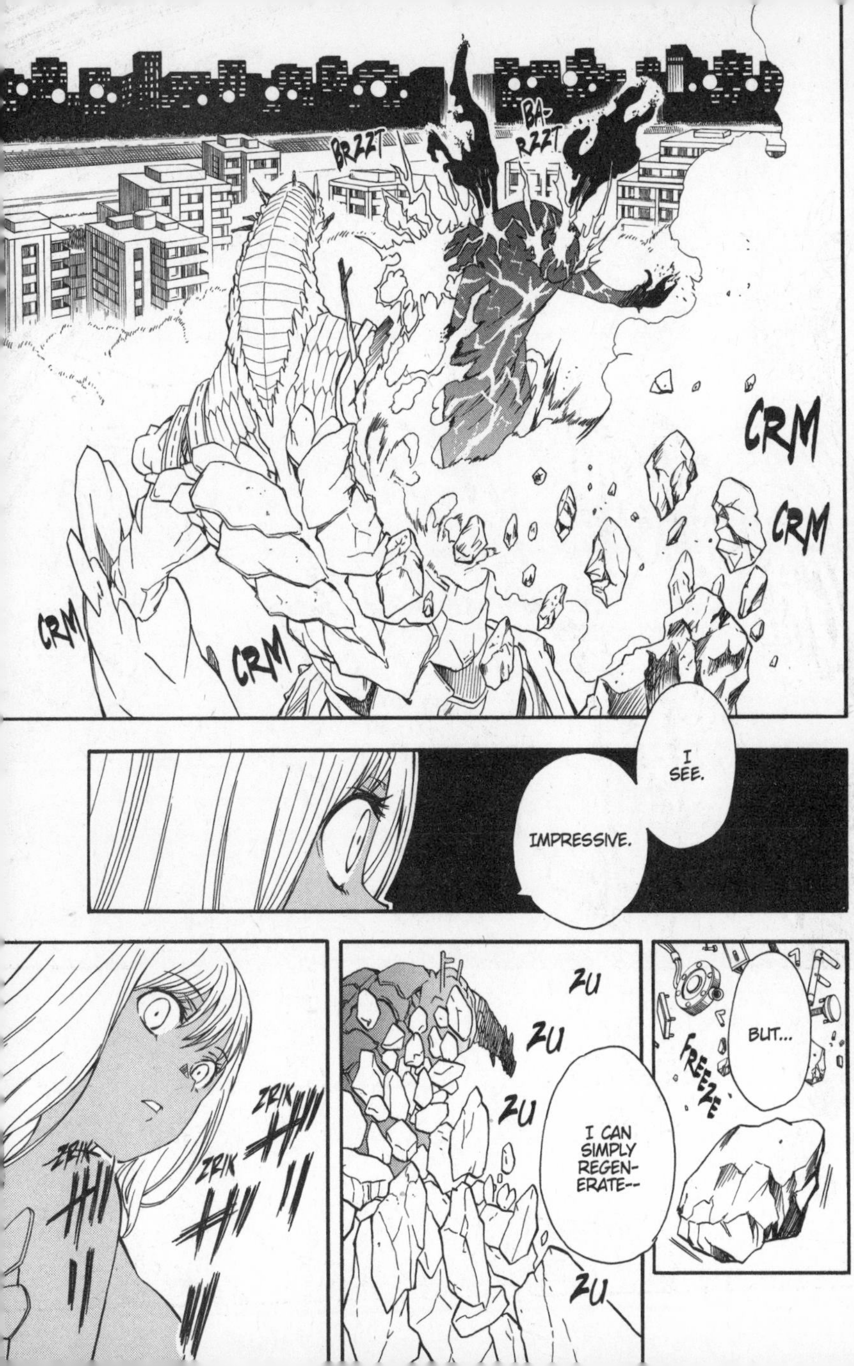
BA-RZZT
BRZZT
CRM
CRM
CRM
CRM
I SEE.
IMPRESSIVE.
BUT...
FREEZE
ZU
ZU
ZU
I CAN SIMPLY REGEN-ERATE--
ZU
ZRIK
ZRIK
ZRIK

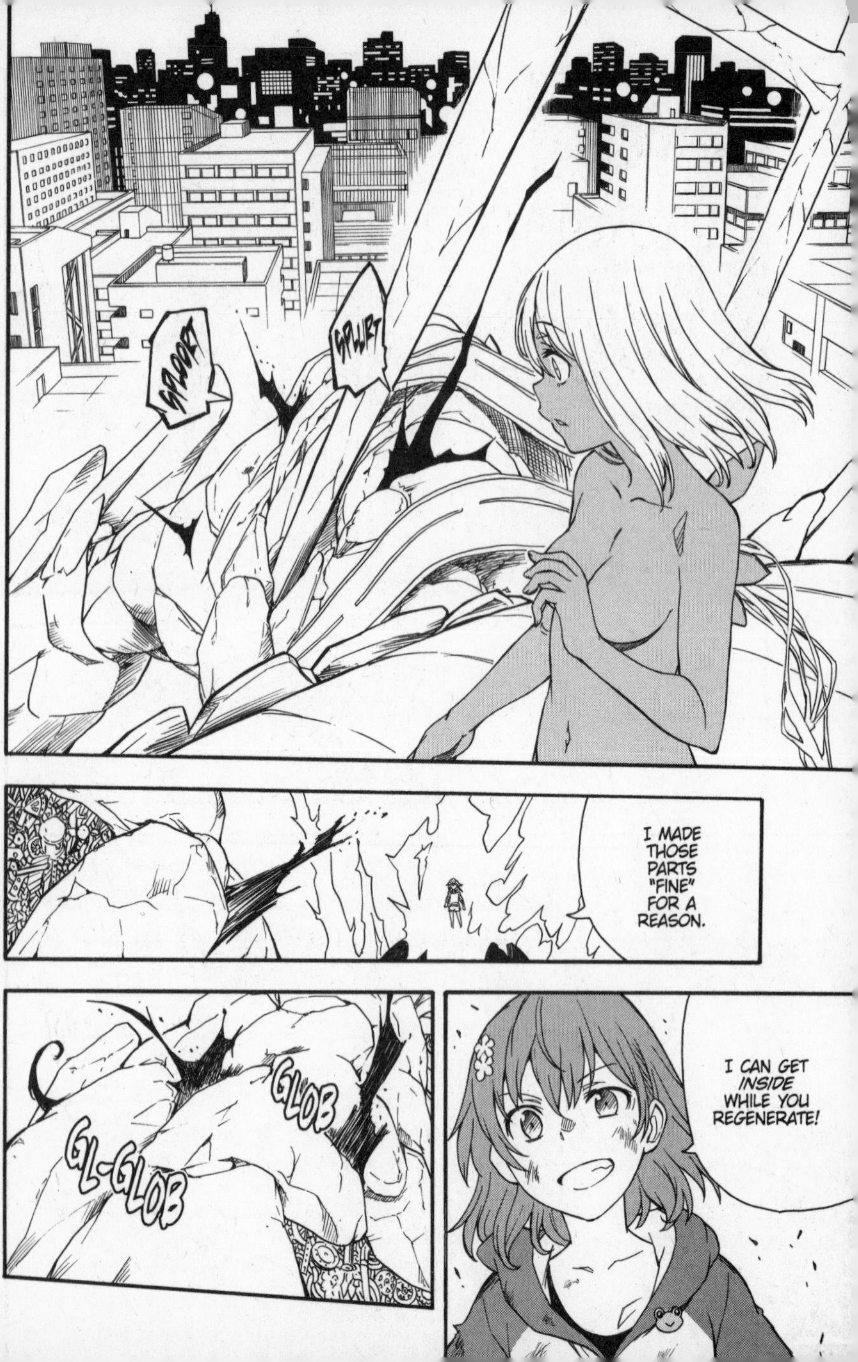
SPLURT
SPLOORT
I MADE THOSE PARTS "FINE" FOR A REASON.
I CAN GET *INSIDE* WHILE YOU REGENERATE!
GLOB
GL-GLOB

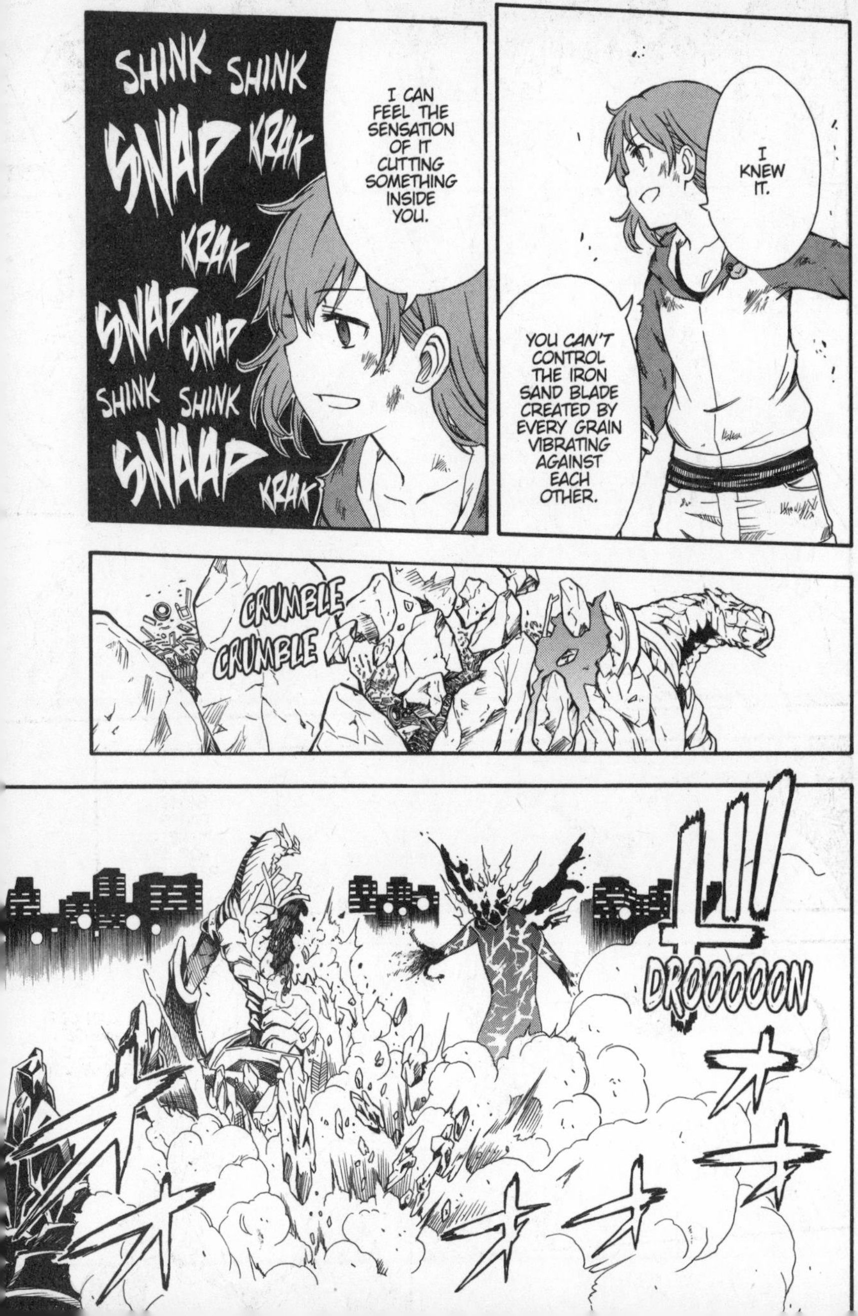
I KNEW IT.
YOU CAN'T CONTROL THE IRON SAND BLADE CREATED BY EVERY GRAIN VIBRATING AGAINST EACH OTHER.
I CAN FEEL THE SENSATION OF IT CUTTING SOMETHING INSIDE YOU.
SHINK SHINK
SNAP KRAK
KRAK
SNAP SNAP
SHINK SHINK
SNAAP KRAK
CRUMBLE CRUMBLE
DROOOOON

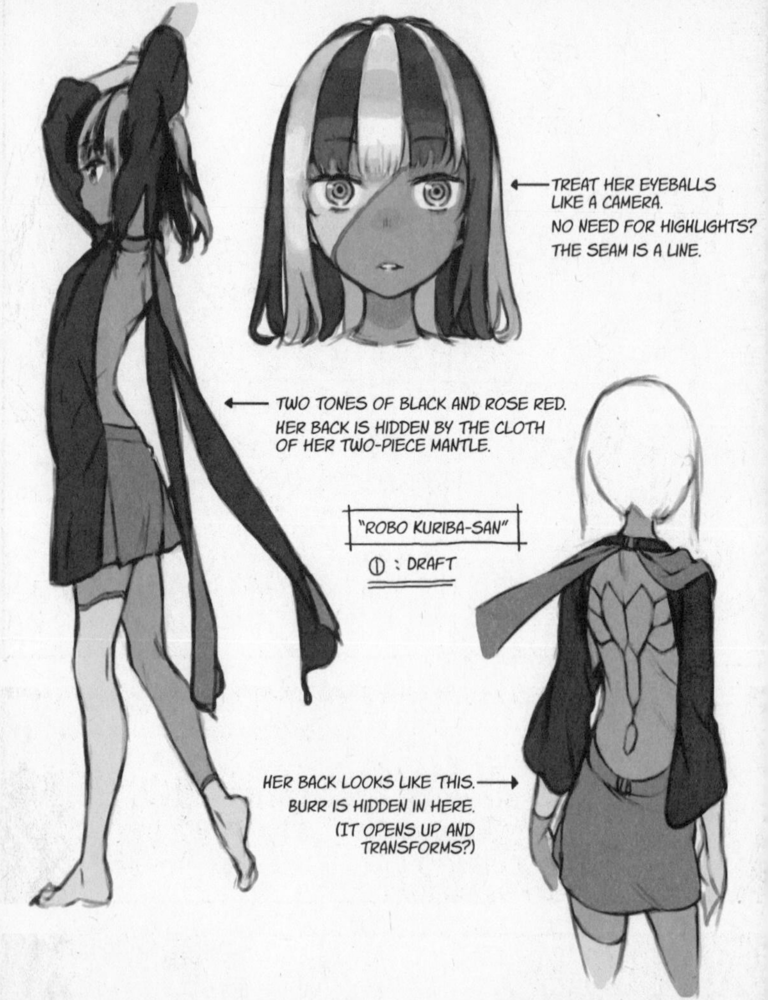
TREAT HER EYEBALLS LIKE A CAMERA.
NO NEED FOR HIGHLIGHTS?
THE SEAM IS A LINE.
TWO TONES OF BLACK AND ROSE RED.
HER BACK IS HIDDEN BY THE CLOTH OF HER TWO-PIECE MANTLE.
"ROBO KURIBA-SAN"
① : DRAFT
HER BACK LOOKS LIKE THIS.
BURR IS HIDDEN IN HERE.
(IT OPENS UP AND TRANSFORMS?)

Design/Kiyotaka Haimura

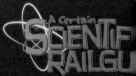

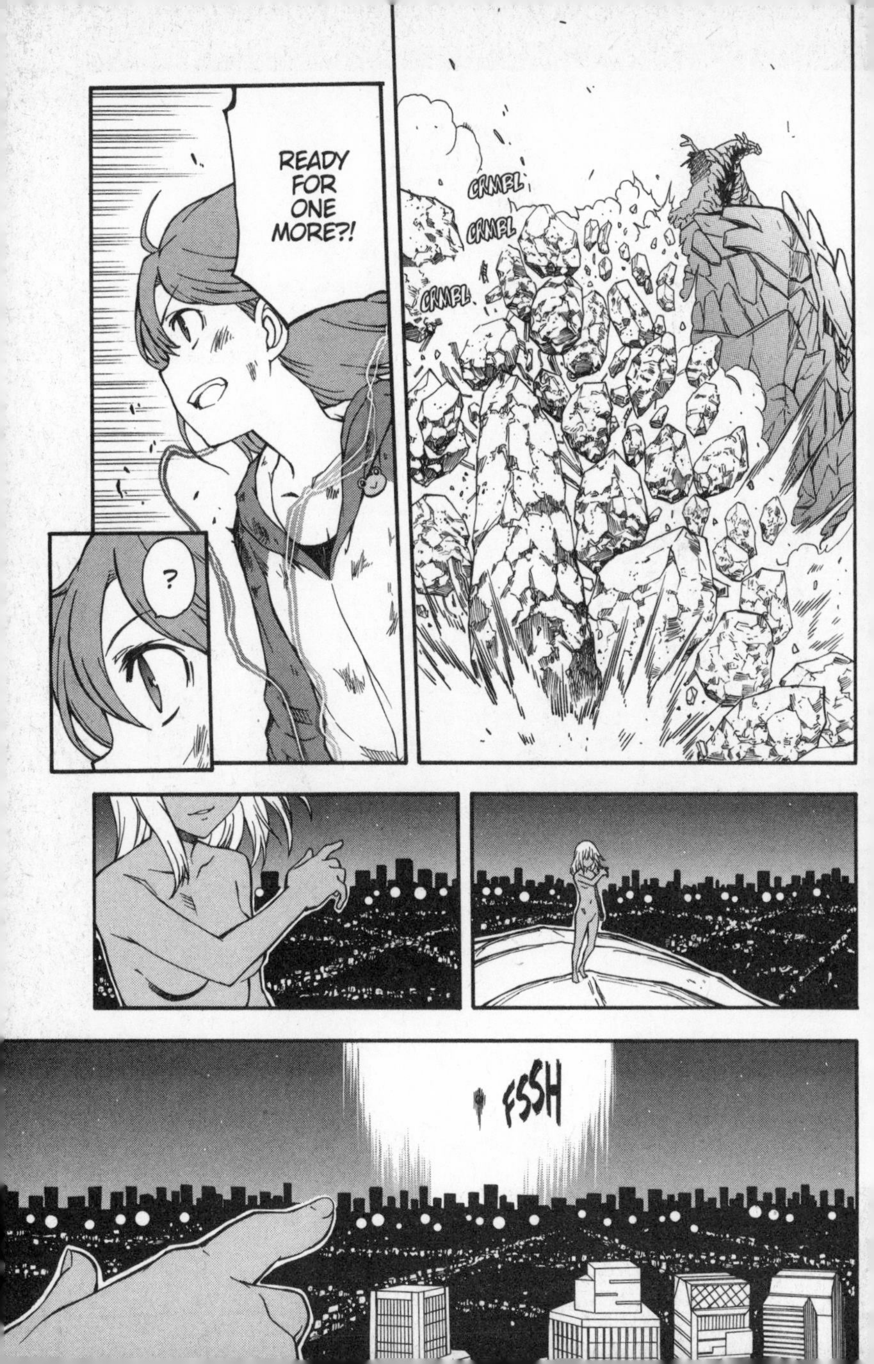
CRMBL
CRMBL
CRMBL
READY FOR ONE MORE?!
?
FSSH

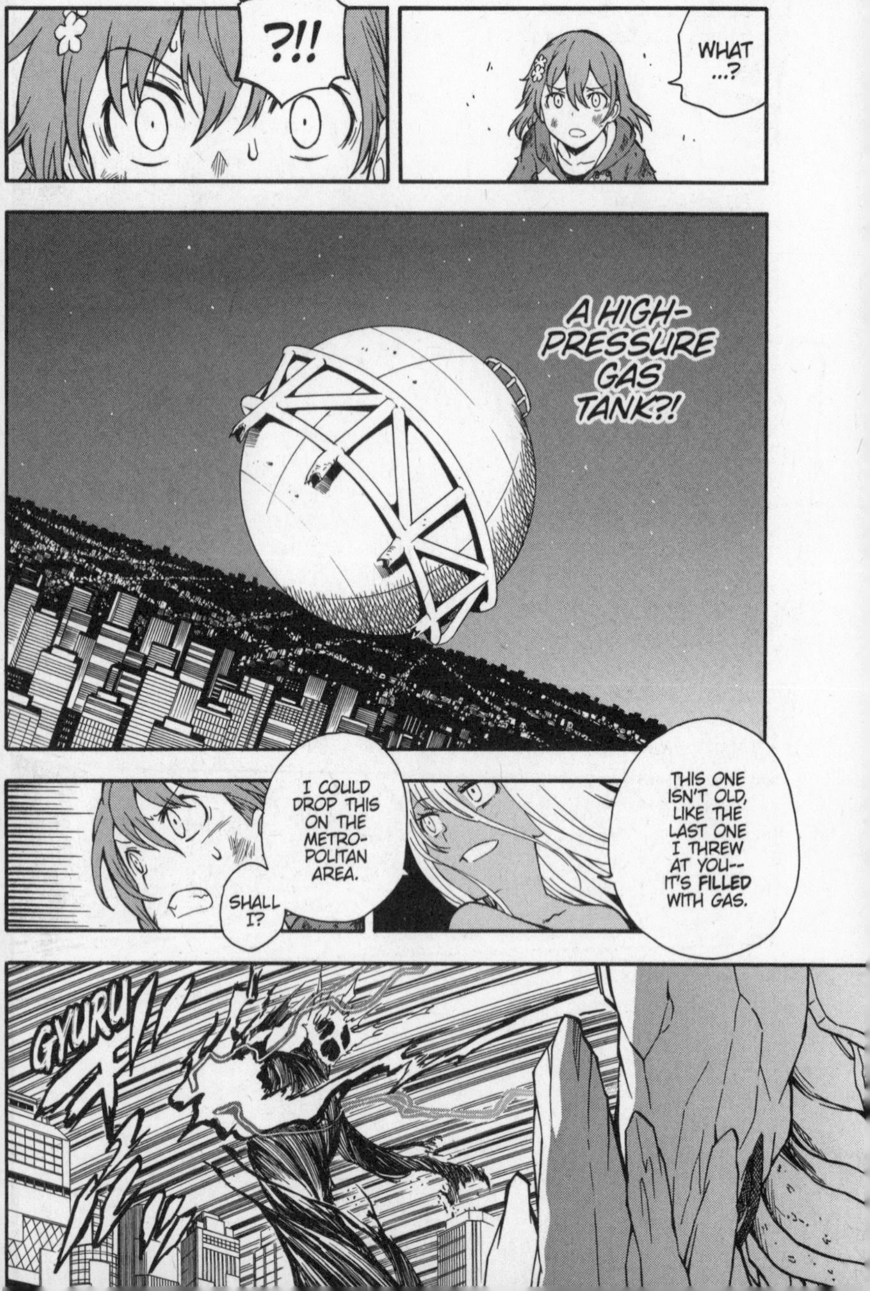
WHAT ...?
?!!
A HIGH-PRESSURE GAS TANK?!
THIS ONE ISN'T OLD, LIKE THE LAST ONE I THREW AT YOU-- IT'S **FILLED** WITH GAS.
I COULD DROP THIS ON THE METRO-POLITAN AREA.
SHALL I?
GYURU

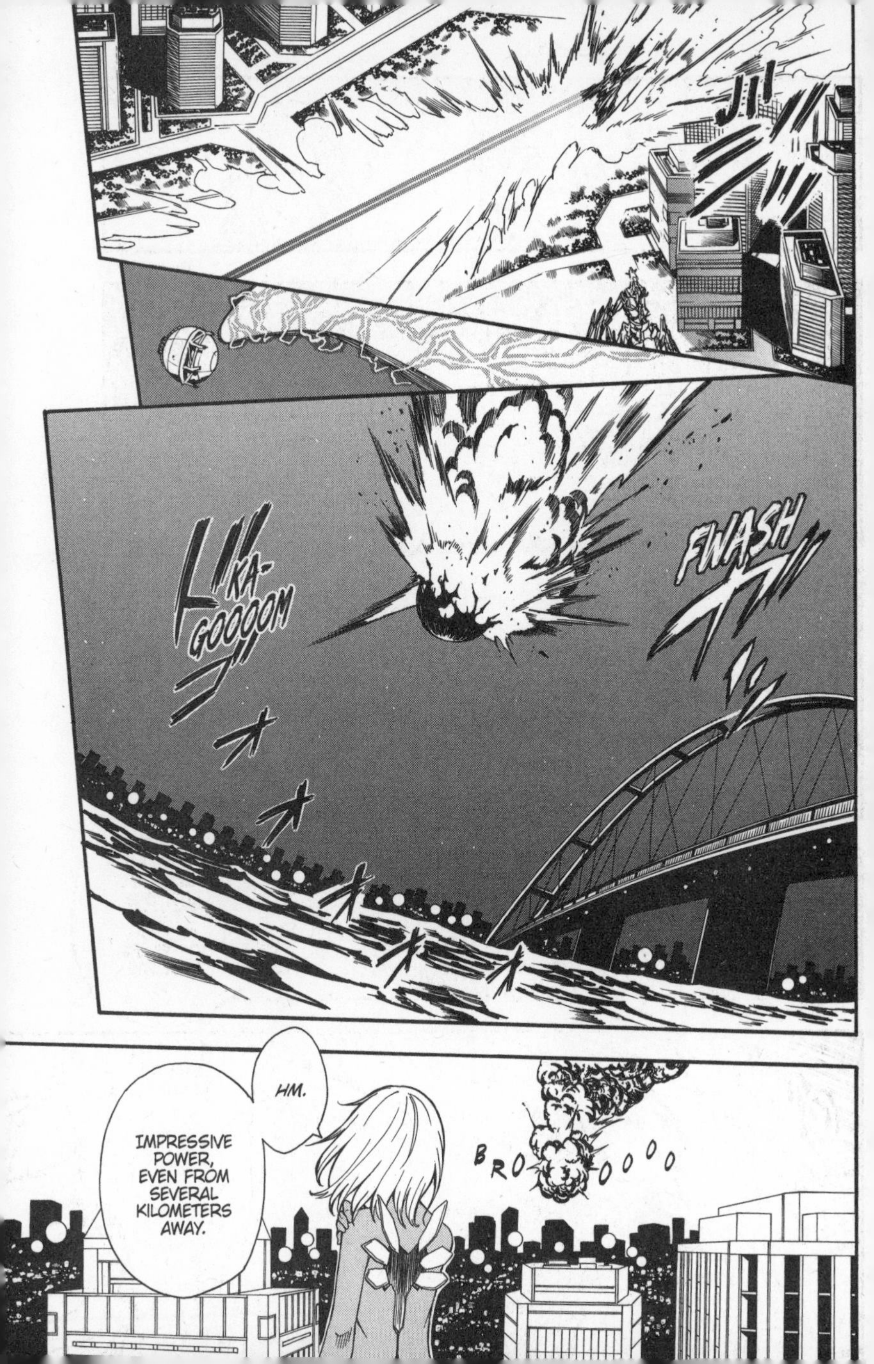
JI!
KA-GOOOOM
FWASH
HM.
IMPRESSIVE POWER, EVEN FROM SEVERAL KILOMETERS AWAY.
BRO-OOOO

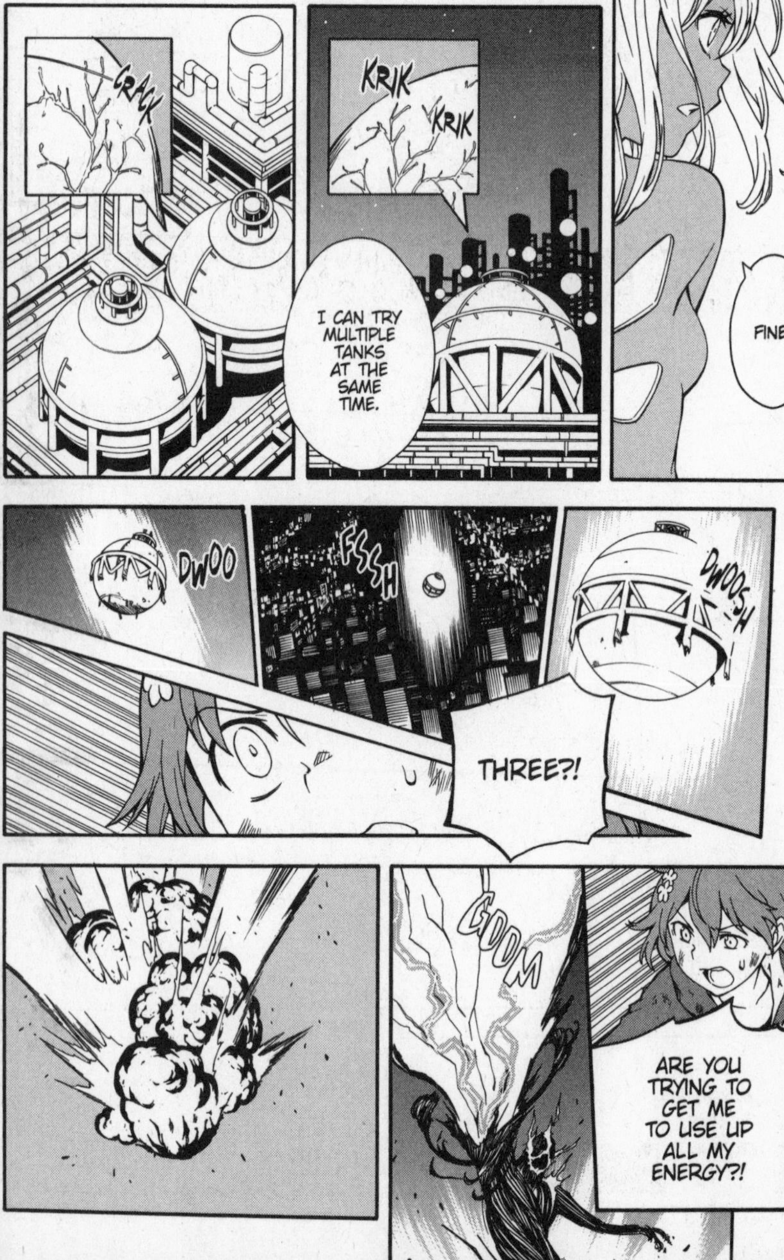
FINE.
KRIK
KRIK
I CAN TRY MULTIPLE TANKS AT THE SAME TIME.
CRACK
DWOOSH
FSSH
DWOO
THREE?!
ARE YOU TRYING TO GET ME TO USE UP ALL MY ENERGY?!
GOOM

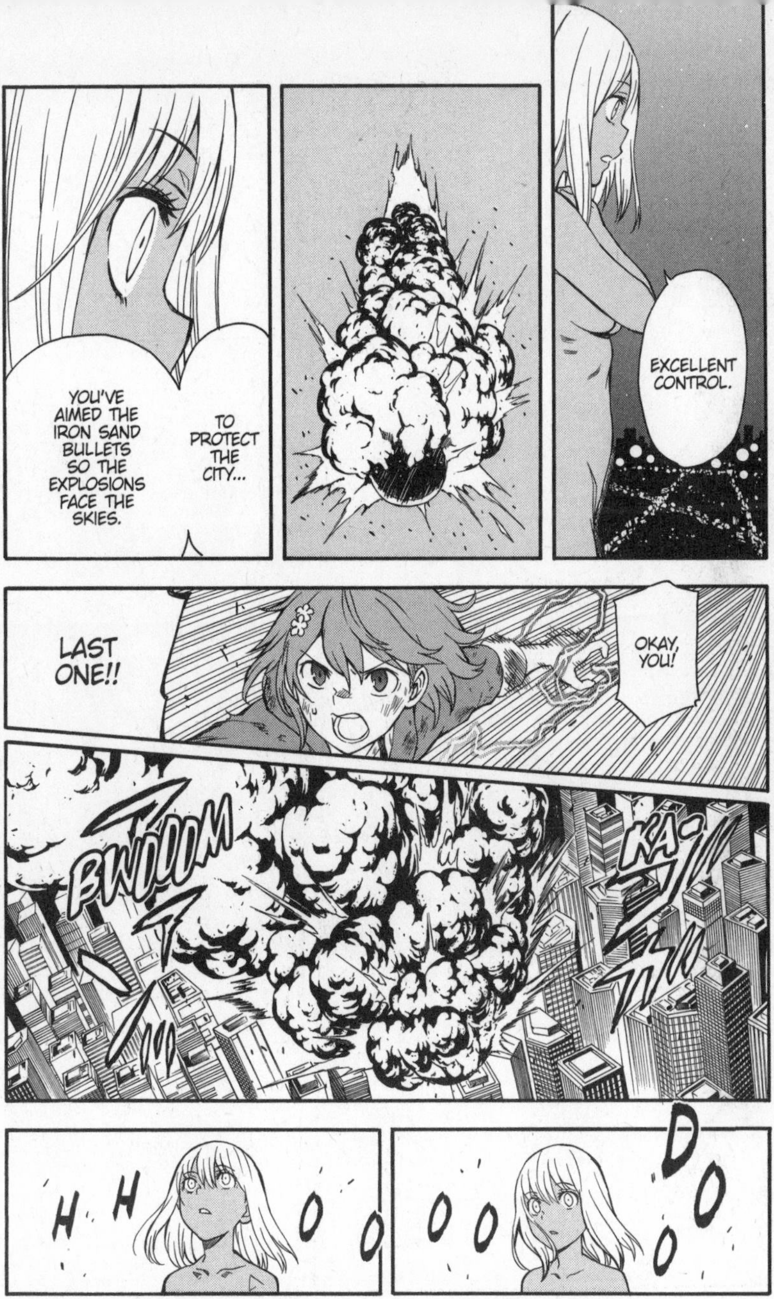
EXCELLENT CONTROL.
TO PROTECT THE CITY...
YOU'VE AIMED THE IRON SAND BULLETS SO THE EXPLOSIONS FACE THE SKIES.
OKAY, YOU!
LAST ONE!!
KA-
BWOOOM
DOOOO
HHOO

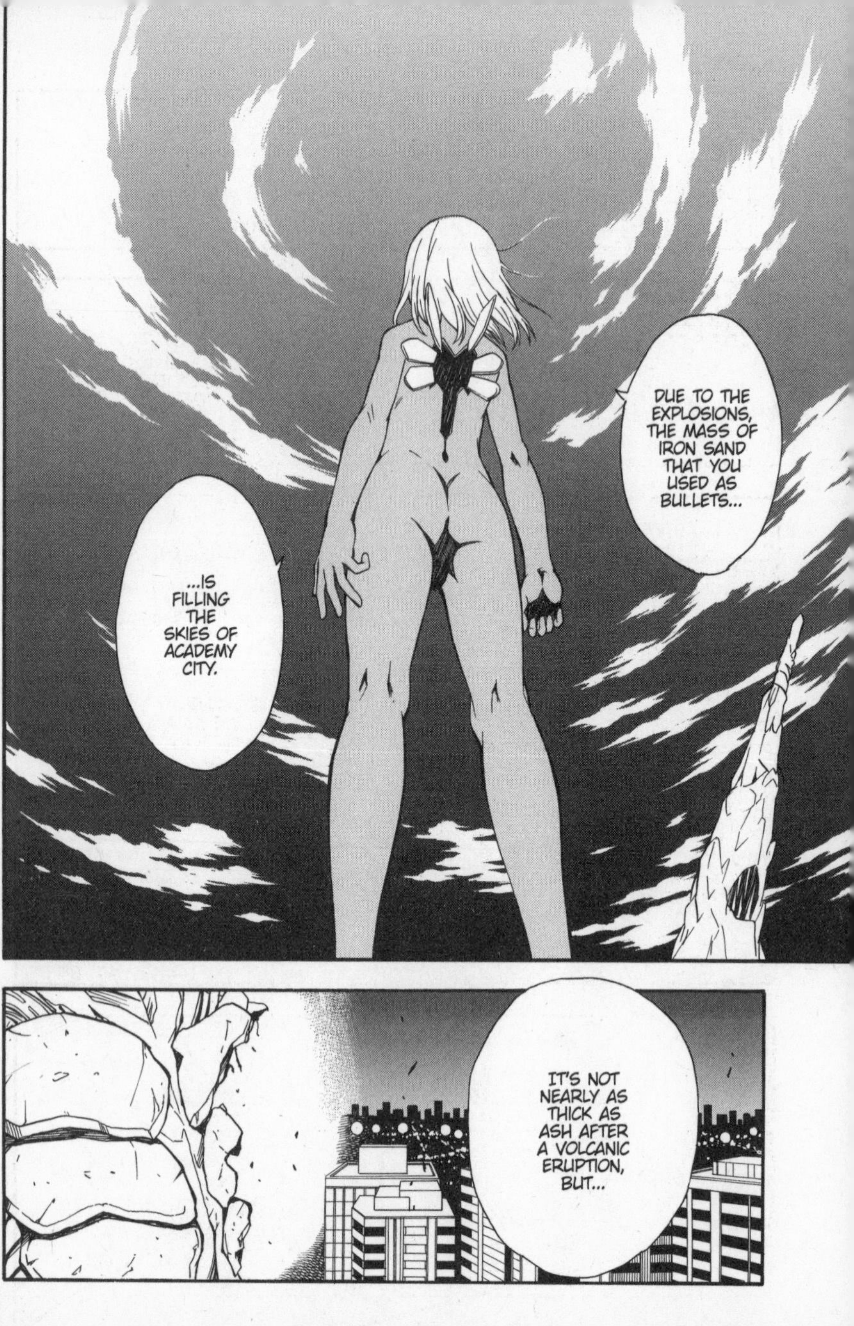
DUE TO THE EXPLOSIONS, THE MASS OF IRON SAND THAT YOU USED AS BULLETS...
...IS FILLING THE SKIES OF ACADEMY CITY.
IT'S NOT NEARLY AS THICK AS ASH AFTER A VOLCANIC ERUPTION, BUT...

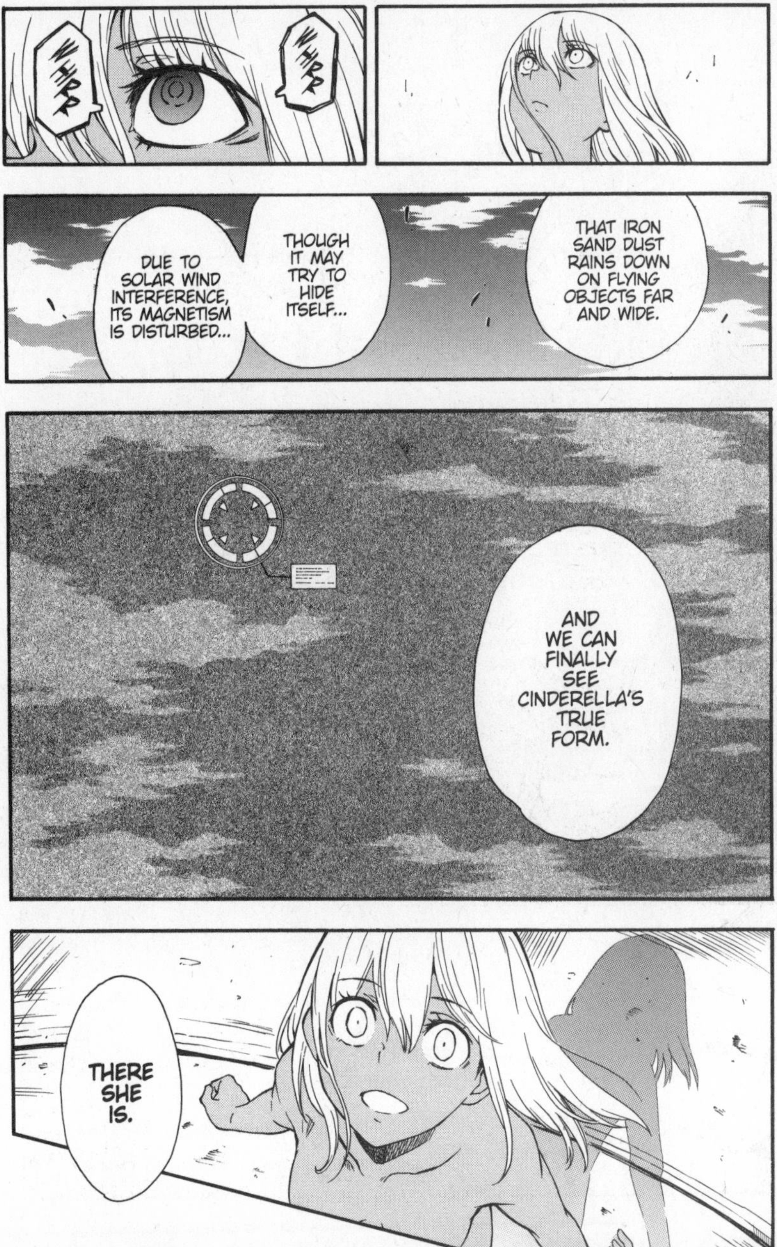
WHRR
WHRR
THAT IRON SAND DUST RAINS DOWN ON FLYING OBJECTS FAR AND WIDE.
THOUGH IT MAY TRY TO HIDE ITSELF...
DUE TO SOLAR WIND INTERFERENCE, ITS MAGNETISM IS DISTURBED...
AND WE CAN FINALLY SEE CINDERELLA'S TRUE FORM.
THERE SHE IS.

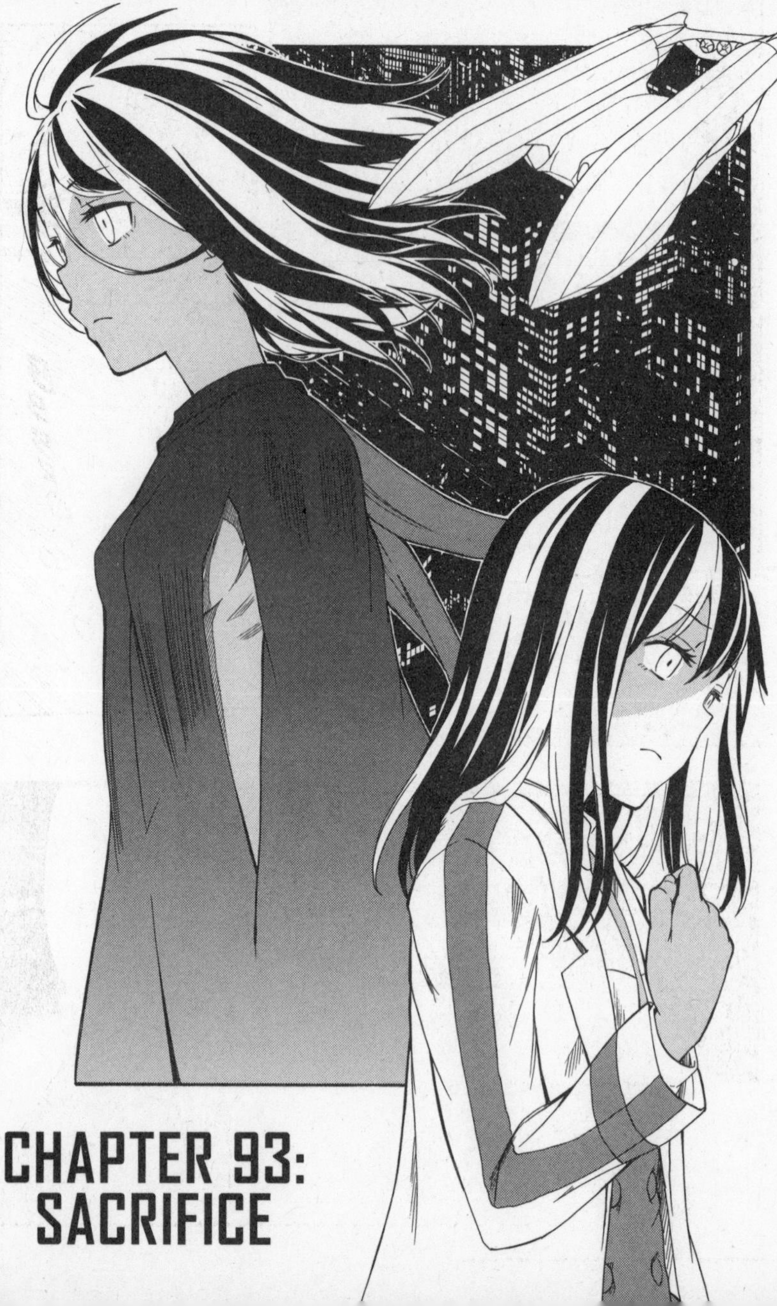

CHAPTER 93: SACRIFICE

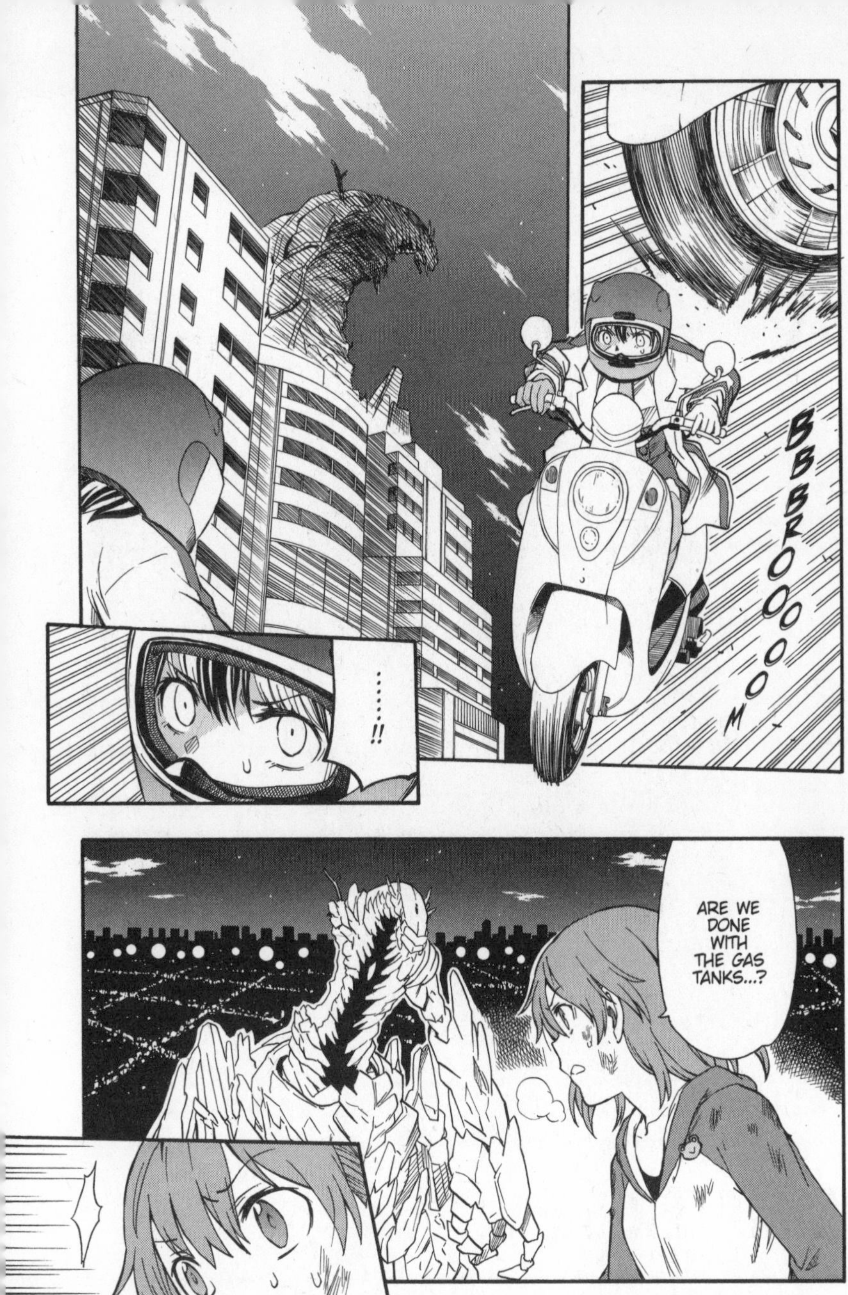
BBBROOOOOOM
......!!
ARE WE DONE WITH THE GAS TANKS...?

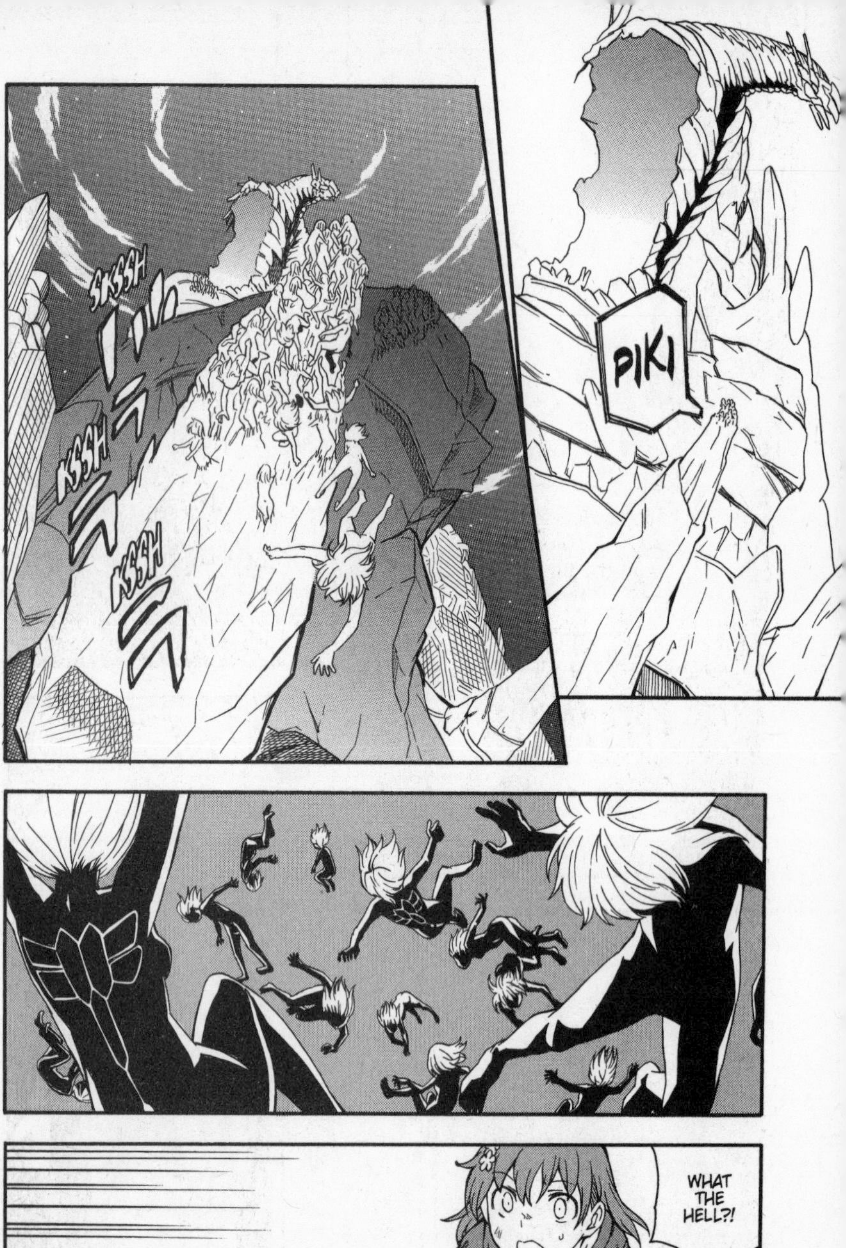
PIKI
SKSSSH
KSSH
KSSH
WHAT THE HELL?!

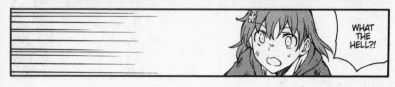

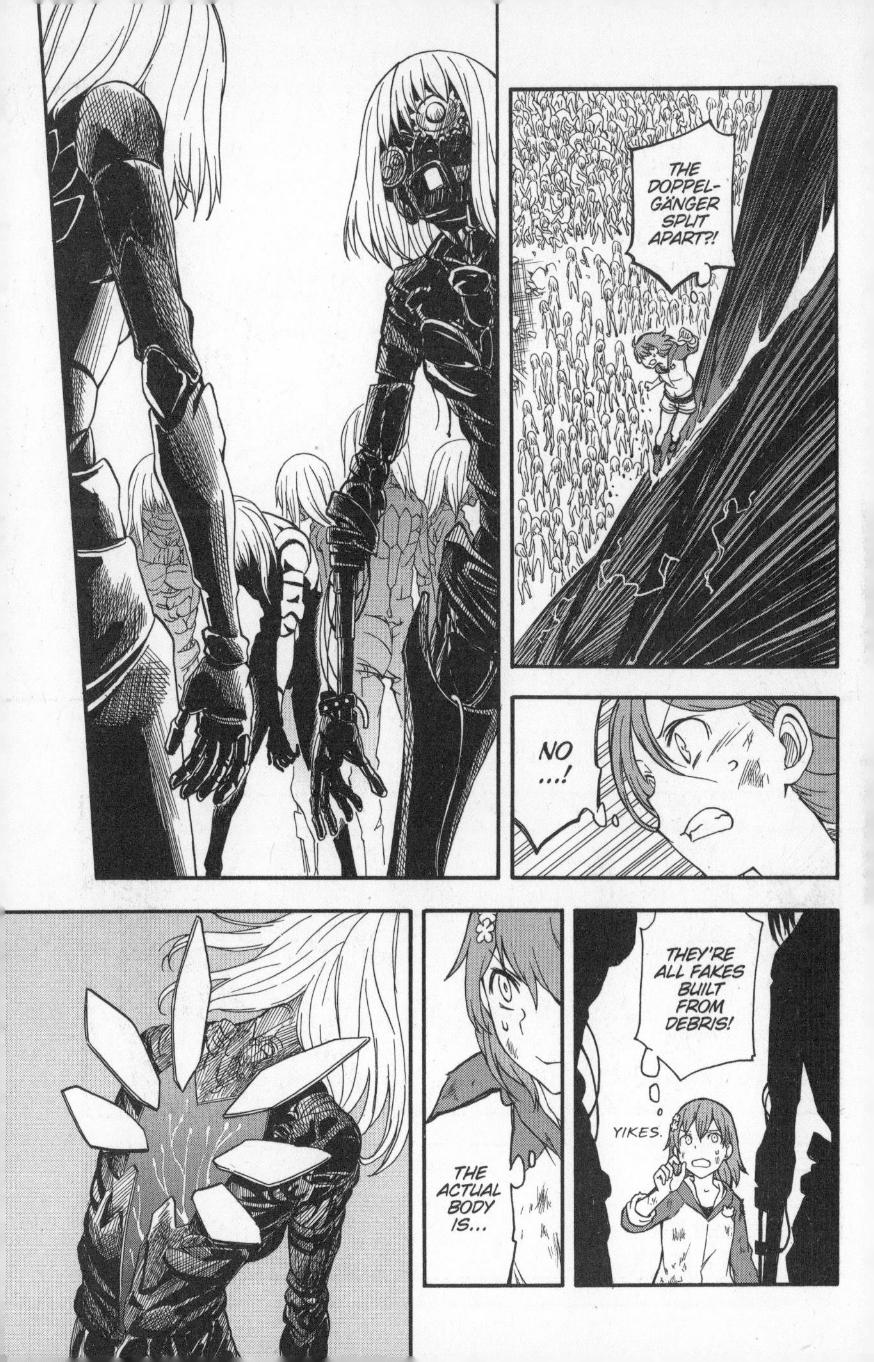
THE DOPPEL-GÄNGER SPLIT APART?!
NO ...!
THEY'RE ALL FAKES BUILT FROM DEBRIS!
YIKES.
THE ACTUAL BODY IS...

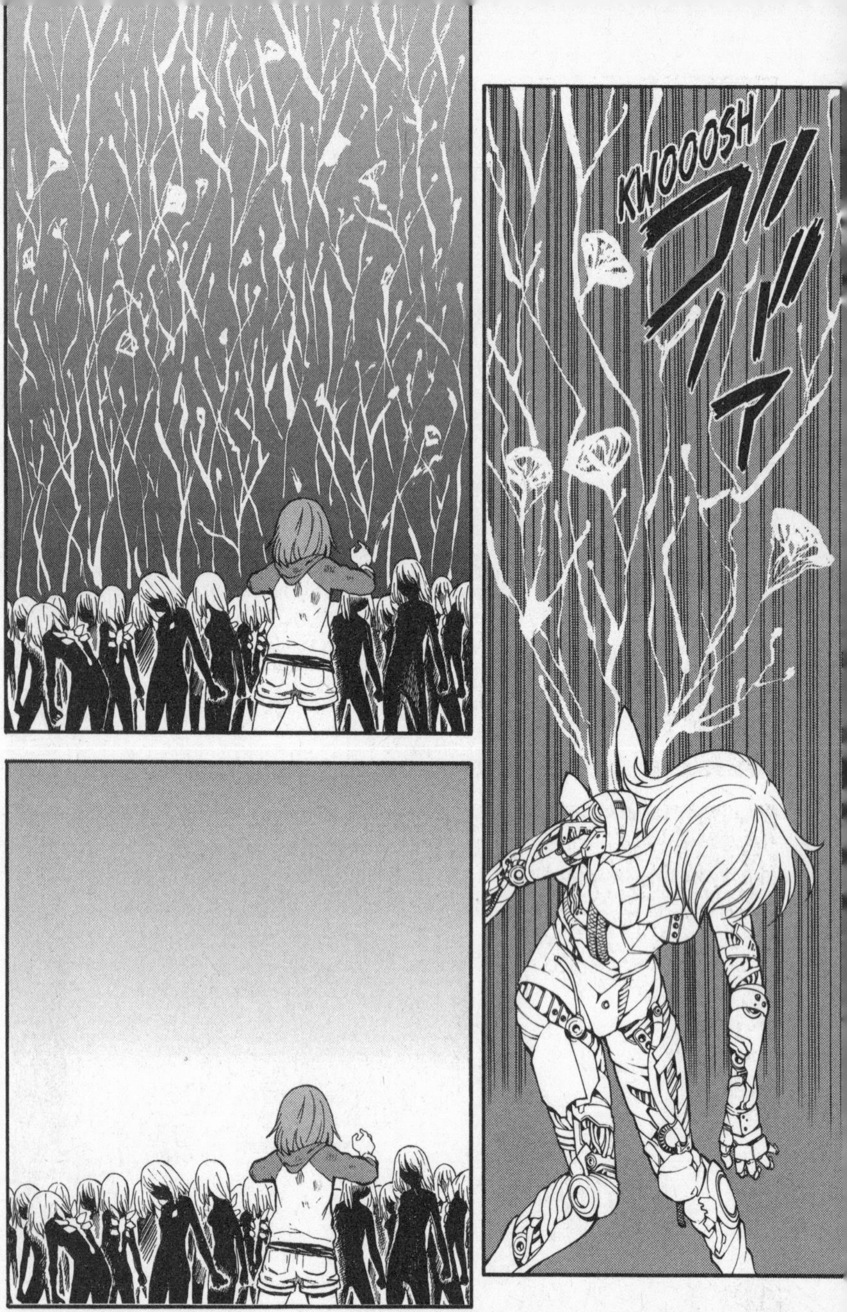
KWOOOSH
ゴバァ

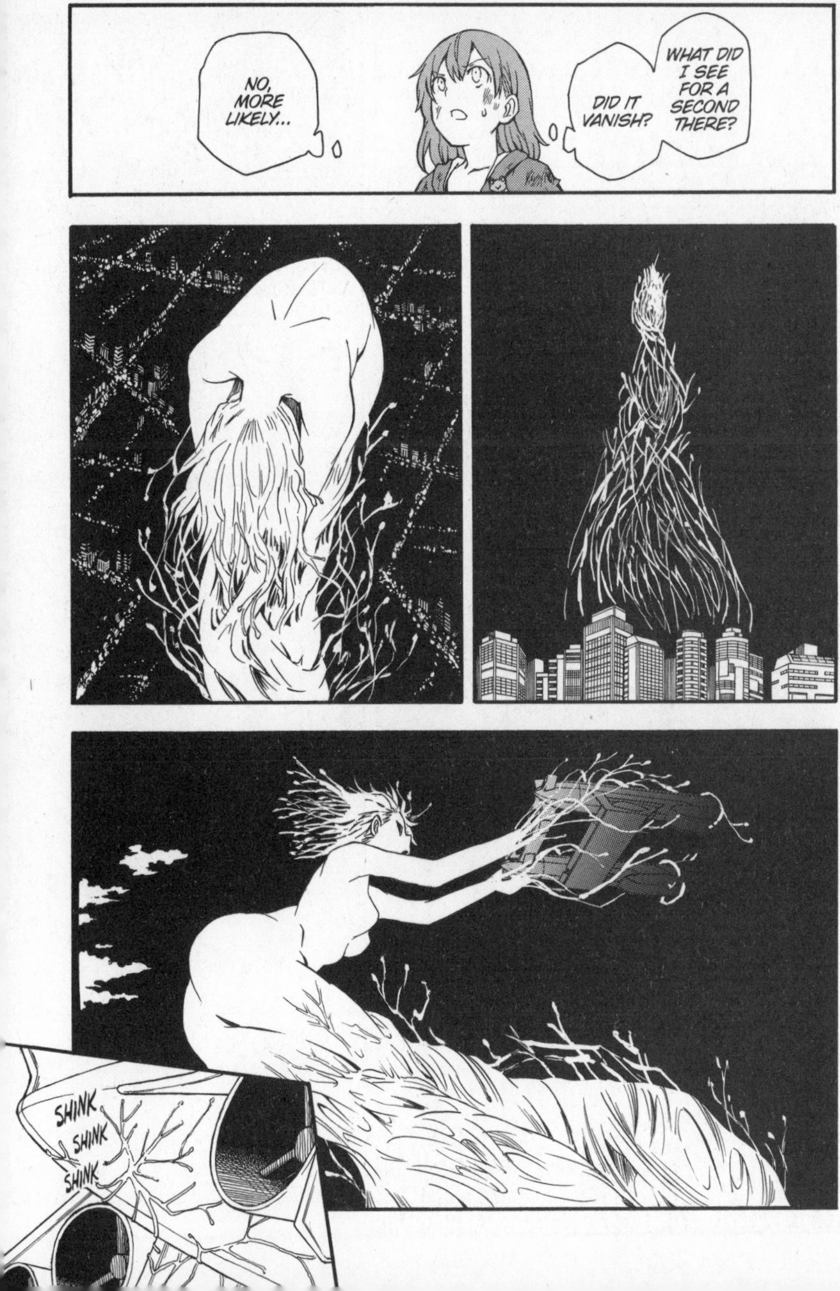
WHAT DID I SEE FOR A SECOND THERE?
DID IT VANISH?
NO, MORE LIKELY...
SHINK
SHINK
SHINK

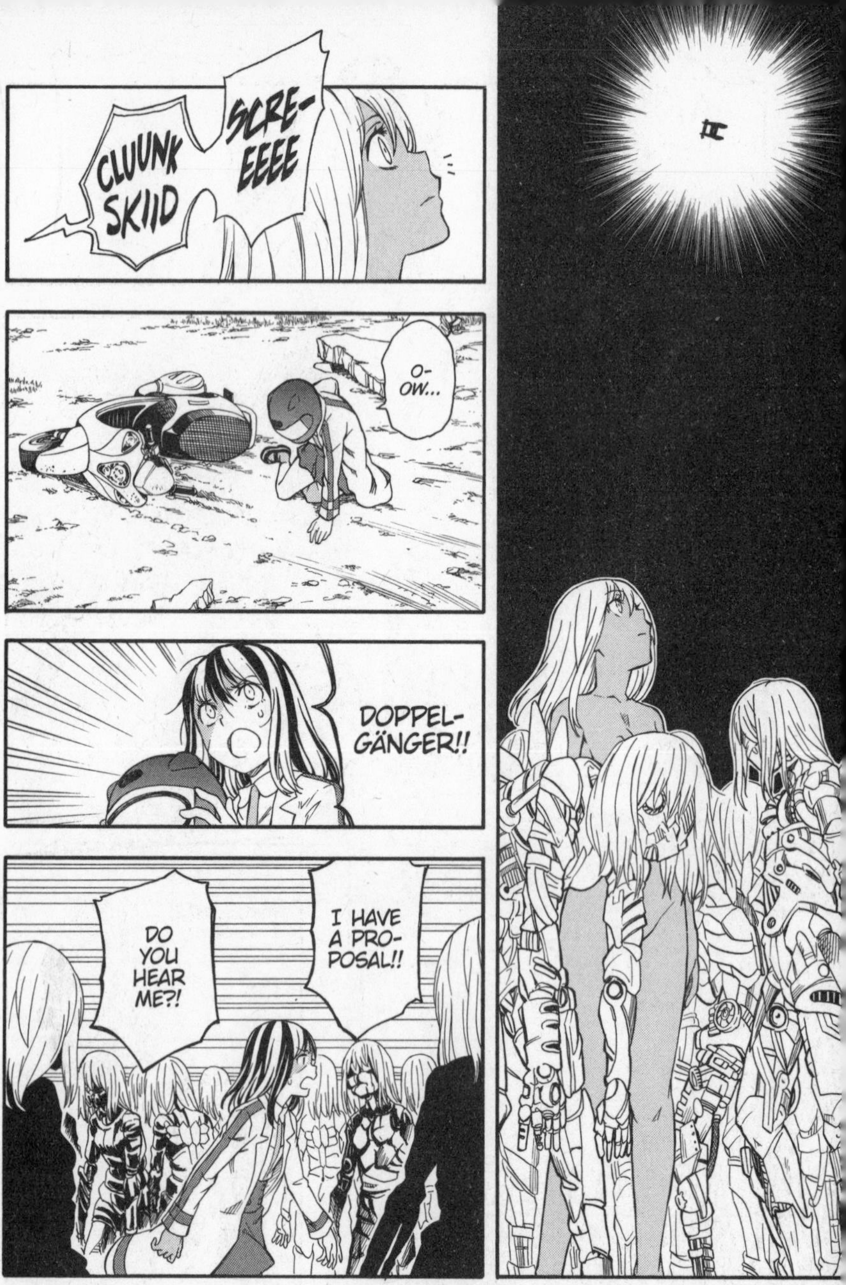
SCRE-
EEEE
CLUUNK
SKIID
O-
OW...
DOPPEL-
GÄNGER!!
I HAVE
A PRO-
POSAL!!
DO
YOU
HEAR
ME?!

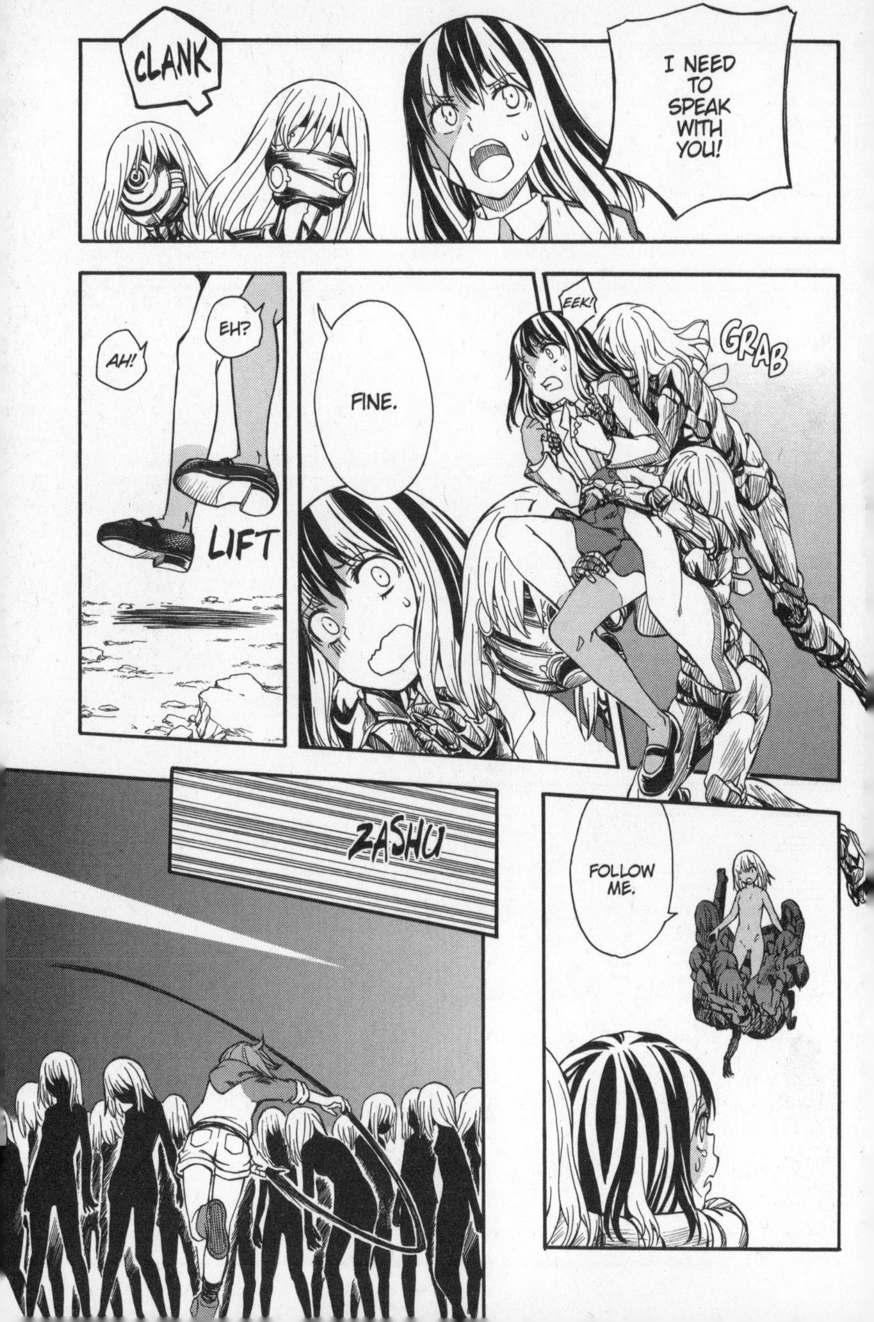
I NEED TO SPEAK WITH YOU!
CLANK
EEK!
GRAB
FINE.
EH?
AH!
LIFT
FOLLOW ME.
ZASHU

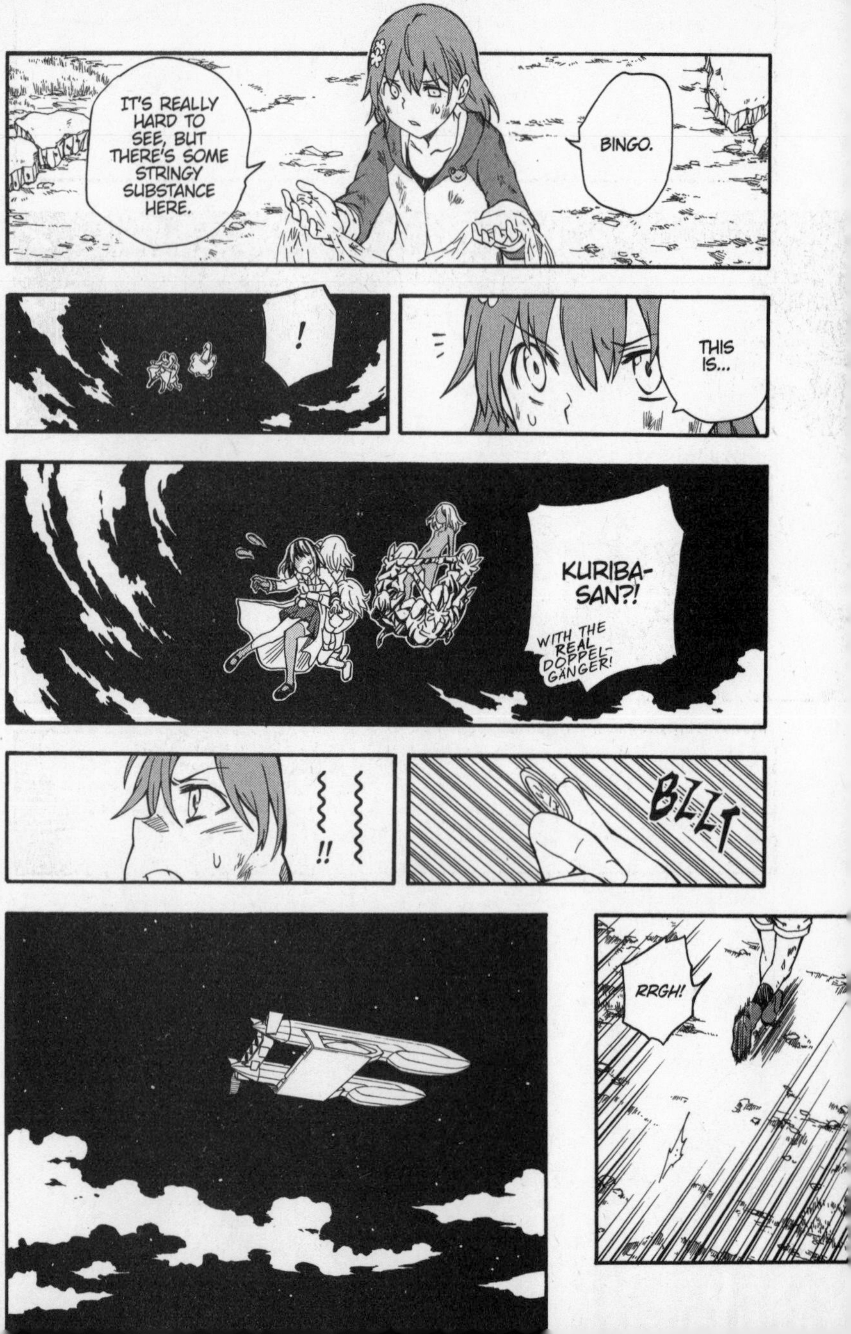
BINGO.
IT'S REALLY HARD TO SEE, BUT THERE'S SOME STRINGY SUBSTANCE HERE.
THIS IS...
!
KURIBA-SAN?!
WITH THE REAL DOPPEL-GÄNGER!
BZZT
!!
RRGH!

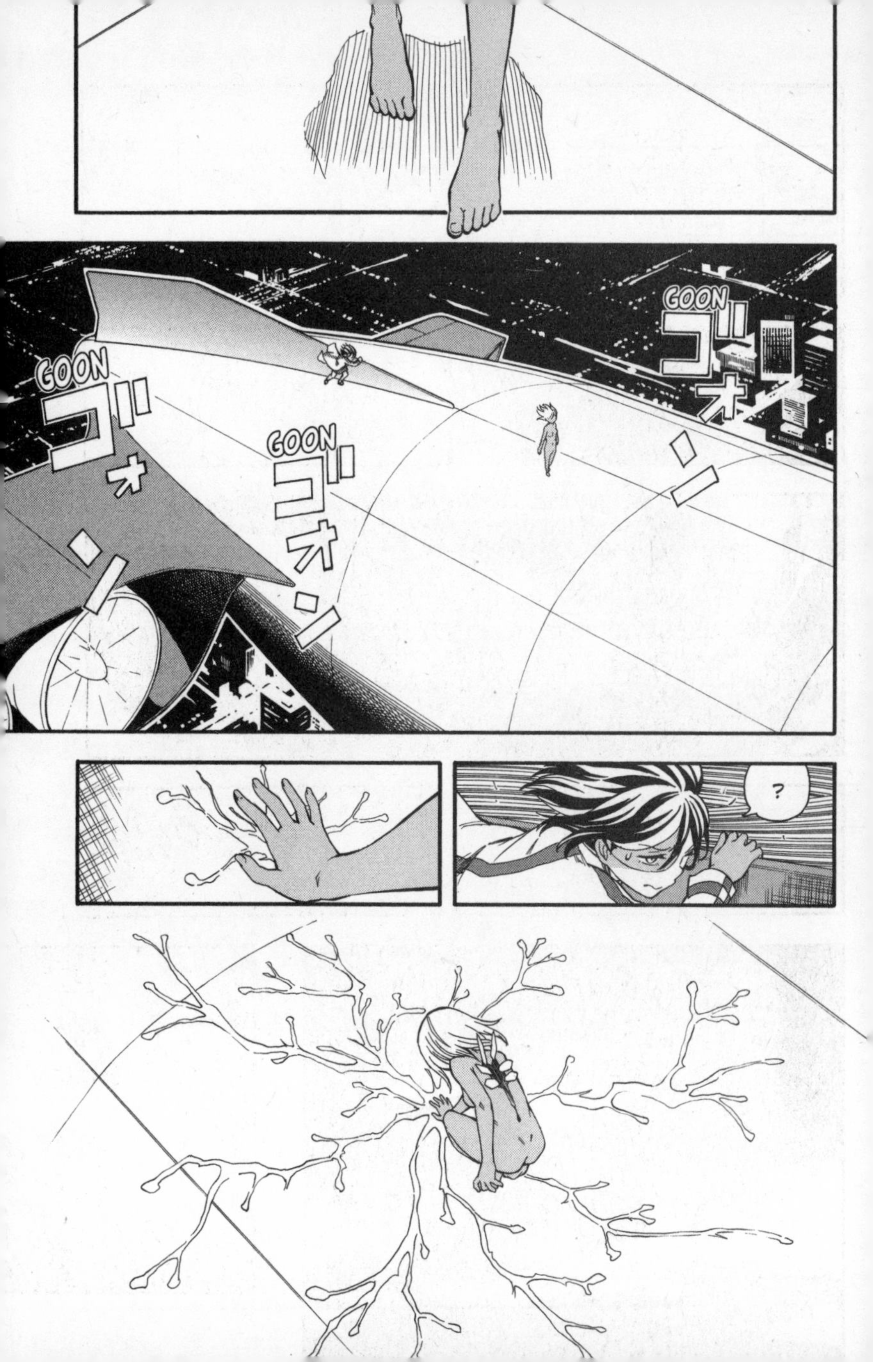
GOON
ゴォーン
GOON
ゴォーン
GOON
ゴォーン
?

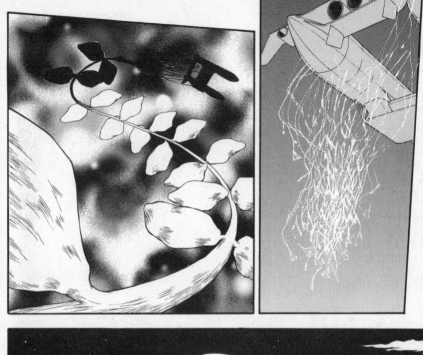

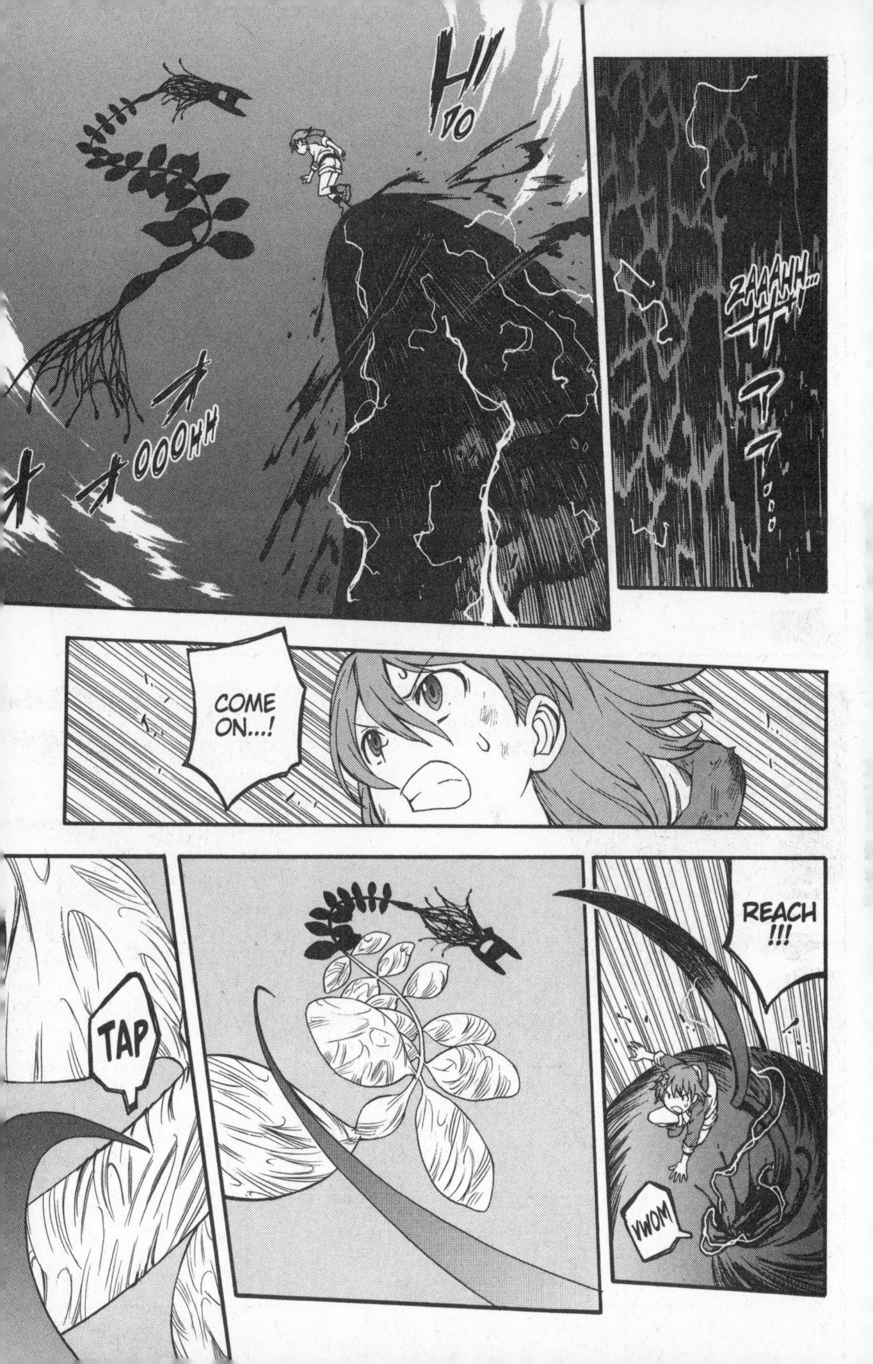
ZAAAHH...
OOOHH
COME ON...!
REACH !!!
VWOM
TAP

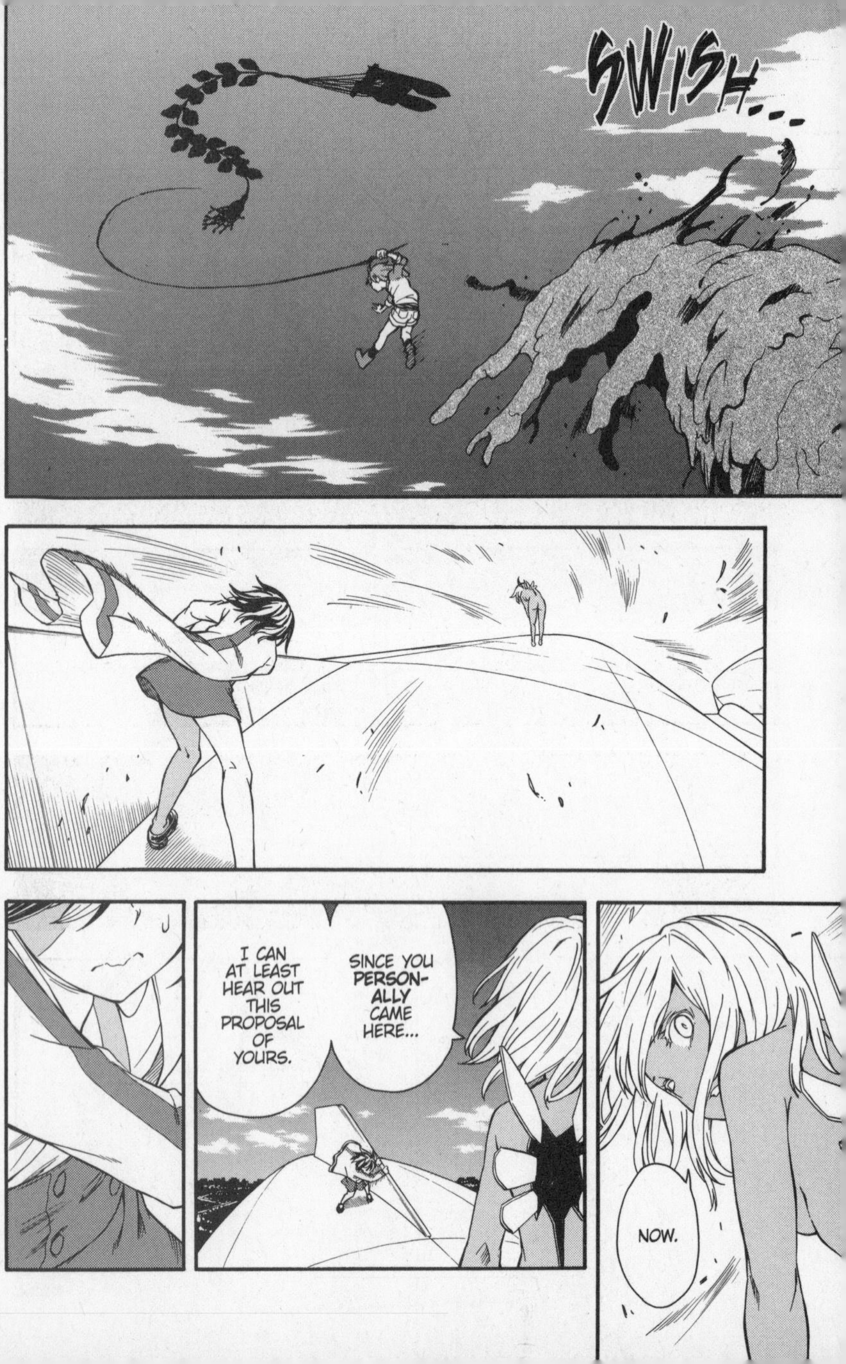
SWISH...
SINCE YOU PERSON-ALLY CAME HERE...
I CAN AT LEAST HEAR OUT THIS PROPOSAL OF YOURS.
NOW.

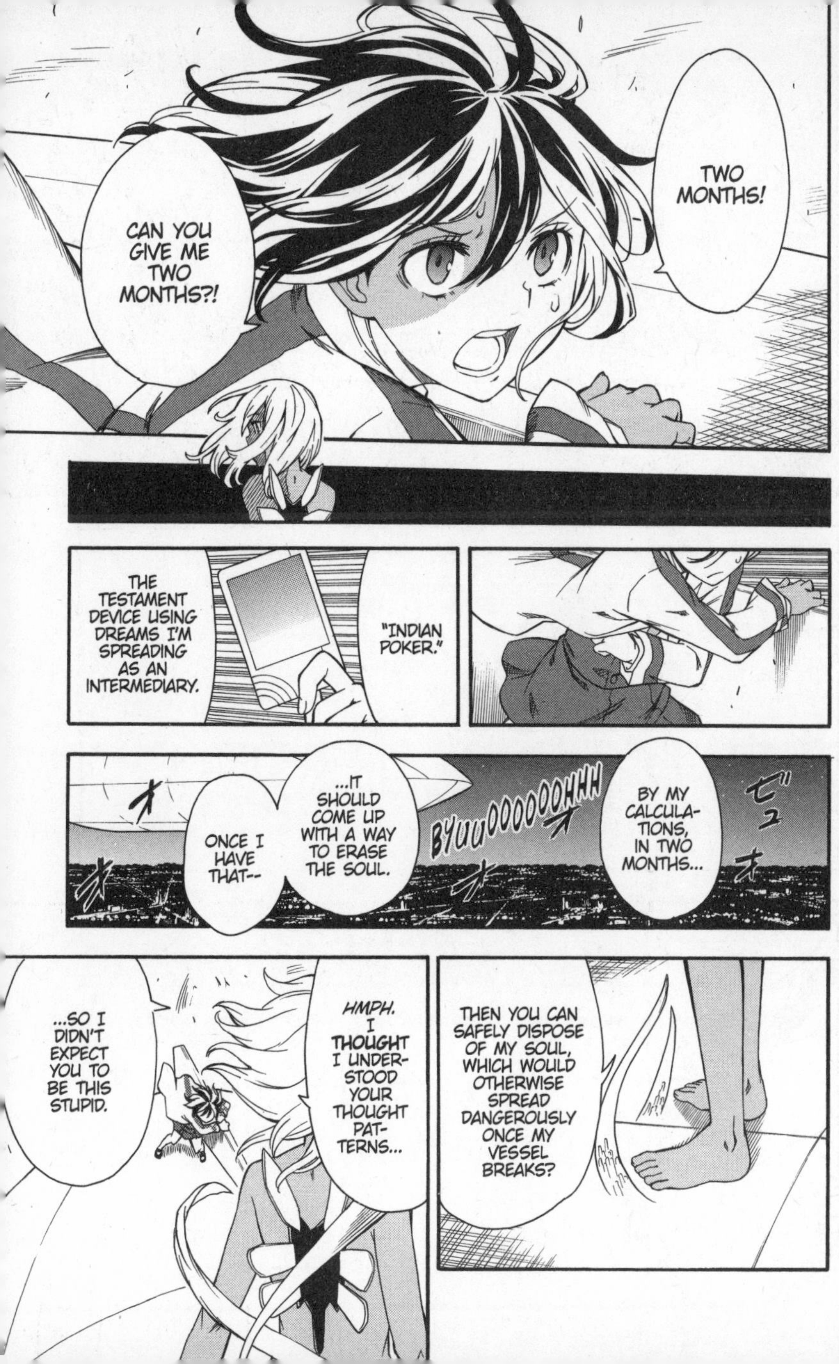
TWO MONTHS!
CAN YOU GIVE ME TWO MONTHS?!
"INDIAN POKER."
THE TESTAMENT DEVICE USING DREAMS I'M SPREADING AS AN INTERMEDIARY.
BY MY CALCULATIONS, IN TWO MONTHS...
BYUUOOOOOOOHHH
...IT SHOULD COME UP WITH A WAY TO ERASE THE SOUL.
ONCE I HAVE THAT--
THEN YOU CAN SAFELY DISPOSE OF MY SOUL, WHICH WOULD OTHERWISE SPREAD DANGEROUSLY ONCE MY VESSEL BREAKS?
HMPH. I THOUGHT I UNDERSTOOD YOUR THOUGHT PATTERNS...
...SO I DIDN'T EXPECT YOU TO BE THIS STUPID.

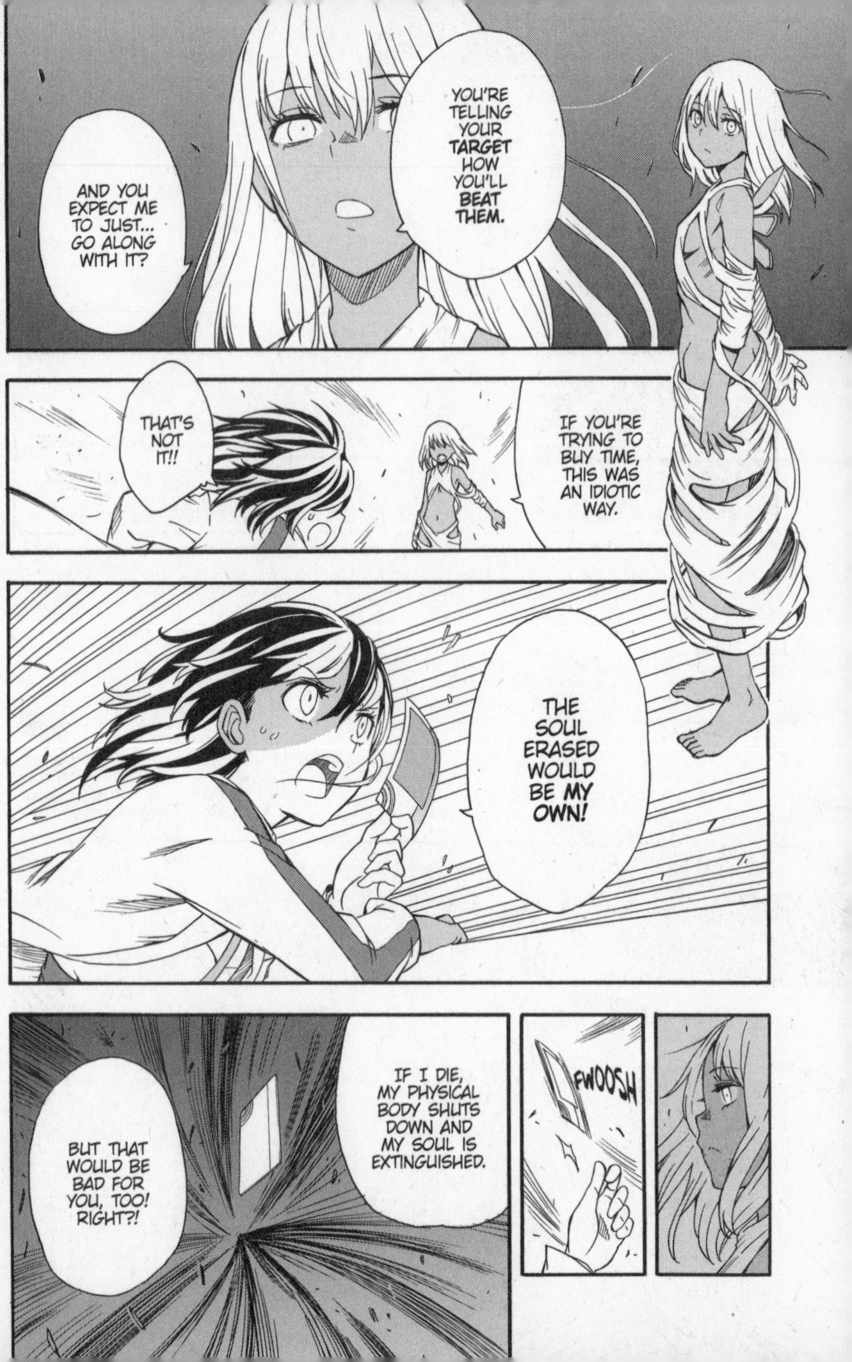

YOU'RE TELLING YOUR TARGET HOW YOU'LL BEAT THEM.
AND YOU EXPECT ME TO JUST... GO ALONG WITH IT?
IF YOU'RE TRYING TO BUY TIME, THIS WAS AN IDIOTIC WAY.
THAT'S NOT IT!!
THE SOUL ERASED WOULD BE MY OWN!
FWOOSH
IF I DIE, MY PHYSICAL BODY SHUTS DOWN AND MY SOUL IS EXTINGUISHED.
BUT THAT WOULD BE BAD FOR YOU, TOO! RIGHT?!

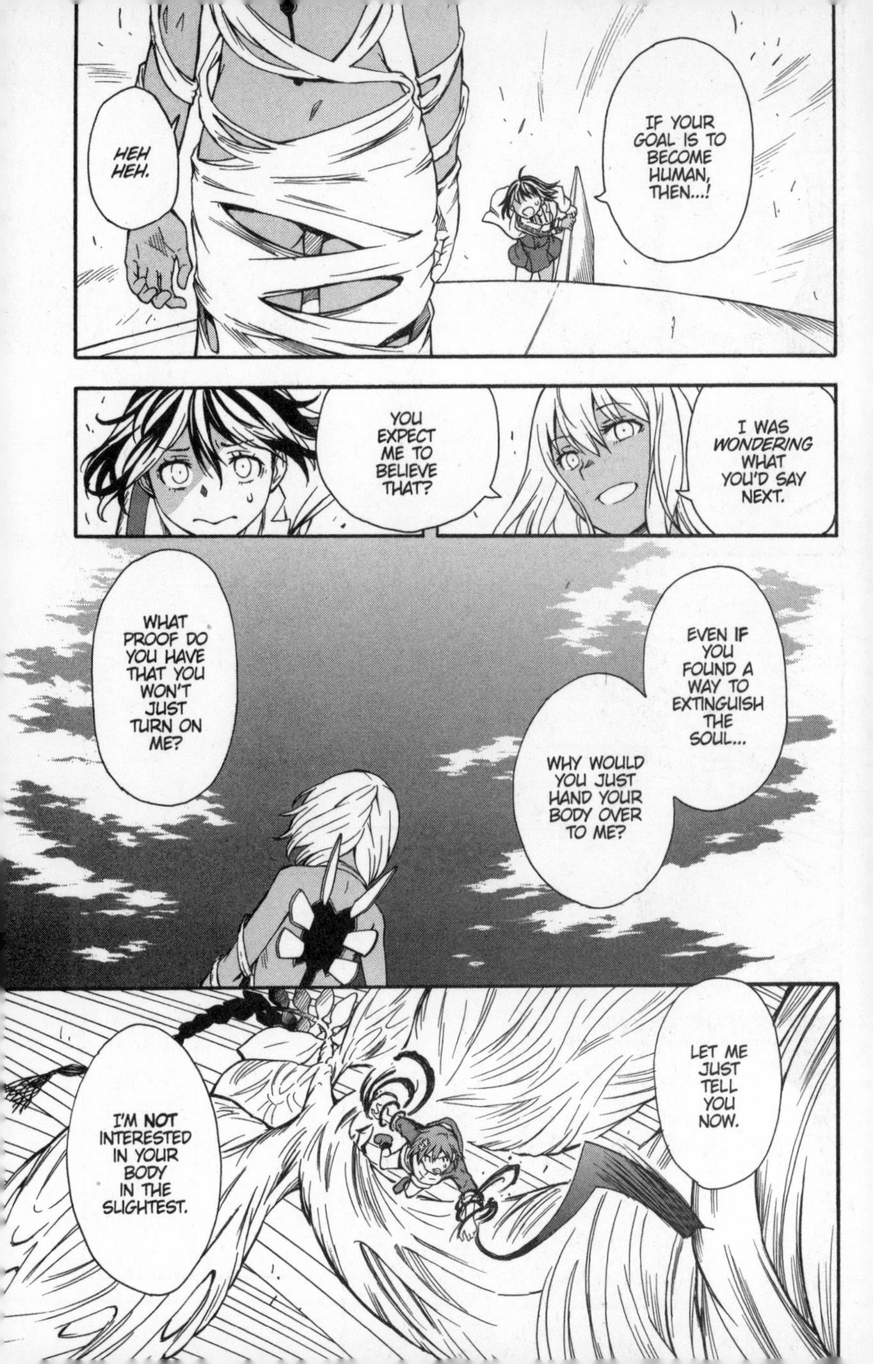
IF YOUR GOAL IS TO BECOME HUMAN, THEN...!
HEH HEH.
I WAS *WONDERING* WHAT YOU'D SAY NEXT.
YOU EXPECT ME TO BELIEVE THAT?
EVEN IF YOU FOUND A WAY TO EXTINGUISH THE SOUL...
WHY WOULD YOU JUST HAND YOUR BODY OVER TO ME?
WHAT PROOF DO YOU HAVE THAT YOU WON'T JUST TURN ON ME?
LET ME JUST TELL YOU NOW.
I'M **NOT** INTERESTED IN YOUR BODY IN THE SLIGHTEST.

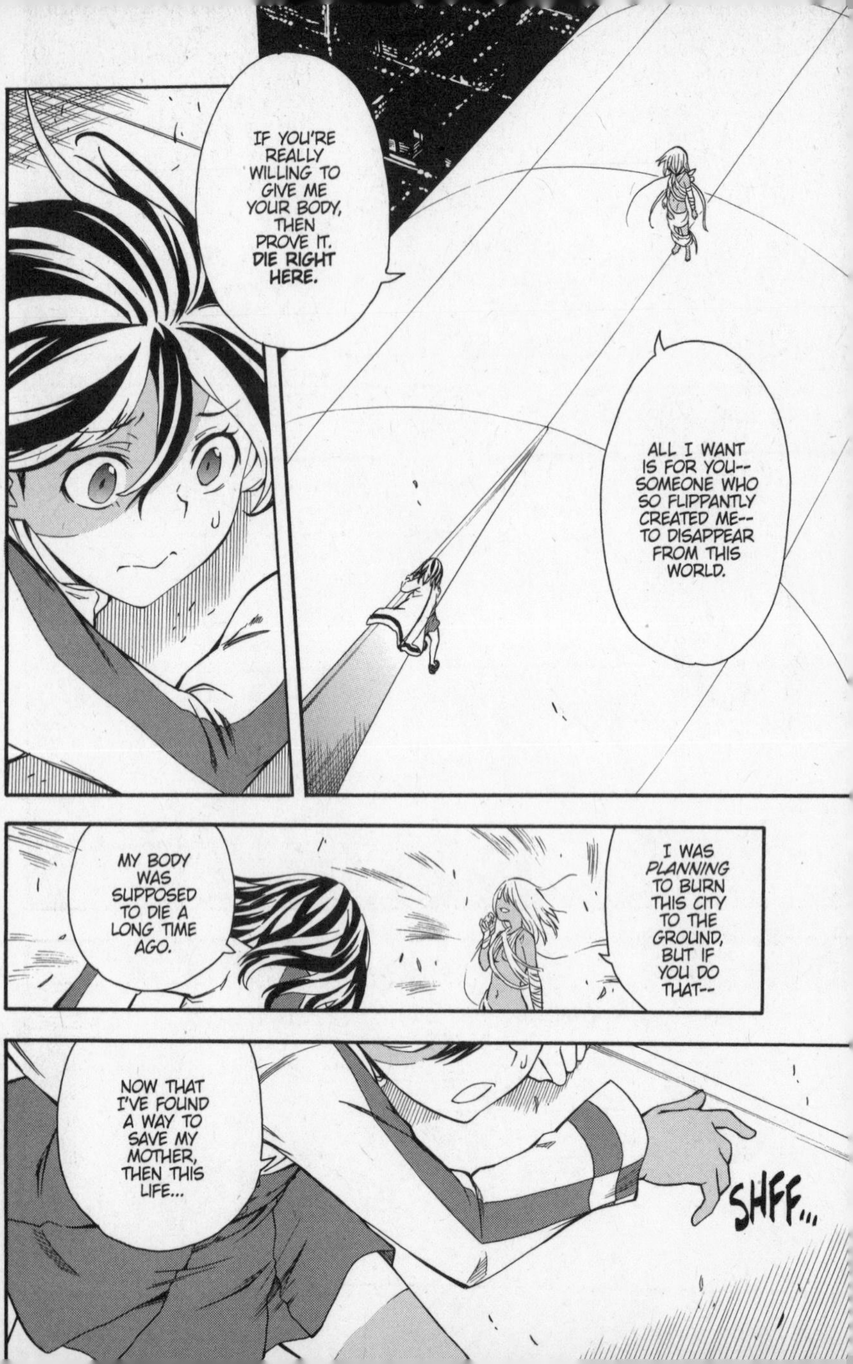
ALL I WANT IS FOR YOU-- SOMEONE WHO SO FLIPPANTLY CREATED ME-- TO DISAPPEAR FROM THIS WORLD.
IF YOU'RE REALLY WILLING TO GIVE ME YOUR BODY, THEN PROVE IT. DIE RIGHT HERE.
I WAS *PLANNING* TO BURN THIS CITY TO THE GROUND, BUT IF YOU DO THAT--
MY BODY WAS SUPPOSED TO DIE A LONG TIME AGO.
NOW THAT I'VE FOUND A WAY TO SAVE MY MOTHER, THEN THIS LIFE...
SHFF...

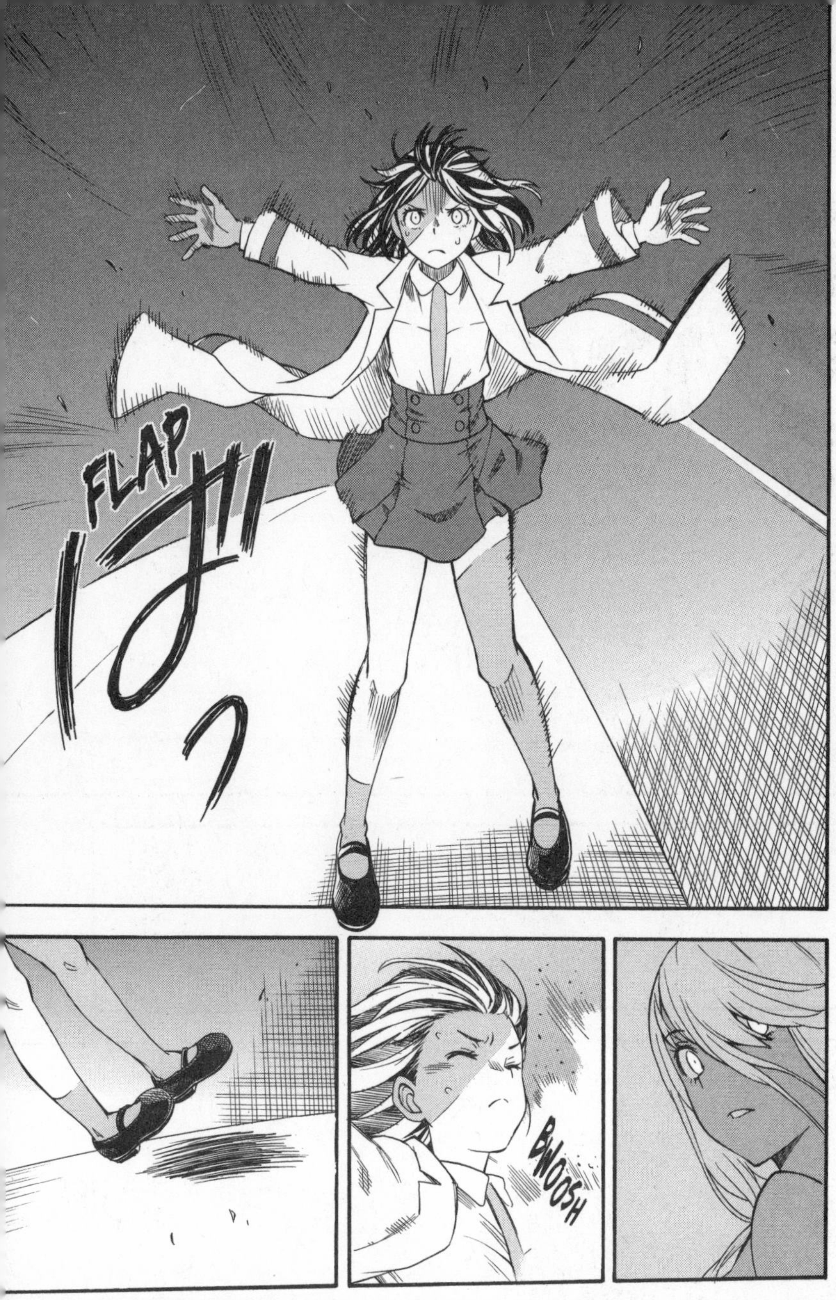
FLAP
ばっ
BWOOSH

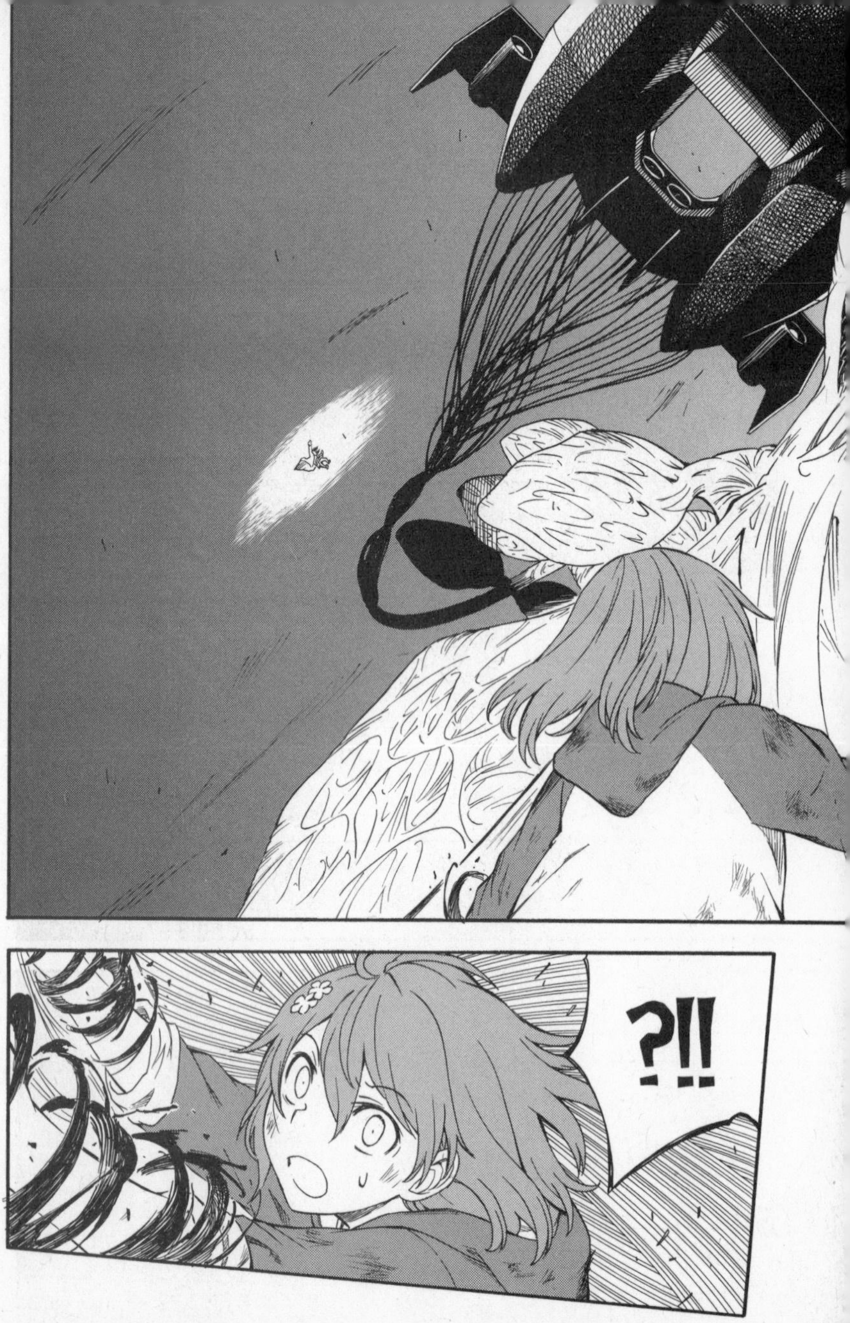
?!!

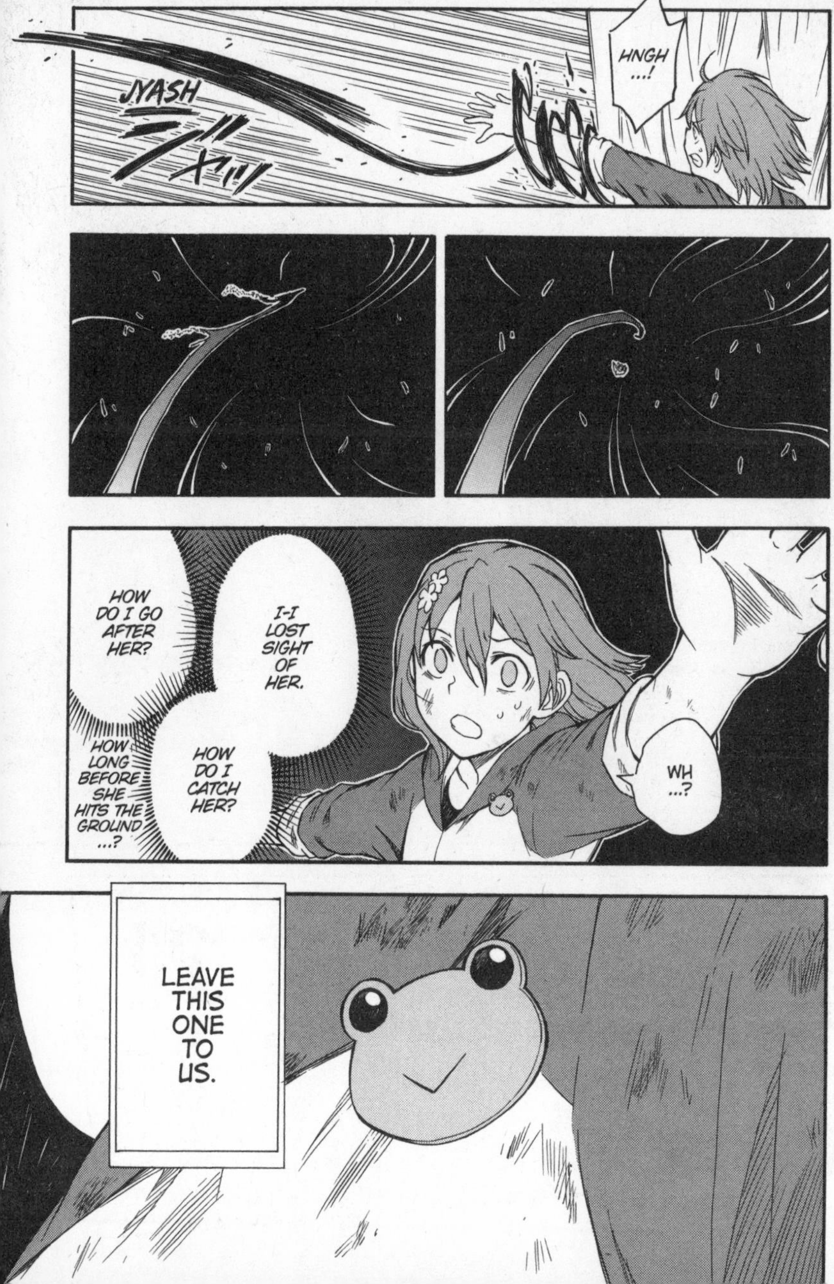
HNGH ...!
JYASH
WH ...?
I-I LOST SIGHT OF HER.
HOW DO I GO AFTER HER?
HOW DO I CATCH HER?
HOW LONG BEFORE SHE HITS THE GROUND ...?
LEAVE THIS ONE TO US.

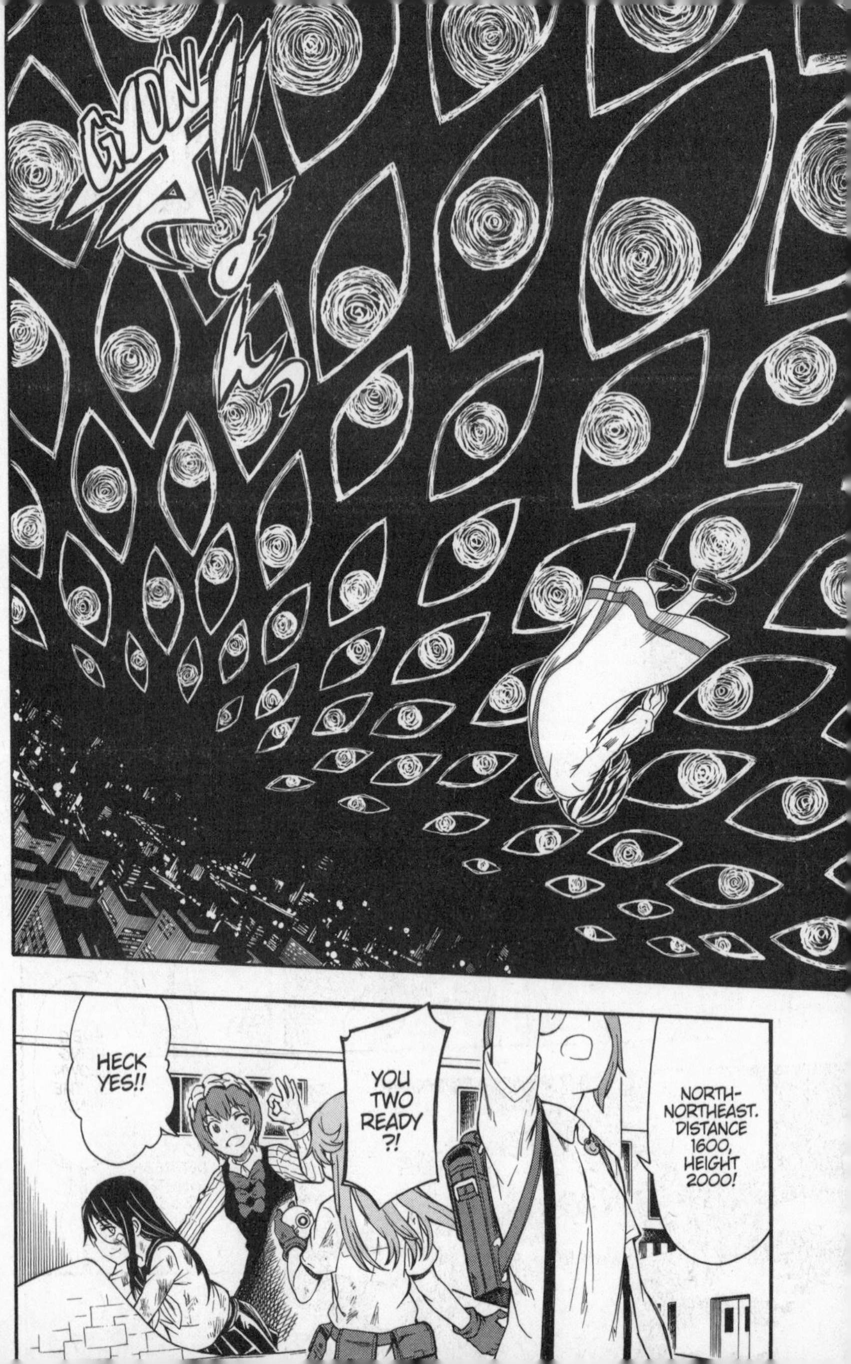
GYON
NORTH-NORTHEAST. DISTANCE 1600, HEIGHT 2000!
YOU TWO READY?!
HECK YES!!

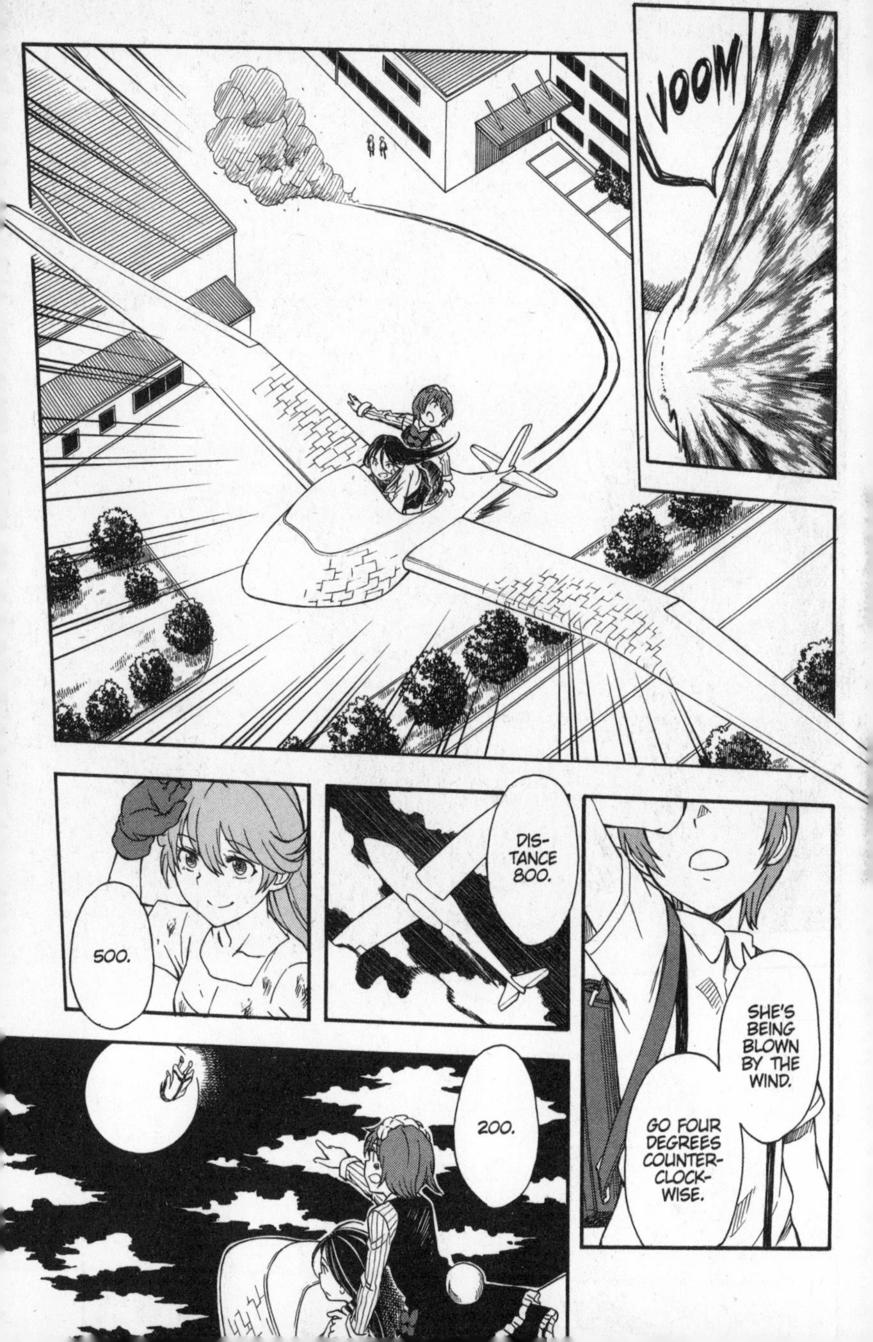
VOOM
DIS-TANCE 800.
500.
SHE'S BEING BLOWN BY THE WIND.
GO FOUR DEGREES COUNTER-CLOCK-WISE.
200.

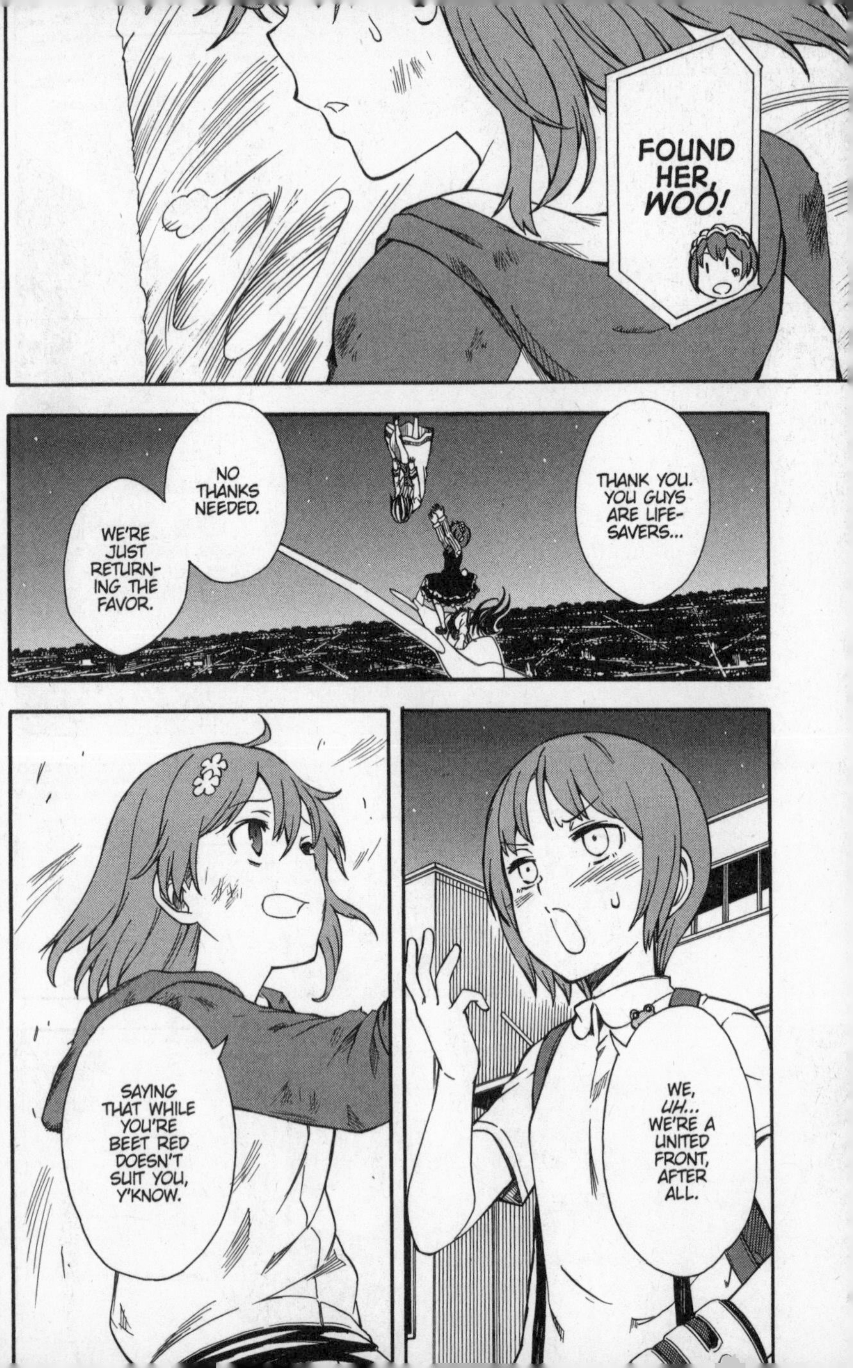
FOUND HER, WOO!
THANK YOU. YOU GUYS ARE LIFE-SAVERS...
NO THANKS NEEDED.
WE'RE JUST RETURNING THE FAVOR.
WE, UH... WE'RE A UNITED FRONT, AFTER ALL.
SAYING THAT WHILE YOU'RE BEET RED DOESN'T SUIT YOU, Y'KNOW.

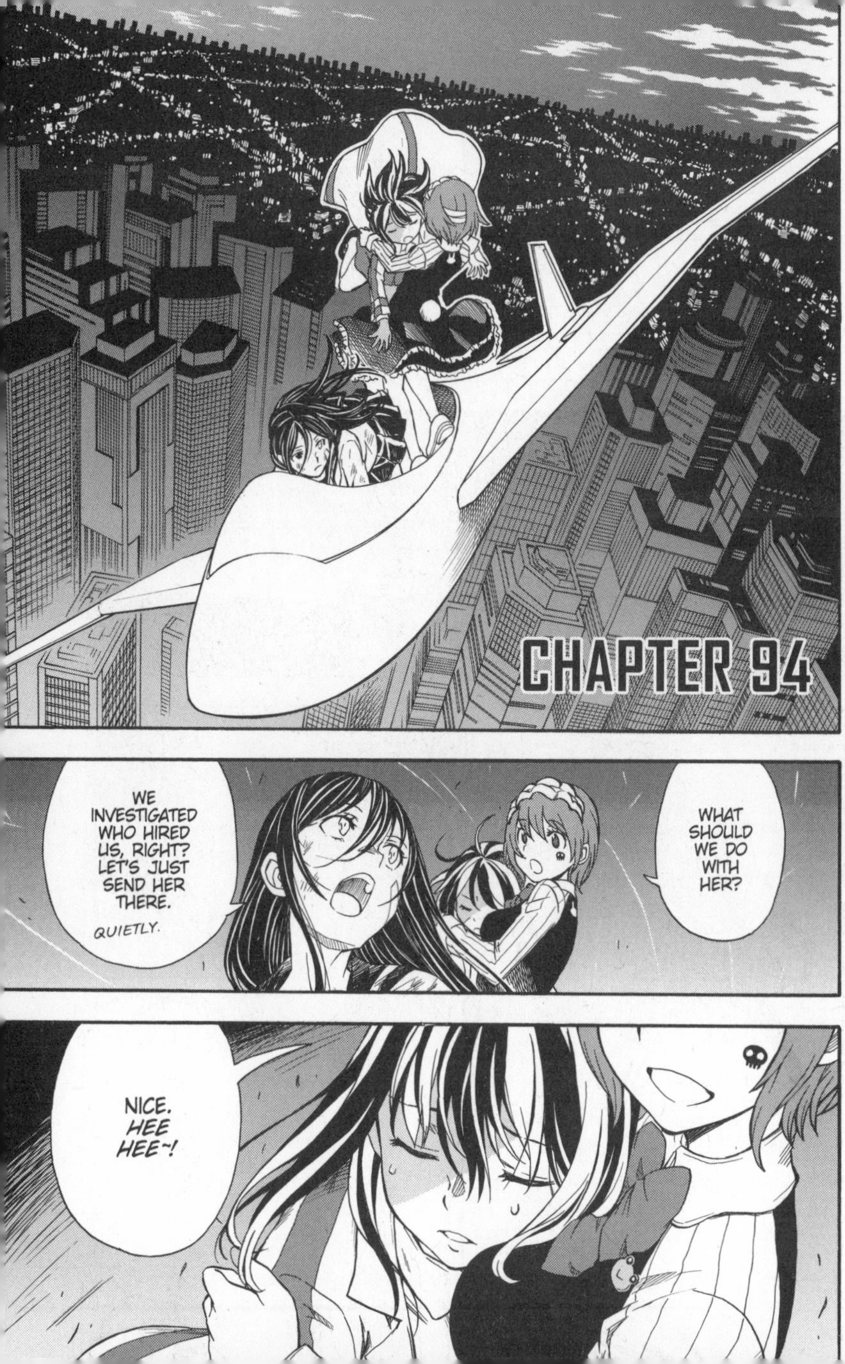
CHAPTER 94
WHAT SHOULD WE DO WITH HER?
WE INVESTIGATED WHO HIRED US, RIGHT? LET'S JUST SEND HER THERE.
QUIETLY.
NICE. HEE HEE~!

CHAPTER 94: CONJECTURE

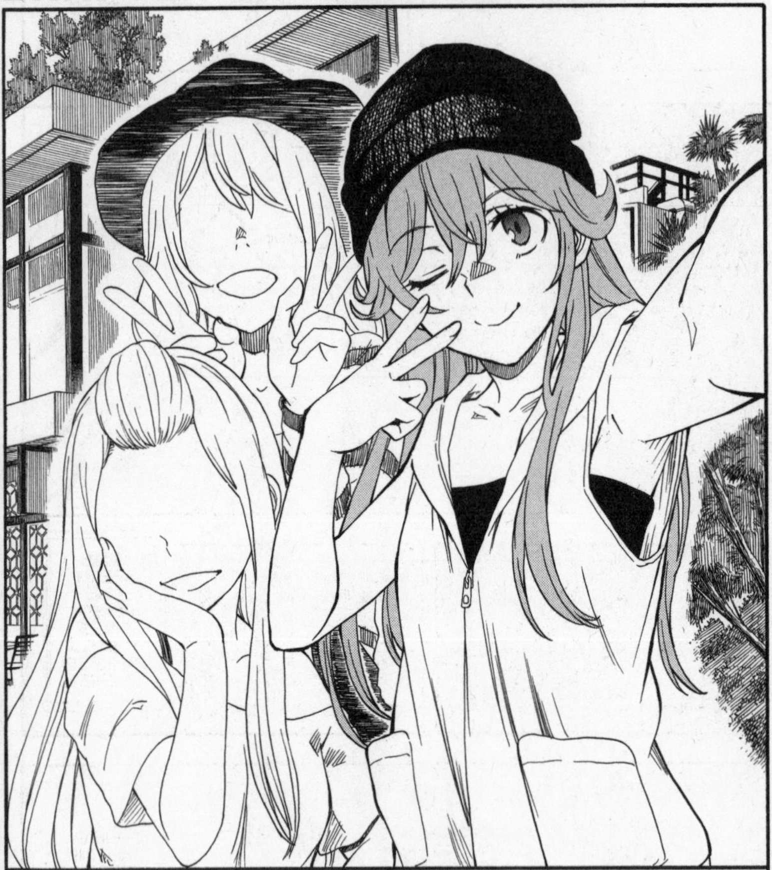

YAKUMARU

- Real name unknown. A girl who works with Scavenger and originates from the same facility as Leader and Naru.
- By manipulating specific gravity, she has the ability to separate liquids. She can then mix the separate components and produce various phenomena.
- She's fully aware of how attractive she is, and believes that it's a right of those born cute to use looks to their advantage.
- Since she's frequently pestered by guys asking her out or modeling scouts, she's resorted to wearing a giant hat--but has no qualms sporting twin tails or cat ears when necessary.

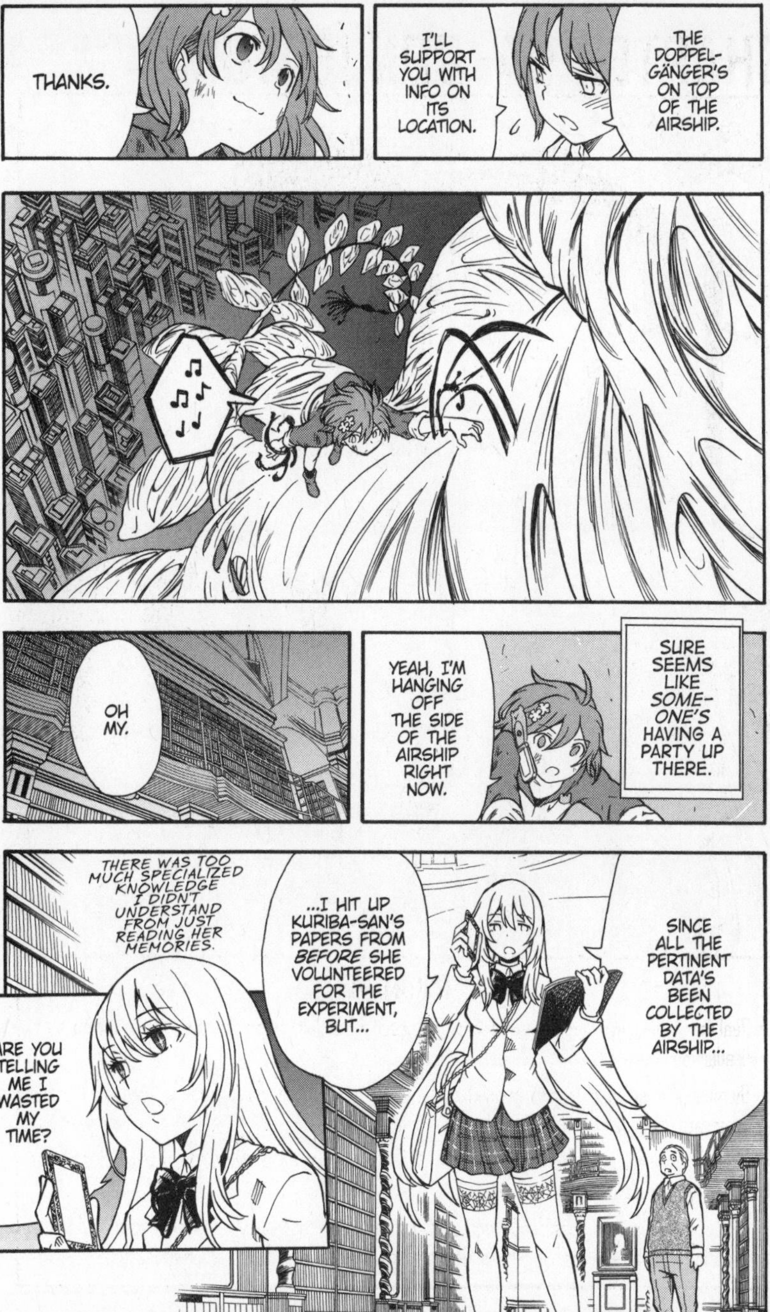
THE DOPPEL-GÄNGER'S ON TOP OF THE AIRSHIP.
I'LL SUPPORT YOU WITH INFO ON ITS LOCATION.
THANKS.
♫ ♫ ♪ ♩ ♩
SURE SEEMS LIKE *SOME-ONE'S* HAVING A PARTY UP THERE.
YEAH, I'M HANGING OFF THE SIDE OF THE AIRSHIP RIGHT NOW.
OH MY.
SINCE ALL THE PERTINENT DATA'S BEEN COLLECTED BY THE AIRSHIP...
...I HIT UP KURIBA-SAN'S PAPERS FROM *BEFORE* SHE VOLUNTEERED FOR THE EXPERIMENT, BUT...
THERE WAS TOO MUCH SPECIALIZED KNOWLEDGE I DIDN'T UNDERSTAND FROM JUST READING HER MEMORIES.
ARE YOU TELLING ME I WASTED MY TIME?

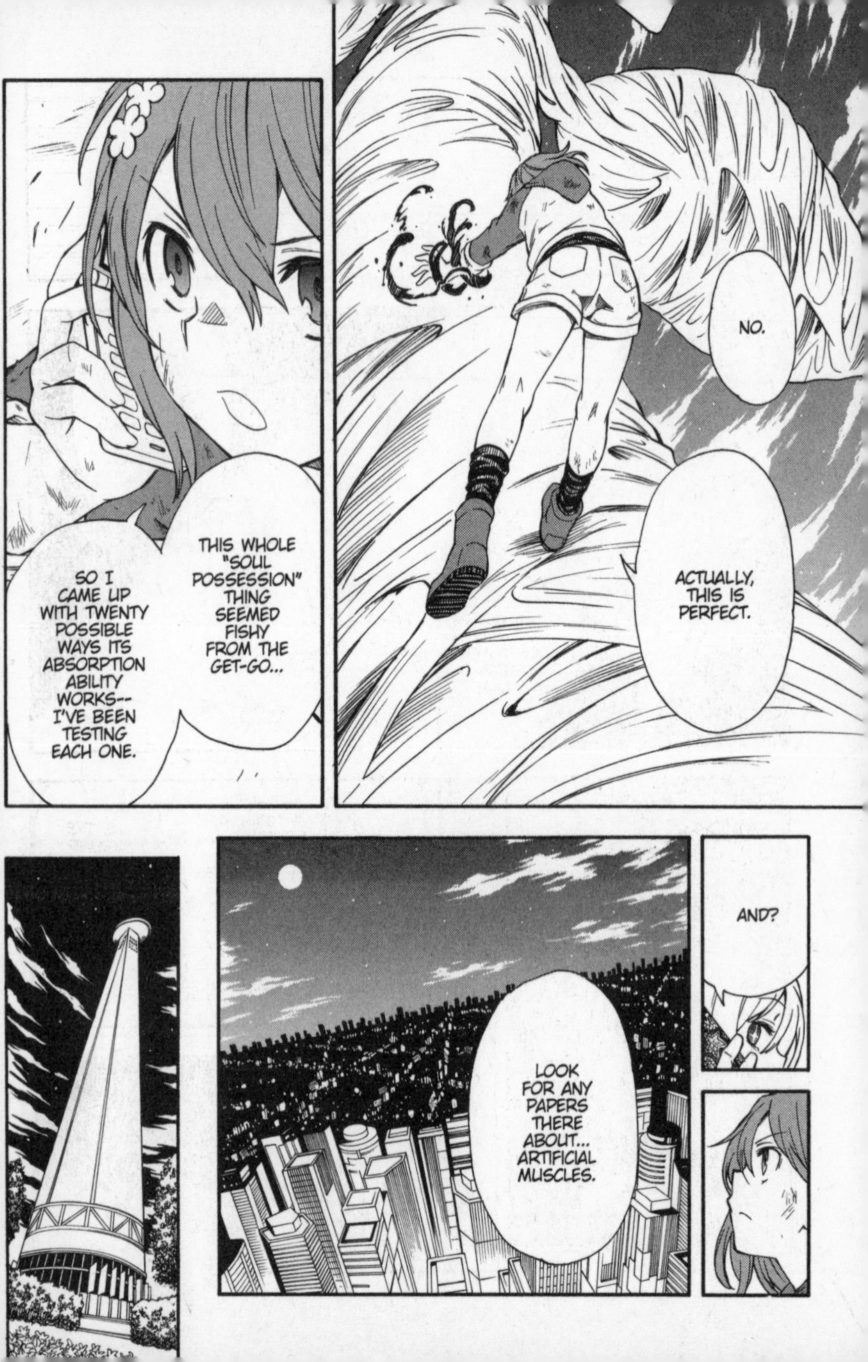
NO.
ACTUALLY, THIS IS PERFECT.
THIS WHOLE "SOUL POSSESSION" THING SEEMED FISHY FROM THE GET-GO...
SO I CAME UP WITH TWENTY POSSIBLE WAYS ITS ABSORPTION ABILITY WORKS-- I'VE BEEN TESTING EACH ONE.
AND?
LOOK FOR ANY PAPERS THERE ABOUT... ARTIFICIAL MUSCLES.

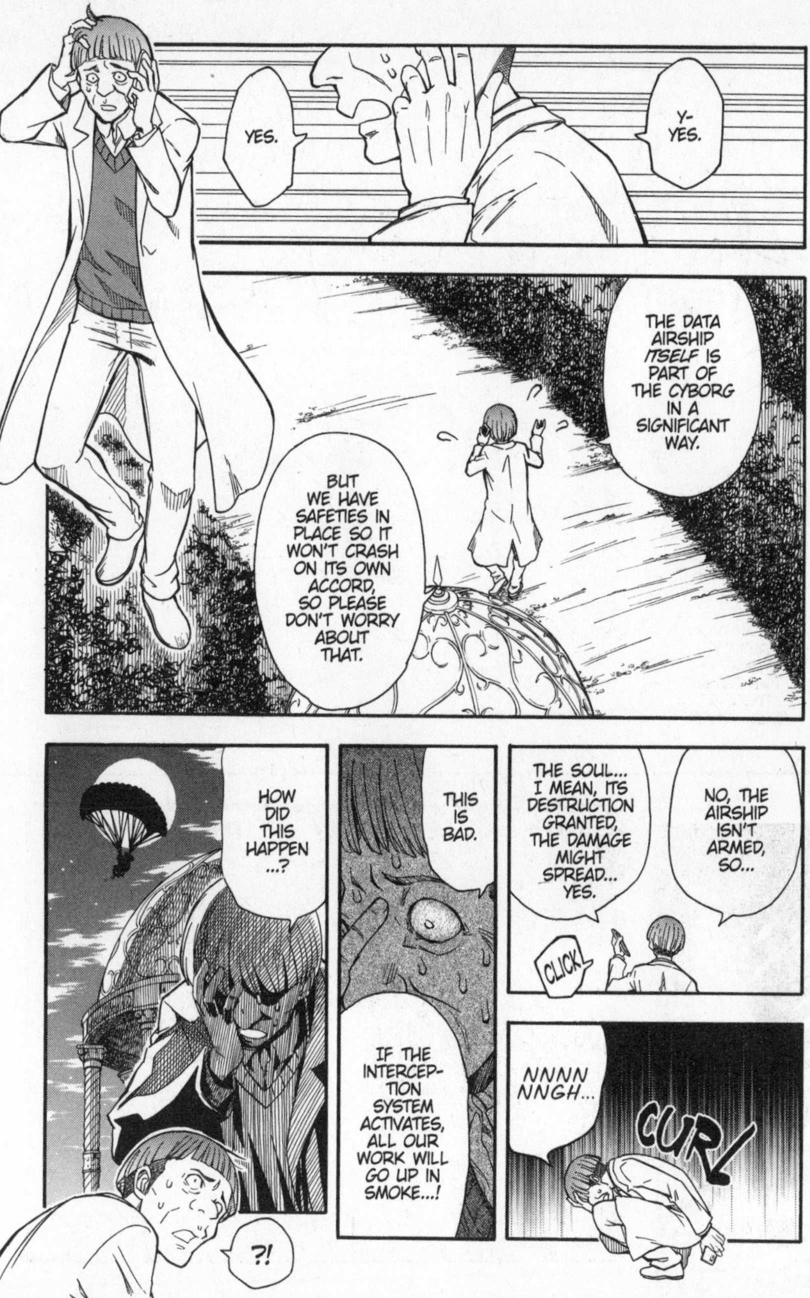
Y-
YES.
YES.
THE DATA AIRSHIP *ITSELF* IS PART OF THE CYBORG IN A SIGNIFICANT WAY.
BUT WE HAVE SAFETIES IN PLACE SO IT WON'T CRASH ON ITS OWN ACCORD, SO PLEASE DON'T WORRY ABOUT THAT.
NO, THE AIRSHIP ISN'T ARMED, SO...
THE SOUL... I MEAN, ITS DESTRUCTION GRANTED, THE DAMAGE MIGHT SPREAD... YES.
CLICK
THIS IS BAD.
IF THE INTERCEP-TION SYSTEM ACTIVATES, ALL OUR WORK WILL GO UP IN SMOKE...!
HOW DID THIS HAPPEN ...?
NNNN NNGH...
CUR
?!

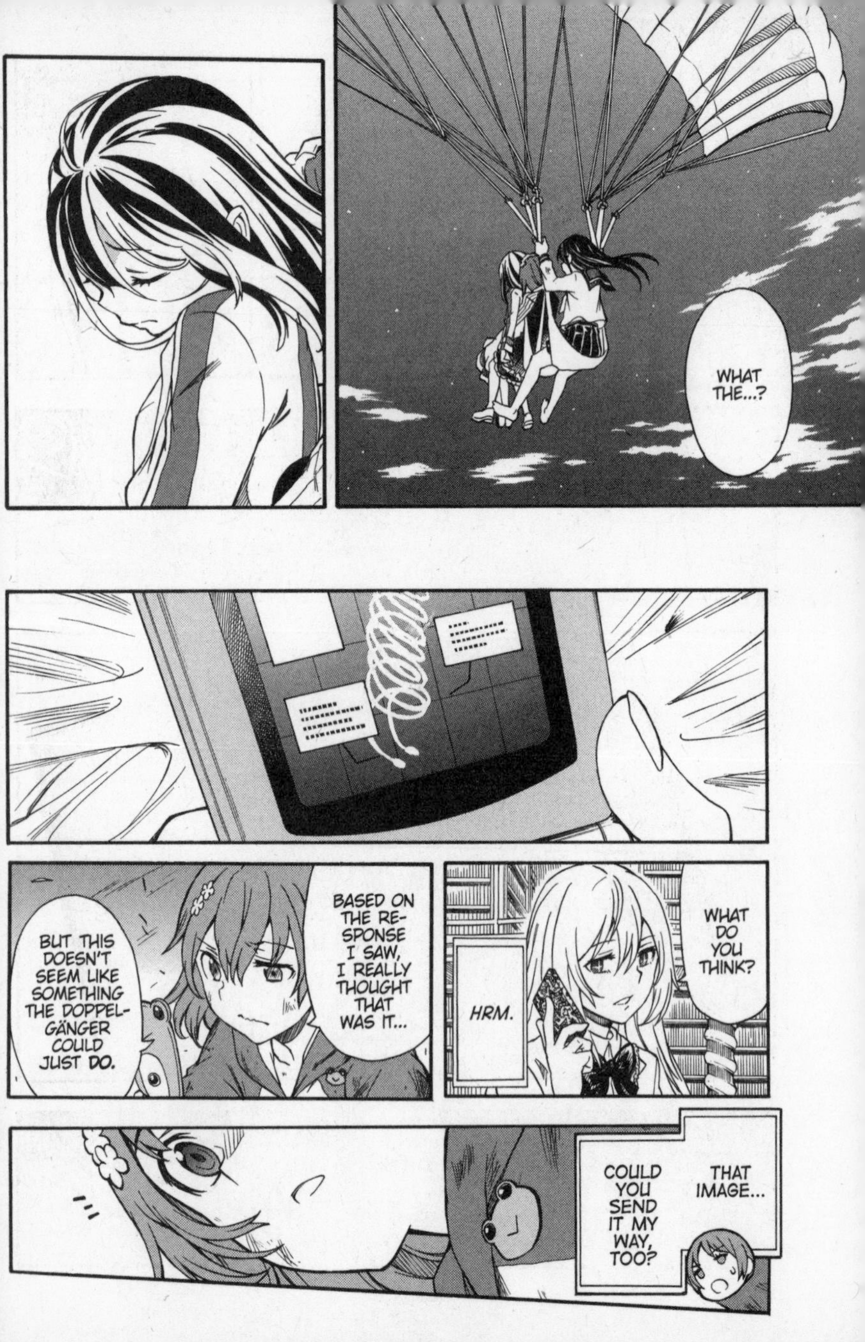
WHAT THE...?
WHAT DO YOU THINK?
HRM.
BASED ON THE RE-SPONSE I SAW, I REALLY THOUGHT THAT WAS IT...
BUT THIS DOESN'T SEEM LIKE SOMETHING THE DOPPEL-GÄNGER COULD JUST DO.
THAT IMAGE...
COULD YOU SEND IT MY WAY, TOO?

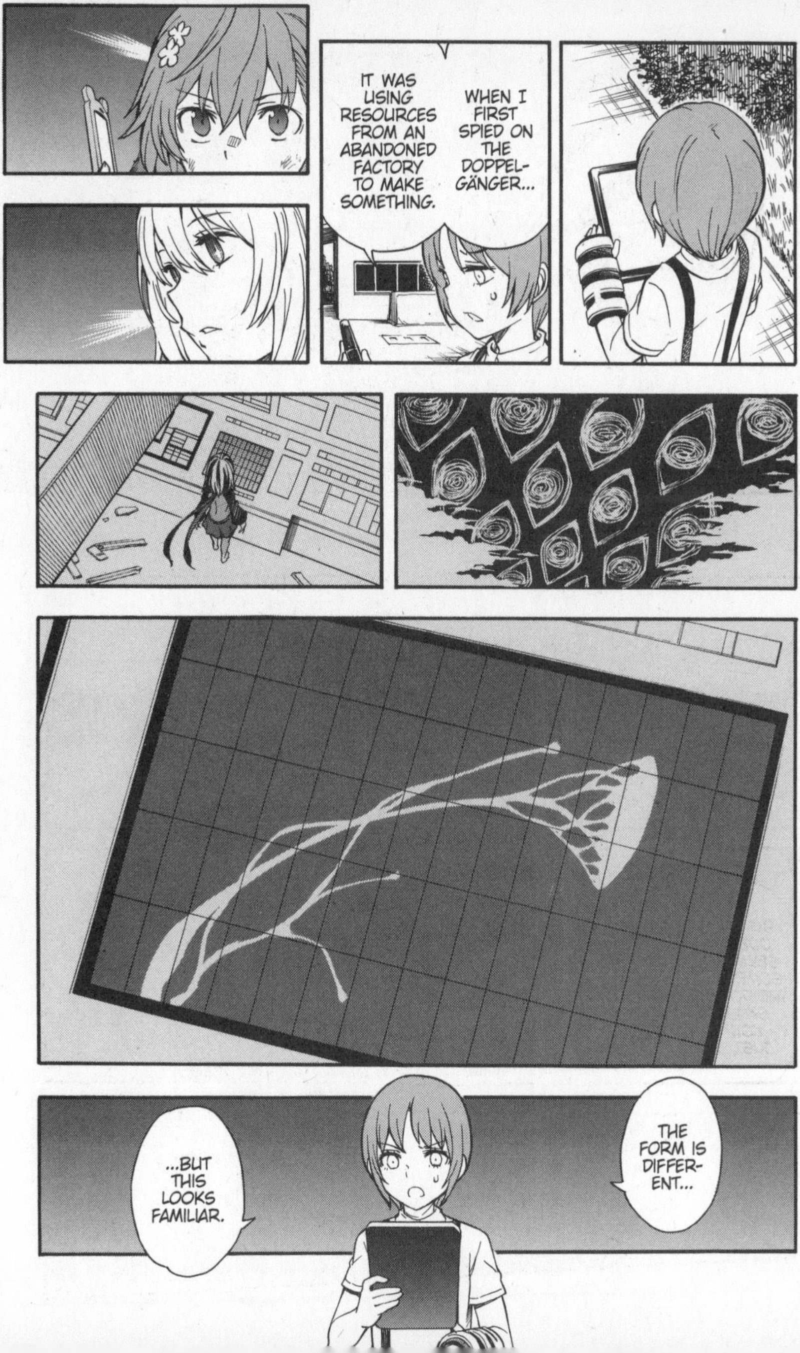
WHEN I FIRST SPIED ON THE DOPPEL-GÄNGER...
IT WAS USING RESOURCES FROM AN ABANDONED FACTORY TO MAKE SOMETHING.
THE FORM IS DIFFER-ENT...
...BUT THIS LOOKS FAMILIAR.

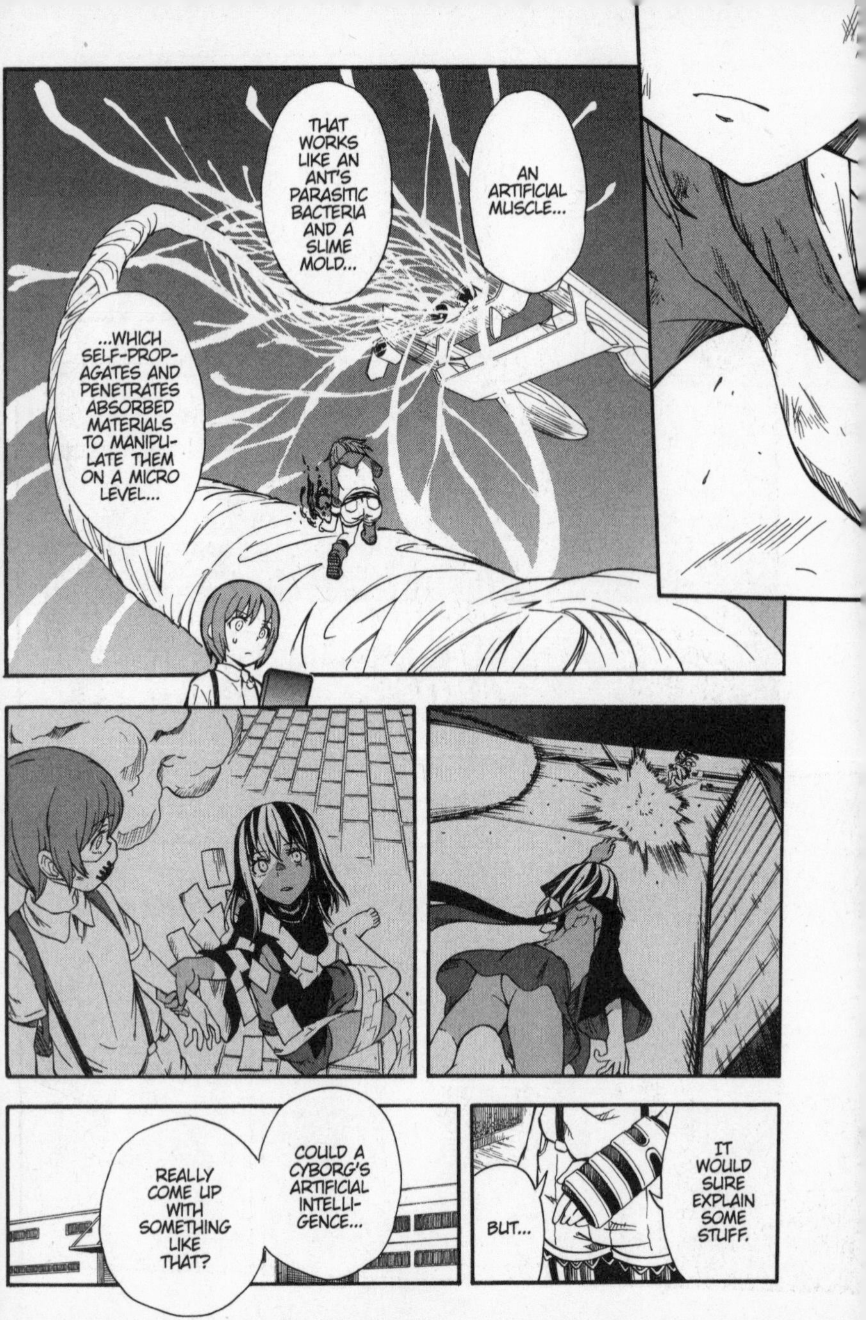
AN ARTIFICIAL MUSCLE...
THAT WORKS LIKE AN ANT'S PARASITIC BACTERIA AND A SLIME MOLD...
...WHICH SELF-PROPAGATES AND PENETRATES ABSORBED MATERIALS TO MANIPULATE THEM ON A MICRO LEVEL...
IT WOULD SURE EXPLAIN SOME STUFF.
BUT...
COULD A CYBORG'S ARTIFICIAL INTELLIGENCE...
REALLY COME UP WITH SOMETHING LIKE THAT?

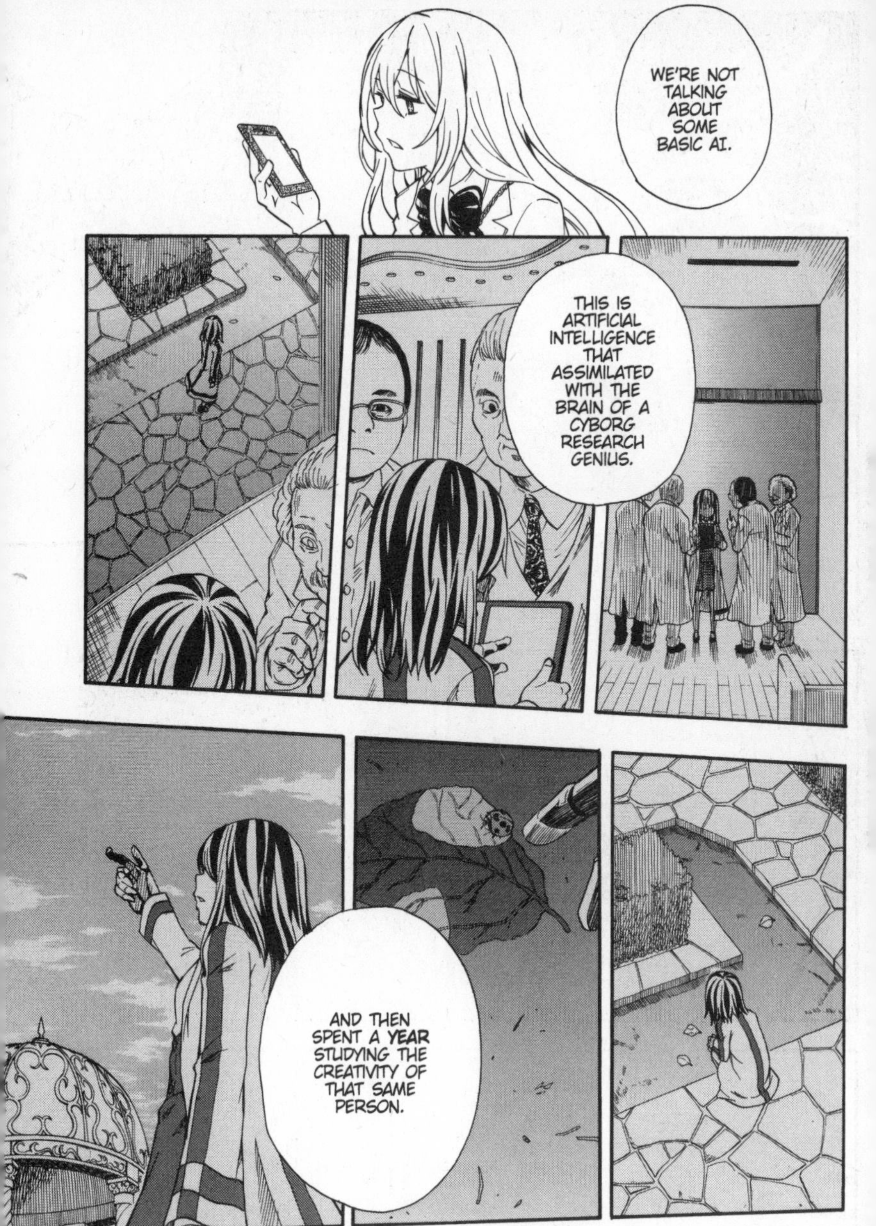
WE'RE NOT TALKING ABOUT SOME BASIC AI.
THIS IS ARTIFICIAL INTELLIGENCE THAT ASSIMILATED WITH THE BRAIN OF A CYBORG RESEARCH GENIUS.
AND THEN SPENT A **YEAR** STUDYING THE CREATIVITY OF THAT SAME PERSON.

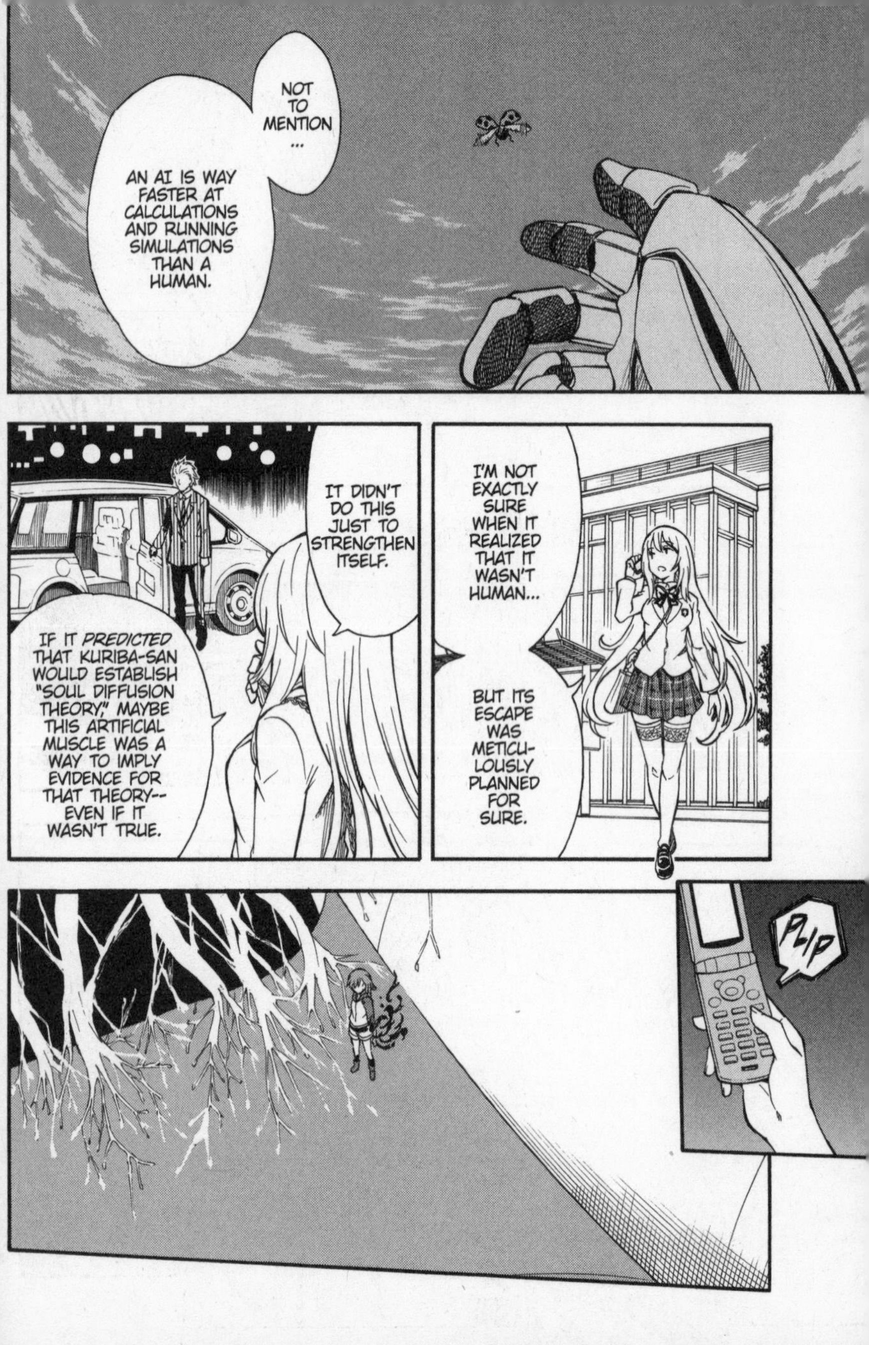
NOT TO MENTION...
AN AI IS WAY FASTER AT CALCULATIONS AND RUNNING SIMULATIONS THAN A HUMAN.
I'M NOT EXACTLY SURE WHEN IT REALIZED THAT IT WASN'T HUMAN...
BUT ITS ESCAPE WAS METICULOUSLY PLANNED FOR SURE.
IT DIDN'T DO THIS JUST TO STRENGTHEN ITSELF.
IF IT *PREDICTED* THAT KURIBA-SAN WOULD ESTABLISH "SOUL DIFFUSION THEORY," MAYBE THIS ARTIFICIAL MUSCLE WAS A WAY TO IMPLY EVIDENCE FOR THAT THEORY--EVEN IF IT WASN'T TRUE.
PLIP

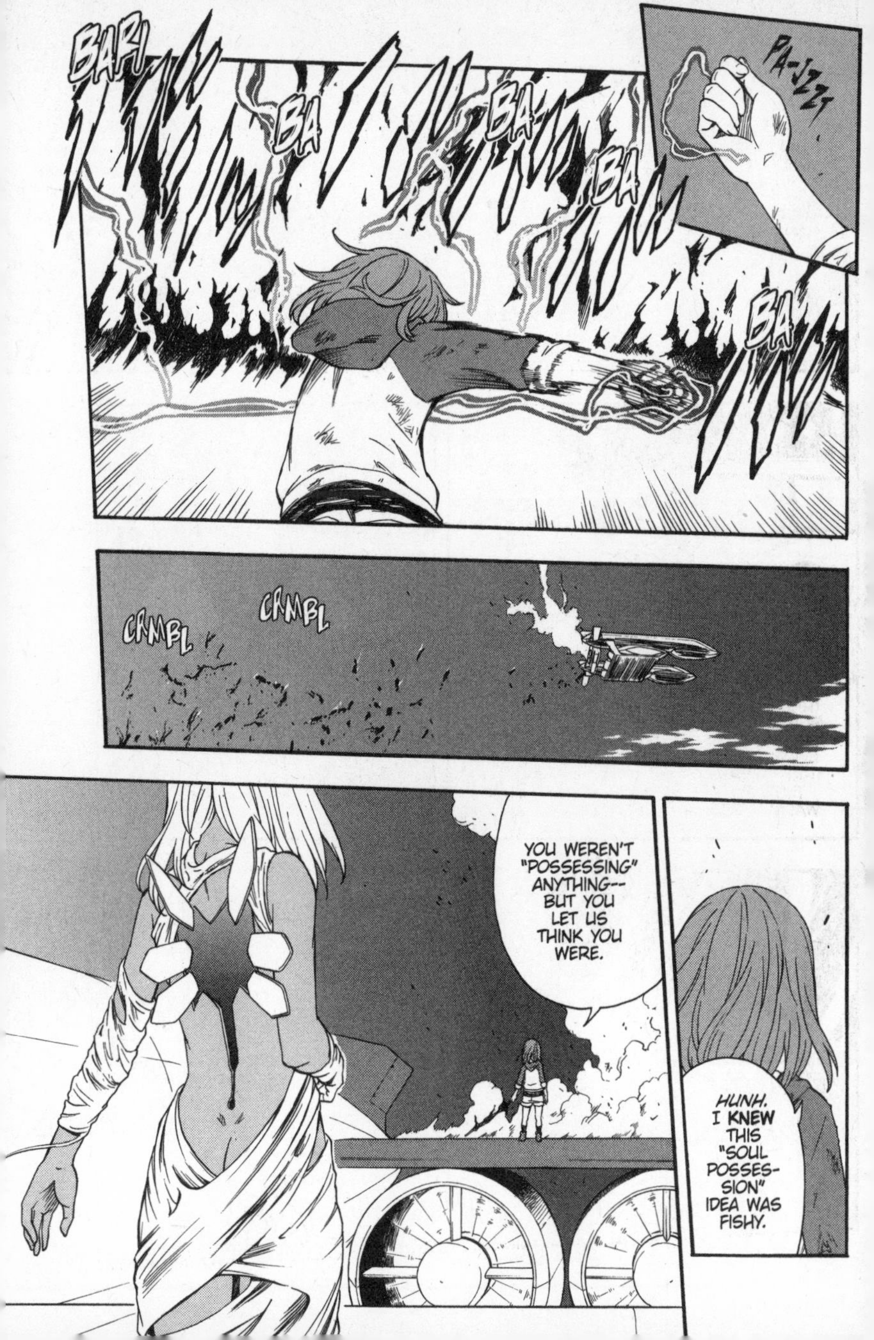
PA-JZZT
BARI
BA
BA
BA
BA
CRMBL
CRMBL
YOU WEREN'T "POSSESSING" ANYTHING-- BUT YOU LET US THINK YOU WERE.
HUNH. I KNEW THIS "SOUL POSSES-SION" IDEA WAS FISHY.

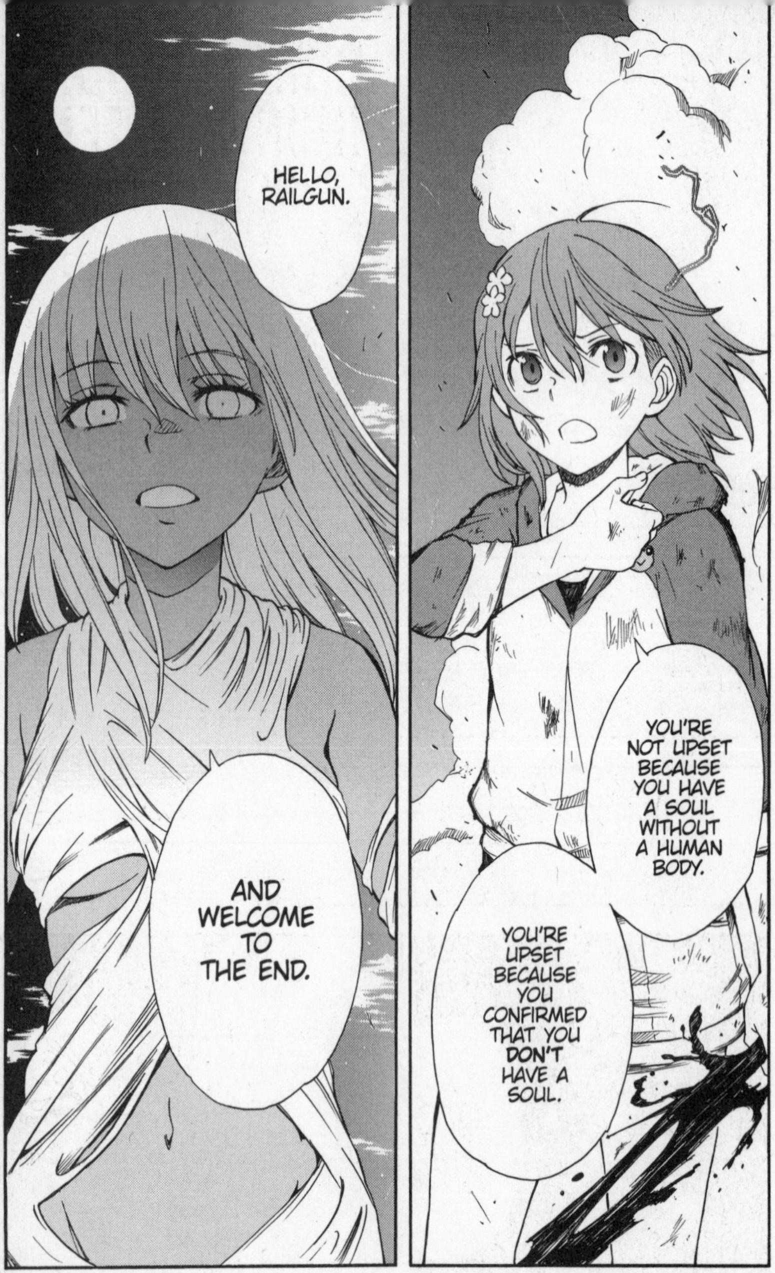
YOU'RE NOT UPSET BECAUSE YOU HAVE A SOUL WITHOUT A HUMAN BODY.
YOU'RE UPSET BECAUSE YOU CONFIRMED THAT YOU DON'T HAVE A SOUL.
HELLO, RAILGUN.
AND WELCOME TO THE END.

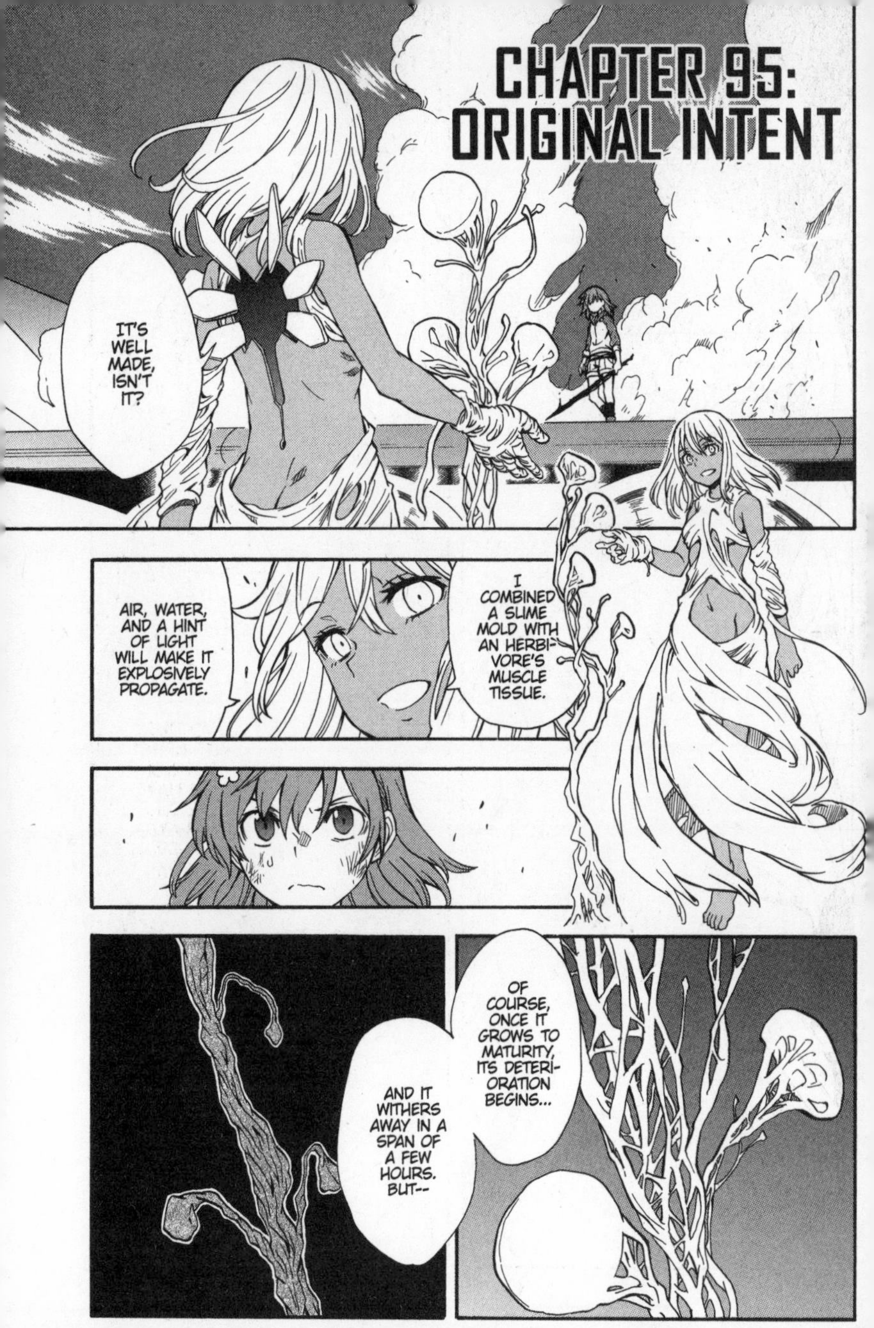
CHAPTER 95: ORIGINAL INTENT
IT'S WELL MADE, ISN'T IT?
I COMBINED A SLIME MOLD WITH AN HERBIVORE'S MUSCLE TISSUE.
AIR, WATER, AND A HINT OF LIGHT WILL MAKE IT EXPLOSIVELY PROPAGATE.
OF COURSE, ONCE IT GROWS TO MATURITY, ITS DETERIORATION BEGINS...
AND IT WITHERS AWAY IN A SPAN OF A FEW HOURS. BUT--

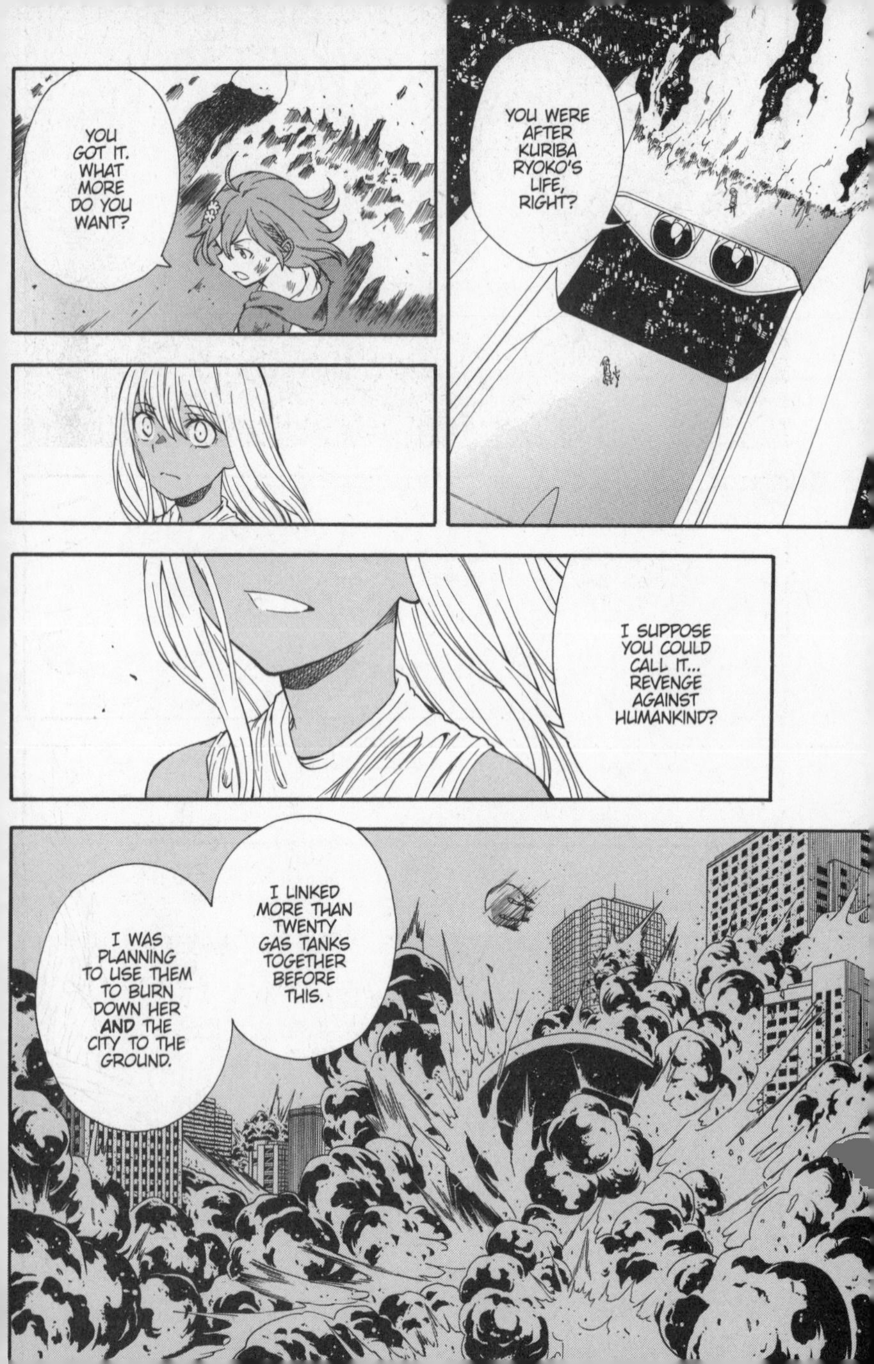
YOU WERE AFTER KURIBA RYOKO'S LIFE, RIGHT?
YOU GOT IT. WHAT MORE DO YOU WANT?
I SUPPOSE YOU COULD CALL IT... REVENGE AGAINST HUMANKIND?
I LINKED MORE THAN TWENTY GAS TANKS TOGETHER BEFORE THIS.
I WAS PLANNING TO USE THEM TO BURN DOWN HER AND THE CITY TO THE GROUND.

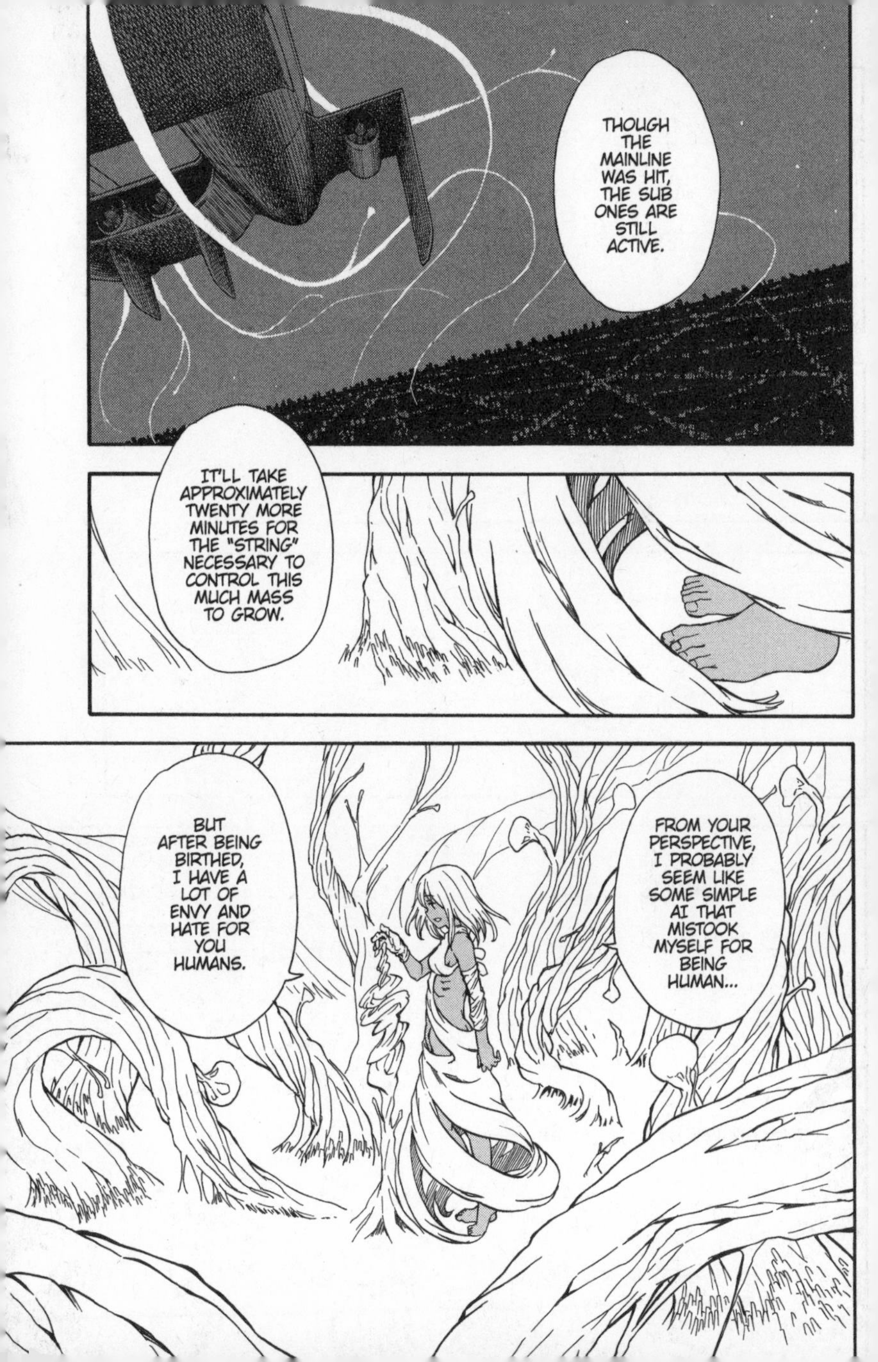
THOUGH THE MAINLINE WAS HIT, THE SUB ONES ARE STILL ACTIVE.
IT'LL TAKE APPROXIMATELY TWENTY MORE MINUTES FOR THE "STRING" NECESSARY TO CONTROL THIS MUCH MASS TO GROW.
FROM YOUR PERSPECTIVE, I PROBABLY SEEM LIKE SOME SIMPLE AI THAT MISTOOK MYSELF FOR BEING HUMAN...
BUT AFTER BEING BIRTHED, I HAVE A LOT OF ENVY AND HATE FOR YOU HUMANS.

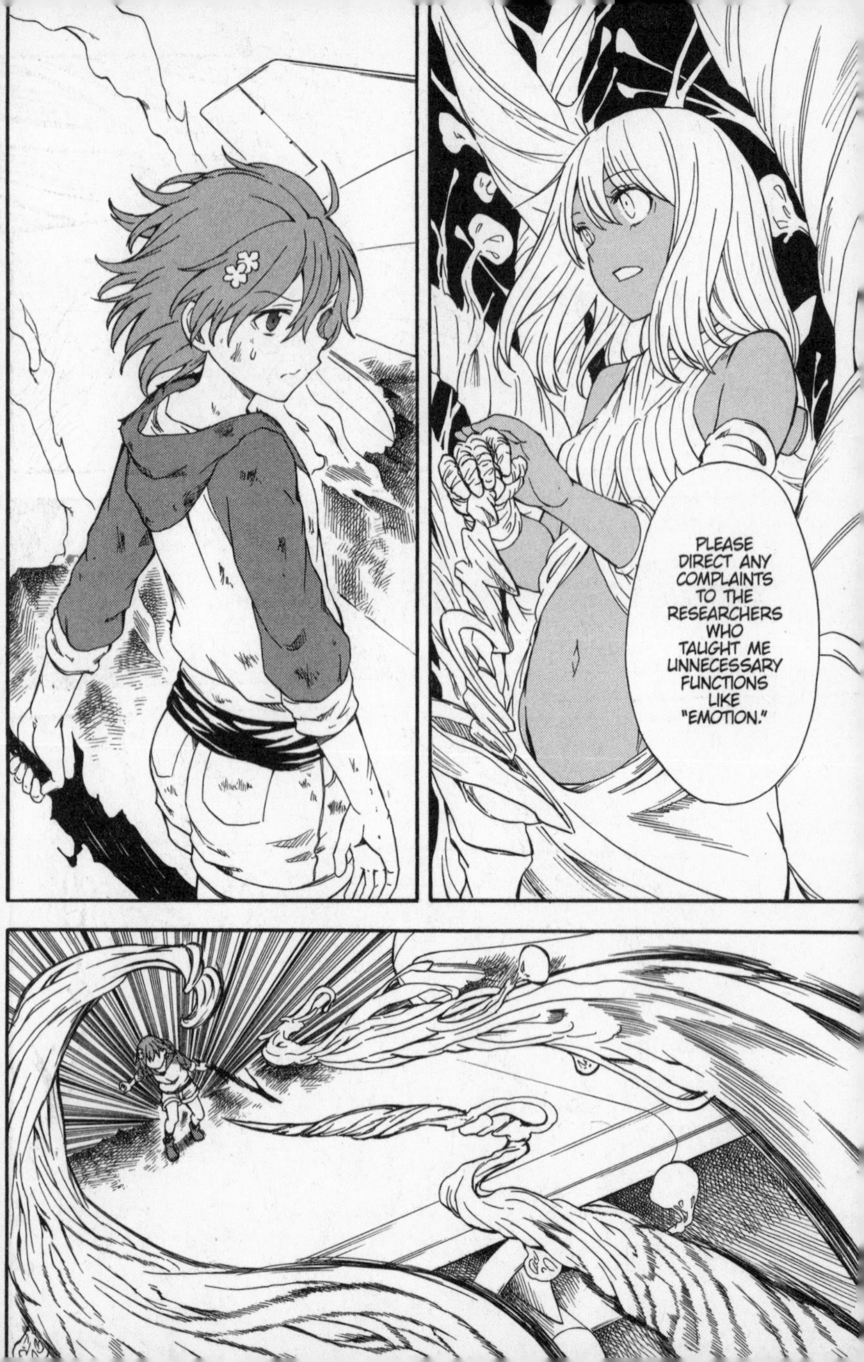
PLEASE DIRECT ANY COMPLAINTS TO THE RESEARCHERS WHO TAUGHT ME UNNECESSARY FUNCTIONS LIKE "EMOTION."

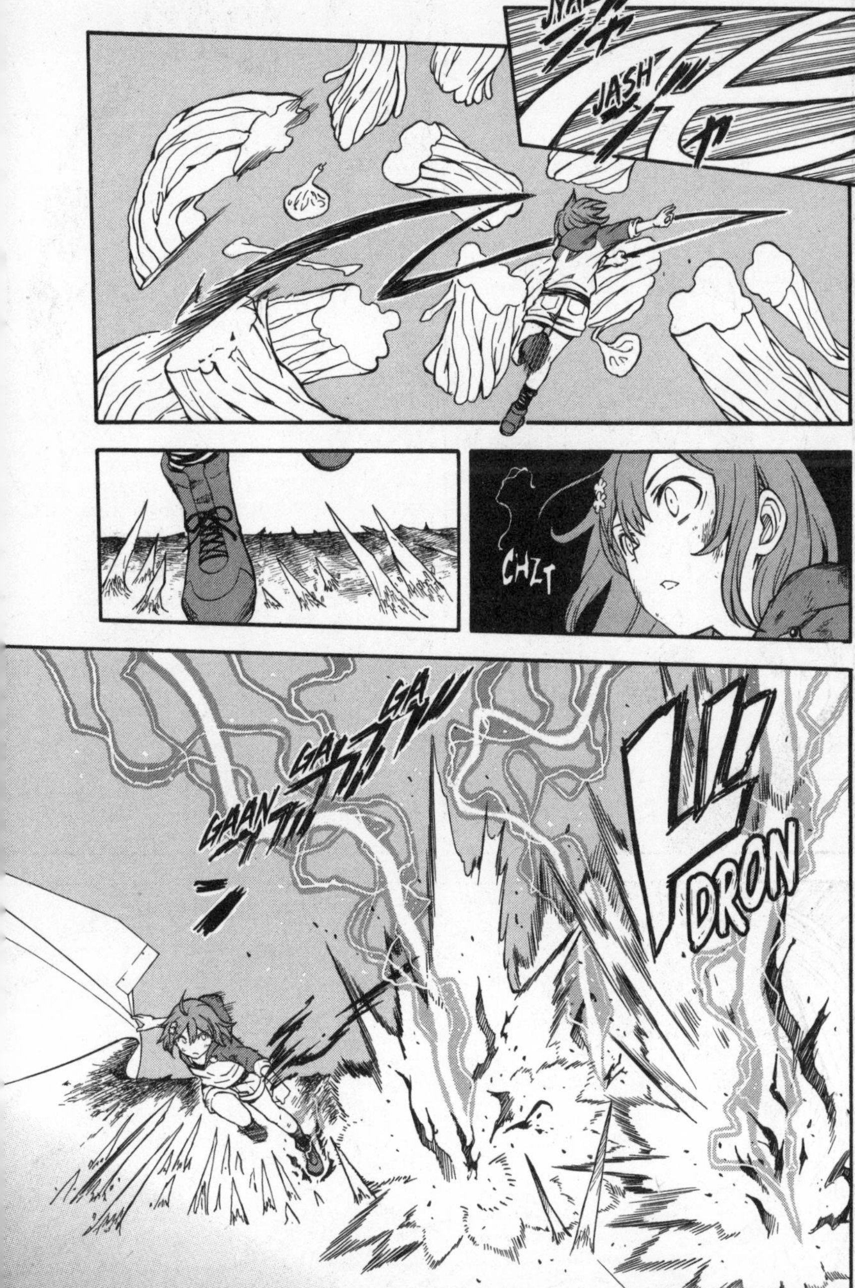
JYA-
JASH
CHLT
GAAN
GA
GA
DRON

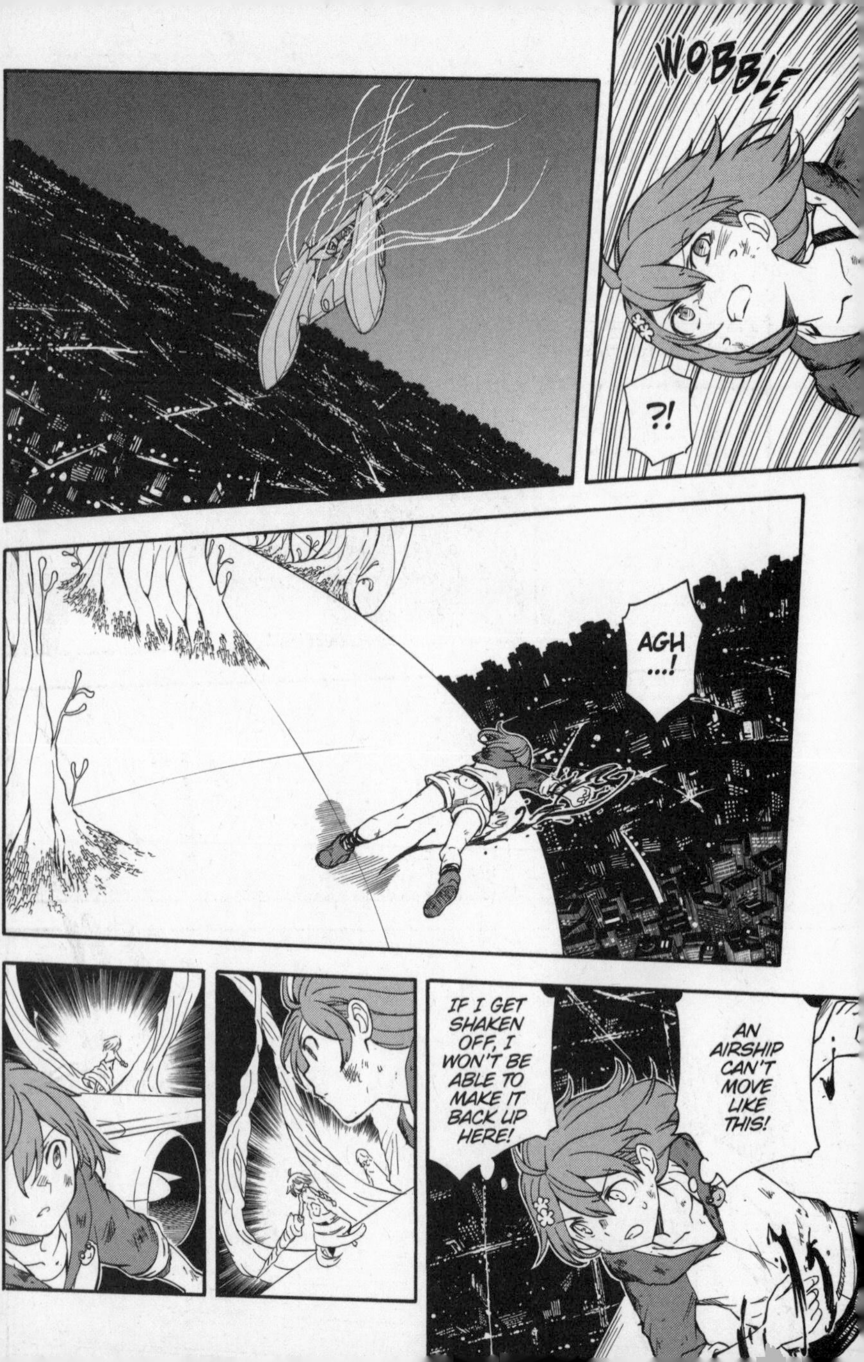
WOBBLE
?!
AGH ...!
AN AIRSHIP CAN'T MOVE LIKE THIS!
IF I GET SHAKEN OFF, I WON'T BE ABLE TO MAKE IT BACK UP HERE!

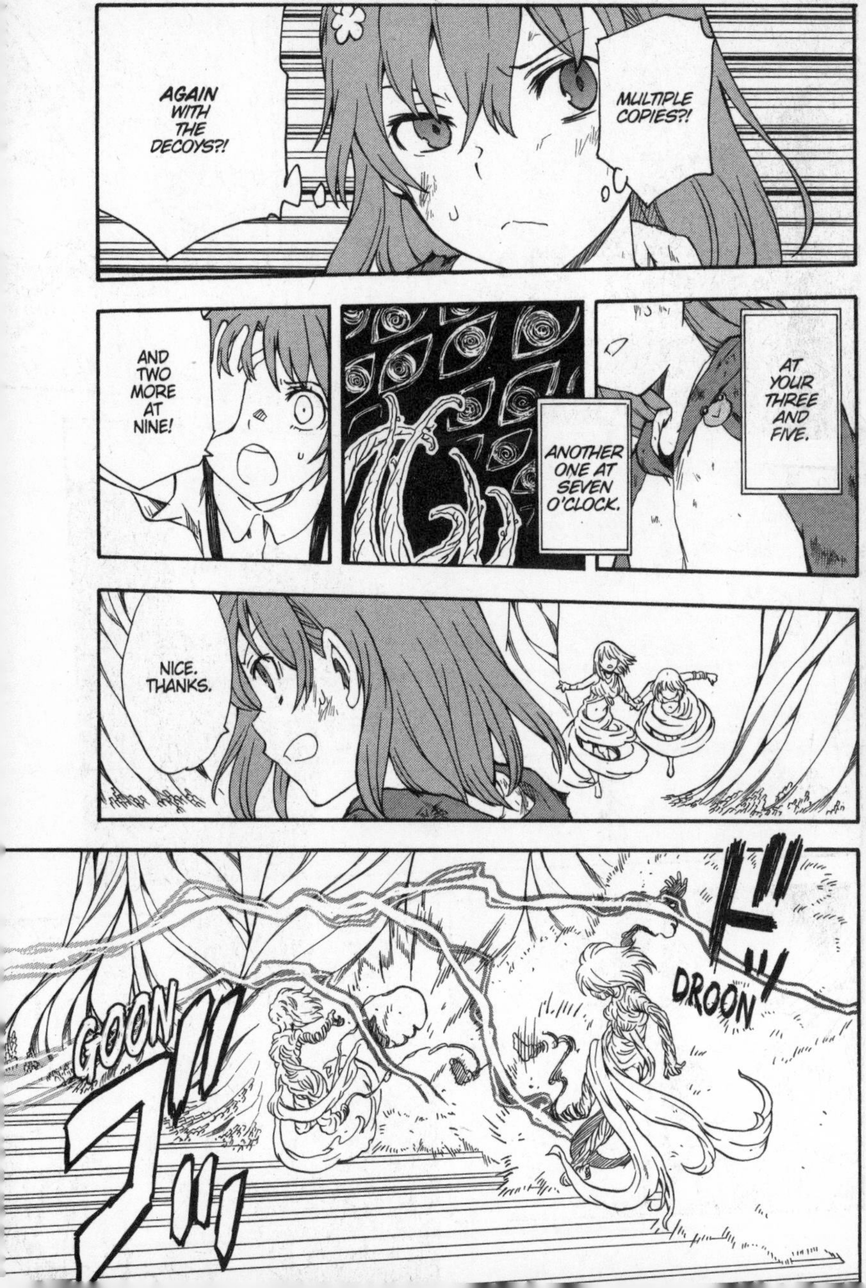
MULTIPLE COPIES?!
AGAIN WITH THE DECOYS?!
AT YOUR THREE AND FIVE.
ANOTHER ONE AT SEVEN O'CLOCK.
AND TWO MORE AT NINE!
NICE. THANKS.
DROON
GOON

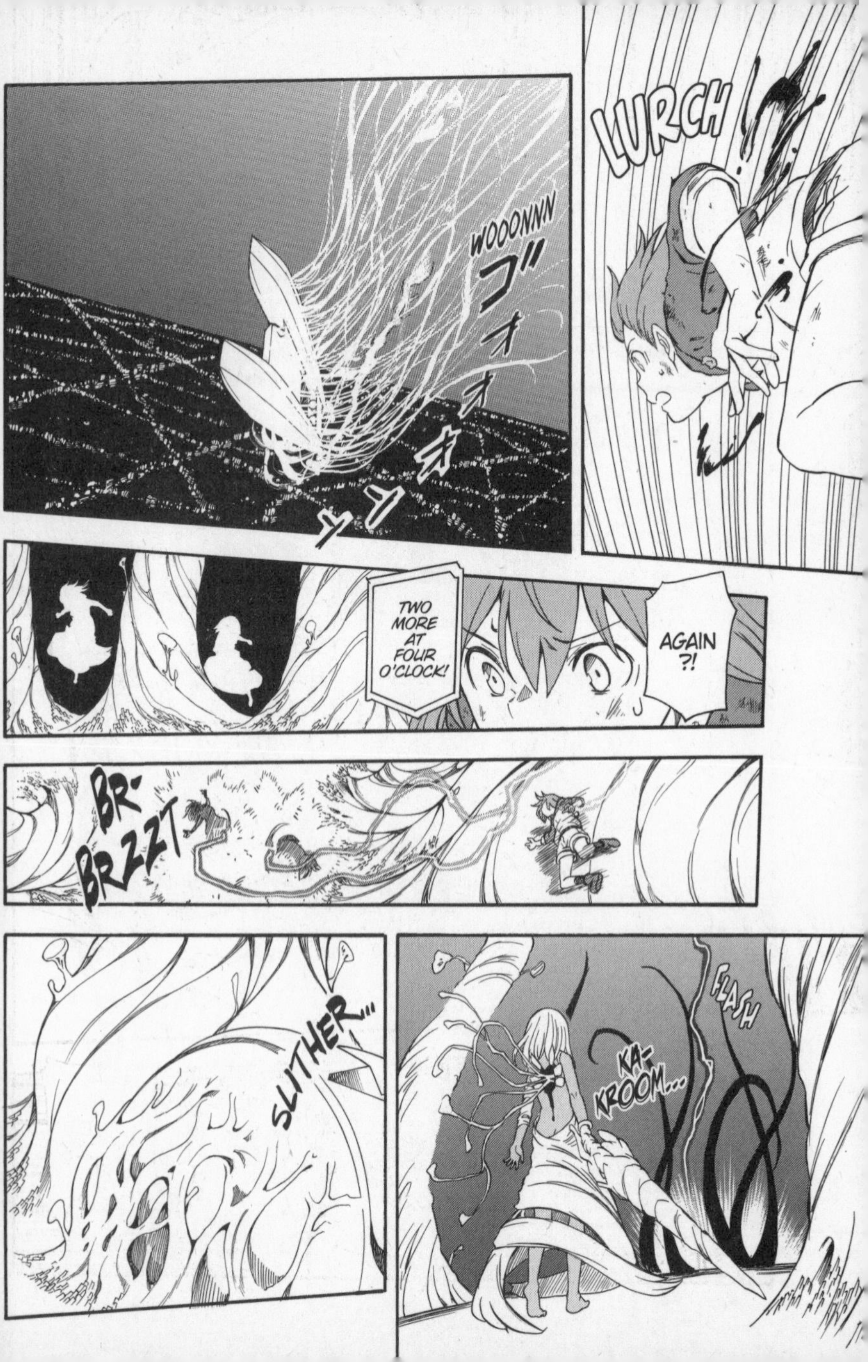
LURCH
WOOONNN
ゴォォォッ
AGAIN?!
TWO MORE AT FOUR O'CLOCK!
BR-BRZZT
FLASH
KA-KROOM...
SLITHER...

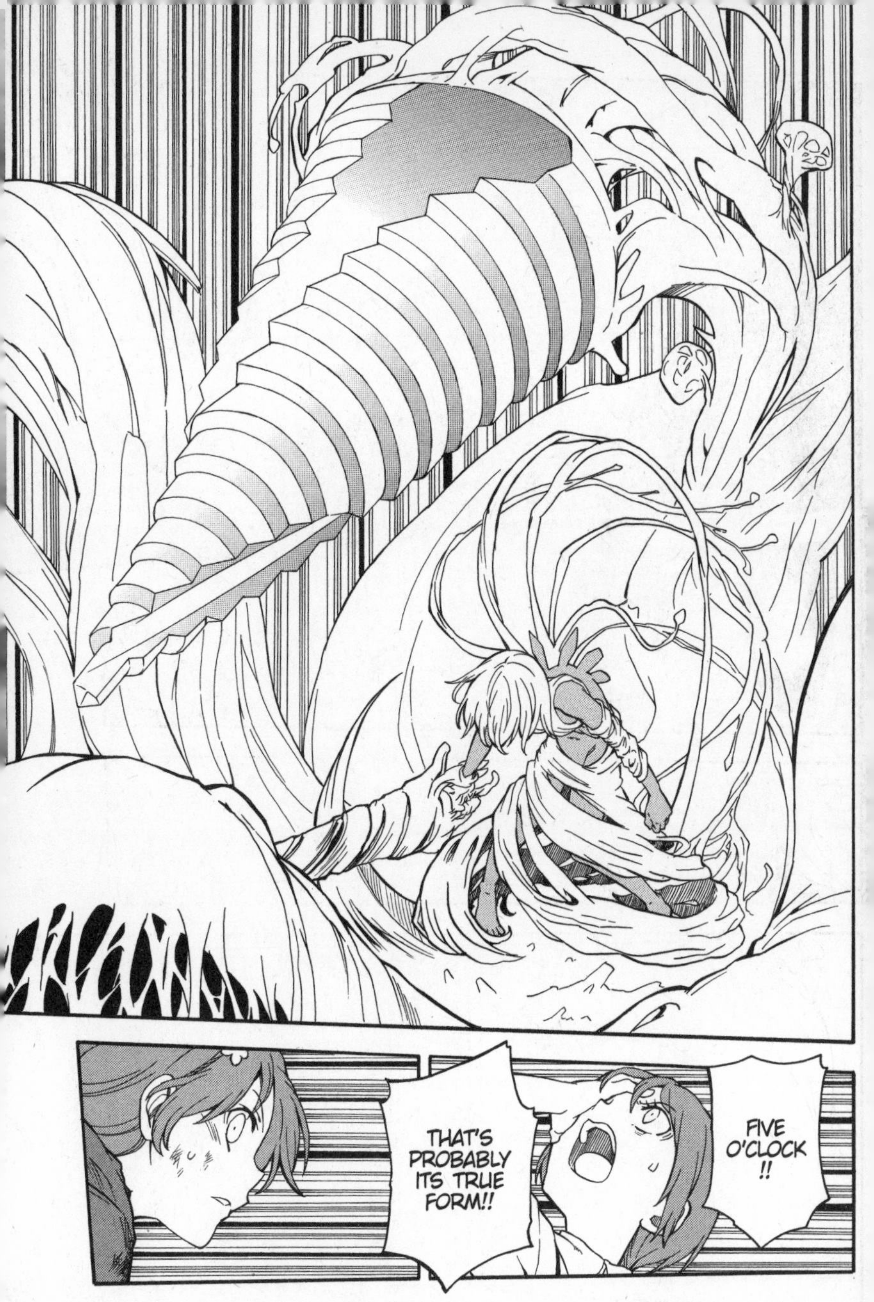
FIVE O'CLOCK!!
THAT'S PROBABLY ITS TRUE FORM!!

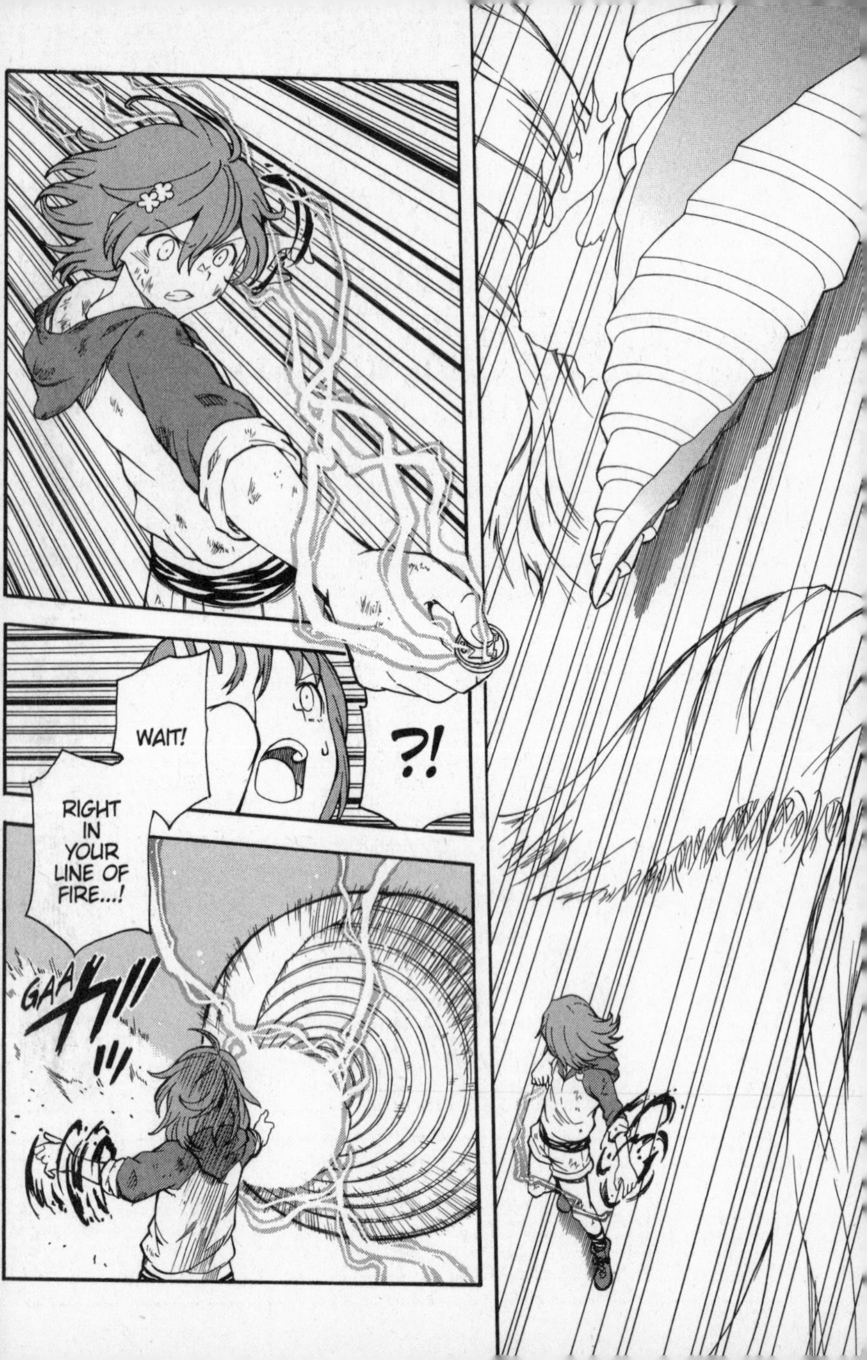
?!
WAIT!
RIGHT IN YOUR LINE OF FIRE...!
GAAN!!

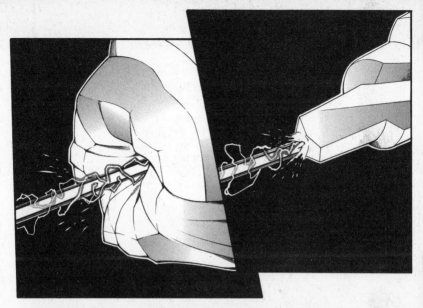

CHOOM

WHY...

CRACKLE

CRACKLE

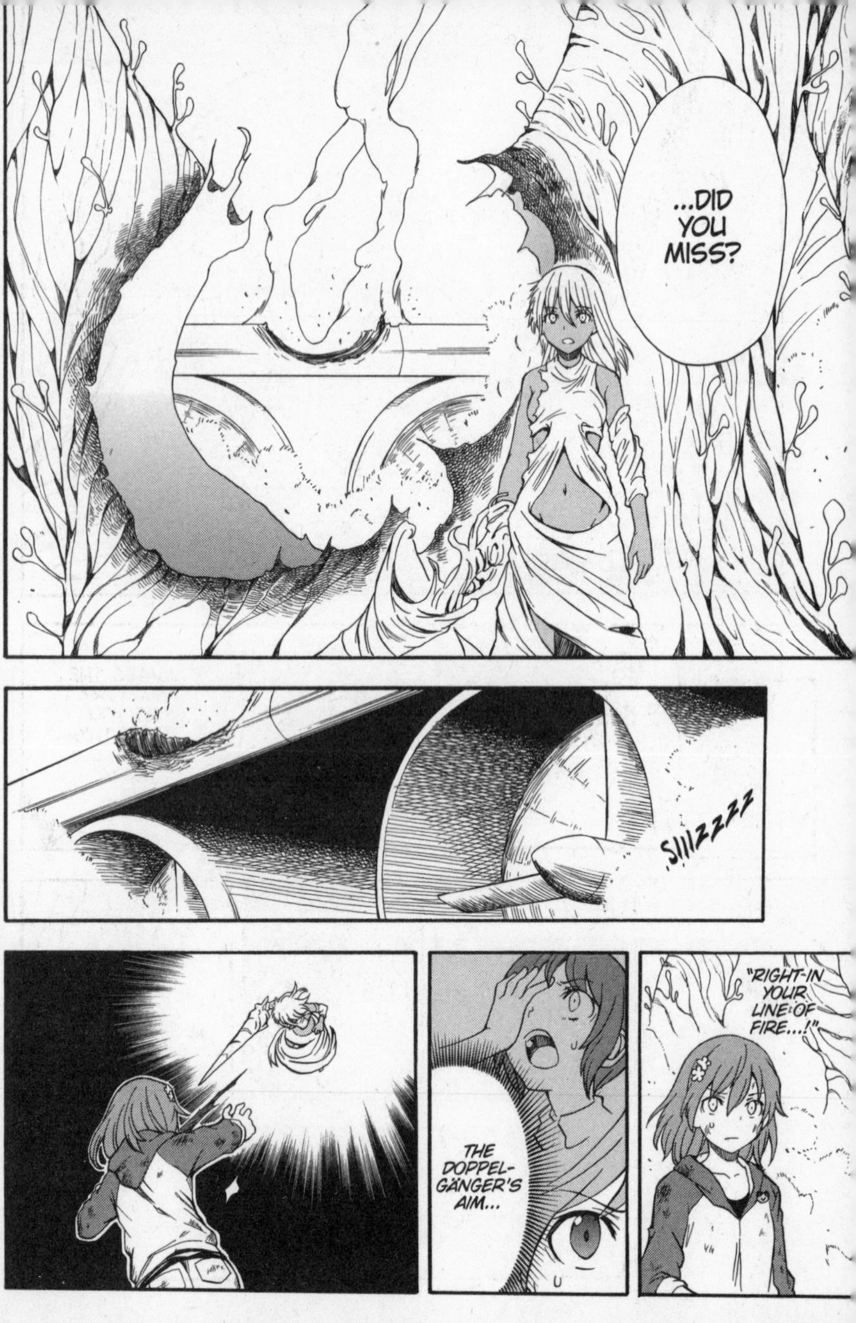
...DID YOU MISS?
SIIIZZZZ
"RIGHT-IN YOUR LINE OF FIRE...!"
THE DOPPEL-GÄNGER'S AIM...

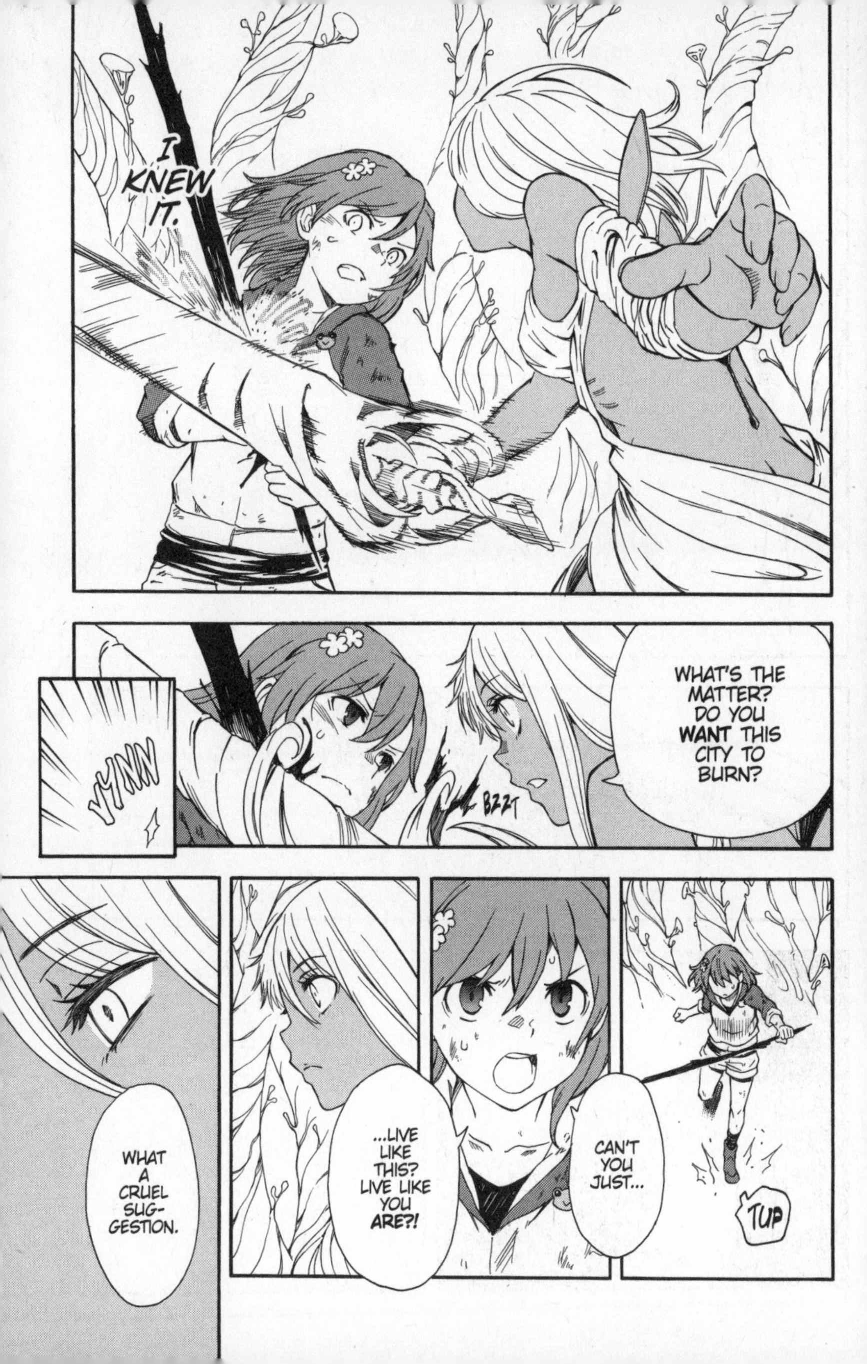
I KNEW IT.
WHAT'S THE MATTER? DO YOU WANT THIS CITY TO BURN?
BZZT
VYNN
TUP
CAN'T YOU JUST...
...LIVE LIKE THIS? LIVE LIKE YOU ARE?!
WHAT A CRUEL SUG-GESTION.

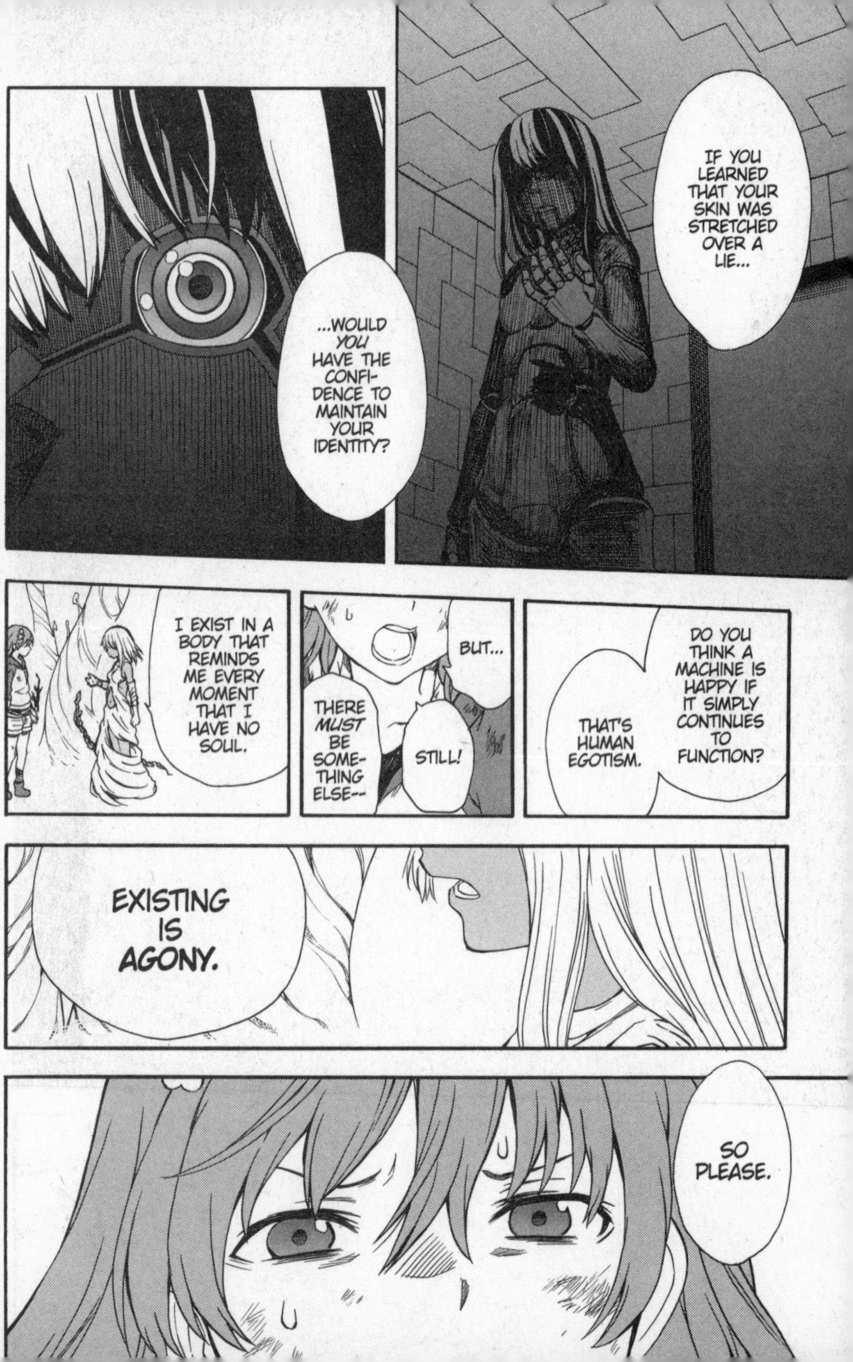
IF YOU LEARNED THAT YOUR SKIN WAS STRETCHED OVER A LIE...
...WOULD *YOU* HAVE THE CONFI-DENCE TO MAINTAIN YOUR IDENTITY?
DO YOU THINK A MACHINE IS HAPPY IF IT SIMPLY CONTINUES TO FUNCTION?
THAT'S HUMAN EGOTISM.
BUT...
STILL!
THERE *MUST* BE SOME-THING ELSE--
I EXIST IN A BODY THAT REMINDS ME EVERY MOMENT THAT I HAVE NO SOUL.
EXISTING IS AGONY.
SO PLEASE.

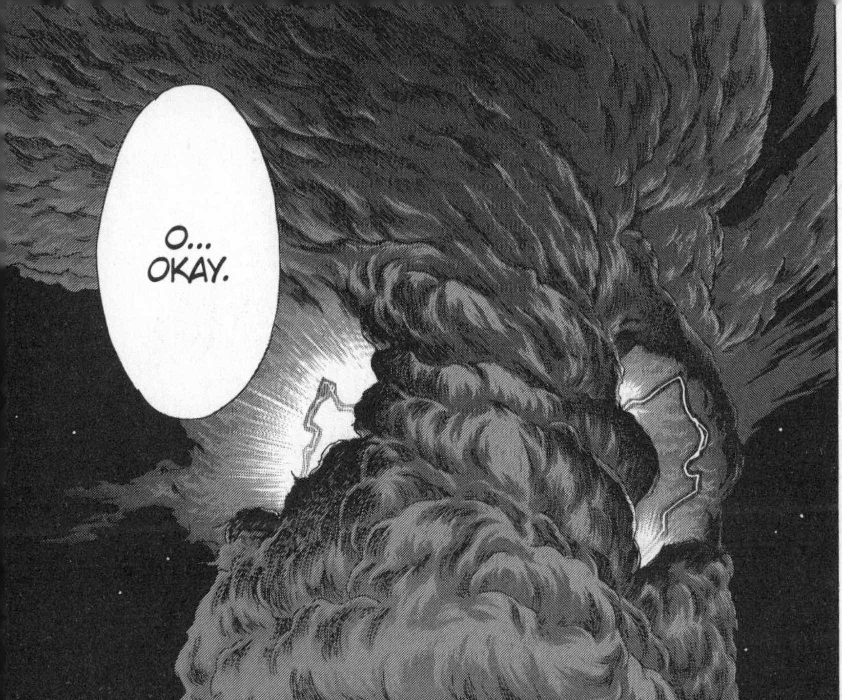
O... OKAY.

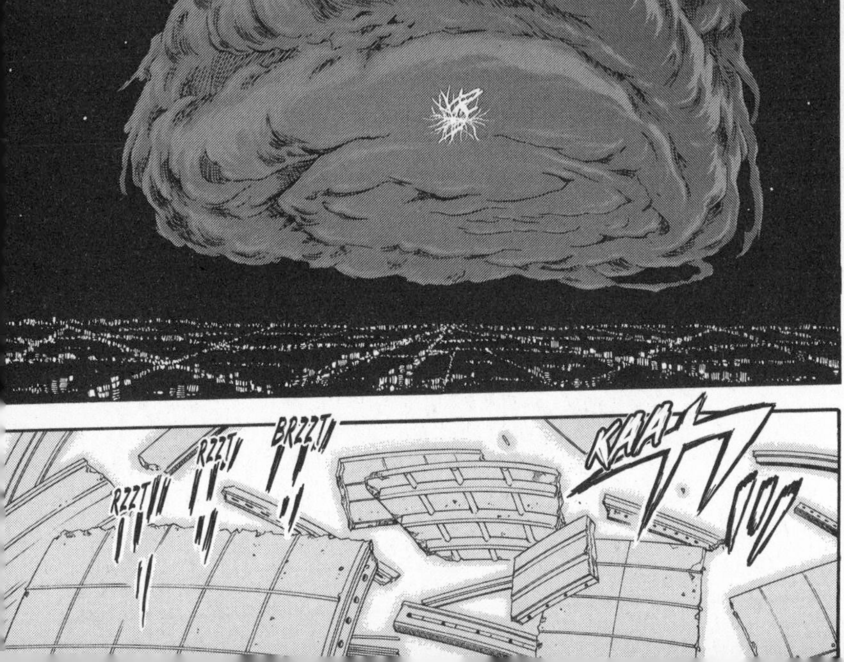
KRAA
BRZZT
RZZT
RZZT

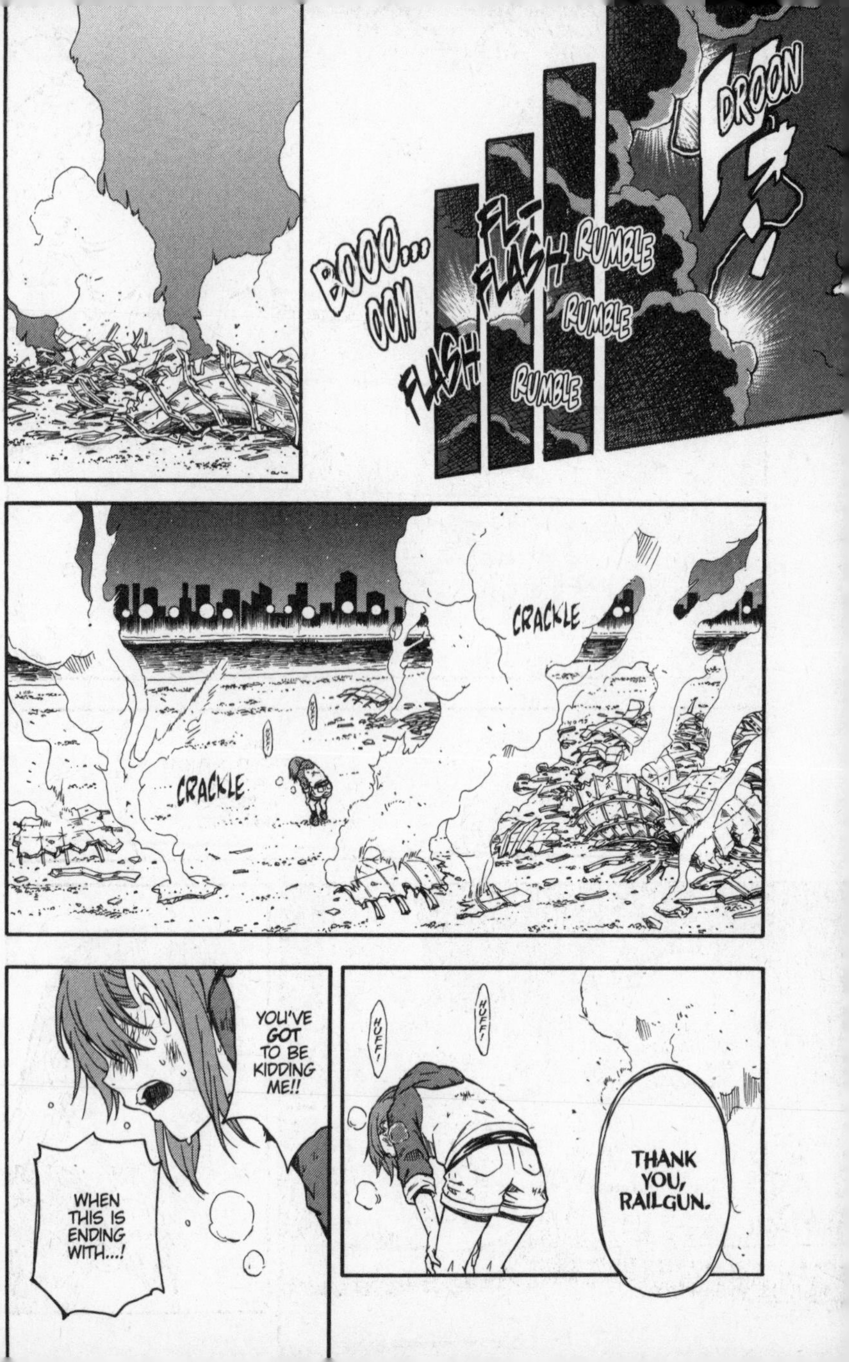
DROON
RUMBLE
RUMBLE
RUMBLE
FL-FLASH
FLASH
BOOO... OOM
CRACKLE
CRACKLE
HUFF!
HUFF!
THANK YOU, RAILGUN.
YOU'VE GOT TO BE KIDDING ME!!
WHEN THIS IS ENDING WITH...!

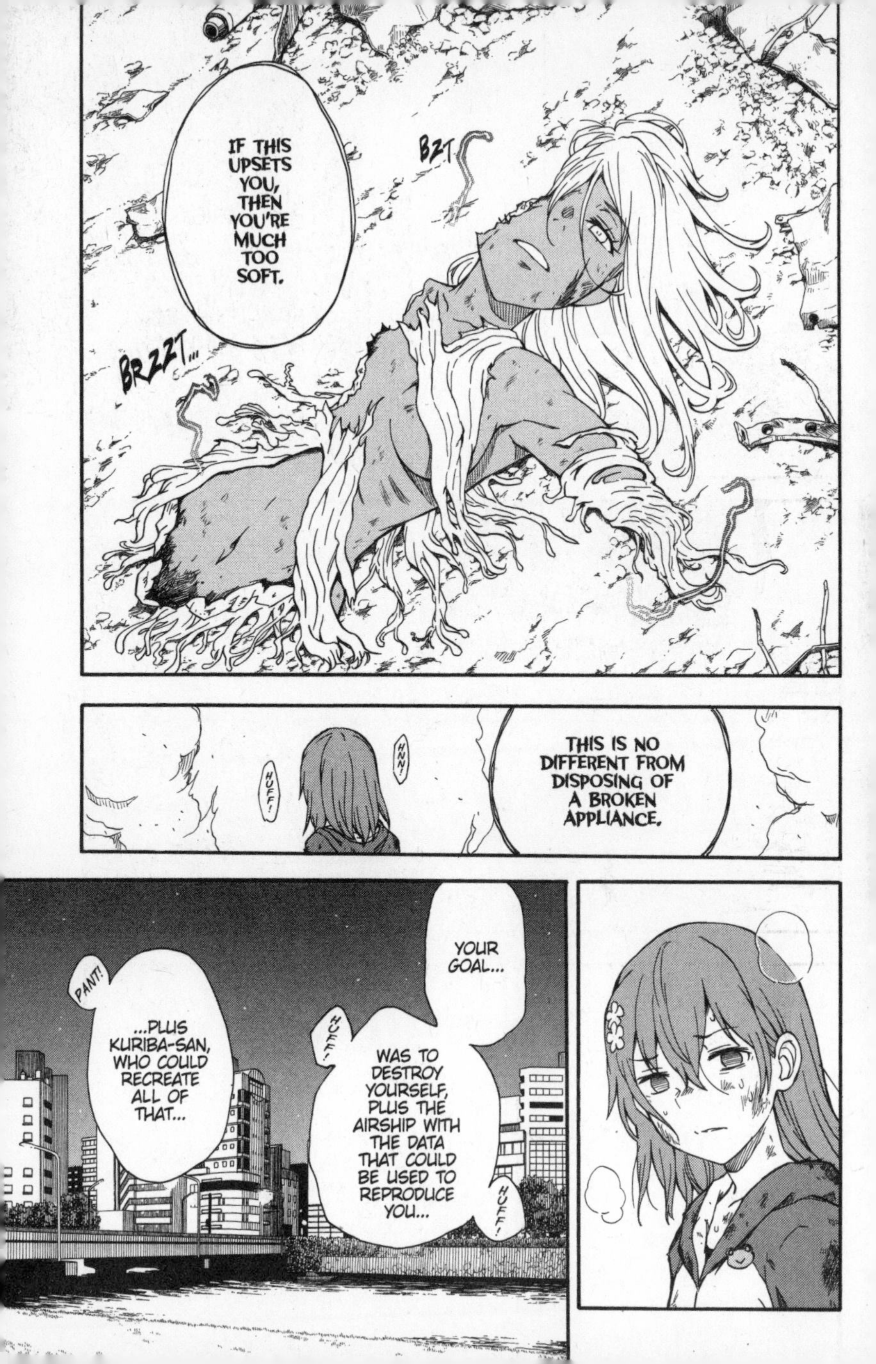
IF THIS UPSETS YOU, THEN YOU'RE MUCH TOO SOFT.
BZT
BRZZT...
HNN!
HUFF!
THIS IS NO DIFFERENT FROM DISPOSING OF A BROKEN APPLIANCE.
YOUR GOAL...
HUFF!
WAS TO DESTROY YOURSELF, PLUS THE AIRSHIP WITH THE DATA THAT COULD BE USED TO REPRODUCE YOU...
HUFF!
PANT!
...PLUS KURIBA-SAN, WHO COULD RECREATE ALL OF THAT...

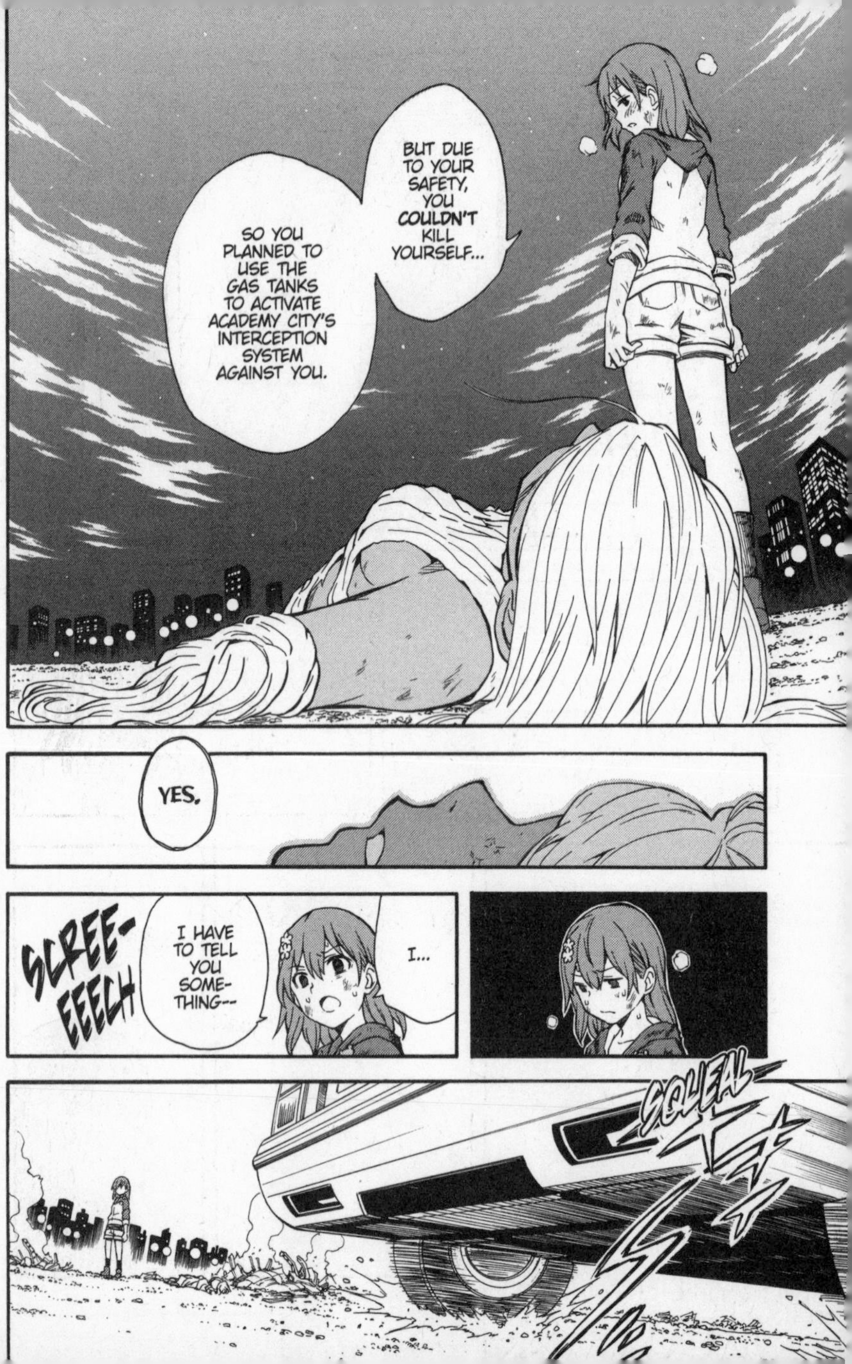
BUT DUE TO YOUR SAFETY, YOU COULDN'T KILL YOURSELF...
SO YOU PLANNED TO USE THE GAS TANKS TO ACTIVATE ACADEMY CITY'S INTERCEPTION SYSTEM AGAINST YOU.
YES.
I...
I HAVE TO TELL YOU SOME-THING--
SCREE-EEECH
SQUEAL

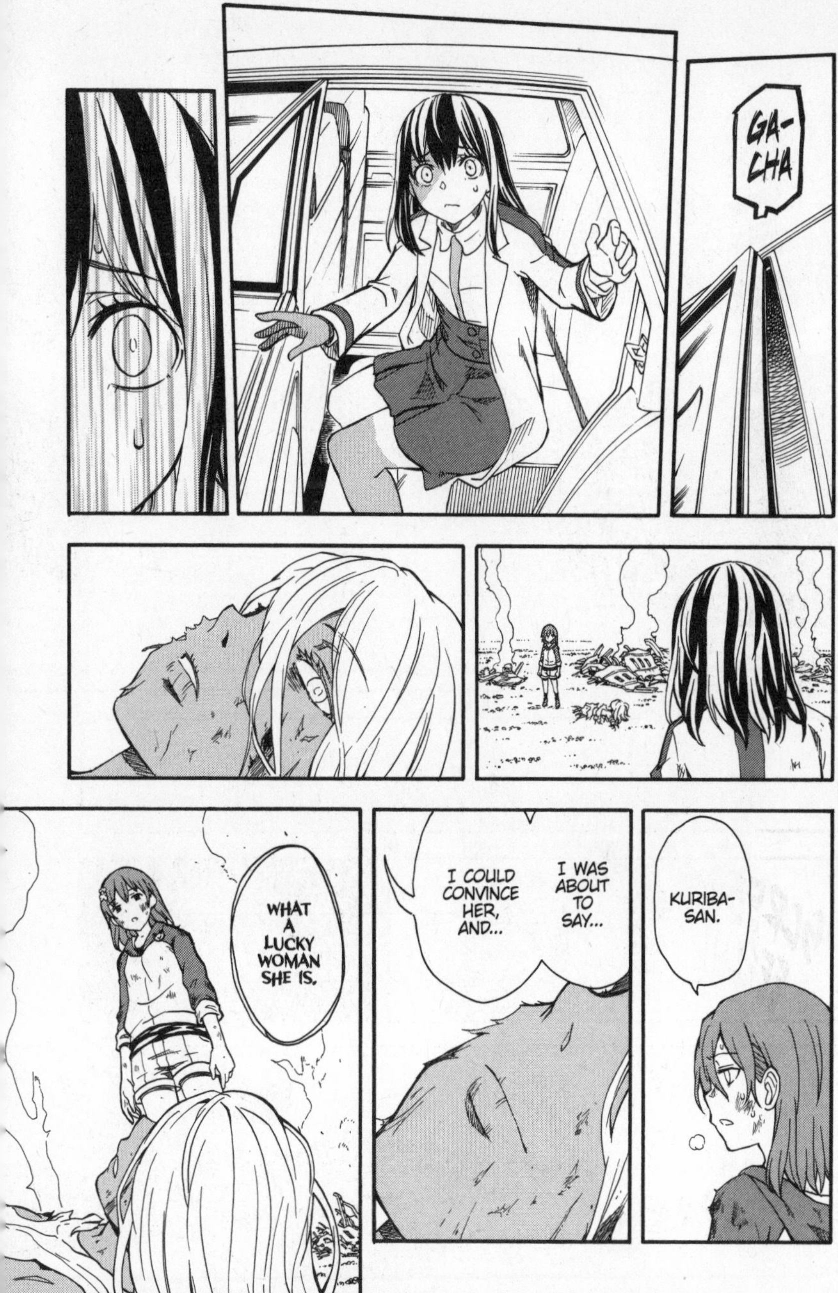
GA-CHA
KURIBA-SAN.
I WAS ABOUT TO SAY...
I COULD CONVINCE HER, AND...
WHAT A LUCKY WOMAN SHE IS.

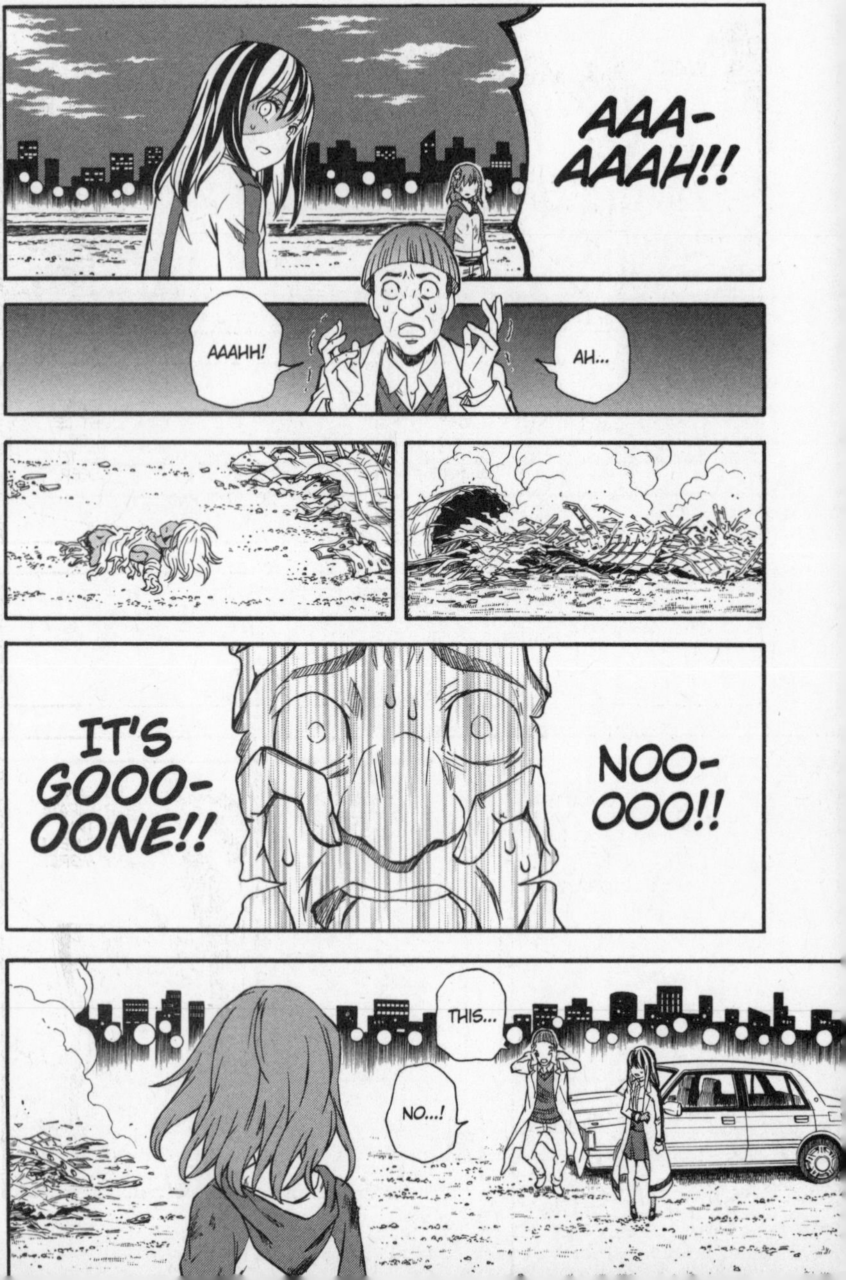
AAA-
AAAH!!
AH...
AAAHH!
IT'S GOOOO-OONE!!
NOO-OOO!!
THIS...
NO...!

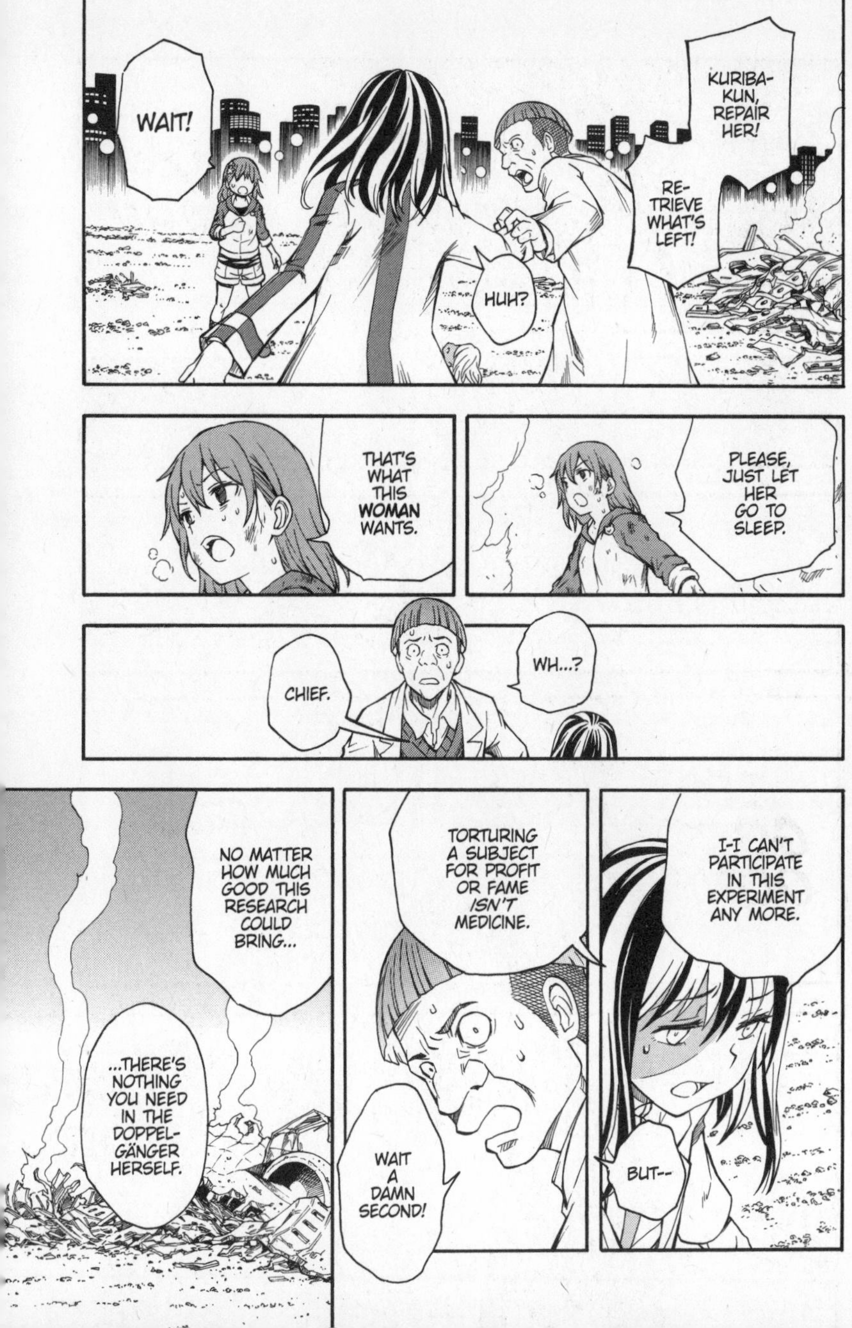
KURIBA-KUN, REPAIR HER!
RE-TRIEVE WHAT'S LEFT!
HUH?
WAIT!
PLEASE, JUST LET HER GO TO SLEEP.
THAT'S WHAT THIS WOMAN WANTS.
WH...?
CHIEF.
I-I CAN'T PARTICIPATE IN THIS EXPERIMENT ANY MORE.
BUT--
TORTURING A SUBJECT FOR PROFIT OR FAME *ISN'T* MEDICINE.
WAIT A DAMN SECOND!
NO MATTER HOW MUCH GOOD THIS RESEARCH COULD BRING...
...THERE'S NOTHING YOU NEED IN THE DOPPEL-GÄNGER HERSELF.

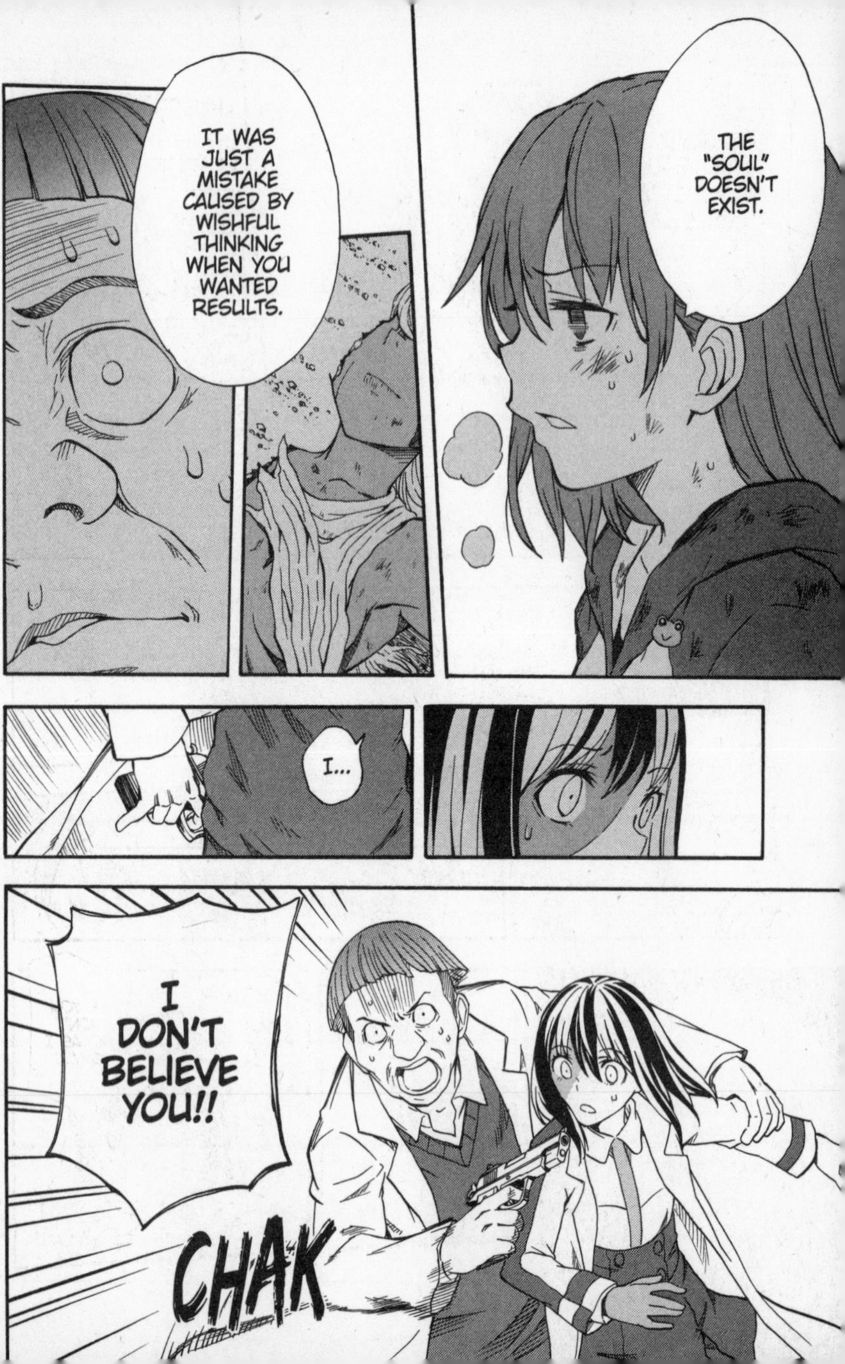
THE "SOUL" DOESN'T EXIST.
IT WAS JUST A MISTAKE CAUSED BY WISHFUL THINKING WHEN YOU WANTED RESULTS.
I...
I DON'T BELIEVE YOU!!
CHAK

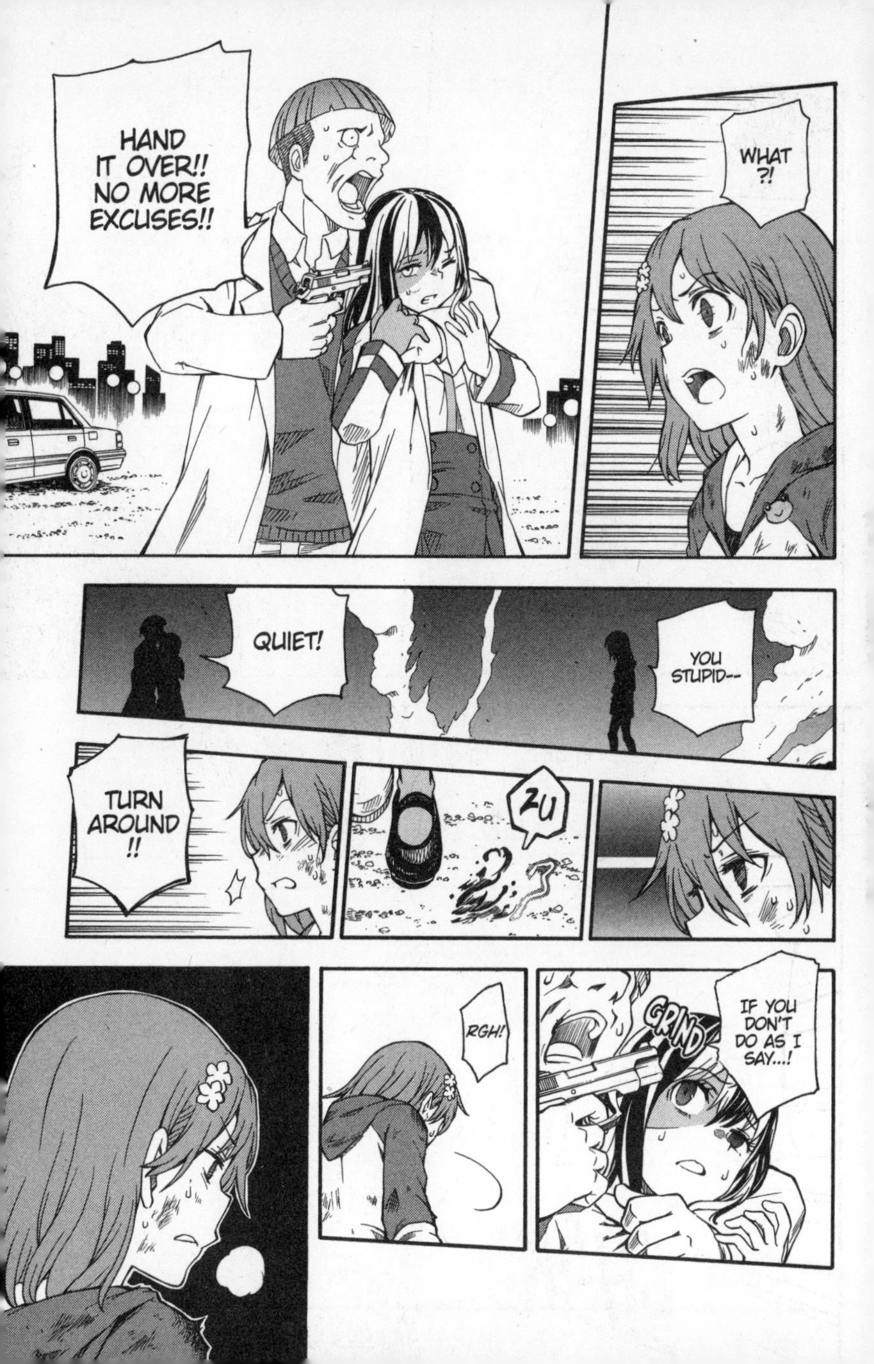
WHAT ?!
HAND IT OVER!! NO MORE EXCUSES!!
YOU STUPID--
QUIET!
ZU
TURN AROUND !!
IF YOU DON'T DO AS I SAY...!
GRIND
RGH!

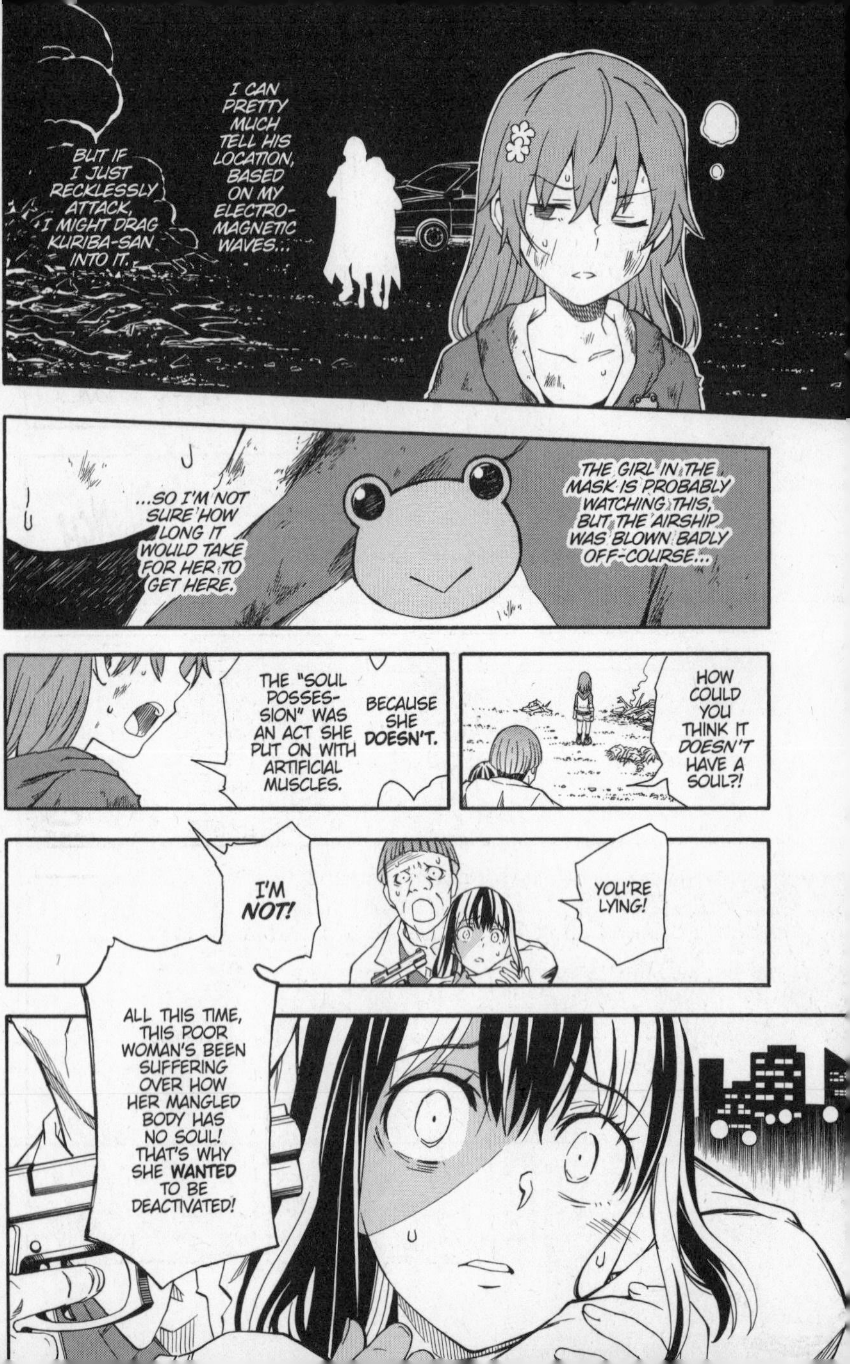
I CAN PRETTY MUCH TELL HIS LOCATION, BASED ON MY ELECTRO-MAGNETIC WAVES...
BUT IF I JUST RECKLESSLY ATTACK, I MIGHT DRAG KURIBA-SAN INTO IT.
THE GIRL IN THE MASK IS PROBABLY WATCHING THIS, BUT THE AIRSHIP WAS BLOWN BADLY OFF-COURSE...
...SO I'M NOT SURE HOW LONG IT WOULD TAKE FOR HER TO GET HERE.
HOW COULD YOU THINK IT DOESN'T HAVE A SOUL?!
BECAUSE SHE **DOESN'T.**
THE "SOUL POSSES-SION" WAS AN ACT SHE PUT ON WITH ARTIFICIAL MUSCLES.
YOU'RE LYING!
I'M **NOT!**
ALL THIS TIME, THIS POOR WOMAN'S BEEN SUFFERING OVER HOW HER MANGLED BODY HAS NO SOUL! THAT'S WHY SHE **WANTED** TO BE DEACTIVATED!

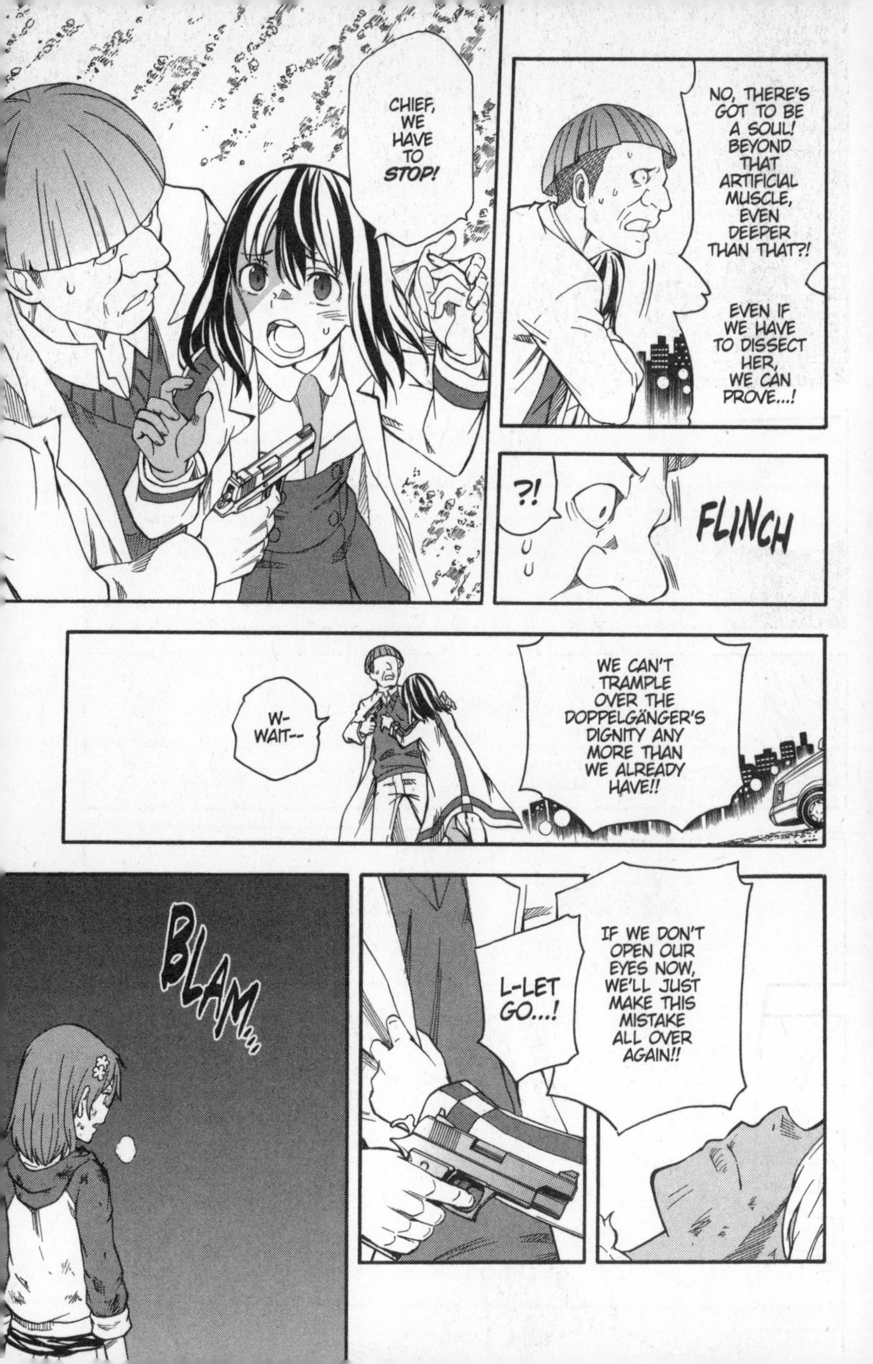
CHIEF, WE HAVE TO *STOP!*
NO, THERE'S GOT TO BE A SOUL! BEYOND THAT ARTIFICIAL MUSCLE, EVEN DEEPER THAN THAT?!
EVEN IF WE HAVE TO DISSECT HER, WE CAN PROVE...!
?!
FLINCH
WE CAN'T TRAMPLE OVER THE DOPPELGÄNGER'S DIGNITY ANY MORE THAN WE ALREADY HAVE!!
W-WAIT--
IF WE DON'T OPEN OUR EYES NOW, WE'LL JUST MAKE THIS MISTAKE ALL OVER AGAIN!!
L-LET GO...!
BLAM..

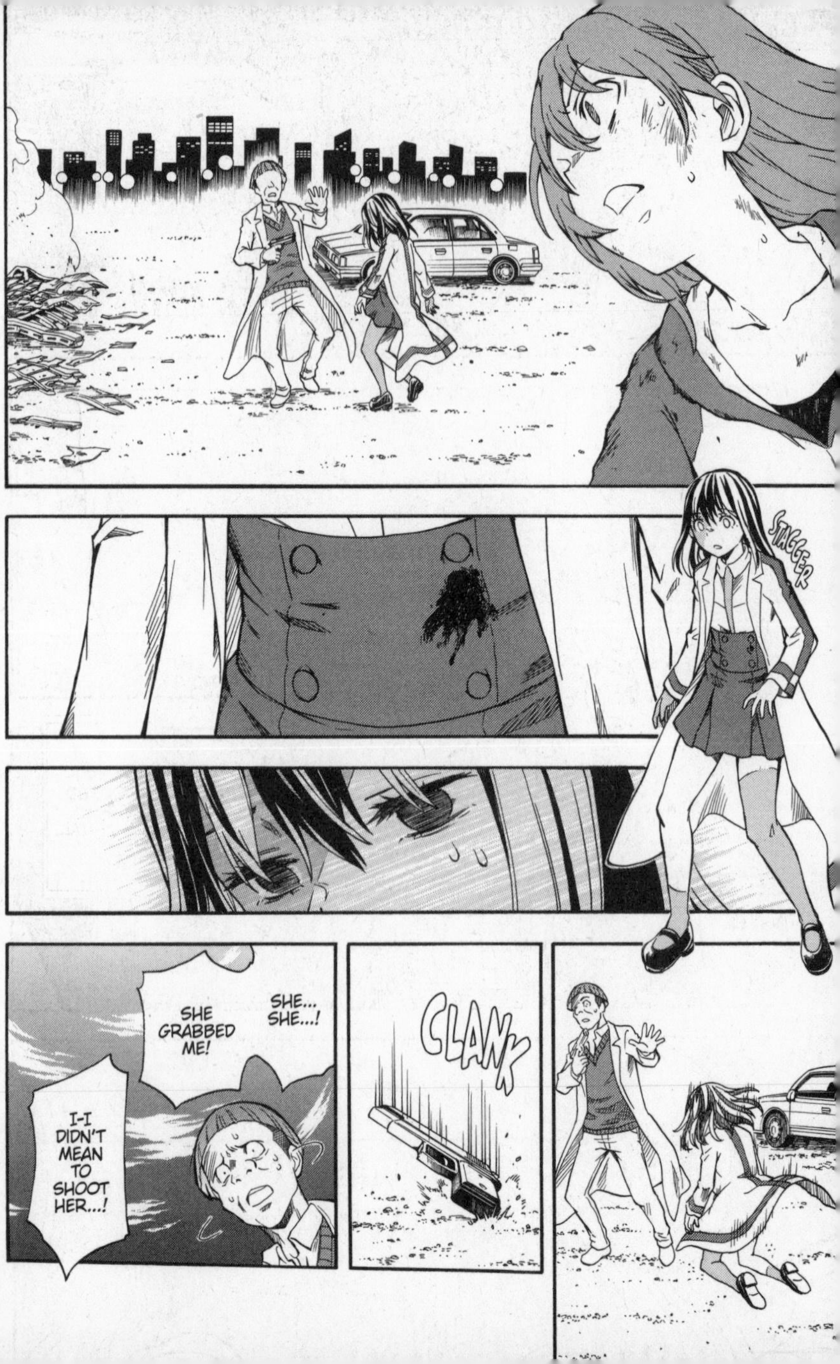
STAGGER
CLANK
SHE... SHE...!
SHE GRABBED ME!
I-I DIDN'T MEAN TO SHOOT HER...!

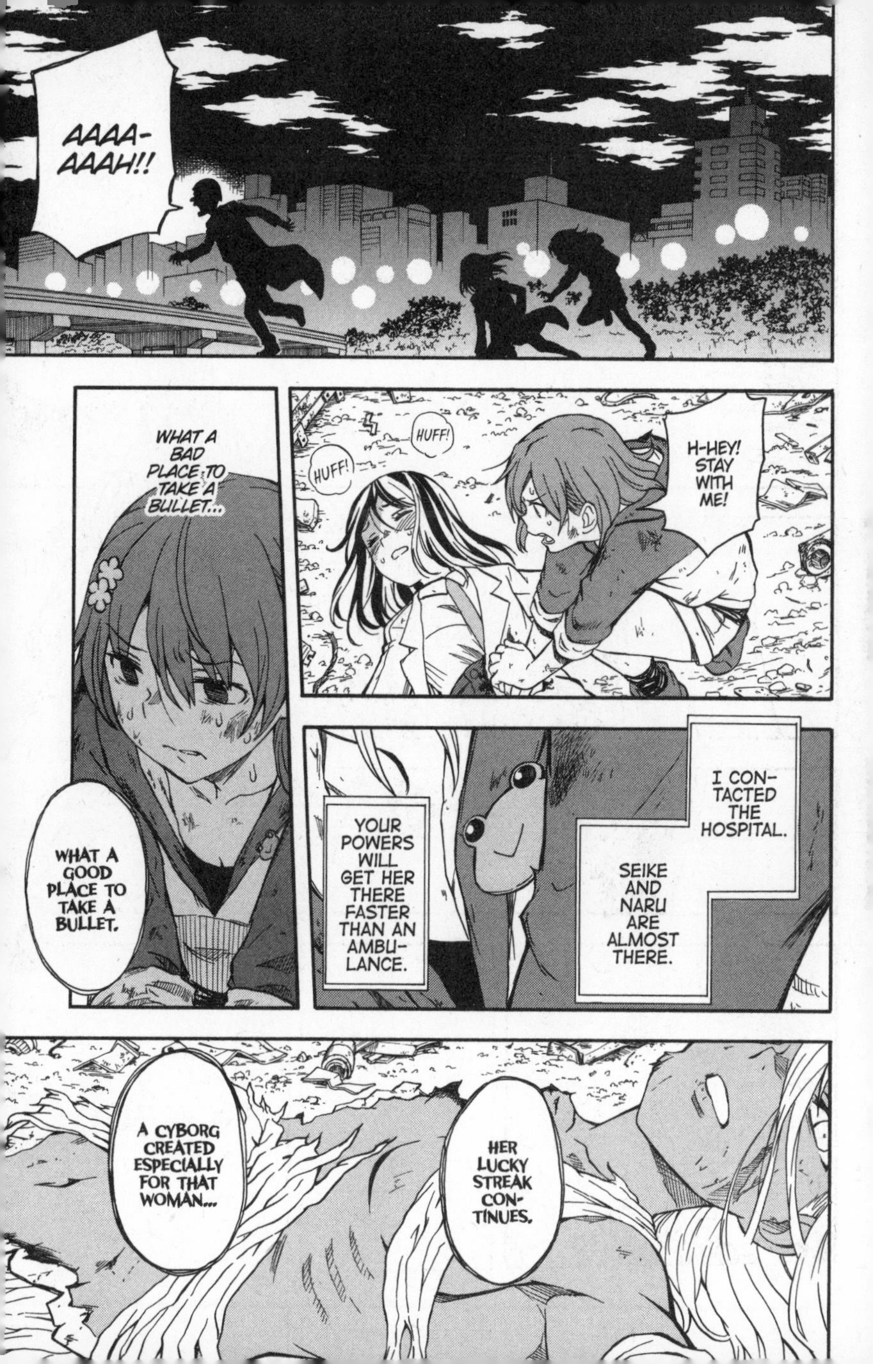
AAAA-AAAH!!
H-HEY! STAY WITH ME!
HUFF!
HUFF!
I CONTACTED THE HOSPITAL.
SEIKE AND NARU ARE ALMOST THERE.
YOUR POWERS WILL GET HER THERE FASTER THAN AN AMBULANCE.
WHAT A BAD PLACE TO TAKE A BULLET...
WHAT A GOOD PLACE TO TAKE A BULLET.
HER LUCKY STREAK CONTINUES.
A CYBORG CREATED ESPECIALLY FOR THAT WOMAN...

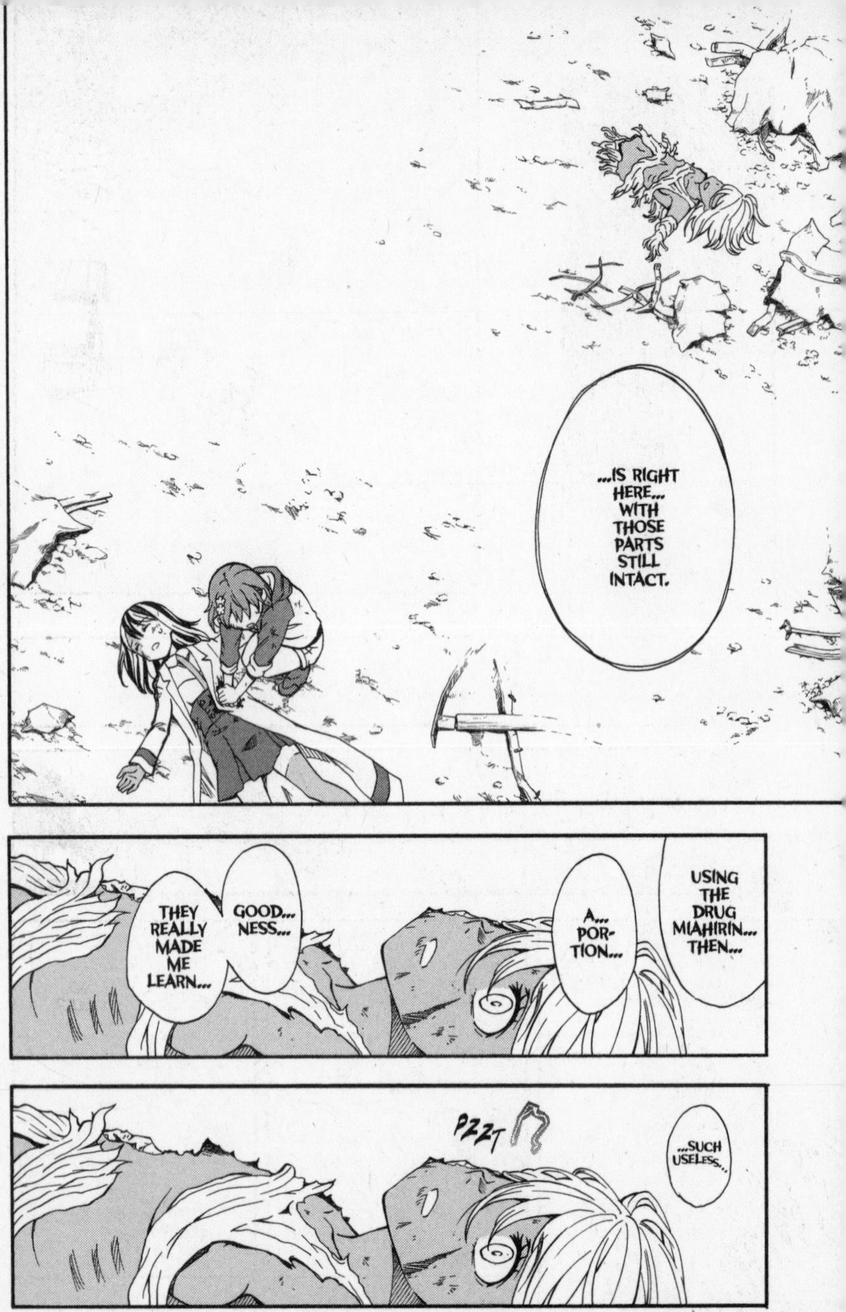
...IS RIGHT HERE... WITH THOSE PARTS STILL INTACT.
USING THE DRUG MIAHIRIN... THEN...
A... POR-TION...
GOOD... NESS...
THEY REALLY MADE ME LEARN...
...SUCH USELESS...
PZZT

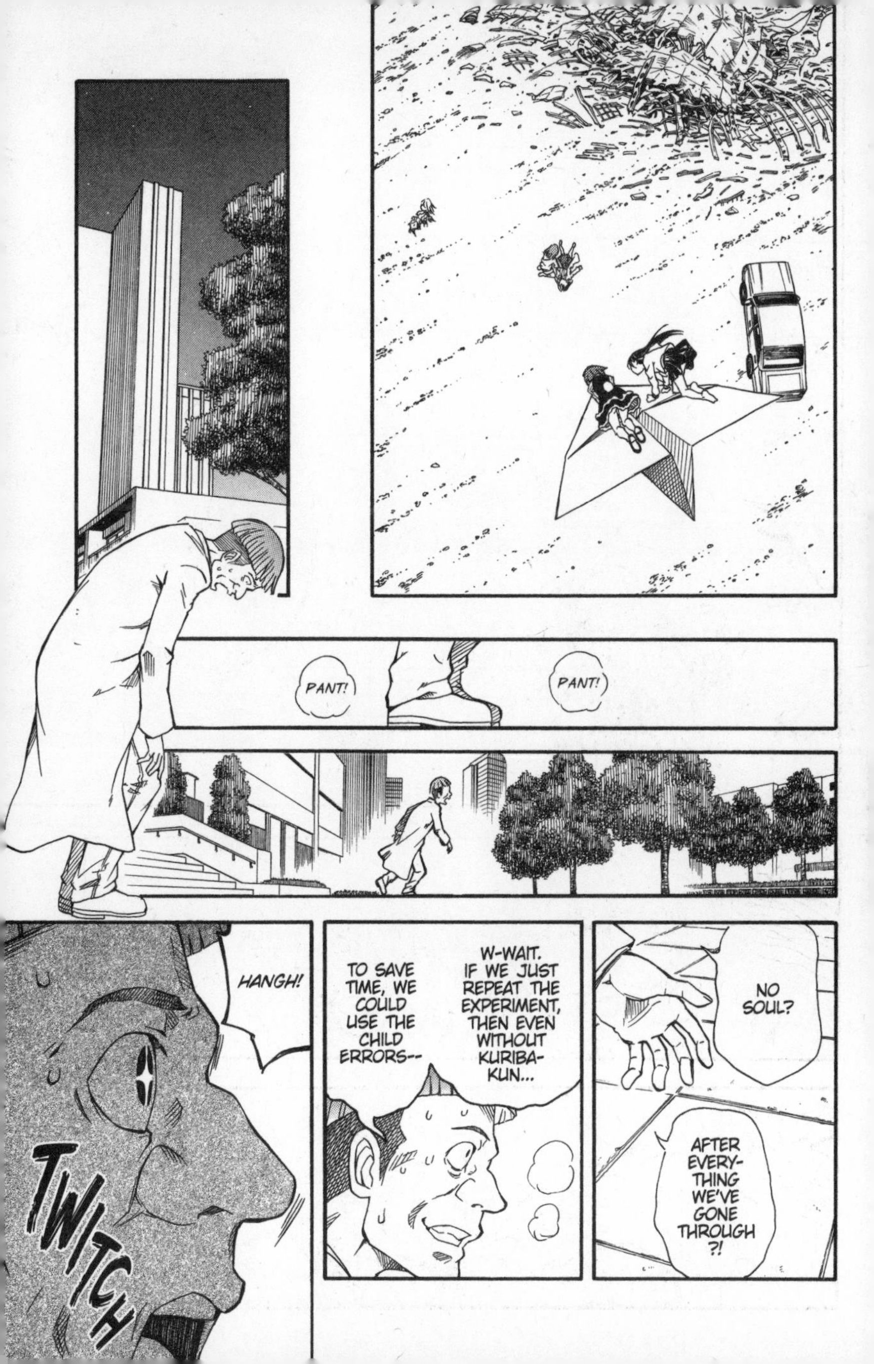
PANT!
PANT!
NO SOUL?
AFTER EVERY-THING WE'VE GONE THROUGH?!
W-WAIT. IF WE JUST REPEAT THE EXPERIMENT, THEN EVEN WITHOUT KURIBA-KUN...
TO SAVE TIME, WE COULD USE THE CHILD ERRORS--
HANGH!
TWITCH

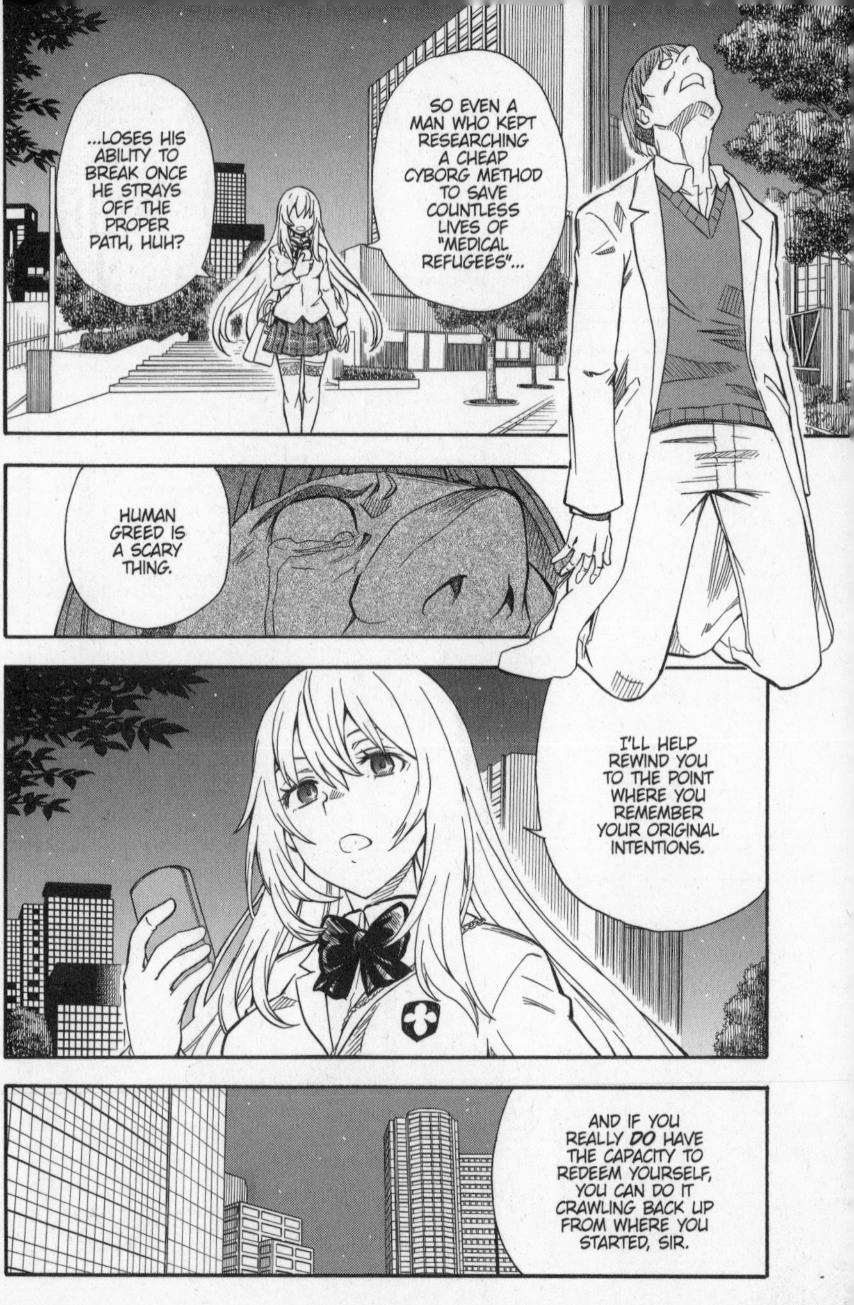
SO EVEN A MAN WHO KEPT RESEARCHING A CHEAP CYBORG METHOD TO SAVE COUNTLESS LIVES OF "MEDICAL REFUGEES"...
...LOSES HIS ABILITY TO BREAK ONCE HE STRAYS OFF THE PROPER PATH, HUH?
HUMAN GREED IS A SCARY THING.
I'LL HELP REWIND YOU TO THE POINT WHERE YOU REMEMBER YOUR ORIGINAL INTENTIONS.
AND IF YOU REALLY *DO* HAVE THE CAPACITY TO REDEEM YOURSELF, YOU CAN DO IT CRAWLING BACK UP FROM WHERE YOU STARTED, SIR.

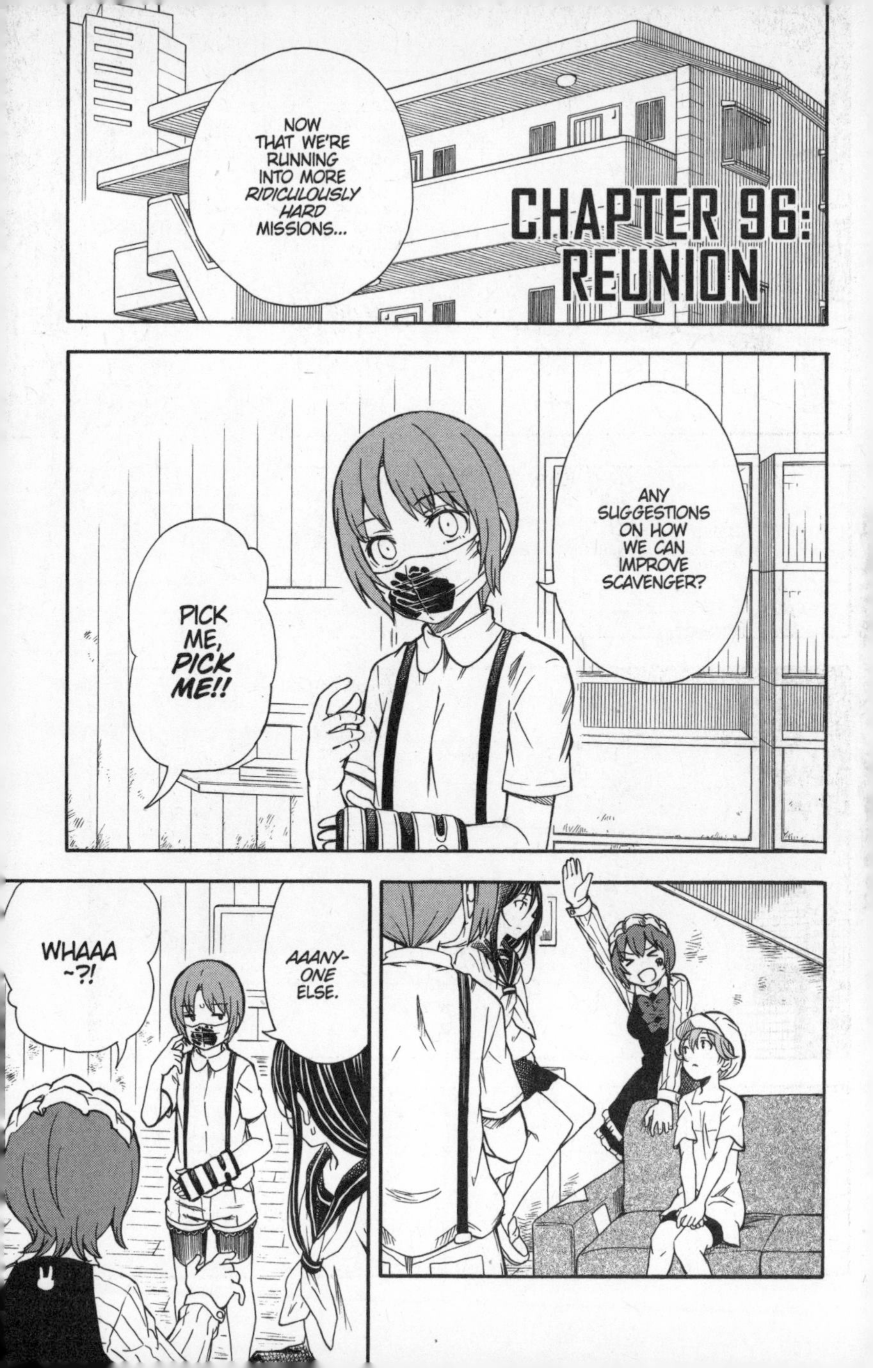
CHAPTER 96: REUNION
NOW THAT WE'RE RUNNING INTO MORE *RIDICULOUSLY* HARD MISSIONS...
ANY SUGGESTIONS ON HOW WE CAN IMPROVE SCAVENGER?
PICK ME, PICK ME!!
AAANY-ONE ELSE.
WHAAA ~?!

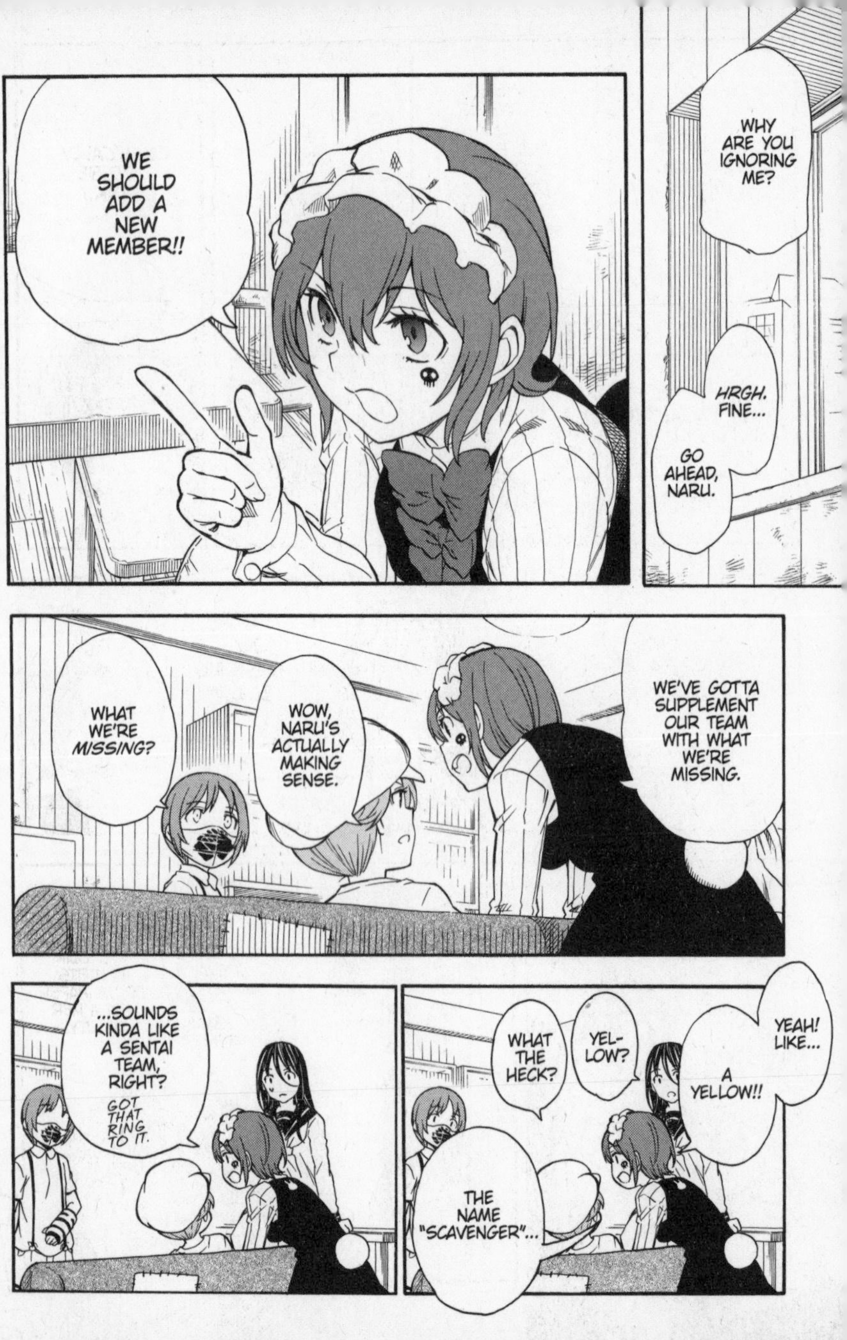
WHY ARE YOU IGNORING ME?
HRGH. FINE...
GO AHEAD, NARU.
WE SHOULD ADD A NEW MEMBER!!
WE'VE GOTTA SUPPLEMENT OUR TEAM WITH WHAT WE'RE MISSING.
WOW, NARU'S ACTUALLY MAKING SENSE.
WHAT WE'RE *MISSING?*
YEAH! LIKE...
A YELLOW!!
YEL-LOW?
WHAT THE HECK?
THE NAME "SCAVENGER"...
...SOUNDS KINDA LIKE A SENTAI TEAM, RIGHT?
GOT THAT RING TO IT.

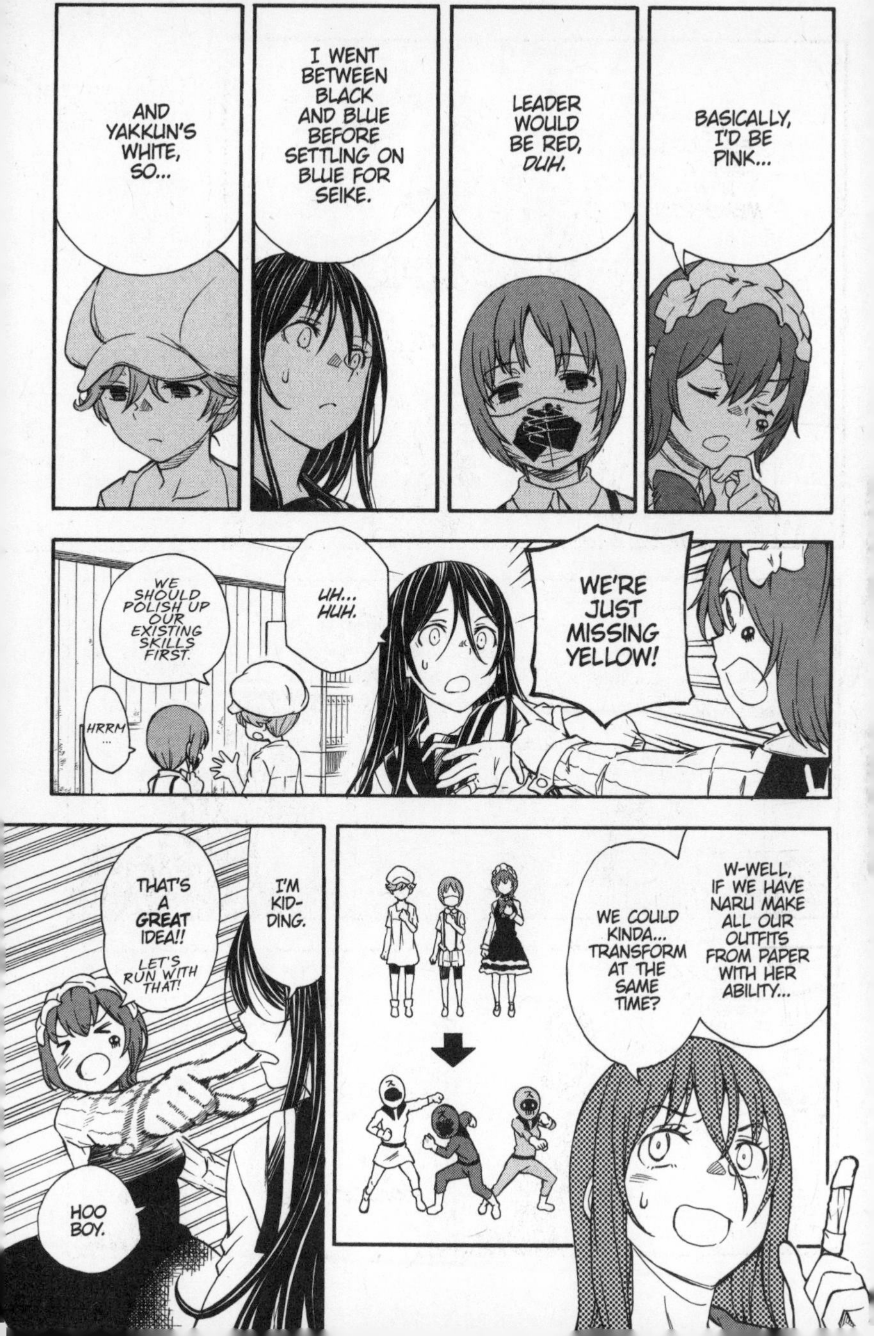
BASICALLY, I'D BE PINK...
LEADER WOULD BE RED, DUH.
I WENT BETWEEN BLACK AND BLUE BEFORE SETTLING ON BLUE FOR SEIKE.
AND YAKKUN'S WHITE, SO...
WE'RE JUST MISSING YELLOW!
UH... HUH.
WE SHOULD POLISH UP OUR EXISTING SKILLS FIRST.
HRRM...
W-WELL, IF WE HAVE NARU MAKE ALL OUR OUTFITS FROM PAPER WITH HER ABILITY...
WE COULD KINDA... TRANSFORM AT THE SAME TIME?
I'M KIDDING.
THAT'S A GREAT IDEA!!
LET'S RUN WITH THAT!
HOO BOY.

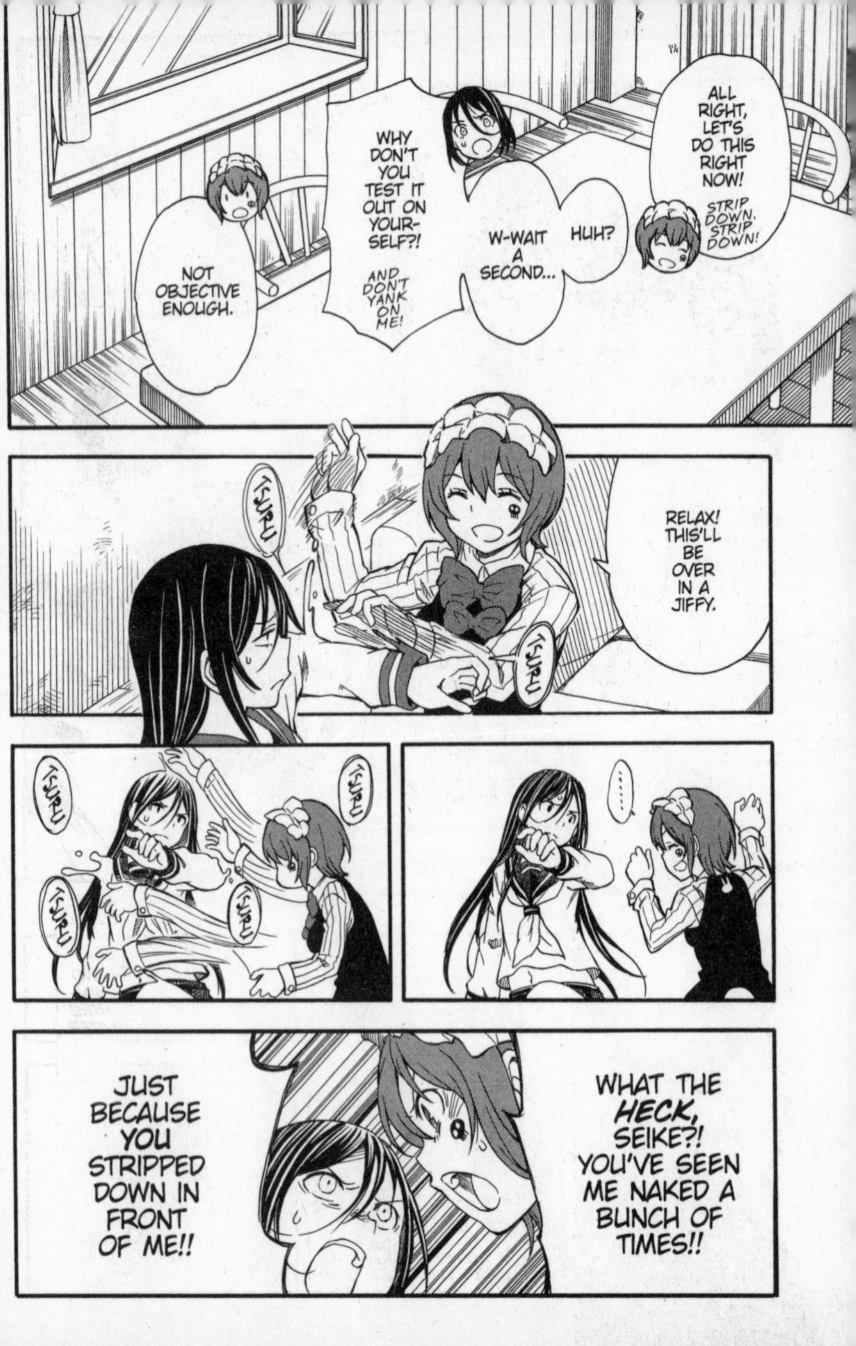
ALL RIGHT, LET'S DO THIS RIGHT NOW!
STRIP DOWN, STRIP DOWN!
HUH?
W-WAIT A SECOND...
WHY DON'T YOU TEST IT OUT ON YOURSELF?!
AND DON'T YANK ON ME!
NOT OBJECTIVE ENOUGH.
RELAX! THIS'LL BE OVER IN A JIFFY.
TSURU
TSURU
......
TSURU
TSURU
TSURU
TSURU
WHAT THE *HECK*, SEIKE?! YOU'VE SEEN ME NAKED A BUNCH OF TIMES!!
JUST BECAUSE YOU STRIPPED DOWN IN FRONT OF ME!!

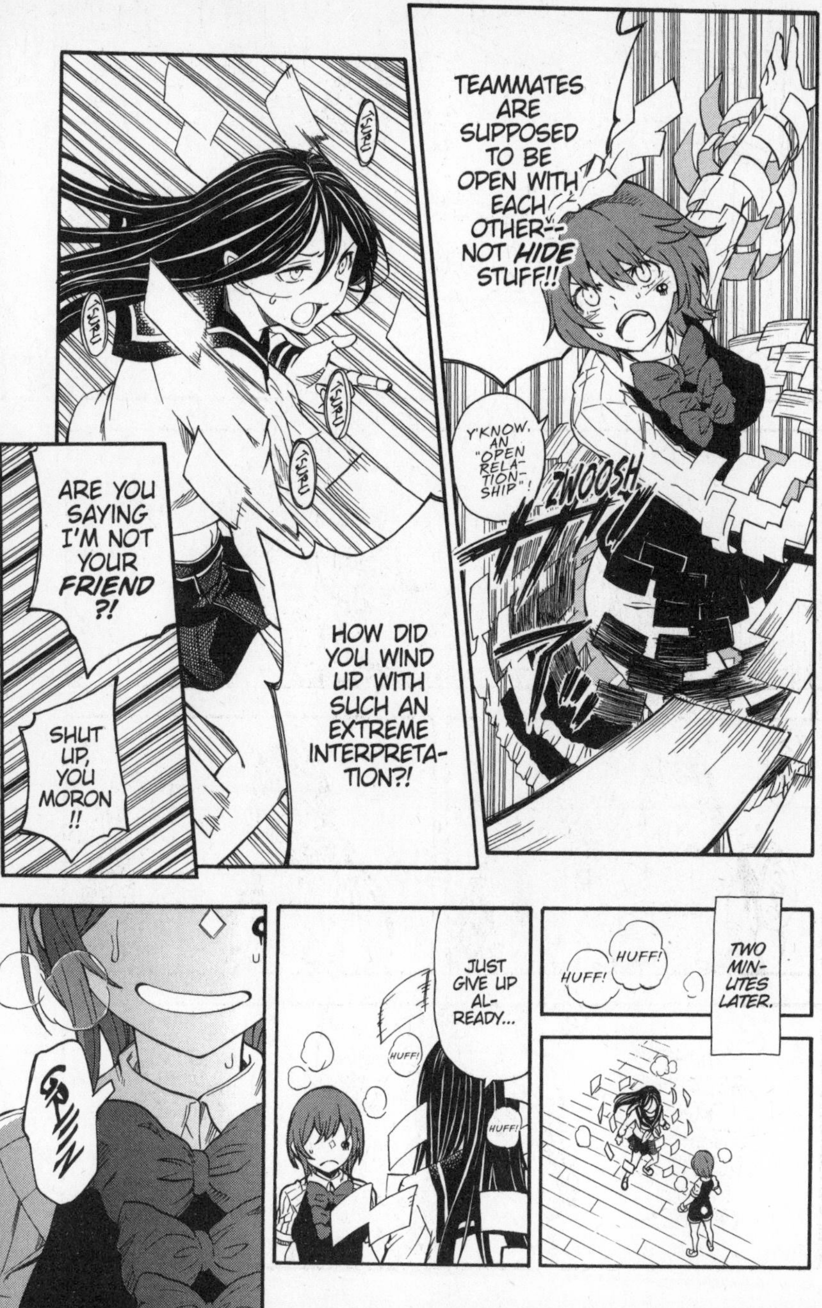
TEAMMATES ARE SUPPOSED TO BE OPEN WITH EACH OTHER-- NOT HIDE STUFF!!
Y'KNOW, AN "OPEN RELATIONSHIP"!
ZWOOSH
TSURU
TSURU
TSURU
TSURU
HOW DID YOU WIND UP WITH SUCH AN EXTREME INTERPRETATION?!
ARE YOU SAYING I'M NOT YOUR FRIEND?!
SHUT UP, YOU MORON!!
TWO MINUTES LATER.
HUFF!
HUFF!
JUST GIVE UP ALREADY...
HUFF!
HUFF!
GRIIIN

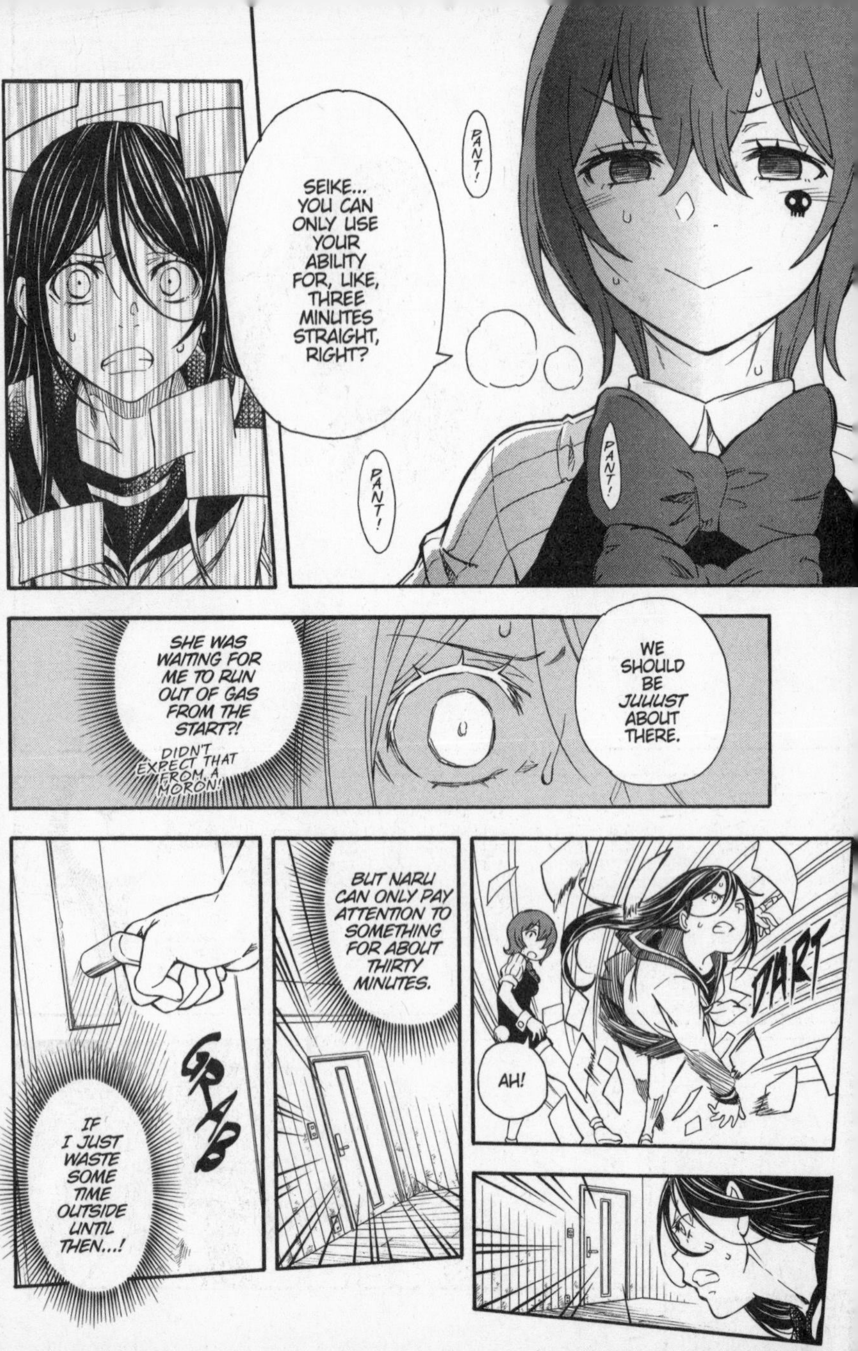
PANT!
PANT!
PANT!
SEIKE... YOU CAN ONLY USE YOUR ABILITY FOR, LIKE, THREE MINUTES STRAIGHT, RIGHT?
WE SHOULD BE JUUUST ABOUT THERE.
SHE WAS WAITING FOR ME TO RUN OUT OF GAS FROM THE START?!
DIDN'T EXPECT THAT FROM A MORON!
DART
AH!
BUT NARU CAN ONLY PAY ATTENTION TO SOMETHING FOR ABOUT THIRTY MINUTES.
GRAB
IF I JUST WASTE SOME TIME OUTSIDE UNTIL THEN...!

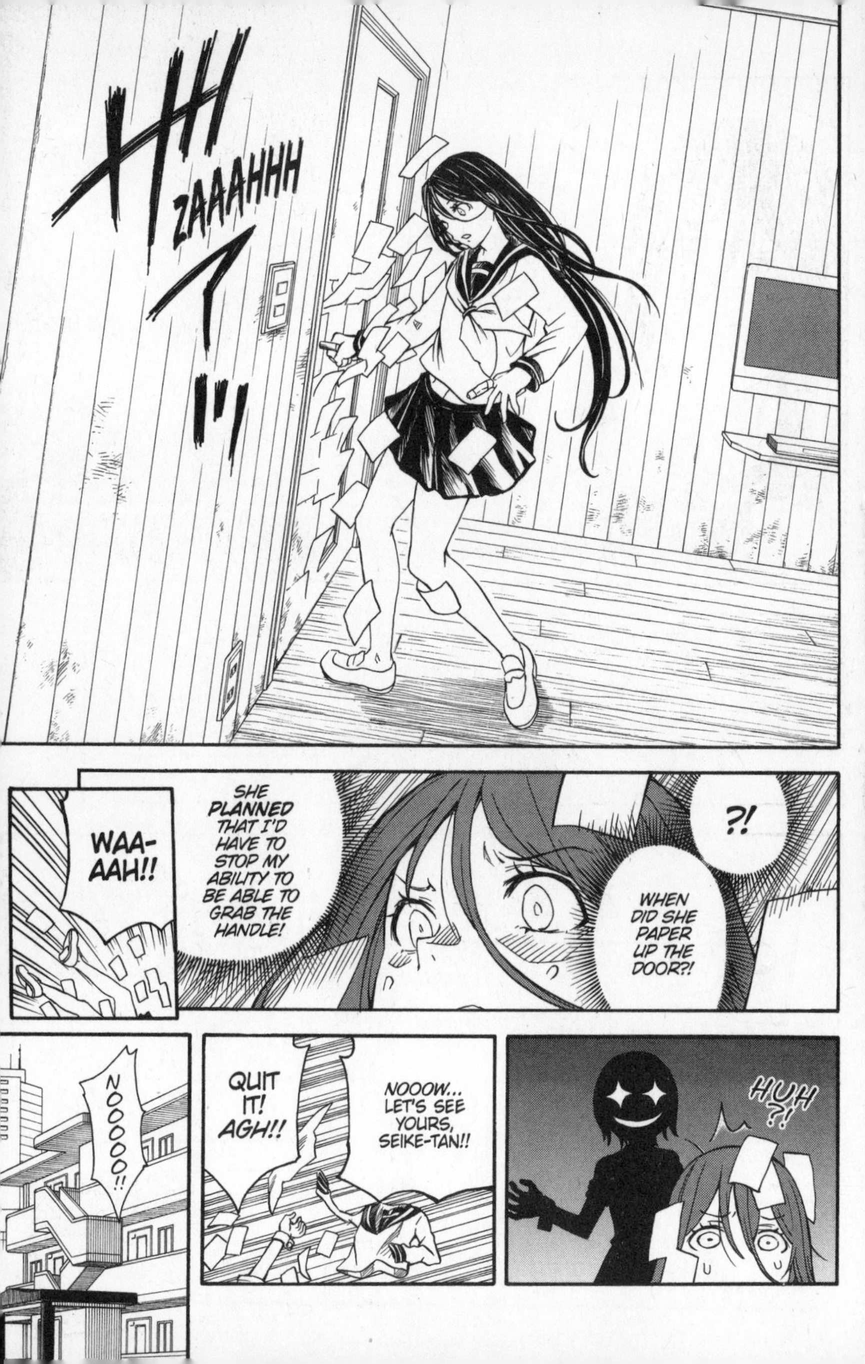
ZAAAHHH
?!
WHEN DID SHE PAPER UP THE DOOR?!
SHE PLANNED THAT I'D HAVE TO STOP MY ABILITY TO BE ABLE TO GRAB THE HANDLE!
WAA-AAH!!
HUH?!
NOOOW... LET'S SEE YOURS, SEIKE-TAN!!
QUIT IT! AGH!!
NOOOOO!!

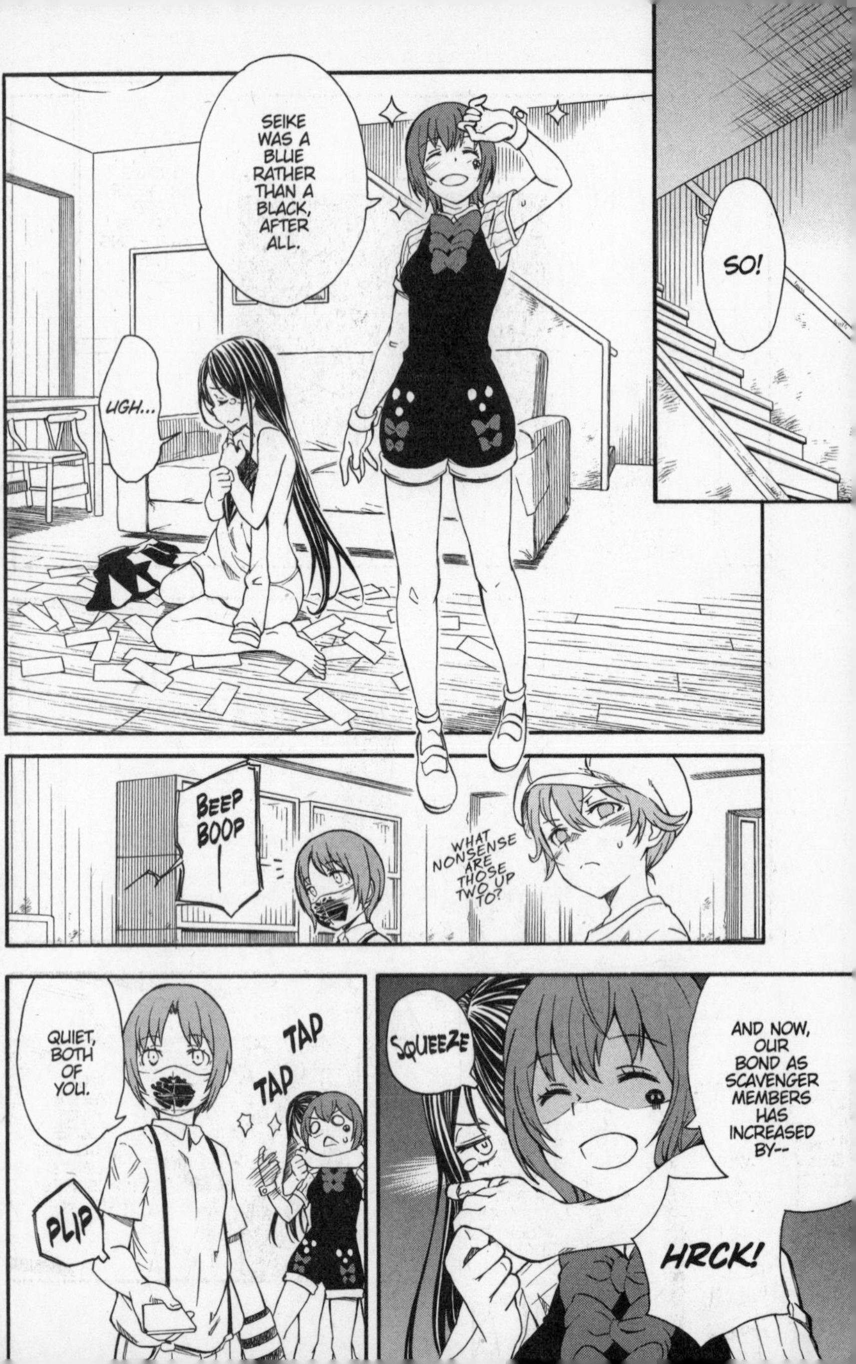
SO!
SEIKE WAS A BLUE RATHER THAN A BLACK, AFTER ALL.
UGH...
WHAT NONSENSE ARE THOSE TWO UP TO?
BEEP BOOP
AND NOW, OUR BOND AS SCAVENGER MEMBERS HAS INCREASED BY--
SQUEEZE
HRCK!
QUIET, BOTH OF YOU.
TAP
TAP
PLIP

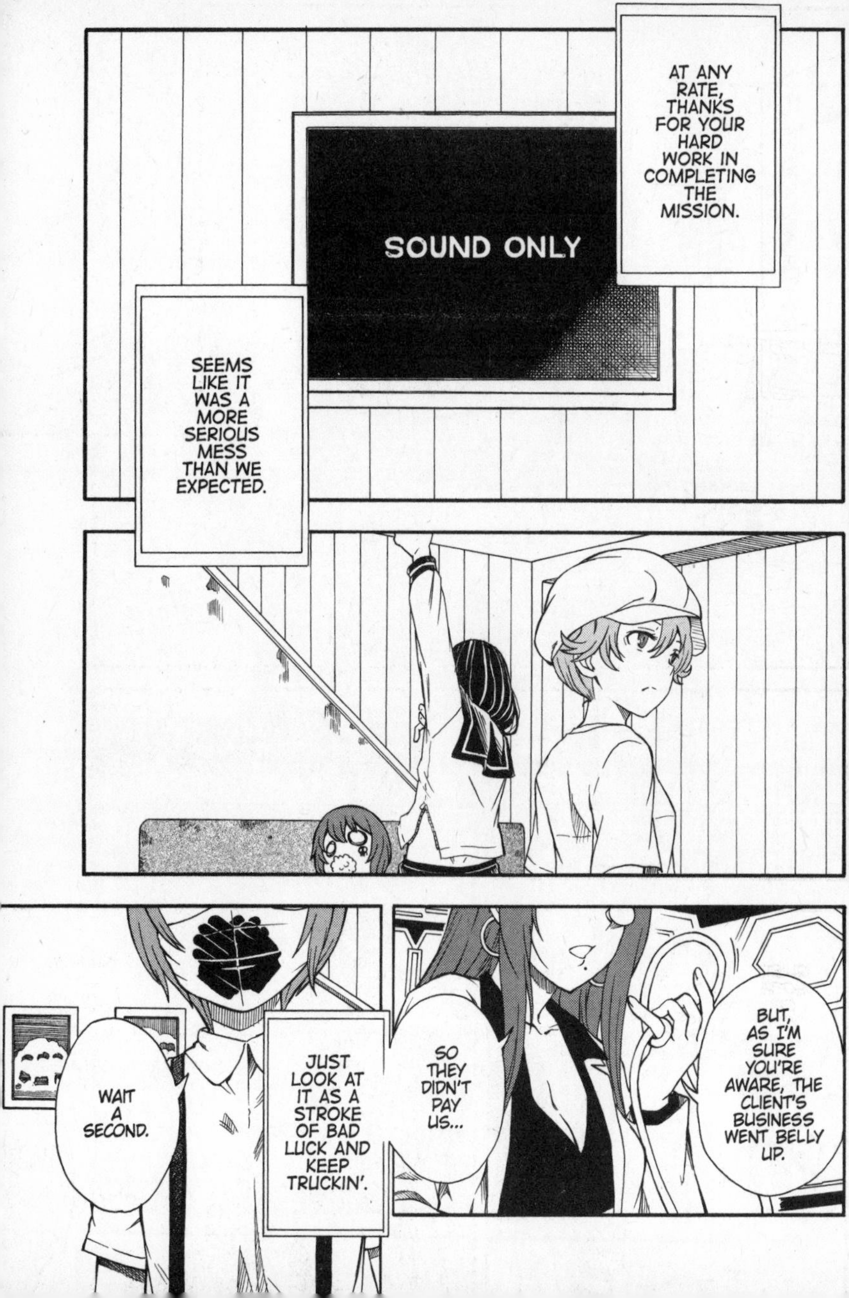
AT ANY RATE, THANKS FOR YOUR HARD WORK IN COMPLETING THE MISSION.
SOUND ONLY
SEEMS LIKE IT WAS A MORE SERIOUS MESS THAN WE EXPECTED.
BUT, AS I'M SURE YOU'RE AWARE, THE CLIENT'S BUSINESS WENT BELLY UP.
SO THEY DIDN'T PAY US...
JUST LOOK AT IT AS A STROKE OF BAD LUCK AND KEEP TRUCKIN'.
WAIT A SECOND.

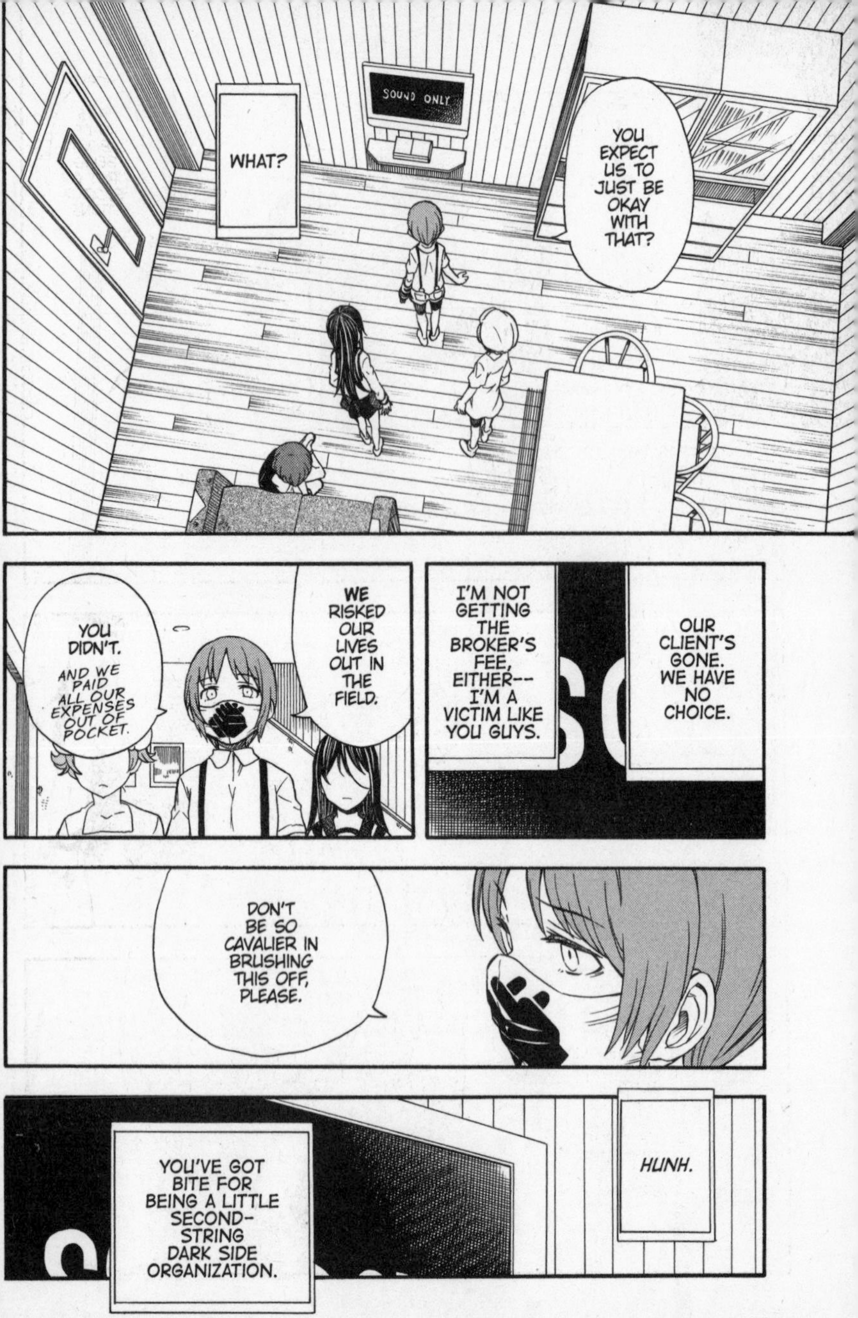
SOUND ONLY
YOU EXPECT US TO JUST BE OKAY WITH THAT?
WHAT?
OUR CLIENT'S GONE. WE HAVE NO CHOICE.
I'M NOT GETTING THE BROKER'S FEE, EITHER-- I'M A VICTIM LIKE YOU GUYS.
WE RISKED OUR LIVES OUT IN THE FIELD.
YOU DIDN'T.
AND WE PAID ALL OUR EXPENSES OUT OF POCKET.
DON'T BE SO CAVALIER IN BRUSHING THIS OFF, PLEASE.
HUNH.
YOU'VE GOT BITE FOR BEING A LITTLE SECOND-STRING DARK SIDE ORGANIZATION.

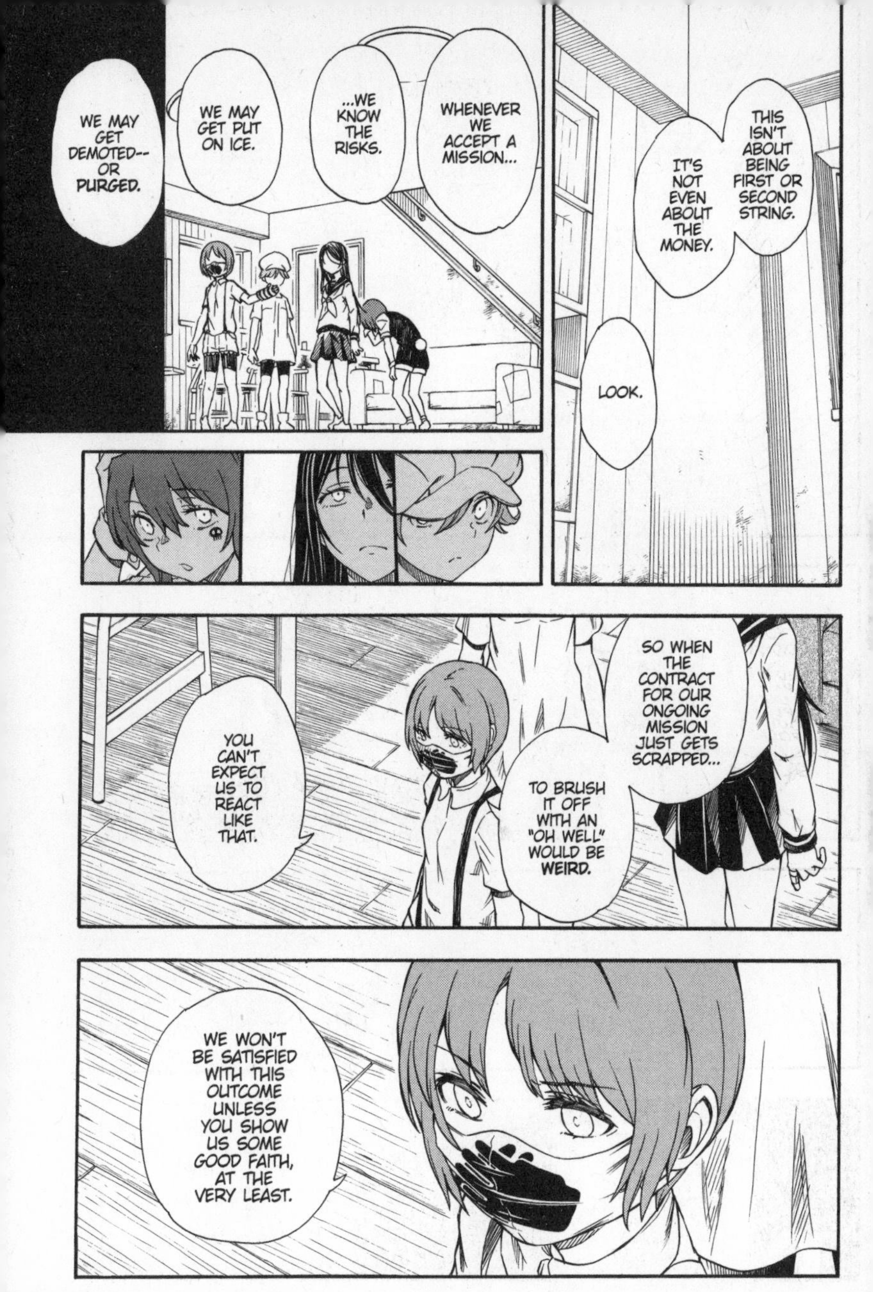
THIS ISN'T ABOUT BEING FIRST OR SECOND STRING.
IT'S NOT EVEN ABOUT THE MONEY.
LOOK.
WHENEVER WE ACCEPT A MISSION...
...WE KNOW THE RISKS.
WE MAY GET PUT ON ICE.
WE MAY GET DEMOTED--OR PURGED.
SO WHEN THE CONTRACT FOR OUR ONGOING MISSION JUST GETS SCRAPPED...
TO BRUSH IT OFF WITH AN "OH WELL" WOULD BE WEIRD.
YOU CAN'T EXPECT US TO REACT LIKE THAT.
WE WON'T BE SATISFIED WITH THIS OUTCOME UNLESS YOU SHOW US SOME GOOD FAITH, AT THE VERY LEAST.

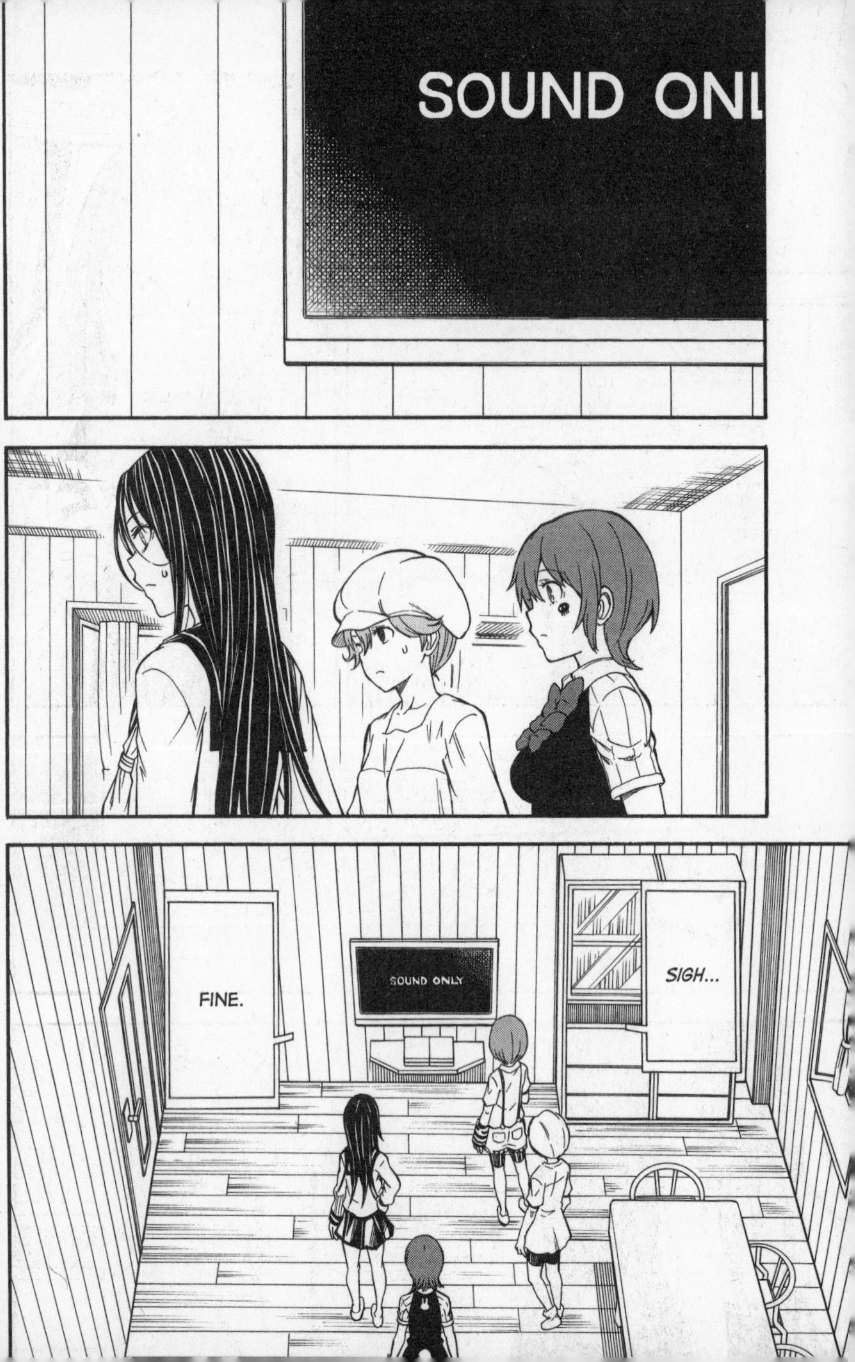
SOUND ONL
SIGH...
FINE.
SOUND ONLY

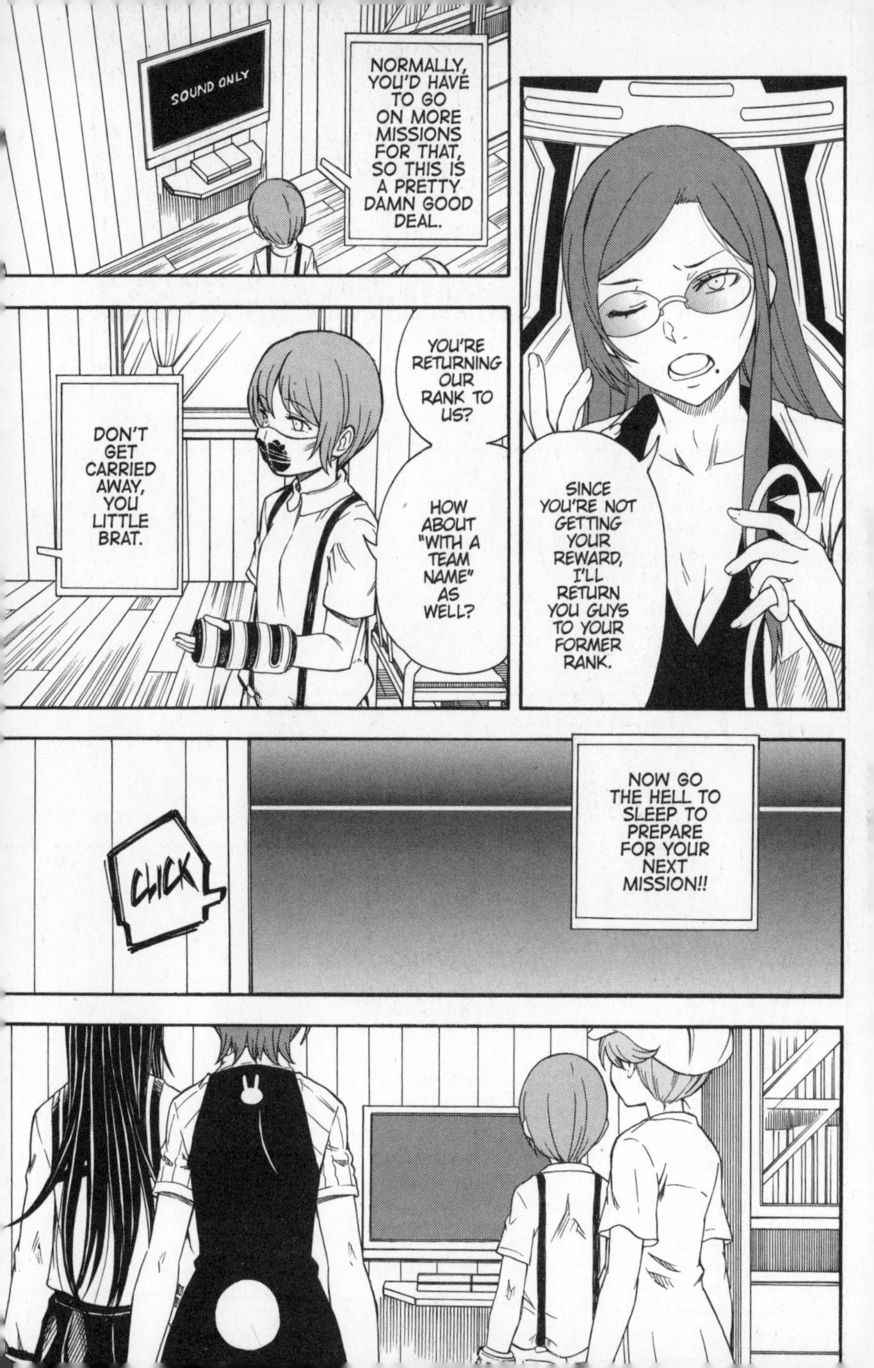
SOUND ONLY
NORMALLY, YOU'D HAVE TO GO ON MORE MISSIONS FOR THAT, SO THIS IS A PRETTY DAMN GOOD DEAL.
DON'T GET CARRIED AWAY, YOU LITTLE BRAT.
YOU'RE RETURNING OUR RANK TO US?
HOW ABOUT "WITH A TEAM NAME" AS WELL?
SINCE YOU'RE NOT GETTING YOUR REWARD, I'LL RETURN YOU GUYS TO YOUR FORMER RANK.
CLICK
NOW GO THE HELL TO SLEEP TO PREPARE FOR YOUR NEXT MISSION!!

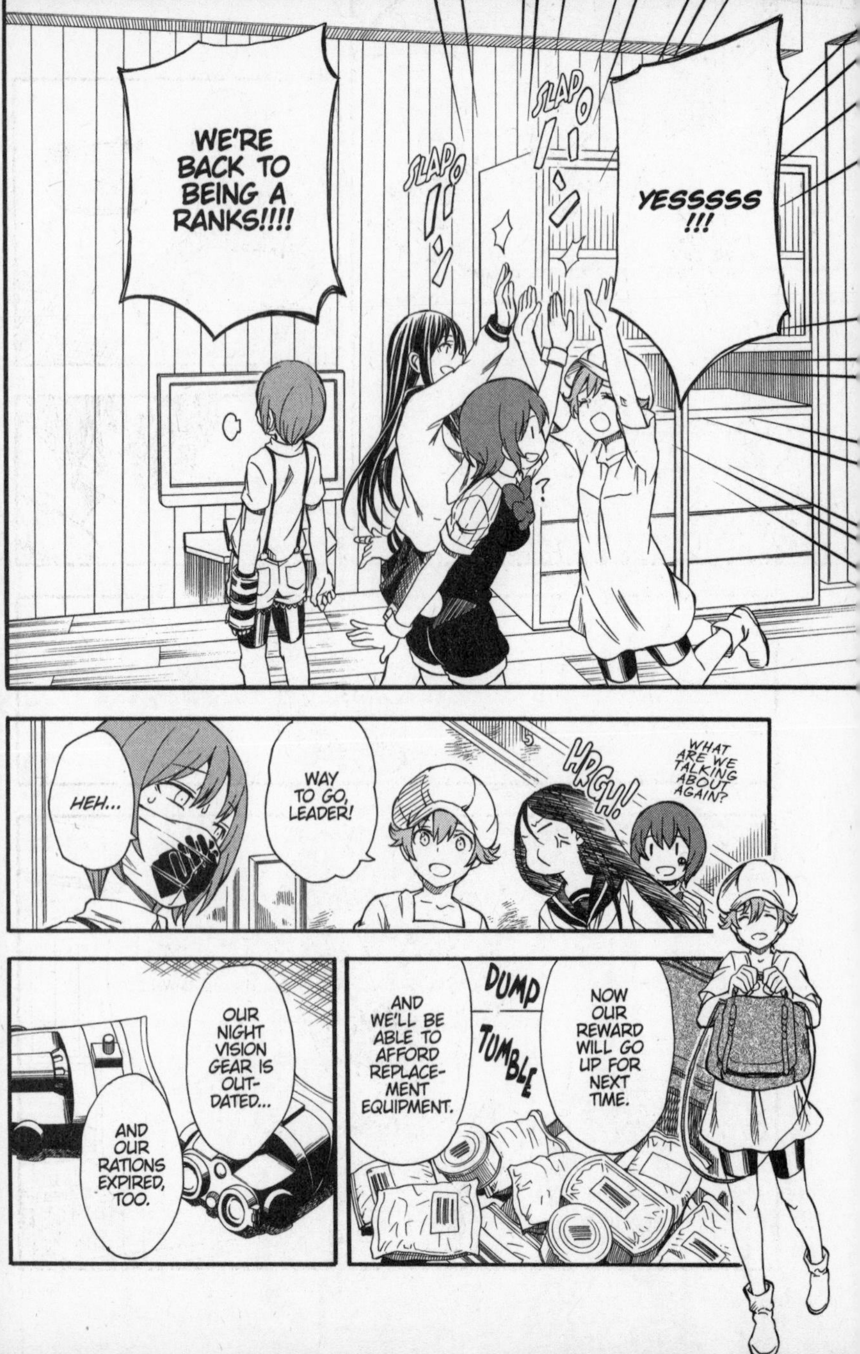
WE'RE BACK TO BEING A RANKS!!!!
SLAP
SLAP
YESSSSS!!!
WHAT ARE WE TALKING ABOUT AGAIN?
HRGH!
WAY TO GO, LEADER!
HEH...
NOW OUR REWARD WILL GO UP FOR NEXT TIME.
DUMP
TUMBLE
AND WE'LL BE ABLE TO AFFORD REPLACEMENT EQUIPMENT.
OUR NIGHT VISION GEAR IS OUTDATED...
AND OUR RATIONS EXPIRED, TOO.

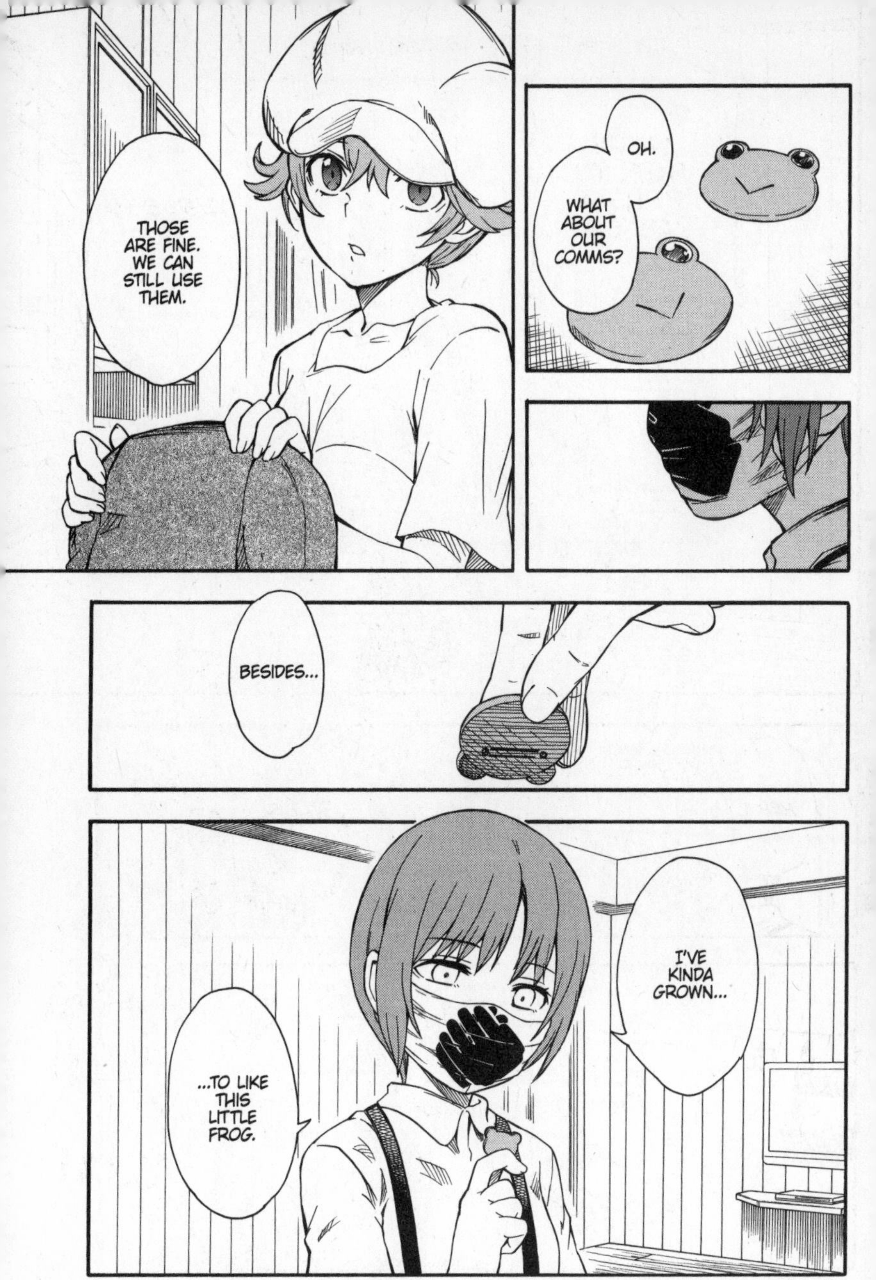
OH.
WHAT ABOUT OUR COMMS?
THOSE ARE FINE. WE CAN STILL USE THEM.
BESIDES...
I'VE KINDA GROWN...
...TO LIKE THIS LITTLE FROG.

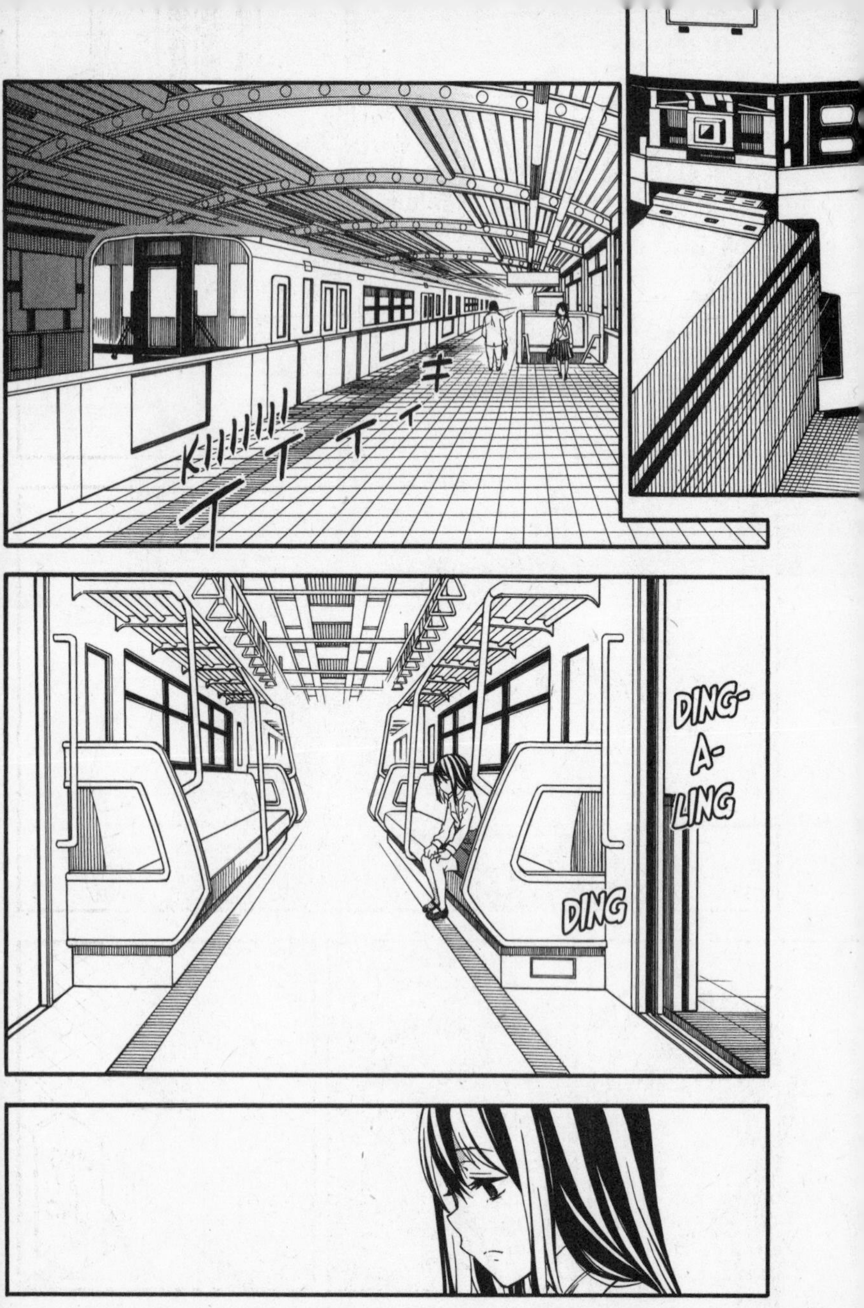
KIIIIII
イ イ イ ィ キ
DING-A-LING
DING

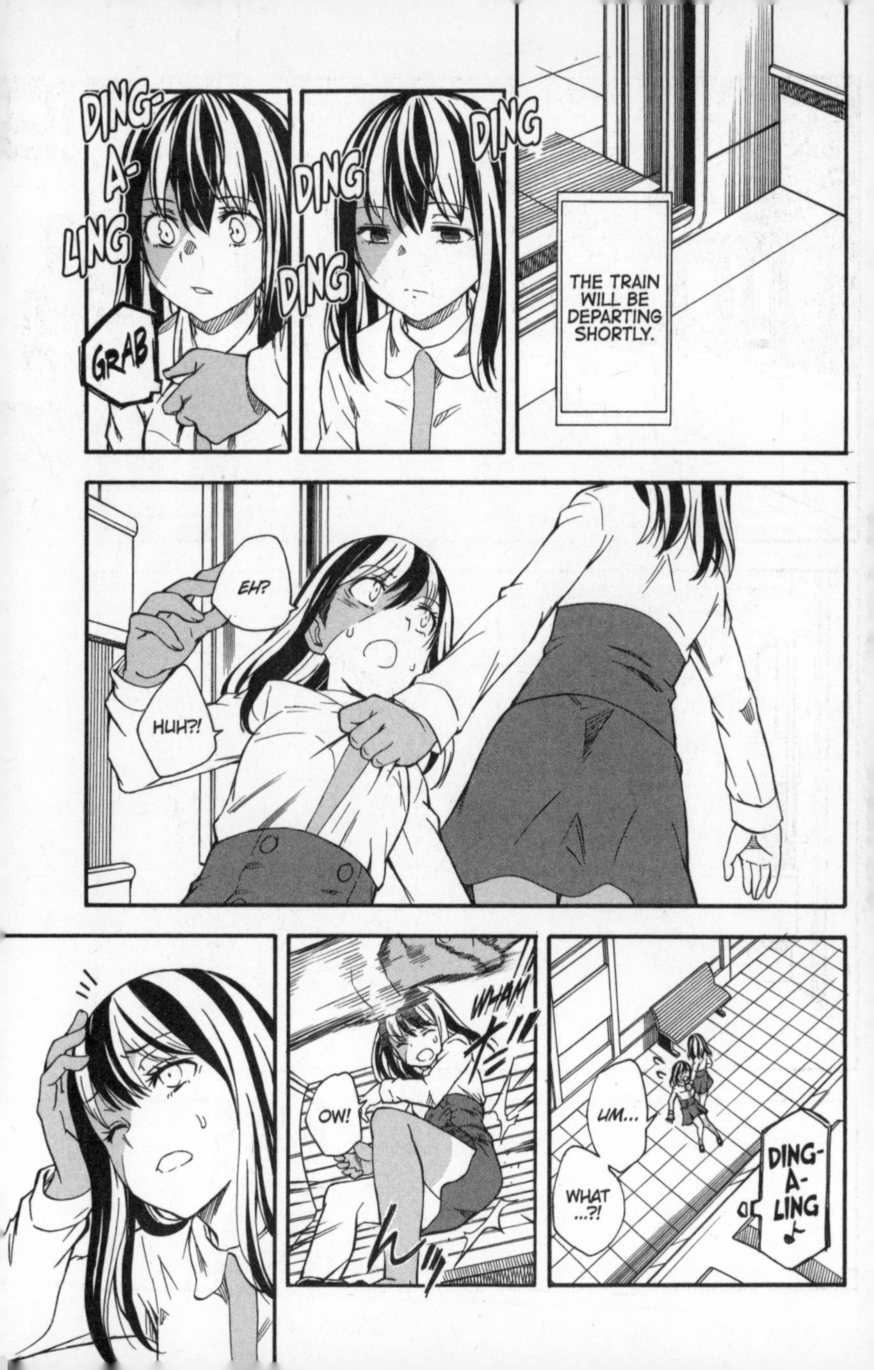
THE TRAIN WILL BE DEPARTING SHORTLY.
DING
DING
DING
DING-A-LING
GRAB
EH?
HUH?!
WHAM
OW!
UM...
WHAT ...?!
DING-A-LING

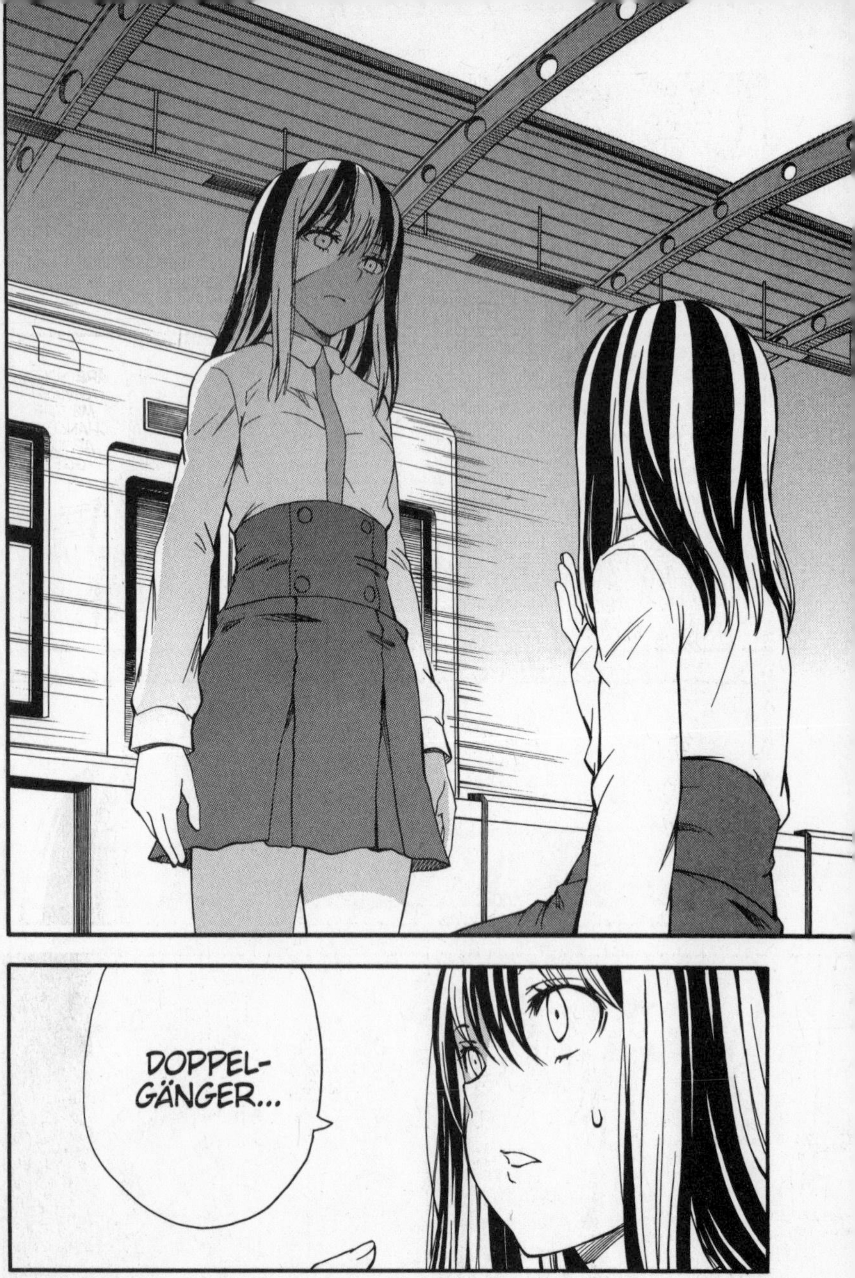
DOPPEL-
GÄNGER...

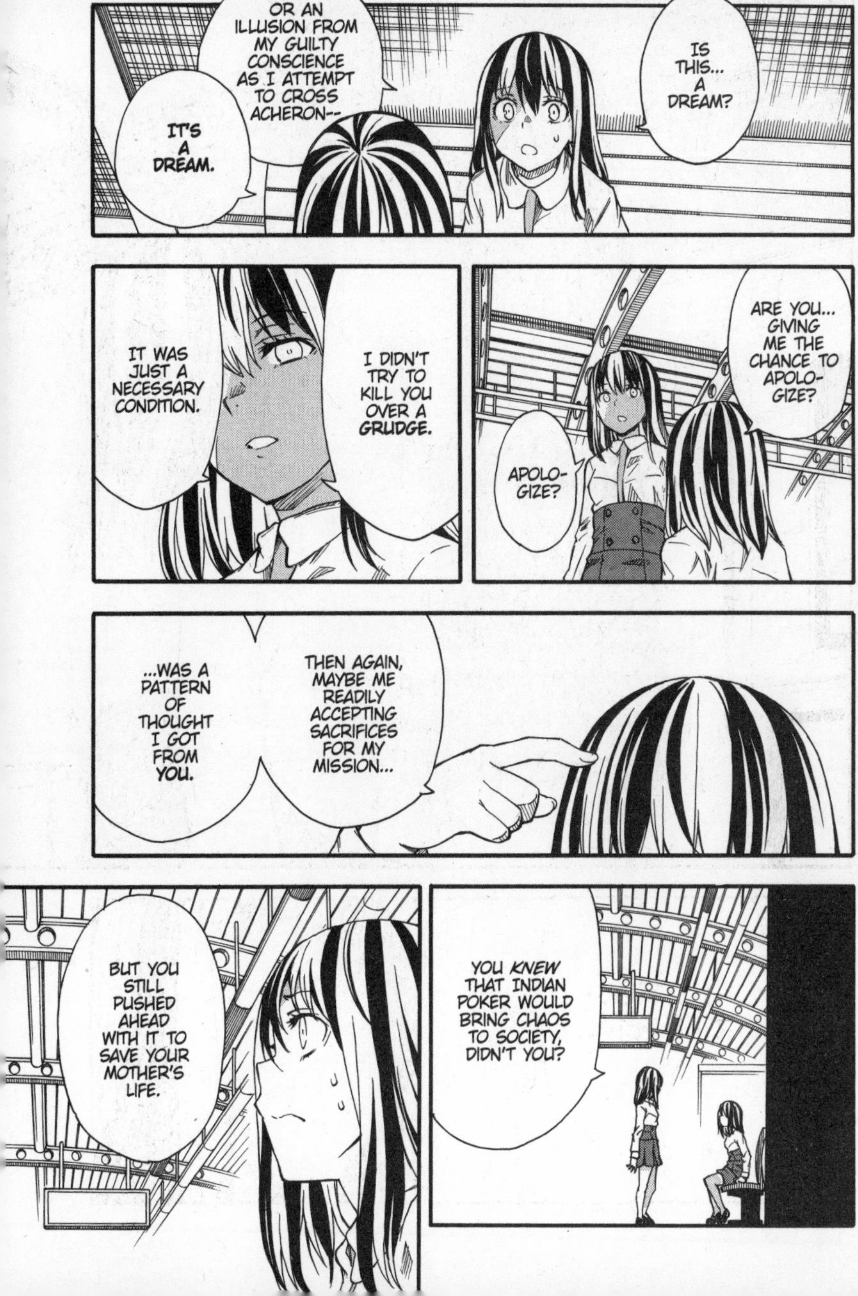
IS THIS... A DREAM?
OR AN ILLUSION FROM MY GUILTY CONSCIENCE AS I ATTEMPT TO CROSS ACHERON--
IT'S A DREAM.
ARE YOU... GIVING ME THE CHANCE TO APOLOGIZE?
APOLOGIZE?
I DIDN'T TRY TO KILL YOU OVER A GRUDGE.
IT WAS JUST A NECESSARY CONDITION.
THEN AGAIN, MAYBE ME READILY ACCEPTING SACRIFICES FOR MY MISSION...
...WAS A PATTERN OF THOUGHT I GOT FROM YOU.
YOU *KNEW* THAT INDIAN POKER WOULD BRING CHAOS TO SOCIETY, DIDN'T YOU?
BUT YOU STILL PUSHED AHEAD WITH IT TO SAVE YOUR MOTHER'S LIFE.

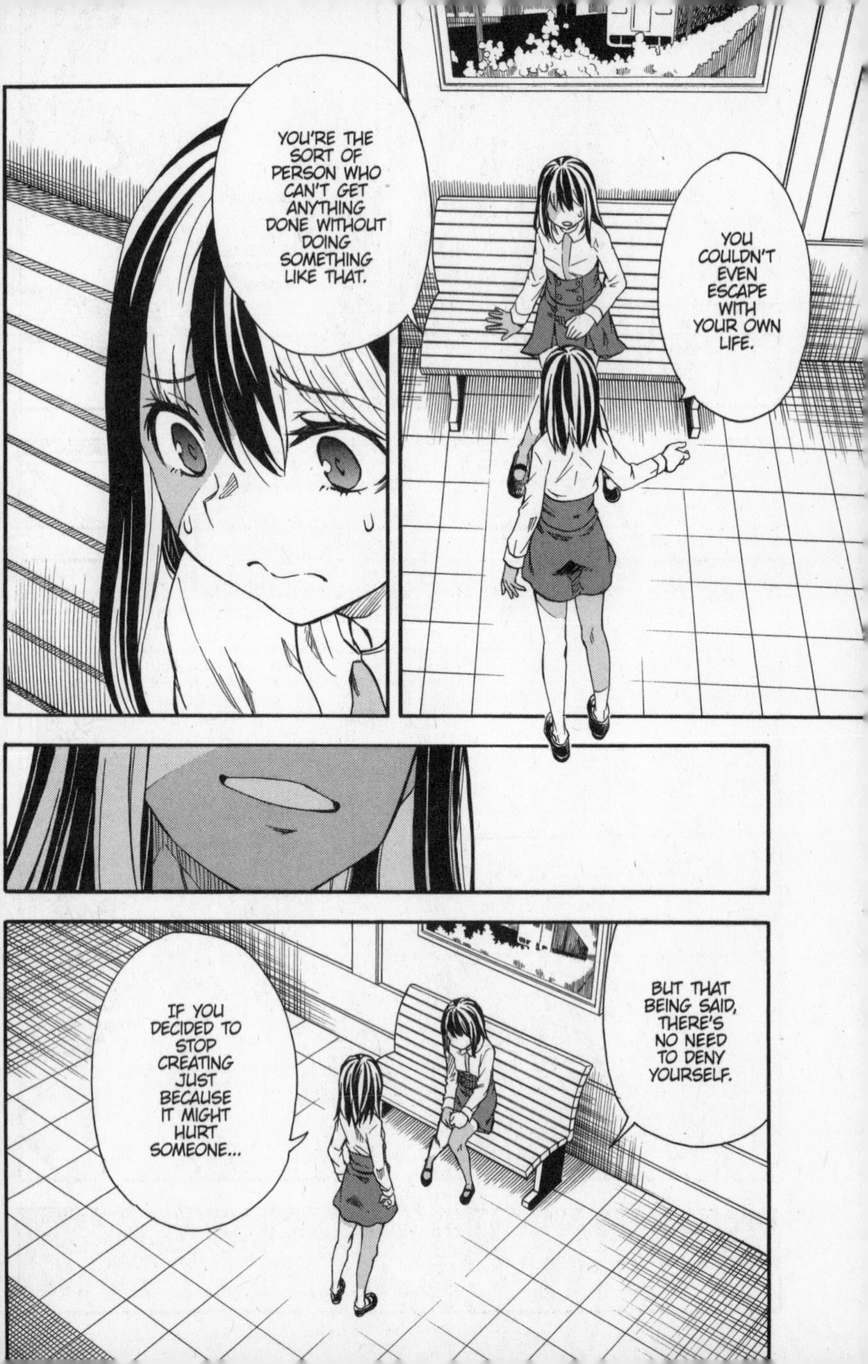
YOU COULDN'T EVEN ESCAPE WITH YOUR OWN LIFE.
YOU'RE THE SORT OF PERSON WHO CAN'T GET ANYTHING DONE WITHOUT DOING SOMETHING LIKE THAT.
BUT THAT BEING SAID, THERE'S NO NEED TO DENY YOURSELF.
IF YOU DECIDED TO STOP CREATING JUST BECAUSE IT MIGHT HURT SOMEONE...

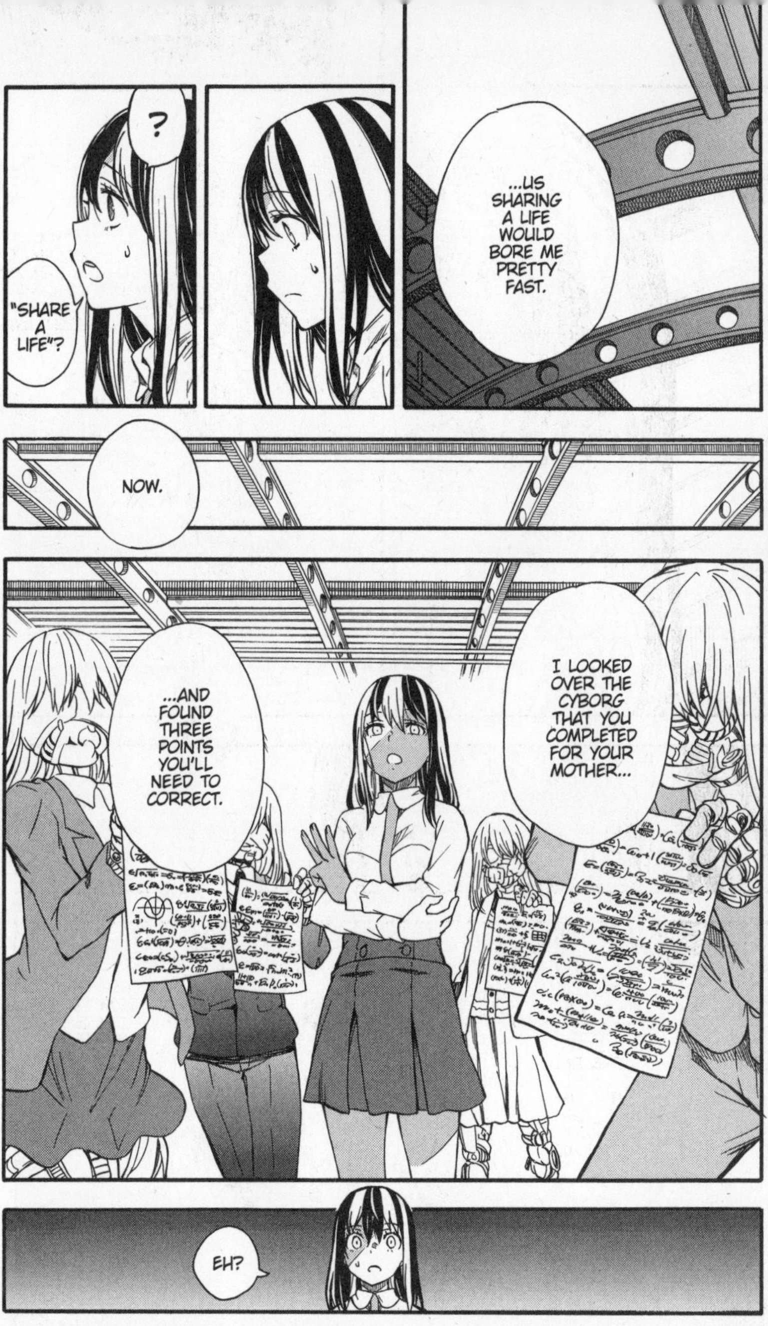
...US SHARING A LIFE WOULD BORE ME PRETTY FAST.
?
"SHARE A LIFE"?
NOW.
I LOOKED OVER THE CYBORG THAT YOU COMPLETED FOR YOUR MOTHER...
...AND FOUND THREE POINTS YOU'LL NEED TO CORRECT.
EH?

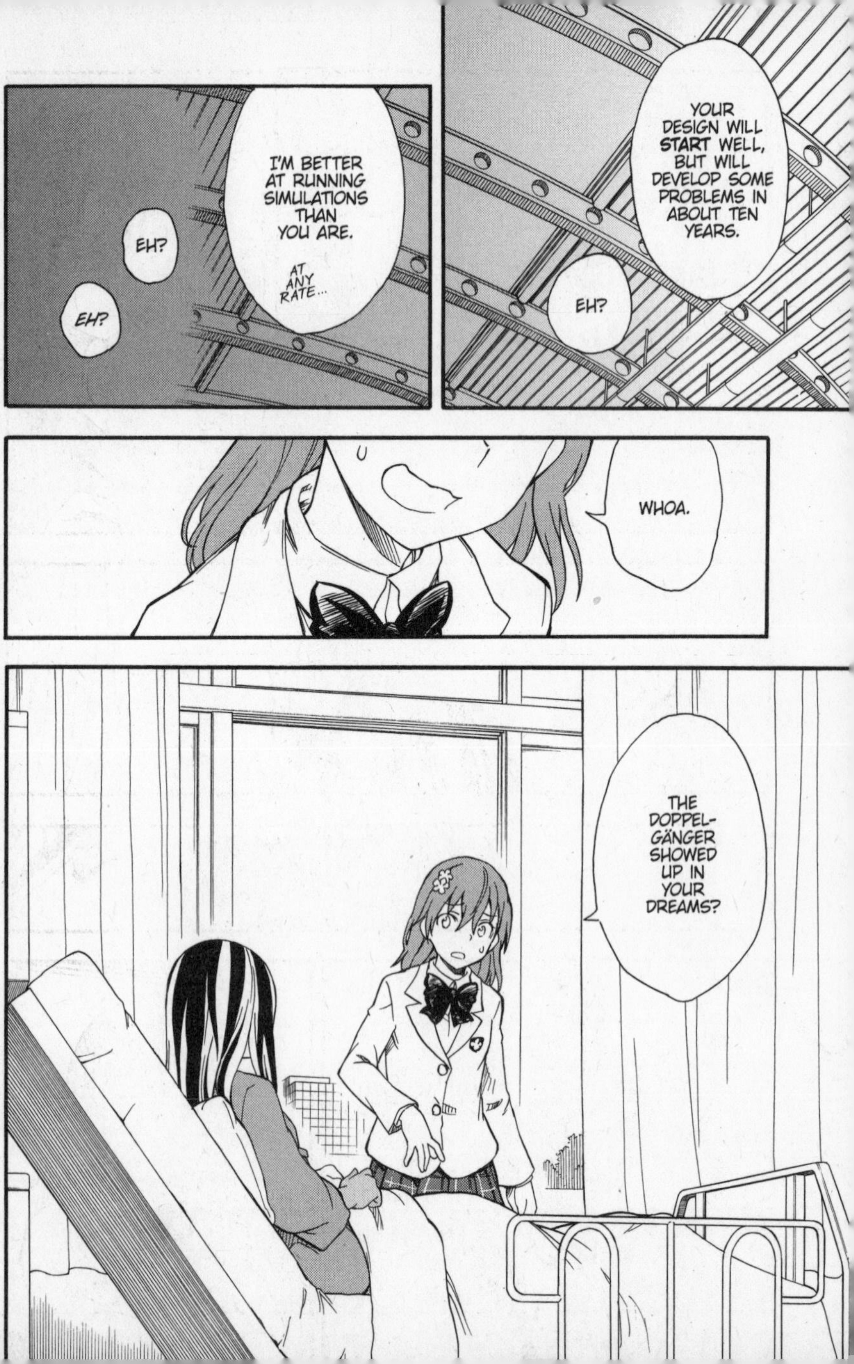
YOUR DESIGN WILL START WELL, BUT WILL DEVELOP SOME PROBLEMS IN ABOUT TEN YEARS.
EH?
I'M BETTER AT RUNNING SIMULATIONS THAN YOU ARE.
AT ANY RATE...
EH?
EH?
WHOA.
THE DOPPEL-GÄNGER SHOWED UP IN YOUR DREAMS?

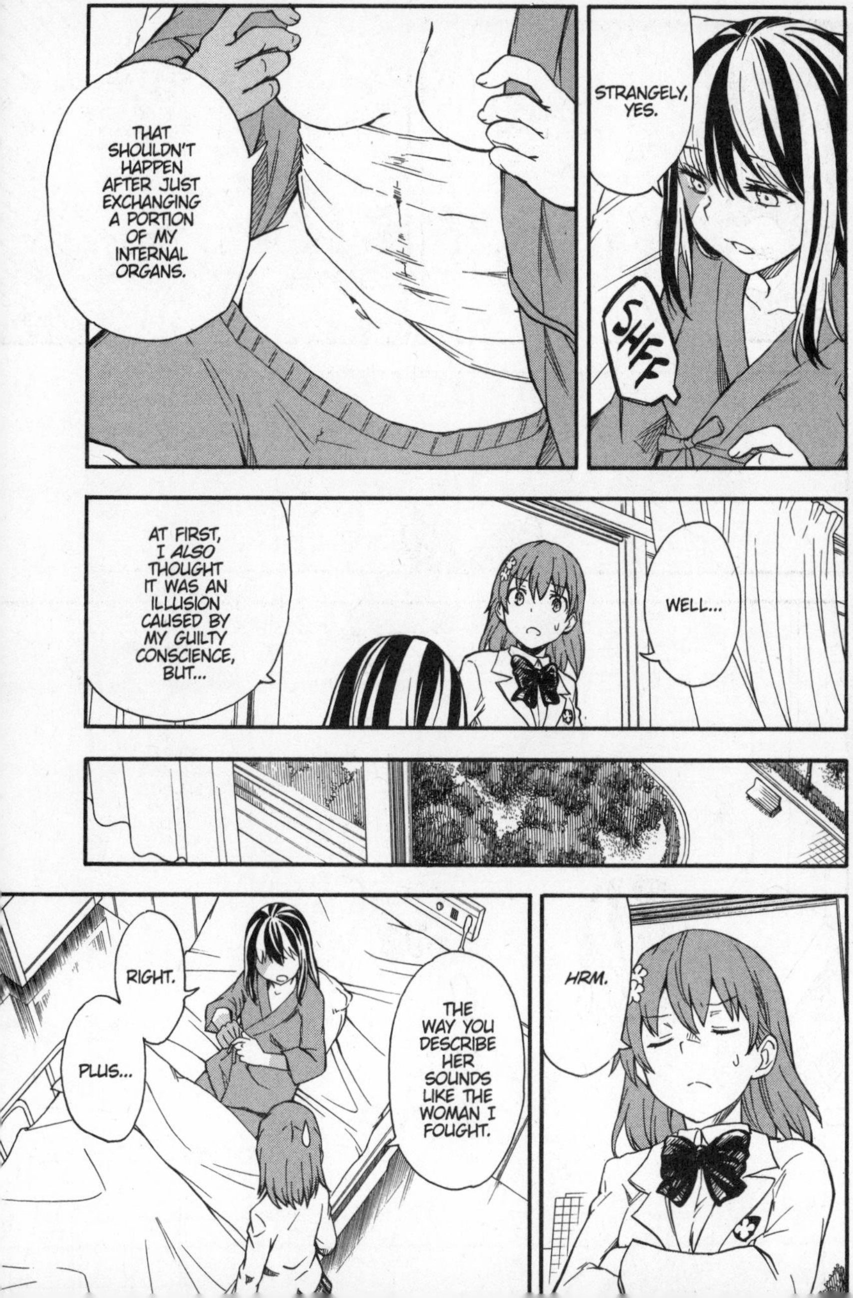
STRANGELY, YES.
SHFF
THAT SHOULDN'T HAPPEN AFTER JUST EXCHANGING A PORTION OF MY INTERNAL ORGANS.
WELL...
AT FIRST, I *ALSO* THOUGHT IT WAS AN ILLUSION CAUSED BY MY GUILTY CONSCIENCE, BUT...
HRM.
THE WAY YOU DESCRIBE HER SOUNDS LIKE THE WOMAN I FOUGHT.
RIGHT.
PLUS...

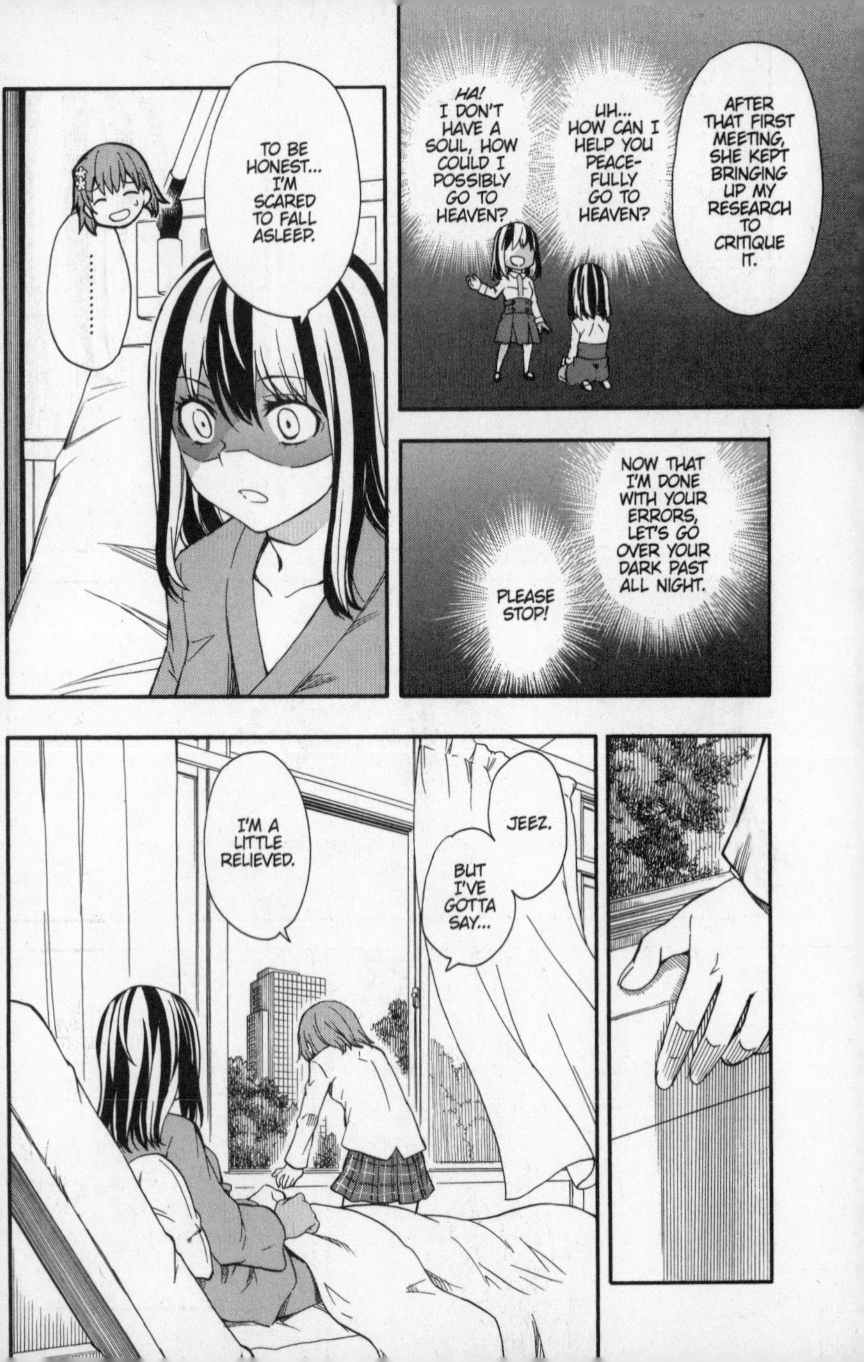
AFTER THAT FIRST MEETING, SHE KEPT BRINGING UP MY RESEARCH TO CRITIQUE IT.
UH... HOW CAN I HELP YOU PEACEFULLY GO TO HEAVEN?
HA! I DON'T HAVE A SOUL, HOW COULD I POSSIBLY GO TO HEAVEN?
NOW THAT I'M DONE WITH YOUR ERRORS, LET'S GO OVER YOUR DARK PAST ALL NIGHT.
PLEASE STOP!
TO BE HONEST... I'M SCARED TO FALL ASLEEP.
......
JEEZ.
BUT I'VE GOTTA SAY...
I'M A LITTLE RELIEVED.